W9-BGY-695

POPULATION LAW AND POLICY

POPULATION LAW AND POLICY

Source Materials and Issues

Stephen L. Isaacs, J. D.
Center for Population and Family Health
Columbia University
New York, New York

HUMAN SCIENCES PRESS
72 Fifth Avenue
NEW YORK, NY 10011
3 Henrietta Street
LONDON, WC2E 8LU

Printed in the United States of America
123456789 987654321

Library of Congress Cataloging in Publication Data

Isaacs, Stephen L.
Population law and policy.

Bibliography
Includes index.
1. Population—Law and legislation. 2. Birth control—Law and legislation. 3. Population—Law and legislation—United States. 4. Birth control—Law and legislation—United States. 5. Population policy. 6. United States—Population policy. I. Title.
K2000.I8 344'.048 *LC* 80-24549
ISBN 0-89885-000-2

To David

ACKNOWLEDGMENT

Many people have given me assistance and encouragement in writing this book. Their willingness to spend time reviewing the manuscript and to make substantive suggestions for its improvement have added immeasurably to the quality of the work. In particular, I wish to express my appreciation to Walter Watson, John Ross, William Sweeney, Richard Clinton, and Elizabeth Preble for their constructive suggestions on the population policy chapters and to Catherine Siener, Allan Rosenfield, Susan Philliber, Peri Rothenberg, Kathy Darabi, and Joy Dryfoos for having so conscientiously gone over sections of the fertility regulation materials. Susan Pasquariella and Judy Wilkinson, the librarians at Columbia University's Center for Population and Family Health, and Barbara Rubin Kessler, reference librarian at the Columbia Law School, were of great help in finding difficult-to-locate source materials.

Very special thanks are due to Jane Zuckerman, for her careful reading of the manuscript and suggestions for its improvement; to Harriet Pilpel, for her encouragement and counsel throughout; to Marianne Lorenzelli, for having tirelessly tracked down materials all over town; to Sydney Spero, whose effort in typing and correcting the manuscript surpassed that which I thought was humanly possible; to Jim Walls, for having reviewed the materials with a sure editorial touch, and to the students in PH8612, my most critical audience, whose perceptions of the strengths and weaknesses of the materials were of incalculable help to me.

Stephen L. Isaacs

SUMMARY OF CONTENTS

CONTENTS

CHAPTER 1

INTRODUCTION

I. INTRODUCTION TO POPULATION LAW AND POLICY

When I first came to Columbia University, I was asked to teach a course on population law and policy for graduate students in the School of Public Health. Naively, I assumed that preparation of such a course would be relatively easy; that I would simply locate the right textbook and assign readings from it. Things did not turn out to be quite so easy, however, for although articles abounded on population policy and on certain legal aspects of population, no single volume existed that covered the entire field. Thus, somebody who wanted to learn about the legal issues surrounding abortion or sterilization might have to sift through a variety of diverse materials, such as law review articles or summaries published in the population journals.[1]

[1]An annotated bibliography of the main reference materials on legal and policy aspects of population is provided in the appendix to this Chapter.

This book attempts to repair this deficiency by providing, in a single volume, the most important materials and issues of population law and policy. As such, it should be of interest to family planning program administrators, public health specialists, physicians, legislators, attorneys, students, international development experts, and clinic counselors, as well as to members of the public interested in population concerns. It covers the following topics:

Fertility Regulation. Chapters 2 through 6 examine the legal aspects of fertility regulation. Because issues related to fertility regulation are so important in contemporary American society, and because they are frequently tested in the courts and considered in the legislatures, they are presented first from a domestic and then from an international perspective. Chapter 2 contains a conceptual framework in which to consider laws relating to fertility regulation; it highlights the tension between the "police power" of the state to make laws to protect the health, safety, welfare, and morality of the people and the "right of privacy" guaranteed by the United States Constitution. Chapter 3 explores legal aspects of abortion, chapter 4 of sterilization, and chapter 5 of contraception. Chapter 6 is devoted to legal aspects of fertility regulation for minors, an issue of considerable current importance.

Incentives, Disincentives, and Other Socioeconomic Laws and Policies. Laws on abortion, sterilization, and contraception tend to affect fertility directly. Other laws, which relate to social and economic conditions, can have a secondary or tertiary effect on demographic behavior. Since any law which affects people's well being might, in the long run, influence child-bearing decisions, comprehensive examination of all laws that might have an indirect influence on fertility is beyond the scope of this book.[2] Chapter 7 does, however, examine some of the laws and policies that most critically, if indirectly, influence fertility, including economic incentives and disincentives, age of marriage, public health measures, housing, and status of women.

Population Policy. International and National Perspectives. Chapter 8 examines population policies and laws from an international

[2]M. COHEN, LAW AND POPULATION CLASSIFICATION PLAN, *Law and Population Monograph* No. 5 (Fletcher School of Law & Diplomacy, 1972), presents a comprehensive listing of those laws which might influence population growth and distribution.

perspective, particularly as they have been formulated within the United Nations' system. The chapter reviews the various definitions of population policy, explores fertility control as a human right, and examines the World Population Plan of Action, the document emanating from the 1974 World Population Conference. This is followed in Chapter 9 by an exploration of the fundamental issues in national population policy formation. Since most of these materials come from countries outside of the United States, the focus of chapters 8 through 9 is international, with particular emphasis on the developing world.

As this outline makes clear, the emphasis of this book is on laws and policies that, directly or indirectly, influence fertility. The focus on fertility is deliberate since that is generally the domain in which governments intervene in order to affect population growth rates. Mortality and migration, the other two variables that influence population growth, composition and distribution, are treated only in passing; the former because it does not present legal and policy issues of the same salience as fertility and the latter because it is such a massive and diffuse topic, worthy of a separate book in itself.

The format of the book is patterned after a law school casebook, modified to meet the needs of the population and public health communities. Each chapter contains excerpts from source materials. These materials have been selected from a wide variety of sources including:

Judicial Decisions. Decisions of courts are of special relevance in the United States and England with their common law tradition. United States Supreme Court decisions, particularly the Court's interpretation of the Constitution, form an important part of the source materials.

Legislation. In the United States the most important legislative body is, of course, the United States Congress, which passes laws authorizing programs (*e.g.,* the Family Planning Services and Population Research Act), as well as laws appropriating money to fund them. Also, state statutes and local ordinances, such as that passed by the Akron, Ohio, municipal council to regulate abortions, can also be of vital importance.

Executive Orders or Decrees. Although these may be important in all countries, they have particular relevance in countries with strong, centralized rule. For example, Argentina's policy banning the distribution of contraceptives was issued in the form of an executive decree.

Administrative Regulations. This includes the regulations of a Health Ministry or Department, a Food and Drug Administration, and the like. Many legal reforms have been, and can be, accomplished simply by changing the regulations of the relevant Ministry. For example, Thai nurses were permitted to distribute oral contraceptives by a change in Ministry of Health regulations. Administrative guidelines of hospitals and health facilities are also included as a source of law. Similarly, professional societies, such as the American Medical Association, have standard setting, licensing, and, sometimes, rule-making authority which forms an important source of population law.

Treaties and International Agreements. These are particularly important to the extent they affect family planning as a human right and transnational population policy.

Religious Strictures. Each of the world's major religions permits or proscribes certain activities related to the family or fertility.

Policy Statements. The sources of population policy are varied and commentators have devoted considerable time to defining what population policy is and where it is found.[3] Some of the sources, in addition to those listed above, are statements and declarations of high-level government officials, social and economic development plans, and plans issued by a national population council.

The source materials are preceded and followed by the author's commentary that provides a conceptual and historical background to the materials, discusses and interprets them, and highlights the major issues left unresolved. An extensive bibliography is provided in the footnotes for those who wish to pursue a topic at greater length.

This format differs considerably from that of the traditional textbook. It is designed to make the reader think about, and come to grips with, the major legal and policy issues that affect population dynamics. It does not provide pat answers to complex questions and,

[3] *See* discussion of this subject, *infra* pp. 349–352.

in fact, highlights the gray areas by raising many questions. Some readers may be disappointed by the degree of uncertainty in the law and others may be put off by the number of policy and legal issues that remain undecided. The benefits of this issues-oriented, casebook approach, however, are many. When a reader finishes the book, he or she will have read the most important legal and policy documents in the field and should understand the state of law and policy, the trends, the important issues yet to be resolved, and the factors likely to be relevant to their resolution.

Many readers will not have a background in population studies; others will lack grounding in legal concepts. For those who need to improve their basic knowledge in the population field, the readings and bibliographic materials cited in Chapters 8 and 9 will provide a useful frame of reference. Probably the best short introductory works to the population field are J. van der Tak, C. Haub, and E. Murphy, *Our Population Predicament: A New Look,* Population Bulletin, vol. 34, no. 5 (*Population Reference Bureau,* 1979); B. Berelson, W. P. Mauldin and S. Segal, *Population: Current Status and Policy Options* (Pop. Council, Center for Policy Studies Working Paper No. 44, 1979), and B. Berelson, *World Population: Status Report—A Guide for the Concerned Citizen, Reports on Population Family Planning* No. 15 (1974).

The remainder of this chapter introduces the non-lawyer to some basic legal concepts. It is not intended to make lawyers out of public health specialists, sociologists, teachers, or family planners, but only to prepare the reader for the legal materials presented in later chapters.

II. INTRODUCTION TO LEGAL CONCEPTS

A. Separation of Powers and Federal-State Relations

The United States Constitution sets forth the functions of the executive, legislative, and judicial branches of government.[4] Although practice has diverged from theory over 200 years, separation of powers remains a concept of great importance. In simplified, somewhat idealized summary, the legislature, composed of representatives elected by the people, makes laws that emerge from the claims

[4]U.S. CONST. articles I through III.

of competing interest groups; the executive branch carries out the laws and has other, specified, functions, and the judiciary resolves cases and controversies brought before it based on a process of reasoned decision-making by which other, similar, cases would be decided the same way.

Similarly, the Constitution distinguishes the function of the federal government from those of state governments. According to the Tenth Amendment to the Constitution, the federal government is one of limited authority and those powers not specifically delegated to the federal government are reserved to the states.[5]

B. Legislation

In civil law countries, such as those of western Europe, legislative codes are supposed to cover every contingency, and courts merely fill in the few interstices that remain. By contrast, in common law countries such as Great Britain and the United States, legislatures supposedly have less authority and courts concomitantly more. In fact, although there are areas of law that remain almost entirely made by judges (the law of torts, for example), civil and common law as practiced are tending to converge. European courts have become increasingly authoritative in interpreting statutes, while in the United States, as the Internal Revenue Code demonstrates, laws can be written that are quite comprehensive.

Legislation in the United States takes the following forms (listed roughly in descending order of political authoritativeness):[6]

The United States Constitution (the "Supreme law of the land" according to Article VI, § 2 of the Constitution)

Treaties (also made the "Supreme law of the land" under the Constitution)

Federal Statutes

Federal Executive Orders and Administrative Regulations

State Constitutions (the supreme law of the state)

State Statutes

[5]The tenth amendment to the U.S. Constitution states "The powers not delegated to the United States by the Constitution, nor prohibited by it to the States, are reserved to the States respectively, or to the people."

[6]N. DOWLING, E. PATTERSON & R. POWELL, MATERIALS FOR LEGAL METHOD (2d Ed. H. Jones, Foundation, 1952).

State Administrative Regulations
Municipal Ordinances

C. The Court System

Although it is not so in all countries, the United States has two court systems: one federal, the other state. Thus, each state has its own court system, as does the federal government. In the states, the lowest courts are criminal courts, civil courts, courts of general jurisdiction, and courts of limited jurisdiction. Criminal courts hear cases brought by the state against people accused of violating the criminal laws, as distinguished from civil courts which hear suits for monetary damages brought between private parties, *e.g.,* a suit for breach of contract. Courts of general jurisdiction can hear either civil or criminal cases, whereas courts of limited jurisdiction are authorized to adjudicate only certain matters, *e.g.,* tax or family matters. The losing party to a suit can appeal to the next higher court, challenging the lower court decision on matters of law. Most states have one intermediate court and a highest court of appeals.

The federal court system, which, according to the Constitution, is empowered to hear, *inter alia,* "cases and controversies arising under this Constitution, the Laws of the United States and Treaties . . .,"[7] is structured similarly.[8] The initial forum is a United States District Court, of which there is at least one in every state. Appeal can be taken to one of the eleven Courts of Appeal. If further appeal is to be taken, the aggrieved party can file a petition for *certiorari* to the United States Supreme Court, composed of nine justices, appointed for life. The Supreme Court, at its discretion, can accept or deny certiorari.

A decision of a court serves as precedent in the area of the court's jurisdiction, so similar cases that arise in the future will be decided in a like manner. The precedential value of a decision does not, however, extend beyond the boundaries of the deciding court's jurisdiction. Thus, decisions of the Court of Appeals for the Second Circuit, which has jurisdiction over federal district courts in New York, Connecticut, and Vermont, must be followed by the federal district courts in those states. The federal district court in Maine, however, which comes under the jurisdiction of the Court of Appeals for the First Circuit, is not bound by a decision of the Court of Appeals for the Second Circuit. Figure 1–1 sets forth in schematic form the U.S. Court System.

Figure 1-1 United States Court System

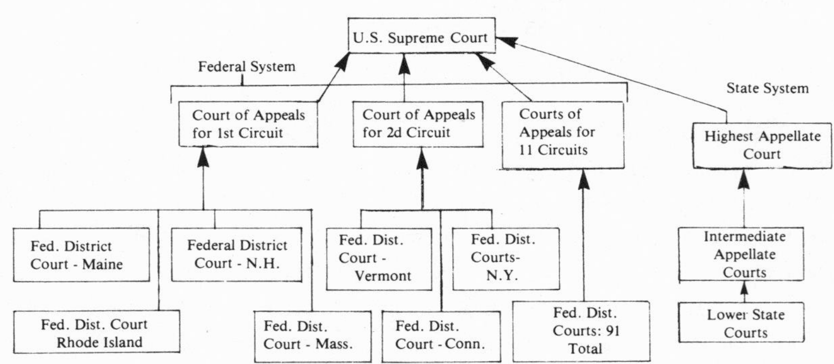

The chart omits elements not required to understand the population law materials such as expedited appeals from three-judge federal district courts, removal from state to federal courts, and distinctions between apoeals and certiorari.

D. Constitutional Litigation

Many of the judicial decisions considered in the chapters on fertility regulation involved challenges to the constitutionality of laws or regulations. Since the early days of American history, courts have had the power to declare both state and federal laws unconstitutional.[9] The constitutionality of a law may be challenged in either state or federal court, and lower court decisions interpreting the Constitution are subject to the process of appeals discussed above. The United States Supreme Court, which can review decisions of lower federal courts and constitutional rulings of the highest court of a state, is the ultimate arbiter of constitutional issues. A decision of the Supreme Court can be overturned only by amending the Constitution.

The power of the courts to review actions of the other branches of government has led to lively Constitutional debate in which courts

[7]U.S.CONST. art. III, §2.

[8]The discussion of the federal court system that follows has omitted some complexities in order to achieve clarity. For a comprehensive analysis, *see* C. WRIGHT, HANDBOOK OF THE LAW OF FEDERAL COURTS (3d Ed., West, 1976).

[9]This was first decided in the case of Marbury v. Madison, 1 Cranch 137 (1803).

have sometimes been accused of judicial lawmaking.[10] This accusation is levied particularly in cases of great social importance where courts enter areas that have been generally considered prerogatives of the legislature, such as the desegregation, one man-one vote, and abortion cases. It raises fascinating social and legal questions: to what extent should judges, who are generally appointed, substitute their judgment for that of popularly elected legislators? What standards should judges use in deciding cases? These issues surface in the context of the fertility regulation and, particularly, the abortion cases.

E. Legal Reasoning

In describing the process of legal reasoning, Edward Levi wrote:[11]*

> The basic pattern of legal reasoning is reasoning by example. It is reasoning from case to case. It is a three-step process described by the doctrine of precedent in which a proposition descriptive of the first case is made into a rule of law and then applied to a next similar situation. The steps are these: similarity is seen between cases; next the rule of law inherent in the first case is announced; then the rule of law is made applicable to the second case. This is a method of reasoning necessary for the law, but it has characteristics which under other circumstances might be considered imperfections.
>
> These characteristics become evident if the legal process is approached as though it were a method of applying general rules of law to diverse facts—in short, as though the doctrine of precedent meant that general rules, once properly determined, remained unchanged, and then were applied, albeit imperfectly, in later cases. If this were the doctrine, it would be disturbing to find that the rules change from case to case and are remade with each case. Yet this change in the rules is the indispensable dynamic quality of law. It occurs because

[10]The key issues of judicial activism or restraint are discussed in A. COX, THE ROLE OF THE SUPREME COURT IN AMERICAN GOVERNMENT (Oxford, 1976). *See also* A. BICKEL, THE LEAST DANGEROUS BRANCH: THE SUPREME COURT AT THE BAR OF POLITICS (Bobbs-Merrill, 1962), and H. Wechsler, *Toward Neutral Principles of Constitutional Law,* 73 HARV. L. REV. 1 (1959).

[11]E. LEVI, AN INTRODUCTION TO LEGAL REASONING 1–2 (Chicago, 1948); for other descriptions of the process of legal reasoning, *see* B. CARDOZO, THE NATURE OF THE JUDICIAL PROCESS (Yale, 1921) and K. LLEWELLYN, THE BRAMBLE BUSH (Oceana, 1930).

*Reprinted with the permission of the University of Chicago.

> the scope of a rule of law, and therefore its meaning, depends upon a determination of what facts will be considered similar to those present when the rule was first announced. The finding of similarity or difference is the key step in the legal process.

Levi's analysis deserves some additional commentary. It mentions the doctrine of precedent, whereby like cases are treated similarly.[12] This doctrine gives stability to the law, but if carried to a logical extreme, could paralyze it. Since, however, no two fact situations are completely alike, a particular court will not be bound to follow the decision of a previous case if one situation can be distinguished from the other. It is, as Levi notes, the judge's duty to determine the similarity or dissimilarity of fact situations. To do this, judges rely on *holding* and *dictum.* The holding of a case is that part of the opinion which is actually necessary to the decision based on the facts of that specific case, *i.e.,* the reason why this *particular* case was decided the way it was. Dictum is often defined as that part of an opinion not necessary to the decision of the case before the court. In some cases, a court will state what it is holding; in others, it will be necessary to dig it out.

The cases analyzed in this book follow a certain pattern. A court (often the Supreme Court) will make a decision based on a certain fact situation. In resolving the case, the court will establish a general principle, one that transcends the specific facts of the case at hand. Further cases, with slightly differing facts, will be considered on the basis of whether or not they fall within the general rule established. For example, in *Griswold v. Connecticut*[13] the Supreme Court ruled that a Connecticut statute which prohibited the use of contraceptives by married couples in their home was unconstitutional. Subsequently, cases with slightly differing fact situations were litigated—cases involving distribution of contraceptives to single people and use of contraceptives by married couples outside their home.

In analyzing the cases contained in this book, it is important to keep three considerations in mind:

What were the facts before the court?

[12]For an article suggesting that judges should have considerable leeway in using precedent to decide constitutional cases, see W. Douglas, *Stare Decisis,* in ESSAYS ON JURISPRUDENCE FROM THE COLUMBIA LAW REVIEW 18 (Columbia, 1963).

[13]381 U.S. 479 (1965), discussed *infra* pp. 49–66.

What did the court actually decide—*i.e.,* what general principle can be extracted from the case?

What is the potential scope or extension of that principle?

F. A Note on Citations

1. Citation system

Citations used in the book generally follow the guidelines of the *Uniform System of Citation,* published by the Columbia, Harvard, Pennsylvania, and Yale law reviews.[14] The abbreviations used are common in legal books and periodicals but may require some explanation for the non-lawyer.

2. Judicial decisions

Judicial decisions are reprinted in court reporter series. For example, decisions of the United States Supreme Court are reprinted in the *United States Reports,* the *U.S. Supreme Court Reporter,* or the *U.S. Supreme Court Reports, Lawyers Edition.*[15] Decisions of the Federal Courts of Appeal are reprinted in the *Federal Reporter* series. Federal and state reporters are available at law libraries. In the text, cases (*e.g., Jones v. Smith*) are followed immediately by a citation. The number preceding the reporter refers to the volume, the number after it to the page. Some of the common abbreviations used in the text are:

> *U.S.* refers to the *United States Reports,* the official reporter of United States Supreme Court opinions. Thus, *United States v. Reynolds,* 345 U.S. 1 (1953) means that the case named *United States versus Reynolds* can be found in volume 345 of the *United States Reports* at page 1, and the case was decided in 1953.
>
> *F. 2d* refers to the *Federal Reporter, Second Series* in which decisions of the U.S. Courts of Appeals are found. Thus, *United States v. One Package,* 86 F. 2d 737 (2d. Cir. 1936) means that the case named *United States versus One Package* can be found on page 737 of the 86th volume of the *Federal Reproter,Second Series* and that the case was decided by the Second Circuit Court of Appeals in 1936.

[14]COLUM. L. REV., HARV. L. REV., U. PA. L. REV. & YALE L. J., A UNIFORM SYSTEM OF CITATION (12th Ed. 1976).

[15]The official Supreme Court reporter, the U.S. REPORTS, is cited throughout the book where possible. Recent decisions are sometimes reported the the SUPREME COURT REPORTER (SUP. CT.) of the LAWYER'S EDITION (L. ED.) before they appear in the official reporter. Where no official citation is available, the SUP. CT. or L. ED. is used.

> *F. Supp.* refers to the *Federal Supplement,* in which decisions of U.S. federal district courts are reported. *James v. Ogilvie,* 310 F. Supp. 661 (N.D. Ill. 1970) means that the case named *James versus Ogilvie* can be found in volume 310 of the *Federal Supplement* at page 661; it was decided by the Federal District Court for the Northern District of Illinois in 1970.

Decisions of state courts are generally reprinted in two places: the state's own law reporter series and the regional series of the West Publishing Company. Some states have more elaborate systems of court reporters. For example, New York State reports decisions of its Court of Appeals (its highest court) in its New York Reports (N.Y.) series, decisions of the Appellate Division (the intermediate appellate court) in its *Appellate Division* (App. Div.) reports series, and lower court decisions in its *Miscellaneous* (Misc.) reports series. Decisions of state courts are cited either by the state reporter or by the relevant West regional reporter which might be:

A. 2d—Atlantic Reporter, Second Series
N.E. 2d—Northeast Reporter, Second Series
S.E. 2d—Southeast Reporter, Second Series
So. 2d—Southern Law Reporter, Second Series
S.W. 2d—Southwest Reporter, Second Series
N.W. 2d—Northwest Reporter, Second Series
P. 2d—Pacific Reporter, Second Series

As an example, *Matter of S.C.E.,* 378 A. 2d 144 (Del. 1977), means that the case, the *Matter of S.C.E.,* can be found on page 144 of the 378th volume of the *Atlantic Reporter,* Second Series; it was decided by the Delaware Supreme Court in 1977.

3. Federal statutes are reported officially in the *Public Laws of the United States* cited as Pub. L. No. . . . For example, Pub. L. No. 91-572 (1970), refers to public law number 572 passed by the 91st Congress in 1970. The West Publishing Company reports federal statutes in its *United States Code* or *United States Code Annotated* series. The citations for these are U.S.C. or U.S.C.A. A citation such as 42 U.S.C. § 602 (1976) means that the text can be found in volume 42 of the 1976 edition of the United States Code, section 602. State statutes are printed in each state's collection of laws.

4. Regulations of Executive Agencies appear in the *Code of Federal Regulations,* cited as the C.F.R. 42 C.F.R § 50 (1980) refers to volume 42 of the *Code of Federal Regulations,* section 50, 1980. Federal regulations also appear in the *Federal Register* in either a preliminary form (when comments are sought), or in a final form.

5. Articles are cited in the following order: author, title, volume, journal, page, date. For example, F. Jaffe, *Public Policy on Fertility Control,* 229 SCIENTIFIC AMERICAN 17 (1973) means that F. Jaffe's article entitled *Public Policy on Fertility Control* appeared in volume 229 of *SCIENTIFIC AMERICAN* at page 17 in 1973. This follows the pattern of legal periodicals, but differs from that of population journals which usually put the volume number after the name of the journal.

APPENDIX: REFERENCE MATERIAL IN POPULATION LAW AND POLICIES

Materials with a United States Focus

FAMILY PLANNING/POPULATION REPORTER. Published by the Alan Guttmacher Institute, this bimonthly publication summarizes the latest court decisions and legislative enactments in the United States.

HUMAN REPRODUCTION LAW REPORTER. A loose-leaf volume which also concentrates on recent developments in United States law. Although it usually appears two to four months later than the *FAMILY PLANNING/POPULATION REPORTER,* this source has the advantage of publishing the entire text of significant laws and court decisions.

FAMILY LAW REPORTER. Published by the Bureau of National Affairs, the FAMILY LAW REPORTER prints the texts of important U.S. decisions and laws. It is written for lawyers and is usually available only in law offices and law school libraries.

DHEW, FAMILY PLANNING, CONTRACEPTION, VOLUNTARY STERILIZATION, AND ABORTION: AN ANALYSIS OF LAWS AND POLICIES IN THE UNITED STATES, EACH STATE AND JURISDICTION (DHEW Publication No. (HSA) 79-5623, 1978). Published by the Health, Education, and Welfare Department, this publication summarizes national and state laws on abortion, contraception, and sterilization. It is current through 1976 with a 1978 addendum.

WASHINGTON MEMO. A monthly newsletter of the Washington office of the Alan Guttmacher Institute focusing on policy and legal developments in the capital.

ABORTION LAW REPORTER, published jointly by NARAL and the Antioch Law School, this loose-leaf publication contains analysis of and excerpts from the latest abortion litigation.

LAW REVIEWS sometimes publish articles on legal aspects of population. For example, the United States Supreme Court decision on abortion provoked an outpouring of scholarly criticism in the law journals. The *JOURNAL OF FAMILY LAW* and the *FAMILY LAW QUARTERLY* are the most likely to publish articles of interest.

Materials with an International Focus

PUBLICATIONS OF THE LAW AND POPULATION PROGRAM, FLETCHER SCHOOL OF LAW AND DIPLOMACY, TUFTS UNIVERSITY. The Law and Population Program has published studies of law and population in a number of countries as well as reviews of the world's laws concerning certain aspects of population (*e.g.,* abortion, sex education, and contraceptives). These studies have appeared as 42 *Law and Population Monographs.*

INTERNATIONAL DIGEST OF HEALTH LEGISLATION. This publication of the World Health Organization digests recently-passed health laws worldwide.

INTERNATIONAL PLANNED PARENTHOOD FEDERATION, LAW FILE. Published monthly, this circular summarized the latest law and policy developments worldwide.

POPULATION & DEVELOPMENT REVIEW. A quarterly publication of the Population Council which contains many useful articles related to international aspects of population and development policy.

POPULATION REPORTS. Published by the Population Information Program of John Hopkins University (and by George Washington University before mid-1978), the *POPULATION REPORTS* series contain comprehensive reviews of all aspects of population.

STUDIES IN FAMILY PLANNING. Although this monthly periodical of the Population Council concentrates on family planning, it contains many important articles with legal or policy ramifications.

CHAPTER 2

THE POLICE POWER AND THE RIGHT OF PRIVACY

I. ANALYTICAL FRAMEWORK: A NOTE ON JUDICIAL BALANCING OF INTERESTS

Chapter 2 and the succeeding four chapters examine the legal issues related to direct means of fertility control—abortion, sterilization, contraception, and the rights of minors to fertility control services. This chapter serves as an introduction to the following four chapters by providing a framework with which to analyze the fertility regulation materials that follow. Although the focus is primarily on the United States and decisions of the United States Supreme Court furnish much of the source material, this chapter should provide a perspective from which to examine international fertility control laws and policies such as sterilization in India or economic disincentives in Singapore.

A large part of the work of the modern United States Supreme Court, particularly as it interprets the Constitution, is given to balancing competing interests, usually the interests of the state versus rights of individuals guaranteed in the Bill of Rights and the Fourteenth Amendment to the Constitution (set forth in the Appendix to this chapter). A number of examples of the tension between individual rights and state authority can be cited: the interest of the state in apprehending criminals versus the right of citizens to be free from unreasonable searches; the interest of the state in protecting public morals by controlling obscenity versus the right of the press to print without governmental restrictions or interference; the interest of the state in maintaining public order versus the right of protesters to assemble and demonstrate.

In the population field, many of the recent legal developments can be more easily understood if viewed in the context of competing rights and interests; specifically, the interest of the state in regulating public health, safety, welfare, and morality (the "police power") weighed against the right of the individual to be free from state interference in the regulation of his or her fertility (the "right of privacy").

To provide a conceptual understanding of these competing rights and interests, this chapter is structured along the following lines: first, an exploration of the police power, with particular reference to the state's authority in the realm of public health, morality, and family life; second, a brief look at "due process" and "equal protection," those constitutionally-protected individual rights that often conflict with the police power, and third, an examination of the right of privacy as established in the seminal case of *Griswold v. Connecticut.*

II. THE POLICE POWER

A. Definition: 16A American Jurisprudence 2d §§360–363 (1979)*

Police power is often said to be a general term used to express the particular right of a government which is inherent in every sovereignty. Thus, it is an inherent power of the states, possessed by every one of them as sovereign.

From what has been said, it follows, as a matter of logic, that the police power is not a grant derived from or under any written constitution, or from the legislature. The term is not found in the Declaration of Independence, the Federal Constitution, or even in most state constitutions . . .

The term *police power,* although generally understood and universally recognized, is somewhat hazy and ambiguous. While there have

*Reprinted with permission from the Lawyers Co-operative Publishing Company, Rochester, New York.

been many attempts to define the police power, it has not received a full and complete definition . . .

While it is generally recognized that it is very difficult and practically impossible to give an exact definition of the police power, many attempts have been made. There is no consensus in favor of any of them, but these definitions are of considerable value as indicating the breadth and scope of this power.

The expression *police power,* although capable of use, and sometimes used, in a restricted sense, is frequently used very broadly to include all legislation and almost every function of civil government. Thus, it has been stated that the police power in effect sums up the whole power of government, and that all other powers are only incidental and ancillary to the execution of the police power; it is that full, final power involved in the administration of law as the means to the attainment of practical justice. And it has been said that the power is only another name for that authority which resides in every sovereignty to pass all laws for the internal regulation and government of the state, that it is the vast residual power of the state, and that it comprises that portion of the sovereignty of the state which is not surrendered by the terms of the Federal Constitution to the federal government . . .

There is considerable authority which speaks of the police power as the power inherent in the state to prescribe, within the limits of the state and federal constitutions, reasonable regulations necessary to preserve the public order, health, safety, and morals . . .

B. Scope of the Police Power

The police power, as is evident from the above excerpt, is something of a misnomer; in reality, it might better have been termed the *governmental power,* for it is the attribute of any sovereign government to make laws for the common good. The extent of the police power—and the deference that courts often give it—in the areas of public health, the family, and morality are explored in the *Jacobson* case and the discussion which follows it.

1. Jacobson v. Massachusetts, 197 U.S. 11 (U.S. Supreme Court 1905)

This case involves the validity, under the Constitution of the United States, of certain provisions in the statutes of Massachusetts relating to vaccination.

The Revised Laws of that Commonwealth, c. 75, §137, provide that "the board of health of a city or town if, in its opinion, it is necessary for the public health or safety shall require and enforce the vaccination and revaccination of all the inhabitants thereof and shall provide them with the means of free vaccination. Whoever, being over twenty-one years of age and not under guardianship, refuses or neglects to comply with such requirement shall forfeit five dollars."

An exception is made in favor of "children who present a certificate, signed by a registered physician, that they are unfit subjects for vaccination." §139.

Proceeding under the above statutes, the Board of Health of the city of Cambridge, Massachusetts, on the twenty-seventh day of February, 1902, adopted the following regulation: "Whereas, smallpox has been prevalent to some extent in the city of Cambridge and still continues to increase; and whereas, it is necessary for the speedy extermination of the disease, that all persons not protected by vaccination should be vaccinated; and whereas, in the opinion of the board, the public health and safety require the vaccination or revaccination of all the inhabitants of Cambridge; be it ordered, that all the inhabitants of the city who have not been successfully vaccinated since March 1, 1897, be vaccinated or revaccinated."

Subsequently, the Board adopted an additional regulation empowering a named physician to enforce the vaccination of persons as directed by the Board at its special meeting of February 27.

The above regulations being in force, the plaintiff in error, Jacobson, was proceeded against by a criminal complaint in one of the inferior courts of Massachusetts. The complaint charged that on the seventeenth day of July, 1902, the Board of Health of Cambridge, being of the opinion that it was necessary for the public health and safety, required the vaccination and revaccination of all the inhabitants thereof who had not been successfully vaccinated since the first day of March, 1897, and provided them with the means of free vaccination, and that the defendant, being over twenty-one years of age and not under guardianship, refused and neglected to comply with such requirement.

The defendant, having been arraigned, pleaded not guilty. The government put in evidence the above regulations adopted by the Board of Health and made proof tending to show that its chairman informed the defendant that by refusing to be vaccinated he would incur the penalty provided by the statute, and would be prosecuted therefor; that he offered to vaccinate the defendant without expense to him; and that the offer was declined and defendant refused to be vaccinated . . .

A verdict of guilty was thereupon returned . . . [and] pursuant to the verdict of the jury, he was sentenced by the court to pay a fine of five dollars. And the court ordered that he stand committed until the fine was paid . . .

Mr. Justice Harlan, after making the foregoing statement, delivered the opinion of the court . . .

. . . we assume for the purposes of the present inquiry that its provisions require, at least as a general rule, that adults not under guardianship and remaining within the limits of the city of Cambridge must submit to the regulation adopted by the Board of Health. Is the statute, so construed, therefore, inconsistent with the liberty which the Constitution of the United States secures to every person against deprivation by the State?

The authority of the State to enact this statute is to be referred to what is commonly called the police power—a power which the State did not surrender when becoming a member of the Union under the Constitution. Although this court has refrained from any attempt to define the limits of that power, yet it has distinctly recognized the authority of a State to enact quarantine laws and "health laws of every description;" indeed, all laws that relate to matters completely within its territory and which do not by their necessary operation affect the people of other States. According to settled principles the police power of a State must be held to embrace, at least, such reasonable regulations established directly by legislative enactment as will protect the public health and the public safety. It is equally true that the State may invest local bodies called into existence for purposes of local administration with authority in some appropriate way to safeguard the public health and the public safety. The mode or manner in which those results are to be accomplished is within the discretion of the State, subject, of course, so far as Federal power is concerned, only to the conditions that no rule prescribed by a State, nor any regulation adopted by a local governmental agency acting under the sanction of state legislation, shall contravene the Constitution of the United States or infringe any right granted or secured by that instrument. A local enactment or regulation, even if based on the acknowledged police powers of a State, must always yield in case of conflict with the exercise by the General Government of any power it possesses under the Constitution, or with any right which that instrument gives or secures.

We come, then, to inquire whether any right given, or secured by the Constitution, is invaded by the statute as interpreted by the state court. The defendant insists that his liberty is invaded when the State subjects him to fine or imprisonment for neglecting or refusing to submit to vaccination; that a compulsory vaccination law is unreasonable, arbitrary and oppressive, and, therefore, hostile to the inherent right of every freeman to care for his own body and health in such way as to him seems best; and that the execution of such a law against one who objects to vaccination, no matter for what reason, is nothing short of an assault upon his person. But the liberty secured by the Constitution of the United States to every person within its jurisdiction does not import an absolute right in each person to be, at all times and in all circumstances, wholly freed from restraint . . .

If the mode adopted by the Commonwealth of Massachusetts for the protection of its local communities against smallpox proved to be distressing, inconvenient or objectionable to some—if nothing more could be reasonably affirmed of the statute in question—the answer is that it was the duty of the constituted authorities primarily to keep in view the welfare, comfort and safety of the many, and not permit the interests of the many to be subordinated to the wishes or convenience of the few. There is, of course, a sphere within which the individual may assert the supremacy of his own will and rightfully dispute the authority of any human government, especially of any free government existing under a written constitution, to interfere with the exercise of that will. But it is equally true that in every well-ordered society charged with the duty of conserving the safety of its members the rights of the individual in respect of his liberty may at times, under the pressure of great dangers, be subjected to such restraint, to be enforced by reasonable regulations, as the safety of the general public may demand . . .

It is said, however, that the statute, as interpreted by the state court, although making an exception in favor of children certified by a registered physician to be unfit subjects for vaccination, makes no exception in the case of adults in like condition. But this cannot be deemed a denial of the equal protection of the laws to adults; for the statute is applicable equally to all in like condition and there are obviously reasons why regulations may be appropriate for adults which could not be safely applied to persons of tender years . . .

The appellant claims that vaccination does not tend to prevent smallpox, but tends to bring about other diseases, and that it does much harm, with no good.

It must be conceded that some laymen, both learned and unlearned, and some physicians of great skill and repute, do not believe that vaccination is a preventive of smallpox. The common belief, however, is that it has a decided tendency to prevent the spread of this fearful disease and to render it less dangerous to those who contract it. While not accepted by all, it is accepted by the mass of the people, as well as by most members of the medical profession. It has been general in our State and in most civilized nations for generations. It is generally accepted in theory and generally applied in practice, both by the voluntary action of the people and in obedience to the command of law. Nearly every State of the Union has statutes to encourage, or directly or indirectly to require, vaccination, and this is true of most nations of Europe . . .

The fact that the belief is not universal is not controlling, for there is scarcely any belief that is accepted by everyone. The possibility that the belief may be wrong, and that science may yet show it to be wrong, is not conclusive; for the legislature has the right to pass laws which,

> according to the common belief of the people, are adapted to prevent the spread of contagious diseases. In a free country, where the government is by the people, through their chosen representatives, practical legislation admits of no other standard of action; for what the people believe is for the common welfare must be accepted as tending to promote the common welfare, whether it does in fact or not. Any other basis would conflict with the spirit of the Constitution, and would sanction measures opposed to a republican form of government. While we do not decide and cannot decide that vaccination is a preventive of smallpox, we take judicial notice of the fact that this is the common belief of the people of the State, and with this fact as a foundation we hold that the statute in question is a health law, enacted in a reasonable and proper exercise of the police power . . .

2. Note on *Jacobson*

a. Scope of Jacobson. How important is the fact that the disease involved, smallpox, is contagious? Should the decision have been the same if the disease were non-communicable? To what extent is *Jacobson* authority for state fluoridation of water? A state ban on smoking? A sterilizing agent in the community water supply? How important is "community belief" to the decision? Justice Harlan states, "It [vaccination] is accepted by the mass of the people, as well as by most members of the medical profession." Would the result have been different if the opinion of the medical community—or the lay community—were less overwhelmingly on one side?

b. State Compulsion. Is *Jacobson* authority for the proposition that a state could "compel" vaccination, even upon an unwilling subject? How important is the penalty for noncompliance (a $5 fine)? Or the exception for children who can prove they are unfit subjects for vaccination? Would the result have been different if the penalty for noncompliance were a short jail term? Forced vaccination? Insofar as it is applicable, would *Jacobson* have provided solid support for the Indian government's "compulsory sterilization" laws? For compulsory sterilization of mental incompetents? For state enforced birth control if the population problem were deemed serious enough?

c. Judicial Deference to Legislatures. Although by now a decision of long standing, *Jacobson* is still cited approvingly in support of the proposition that people do not have unlimited control of their own bodies. It also illustrates the deference courts pay to legislatures in the realm of public health legislation. The major chipping away at this deference has come in the cases considered in this and the succeeding chapters.

3. State Regulation of Family Life

The state has the power to regulate many aspects of domestic relations, ranging from marriage and divorce to child support. It is, of course, within the state's power to limit the number of spouses an individual can have to one at a time, even when this conflicts with religious beliefs. In *Reynolds v. United States,* 98 U.S. 145 (1878), the defendant, a Mormon having two wives, was charged with violating a law prohibiting bigamy. The Supreme Court upheld his conviction, stating:

> In our opinion, the statute immediately under consideration is within the legislative power of Congress. It is constitutional and valid as prescribing a rule of action for all those residing in the Territories, and in places over which the United States have exclusive control. This being so, the only question which remains is, whether those who make polygamy a part of their religion are excepted from the operation of the statute. If they are, then those who do not make polygamy a part of their religious belief may be found guilty and punished, while those who do, must be acquitted and go free. This would be introducing a new element into criminal law. Laws are made for the government of actions, and while they cannot interfere with mere religious belief and opinions, they may with practices. Suppose one believed that human sacrifices were a necessary part of religious worship, would it be seriously contended that the civil government under which he lived could not interfere to prevent a sacrifice? Or if a wife religiously believed it was her duty to burn herself upon the funeral pyre of her dead husband, would it be beyond the power of the civil government to prevent her carrying her belief into practice?
>
> So here, as a law of the organization of society under the exclusive dominion of the United States, it is provided that plural marriages shall not be allowed. Can a man excuse his practices to the contrary because of his religious belief? To permit this would be to make the professed doctrines of religious belief superior to the law of the land, and in effect to permit every citizen to become law unto himself. Government could exist only in name under such circumstances . . .

Although it is an old case and attitudes of courts toward the free exercise of religion have evolved since 1878[1] and notwithstanding

[1] *See, e.g.,* Arizona v. Whittingham, 504 P. 2d 950 (Ariz. 1973), *cert. denied* 417 U.S. 946 (1974) upholding the use of peyote in a bona fide religious wedding ceremony.

criticism of its underlying rationale,[2] *Reynolds* has survived and is considered good law.

Professor Luke Lee has asked: if the state has the power to regulate the intimacies of family life, even to the extent of prohibiting more than one wife and compelling children to go to school, why does it not have the authority to order sterilizations after a specified number of children?[3]

4. State Regulation of Morality

Consider the traditional definition of the police power: "the power inherent in a government to enact laws, within constitutional limits, to promote the order, safety, health, *morals* and general welfare of society."[4] Why does the state have an interest in promoting morality? What is the extent of the state's power to legislate morality? What, if any, are the state's limits in promoting morality? How is morality to be defined? As "traditional morality"? As "contemporary morality?" Is it a legislative, judicial, or executive function to provide the definition?

The issues for and against state involvement in morality were most clearly articulated more than a decade ago in England in the context of what has become known as "the Hart-Devlin debate." Responding to the recommendation of the Wolfenden Committee in England that homosexuality should be decriminalized, Lord Devlin stated, "We should ask ourselves in the first instance whether, looking at it [the practice of homosexuality] calmly and dispassionately, we regard it as a vice so abominable that its mere presence is an offense. If that is the genuine feeling of the society in which we live, I do not see how society can be denied the right to eradicate it."[5] He justified this position on two grounds: first, a shared morality is necessary to a society's existence and, therefore, society has the right to suppress immoral behavior in order to prevent its own disintegration and, second, that a majority of a

[2] *See, e.g.,* H. CLARK, JR., THE LAW OF DOMESTIC RELATIONS IN THE UNITED STATES 62 (West, 1968).

[3] L. Lee, *Compulsory Sterilization and Human Rights,* POPULI, vol. 3, no. 4, p. 2 (1976). *See also* Justice Goldberg's comment on this subject in Griswold v. Connecticut, pp. 53–54, *infra.*

[4] 16 C.J.S., § 174 (1956) (emphasis added).

[5] P. DEVLIN, THE ENFORCEMENT OF MORALS 17 (Oxford, 1965).

community views certain behavior as immoral gives legislators the right, or even the duty, to act on that consensus and suppress the offensive conduct.[6]

H.L.A. Hart, and others who responded to Lord Devlin, questioned whether so-called immoral behavior would, in fact, cause society to disintegrate and, more importantly, argued that the enforcement of morality by itself is not sufficient to justify criminal sanctions.[7] Proponents of the view that society should not legislate morality ultimately rely on the utilitarian philosophy of John Stuart Mill, as expressed below, or some variation thereof:

> The only purpose for which power can be rightfully exercised over any member of a civilized community, against his will, is to prevent harm to others. His own good, either physical or moral, is not a sufficient warrant.[8]

However, only the most unreconstructed utilitarian accepts Mill's postulation without reservation. Does not government have some right to legislate on frankly paternalistic grounds? To keep pornographic books out of the hands of children? To keep an individual from inflicting physical harm on himself? How can paternalistic legislation—*e.g.*, a requirement of safety belts in automobiles—be distinguished from morality enforcement—*e.g.*, prohibiting homosexual activity? Is there a distinction between government's protecting an individual from physical harm and protecting him from moral harm?[9]

Notwithstanding the debate about whether the government should legislate morality and the justification for and scope of governmental paternalism, recent U.S. Supreme Court decisions have

[6]R. Dworkin, *Lord Devlin and the Enforcement of Morals,* 75 YALE L.J. 986 (1966).

[7]H. HART, THE CONCEPT OF LAW (Oxford, 1961).

[8]J. MILL, ON LIBERTY 13 (Bobbs-Merrill, 1956); for a cogent analysis of the utilitarian position, *see* H. HART, *The Shell Foundation Lectures, 1978–1979: Utilitarianism and Natural Rights,* 53 TULANE L. REV. 663 (1979), and *Between Utility and Rights,* 79 COLUM. L. REV. 828 (1979). *See also* J. RAWLS, A THEORY OF JUSTICE (Harvard, 1971).

[9]For analyses of the issues involved in governmental regulation of morality, *see* R. Dworkin, *Lord Devlin and the Enforcement of Morals,* supra n.6., R. Sartorius, *The Enforcement of Morality,* 81 YALE L.J. 891 (1972), and T. Hindes, *Morality Enforcement through the Criminal Law and the Modern Doctrine of Substantive Due Process,* 126 U.PA. L.REV. 344 (1977).

made it clear that promoting morality is considered a legitimate state interest.[10] As Justice Brennan said dissenting in *Paris Adult Theater I v. Slaton,* 413 U.S. 49, 108–109 (1973):

> The traditional description of state police power does embrace the regulation of morals as well as the health, safety, and general welfare of the citizenry . . . And much legislation—compulsory public education laws, civil rights laws, even the abolition of capital punishment—is grounded, at least in part, on a concern with the morality of the community.

III. DUE PROCESS AND EQUAL PROTECTION OF THE LAWS

A. The Concepts of Due Process and Equal Protection of the Laws: F. Grad, Public Health Law Manual 28–31 (APHA, 1975)*

In considering constitutional protections under bills of rights, it is essential to recall that we are operating under a dual form of government. Because ours is a federal government, constitutional protections both under the federal and under the relevant state bill of rights must be considered. To a great extent, the state and federal bills of rights duplicate protections, so that many of the people's rights secured in state constitutions against the state government are similarly guaranteed by the first ten amendments to the Constitution of the United States against interference by the National Government. Furthermore, many of the personal and political protections of the first ten amendments of the National Constitution have been made applicable to the states through the Fourteenth Amendment of the National Constitution:

> No State shall make or enforce any law which shall abridge the privileges or immunities of citizens of the United States; nor shall any State deprive any person of life, liberty, or property, without due process of law; nor deny to any person within its jurisdiction the equal protection of the laws.

This means that in looking for protection against certain improper exercises of power by his own state government, a person need not

[10] *See Paris Adult Theatre I v. Slaton,* 413 U.S. 49 (1973); *Poe v. Ullman,* 367 U.S. 497 (1961), Justice Harlan dissenting; *Doe v. Commonwealth's Attorney,* 425 U.S. 901 (1976).

*Reprinted with permission from the American Public Health Association.

look to his own state constitution and its bill of rights alone, but he may also look for such protection to the National Government and its courts. Of course, as a reading of the Fourteenth Amendment will tell, it does not expressly make the entire National Bill of Rights applicable to the states. But the Fourteenth Amendment has been constructed to prohibit the states—and this includes all local political subdivisions, such as municipalities and health districts as well—from abridging those guarantees of the National Bill of Rights which are "fundamental to a concept of ordered liberty." Thus, a person who believes that his constitutionally guaranteed liberties have been invaded by some state law or regulation, or by some action or decision of a state or local health department may seek his remedy in a state court, under the state bill of rights, and he may seek further protection in the Federal courts, or through the state courts and then to the United States Supreme Court, for the protection of any of the rights guaranteed by the Federal Constitution through the Fourteenth Amendment.

In reviewing state legislation and state action for compliance with the requirements of the Fourteenth Amendment, the courts have relied most heavily on the "equal protection" and "due process" clauses. A brief consideration of both of these clauses is therefore necessary.

The Meaning of "Equal Protection"

The prohibition against the denial "to any person" of the "equal protection of the laws" is found in a number of state bills of rights as well as in the Federal. The equal protection clause concerns itself with the comparative treatment of individuals. It insures that no greater burden is placed by government action on one person than on another in similar circumstances or that government does not discriminate unfairly in the granting of privileges. This does not mean that the government cannot differentiate between different persons or activities on reasonable grounds. For instance, in the public health field it is perfectly proper for a health department to make different regulations for different kinds of food establishments, varying the severity of the requirements with the potential risk to public health imposed by each, or to impose different licensing and other requirements on wholesalers and on retailers of milk, or frozen desserts, or shellfish, again depending on the relative extent of the risk of each operation. So, too, when distributing a scarce and much sought-after new vaccine —such as in the early days of the Salk vaccine—the government may establish priorities to see that children, pregnant women, or other persons who are in a special category are preferred. While permitting reasonable classification, the equal protection clause outlaws distinctions not based on rational grounds. It would not be a proper classification to require a higher license fee for a particular trade in one part of a jurisdiction than in another—unless it could be shown that inspection and administration costs differ significantly in one from the other. And it would clearly be an improper classification to deny the benefit of a new vaccine to children with red hair while granting it to blonde or brunette children that are otherwise similarly situated. The question of proper classification is a recurring one in public health law and regulation; while it has constitutional "equal protection" ramification, it is essentially a problem of fairness to be honestly resolved not by reference to constitutional theory, but by reference to the precise facts of the situation. Unless a meaningful factual difference exists between two activities, two persons, or two situations, the Constitution requires that they be treated alike.

The Meaning of "Due Process"

Unlike the "equal protection" clause, which focuses on the comparative treatment of persons and situations, the "due process" clause focuses on the individual treatment accorded to any person. The requirement of "due process" insures that no person shall be deprived of those rights which are "implicit in the concept of ordered liberty" and it guarantees that every individual shall be treated with at least a minimum of "decency and fairness." In so far as the guarantees of the Federal Bill of Rights are applicable to the states through the Fourteenth Amendment, this is accomplished through the requirements of "due process." So far, the United States Supreme Court has held that this guarantee of fundamental fairness includes at least the following guarantees:

From the First Amendment, the establishment clause (separation of Church and State), freedom of religion, freedom of speech and press, and the right of assembly.

From the Fourth Amendment, freedom from unreasonable searches and seizures.

From the Fifth Amendment, protection of the privilege against self-incrimination.

From the Sixth Amendment, the right to a fair, impartial public trial with the assistance of counsel, in cases of felony and in cases of lesser offenses when the Supreme Court considers it essential, and from the Eighth Amendment, freedom from cruel and unusual punishment.

Some provisions of the Federal Bill of Rights do not apply to the states, though many state bills of rights may in fact provide for them, such as, for instance, in the Fifth Amendment the right to grand jury indictment, and in the Sixth and Seventh Amendments, the right to trial by jury in both civil and criminal cases.

In sum, the Supreme Court has refused to issue a rigid definition of the phrase "due process of law," but it is clear that it includes all of the procedural and legal protections which all of us traditionally enjoy and expect to maintain. While "due process" may give rise to many technical legal problems in specific instances, it is probably fair to say that any state action—including action by a state or local health department—that rides roughshod over normal expection, that is an arbitrary exercise of naked power, or that goes completely counter to established and expected ways of dealing with particular problems is in danger of being held a violation of due process of law.

B. Note on Judicial Analysis of Due Process and Equal Protection[11]

Historically, the United States Supreme Court's adjudication of due process cases has differed considerably from its treatment of equal protection cases. In the early years of the twentieth century, the Supreme Court struck down various socially progressive enactments on the grounds that they violated "substantive due process," particularly the liberty of contract guaranteed by the Fourteenth Amendment. For example, the Court, in *Lochner v. New York,* 198 U.S. 45 (1905), held unconstitutional a New York law limiting bakers to working 60 hours a week. This now-discredited period of giving an economic interpretation to substantive due process came to an end in the mid-1930's. Justice Roberts enunciated the new standards:[12]

> If the laws passed are seen to have a reasonable relation to a proper legislative purpose, and are neither arbitrary nor discriminatory, the requirements of due process are satisfied . . .

The court maintained this *laissez-faire* attitude toward due process cases—in some instances even going out of its way to articulate possible legislative motives[13] until recently when it began demanding a more exacting standard where fundamental personal rights were concerned.[14]

[11]For an excellent examination of this topic, *see* S. Bice, *Standards of Judicial Review under the Equal Protection and Due Process Clauses,* 50 SO. CALIF. L. REV. 689 (1977).

[12]Nebbia v. New York, 291 U.S. 502, 503 (1934).

[13]*See, e.g.*, Williamson v. Lee Optical Co., 348 U.S. 483 (1955).

[14]The criteria for determining whether a right is fundamental or not is examined on pp. 60–61, *infra*.

In contrast to the judicial activism shown in the early substantive due process cases, the Court has traditionally utilized a standard of review in equal protection cases that was very deferential toward legislatures. It would scrutinize challenged legislation to see whether it was reasonably-related to a permissible legislative purpose. In the 1960's the Warren Court began to use the equal protection clause as a major interventionist tool where fundamental personal rights or "suspect" classifications[15] were involved.

During the 1960's and 1970's, the Supreme Court's analysis of due process and equal protection cases tended to converge as it developed stricter standards of scrutiny where fundamental personal rights, particularly those involving privacy, were infringed.

What, then, is the current mode of analysis of due process and equal protection cases, particularly where rights of privacy may have been infringed?

(1) The court will determine whether a "fundamental right" is involved.[16]

(2) If a fundamental right is found to be involved, the court will give "strict scrutiny" to the challenged law and require the state to demonstrate a "compelling" reason why the law was necessary. It will examine both the ends (is the end within the police power of the state? is it a legitimate governmental objective?) and the means (is the law "necessary" to meet the state's objective? is there a compelling reason for its enactment?). The court will also examine whether the law is "narrowly drawn," *i.e.*, whether the state's goal could be achieved by a less broad statute that would be less harmful to fundamental rights. Where fundamental rights are involved, a law must pass, in Justice Harlan's words in *Poe v. Ullman,* p. 58, *infra,* "a more rigorous Constitutional test than that going merely to the plausibility of its underlying rationale." Under the "compelling state interest" test, the state rarely prevails.[17]

(3) If the court finds that no fundamental rights are involved, it then imposes a much more lenient test; is the legislation "rationally

[15]To date, race and alienage have been considered suspect classes. Illegitimacy may be one. In 1973 four Supreme Court justices found that classification by sex was suspect, but this view has never commanded a majority.

[16]And where an equal protection argument is made, whether a suspect class is involved.

[17]Using the more rigorous "compelling state interest" test, the government has prevailed in the Supreme Court only two times, both in the context of treatment of Japanese during World War II. Korematsu v. United States, 323 U.S. 214 (1944) and Hirabayashi v. United States, 320 U.S. 81 (1943).

related" to a permissible state interest. As in (2) above, it will examine both the ends (is this within the police power of the state?) and the means (is it a reasonable way of achieving the goal?). The state rarely loses under this test.

For application of this mode of analysis in an equal protection context, see Justice Powell's opinion in *Maher v. Roe,* pp. 90–90, *infra.,* and for a criticism of it, see Justice Marshall's dissent in the same case, pp. 96–97, *infra.*[18]

IV. THE RIGHT OF PRIVACY

A key concept considered in the cases relating to abortion, sterilization, and contraception is that of the right of privacy. This was recognized as a constitutionally-protected right in *Griswold v. Connecticut,* excerpted below, in which the Supreme Court struck down a Connecticut statute that prohibited even the use of contraceptives. *Griswold* is followed in the text by Justice Harlan's dissent in *Poe v. Ullman,* an earlier challenge to Connecticut's birth control law which the Supreme Court refused to hear, and then by an examination of the major issues related to the right of privacy.

A. Griswold v. Connecticut, 381 U.S. 479 (U.S. Supreme Court 1965)

Mr. Justice Douglas delivered the opinion of the Court.

Appellant Griswold is Executive Director of the Planned Parenthood League of Connecticut. Appellant Buxton is a licensed physician and a professor at the Yale Medical School who served as Medical Director for the League at its Center in New Haven—a center open and operating from November 1 to November 10, 1961, when appellants were arrested.

They gave information, instruction, and medical advice to *married persons* as to the means of preventing conception. They examined the wife and prescribed the best contraceptive device or material for her use. Fees were usually charged, although some couples were serviced free.

[18] *See also* G. GUNTHER, CONSTITUTIONAL LAW: CASES AND MATERIALS, 657–690 (9th ed., Foundation, 1975).

The statutes whose constitutionality is involved in this appeal are § § 53–32 and 54–196 of the General Statutes of Connecticut (1958 rev.). The former provides:

> "Any person who uses any drug, medicinal article or instrument for the purpose of preventing conception shall be fined not less than fifty dollars or imprisoned not less than sixty days nor more than one year or be both fined and imprisoned."

Section 54–196 provides:

> "Any person who assists, abets, counsels, causes, hires, or commands another to commit any offense may be prosecuted and punished as if he were the principal offender."

The appellants were found guilty as accessories and fined $100 each, against the claim that the accessory statute as so applied violated the Fourteenth Amendment. The Appellate Division of the Circuit Court affirmed. The Supreme Court of Errors affirmed that judgment . . .

We do not sit as a super-legislature to determine the wisdom, need, and propriety of laws that touch economic problems, business affairs, or social conditions. This law, however, operates directly on an intimate relation of husband and wife and their physician's role in one aspect of that relation.

The association of people is not mentioned in the Constitution nor in the Bill of Rights. The right to educate a child in a school of the parents' choice—whether public or private or parochial—is also not mentioned. Nor is the right to study any particular subject or any foreign language. Yet the First Amendment has been construed to include certain of those rights.

By *Pierce v. Society of Sisters,* 268 U. S. 510 (1925), the right to educate one's children as one chooses is made applicable to the States by the force of the First and Fourteenth Amendments. By *Meyer v. Nebraska,* 262 U.S. 390 (1923) the same dignity is given the right to study the German language in a private school. In other words, the State may not, consistently with the spirit of the First Amendment, contract the spectrum of available knowledge. The right of freedom of speech and press includes not only the right to utter or to print, but the right to distribute, the right to receive, the right to read . . . and freedom of inquiry, freedom of thought, and freedom to teach . . . —indeed the freedom of the entire university community. . . . Without those peripheral rights the specific rights would be less secure. And so we reaffirm the principle of the *Pierce* and the *Meyer* cases.

In *NAACP v. Alabama,* 357 U.S. 449, 462, we protected the "freedom to associate and privacy in one's associations," noting that freedom of association was a peripheral First Amendment right. . . . In other words, the First Amendment has a penumbra where privacy is protected from governmental intrusion. In like context, we have protected forms of "association" that are not political in the customary sense but pertain to the social, legal, and economic benefit of the members. . . .

The foregoing cases suggest that specific guarantees in the Bill of Rights have penumbras, formed by emanations from those guarantees that help give them life and substance. See *Poe v. Ullman,* 367 U.S. 497, 516–522 (dissenting opinion). Various guarantees create zones of privacy. The right of association contained in the penumbra of the First Amendment is one, as we have seen. The Third Amendment in its prohibition against the quartering of soldiers "in any house" in time of peace without the consent of the owner is another facet of that privacy. The Fourth Amendment explicitly affirms the "right of the people to be secure in their persons, houses, papers, and effects, against unreasonable searches and seizures." The Fifth Amendment in its Self-Incrimination Clause enables the citizen to create a zone of privacy which government may not force him to surrender to his detriment. The Ninth Amendment provides: "The enumeration in the Constitution, of certain rights, shall not be construed to deny or disparage others retained by the people. . . ."

The present case, then, concerns a relationship lying within the zone of privacy created by several fundamental constitutional guarantees. And it concerns a law which in forbidding the *use* of contraceptives rather than regulating their manufacture or sale, seeks to achieve its goals by means having a maximum destructive impact upon that relationship. Such a law cannot stand in light of the familiar principle, so often applied by this Court, that a "governmental purpose to control or prevent activities constitutionally subject to state regulation may not be achieved by means which sweep unneccessarily broadly and thereby invade the area of protected freedoms." *NAACP v, Alabama,* 377 U.S. 288, 307. Would we allow the police to search the sacred precincts of marital bedrooms for telltale signs of the use of contraceptives? The very idea is repulsive to the notions of privacy surrounding the marriage relationship.

We deal with a right of privacy older than the Bill of Rights—older than our political parties, older than our school system. Marriage is a coming together for better or worse, hopefully enduring, and intimate to the degree of being sacred. It is an association that promotes a way of life, not causes; a harmony in living, not political faiths; a bilateral loyalty, not commercial or social projects. Yet it is an association for as noble a purpose as any involved in our prior decisions. Reversed.

Mr. Justice Goldberg, whom The Chief Justice and Mr. Justice Brennan join, concurring.

I agree with the Court that Connecticut's birth-control law unconstitutionally intrudes upon the right of marital privacy, and I join in its opinion and judgment. Although I have not accepted the view that "due process" as used in the Fourteenth Amendment incorporates all of the first eight Amendments . . . I do agree that the concept of liberty protects those personal rights that are fundamental, and is not confined to the specific terms of the Bill of Rights. My conclusion that the concept of liberty is not so restricted and that it embraces the right of marital privacy though that right is not mentioned explicitly in the Constitution is supported both by numerous decisions of this Court, referred to in the Court's opinion, and by the language and history of the Ninth Amendment. In reaching the conclusion that the right of marital privacy is protected, as being within the protected penumbra of specific guarantees of the Bill of Rights, the Court refers to the Ninth Amendment. . . . I add these words to emphasize the relevance of that Amendment to the Court's holding. . . .

This court, in a series of decisions, has held that the Fourteenth Amendment absorbs and applies to the States those specifics of the first eight amendments which express fundamental personal rights. The language and history of the Ninth Amendment reveal that the Framers of the Constitution believed that there are additional fundamental rights, protected from governmental infringement, which exist alongside those fundamental rights specifically mentioned in the first eight constitutional amendments.

The Ninth Amendment reads, "The enumeration in the Constitution, of certain rights, shall not be construed to deny or disparage others retained by the people." The Amendment is almost entirely the work of James Madison. It was introduced in Congress by him and passed the House and Senate with little or no debate and virtually no change in language. It was proffered to quiet expressed fears that a bill of specifically enumerated rights could not be sufficiently broad to cover all essential rights and that the specific mention of certain rights would be interpreted as a denial that others were protected. . . .

To hold that a right so basic and fundamental and so deep-rooted in our society as the right of privacy in marriage may be infringed because that right is not guaranteed in so many words by the first eight amendments to the Constitution is to ignore the Ninth Amendment and to give it no effect whatsoever. . . .

In determining which rights are fundamental, judges are not left at large to decide cases in light of their personal and private notions. Rather, they must look to the "traditions and [collective] conscience of our people" to determine whether a principle is "so rooted [there] . . . as to be ranked as fundamental." *Snyder v. Massachusetts,* 291

U.S. 97, 105. The inquiry is whether a right involved "is of such a character that it cannot be denied without violating those "fundamental principles of liberty and justice which lie at the base of all our civil and political institutions. . . ." *Powell v. Alabama,* 287 U.S. 45, 67. . . .

I agree fully with the Court that, applying these tests, the right of privacy is a fundamental personal right, emanating "from the totality of the constitutional scheme under which we live." . . . Mr. Justice Brandeis, dissenting in *Olmstead v. United States,* 277 U.S. 438, 478, comprehensively summarized the principles underlying the Constitution's guarantees of privacy:

> "The protection guaranteed by the [Fourth and Fifth] Amendments is much broader in scope. The makers of our Constitution undertook to secure conditions favorable to the pursuit of happiness. They recognized the significance of man's spiritual nature, of his feelings and of his intellect. They knew that only a part of the pain, pleasure and satisfactions of life are to be found in material things. They sought to protect Americans in their beliefs, their thoughts, their emotions and their sensations. They conferred, as against the Government, the right to be let alone —the most comprehensive of rights and the right most valued by civilized men" . . .

The entire fabric of the Constitution and the purposes that clearly underlie its specific guarantees demonstrate that the rights to marital privacy and to marry and raise a family are of similar order and magnitude as the fundamental rights specifically protected . . .

The logic of the dissents would sanction federal or state legislation that seems to me even more plainly unconstitutional than the statute before us. Surely the Government, absent a showing of a compelling subordinating state interest, could not decree that all husbands and wives must be sterilized after two children have been born to them. Yet by their reasoning such an invasion of marital privacy would not be subject to constitutional challenge because, while it might be "silly," no provision of the Constitution specifically prevents the Government from curtailing the marital right to bear children and raise a family. While it may shock some of my Brethren that the Court today holds that the Constitution protects the right of marital privacy, in my view it is far more shocking to believe that the personal liberty guaranteed by the Constitution does not include protection against such totalitarian limitation of family size, which is at complete variance with our constitutional concepts. Yet, if upon a showing of a slender basis of rationality, a law outlawing voluntary birth control by married persons is valid, then, by the same reasoning, a law requiring compulsory birth control also would seem to be valid. In my view, however, both types of law would unjustifiably intrude upon rights of marital privacy which are constitutionally protected.

In a long series of cases this Court has held that where fundamental personal liberties are involved, they may not be abridged by the States simply on a showing that a regulatory statute has some rational relationship to the effectuation of a proper state purpose. "Where there is a significant encroachment upon personal liberty, the State may prevail only upon showing a subordinating interest which is compelling," *Bates v. Little Rock,* 361 U.S. 516, 524. The law must be shown "necessary, and not merely rationally related, to the accomplishment of a permissible state policy."

Although the Connecticut birth-control law obviously encroaches upon a fundamental personal liberty, the State does not show that the law serves any "subordinating [state] interest which is compelling" or that it is "necessary . . . to the accomplishment of a permissible state policy." The State, at most, argues that there is some rational relation between this statute and what is admittedly a legitimate subject of state concern—the discouraging of extra-marital relations. It says that preventing the use of birth-control devices by married persons helps prevent the indulgence by some in such extra-marital relations. The rationality of this justification is dubious, particularly in the light of the unmarried as well as married, of birth-control devices for the prevention of disease, as distinguished from the prevention of conception. . . . But, in any event, it is clear that the state interest in safeguarding marital fidelity can be served by a more discriminately tailored statute, which does not, like the present one, sweep unnecessarily broadly, reaching far beyond the evil sought to be dealt with and intruding upon the privacy of all married couples. . . . The State of Connecticut does have statutes, the constitutionality of which is beyond doubt, which prohibit adultery and fornication. . . . These statutes demonstrate that means for achieving the same basic purpose of protecting marital fidelity are available to Connecticut without the need to "invade the area of protected freedoms." . . .

Finally, it should be said of the Court's holding today that it in no way interferes with a State's proper regulation of sexual promiscuity or misconduct. . . .

Mr. Justice Harlan, concurring in the judgment.

I fully agree with the judgment of reversal, but find myself unable to join the Court's opinion. . . .

In my view, the proper constitutional inquiry in this case is whether this Connecticut statute infringes the Due Process Clause of the Fourteenth Amendment because the enactment violates basic values "implicit in the concept of ordered liberty," *Palko v. Connecticut,* 302

U.S. 319, 325. For reasons stated at length in my dissenting opinion in *Poe v. Ullman,* I believe that it does. While the relevant inquiry may be aided by resort to one or more of the provisions of the Bill of Rights, it is not dependent on them or any of their radiations. The Due Process Clause of the Fourteenth Amendment stands, in my opinion, on its own bottom. . . .

Mr. Justice White, concurring in the judgment.

. . . The Connecticut anti-contraceptive statute . . . forbids all married persons the right to use birth-control devices, regardless of whether their use is dictated by considerations of family planning . . . health, or even of life itself. . . . And the clear effect of these statutes, as enforced, is to deny disadvantaged citizens of Connecticut, those without either adequate knowledge or resources to obtain private counseling, access to medical assistance and up-to-date information in respect to proper methods of birth controls. . . . In my view, a statute with these effects bears a substantial burden of justification when attacked under the Fourteenth Amendment.

An examination of the justification offered, however, cannot be avoided by saying that the Connecticut anti-use statute invades a protected area of privacy and association or that it demeans the marriage relationship. The nature of the right invaded is pertinent, to be sure, for statutes regulating sensitive areas of liberty do, under the cases of this Court, require "strict scrutiny," *Skinner v. Oklahoma,* 316 U.S. 535, 541, and "must be viewed in the light of less drastic means for achieving the same basic purpose." *Shelton v. Tucker*, 364 U.S. 479, 488. "Where there is a significant encroachment upon personal liberty, the State may prevail only upon showing a subordinating interest which is compelling." *Bates v. Little Rock,* 361 U.S. 516, 524. . . .

In these circumstances one is rather hard pressed to explain how the ban on use by married persons in any way prevents use of such devices by persons engaging in illicit sexual relations and thereby contributes to the State's policy against such relationships. Neither the state courts nor the State before the bar of this Court has tendered such an explanation. . . . At most the broad ban is of marginal utility to the declared objective. A statute limiting its prohibition on use to persons engaging in the prohibited relationship would serve the end posited by Connecticut in the same way, and with the same effectiveness, or ineffectiveness, as the broad anti-use statute under attack in this case. I find nothing in this record justifying the sweeping scope of this statute, with its telling effect on the freedoms of married persons, and therefore conclude that it deprives such persons of liberty without due process of law.

Mr. Justice Black, with whom Mr. Justice Stewart joins, dissenting.

. . . I do not to any extent whatever base my view that this Connecticut law is constitutional on a belief that the law is wise or that its policy is a good one. In order that there may be no room at all to doubt why I vote as I do, I feel constrained to add that the law is every bit as offensive to me as it is to my Brethren of the majority and my Brothers Harlan, White and Goldberg who, reciting reasons why it is offensive to them, hold it unconstitutional. There is no single one of the graphic and eloquent strictures and criticisms fired at the policy of this Connecticut law either by the Court's opinion or by those of my concurring Brethren to which I cannot subscribe—except their conclusion that the evil qualities they see in the law make it unconstitutional. . . .

The Court talks about a constitutional "right of privacy" as though there is some constitutional provision or provisions forbidding any law ever to be passed which might abridge the "privacy" of individuals. But there is not. There are, of course, guarantees in certain specific constitutional provisions which are designed in part to protect privacy at certain times and places with respect to certain activities. Such, for example, is the Fourth Amendment's guarantee against "unreasonable searches or seizures." . . .

The due process argument which my Brothers Harlan and White adopt here is based, as their opinions indicate, on the premise that this Court is vested with power to invalidate all state laws that it considers to be arbitrary, capricious, unreasonable, or oppressive, or on this Court's belief that a particular state law under scrutiny has no "rational or justifying" purpose, or is offensive to a "sense of fairness and justice." If these formulas based on "natural justice," or others which mean the same thing, are to prevail, they require judges to determine what is or is not constitutional on the basis of their own appraisal of what laws are unwise or unnecessary. The power to make such decisions is of course that of a legislative body. . . .

. . . My point is that there is no provision of the Constitution which either expressly or impliedly vests power in this Court to sit as a supervisory agency over acts of duly constituted legislative bodies and set aside their laws because of the Court's belief that the legislative policies adopted are unreasonable, unwise, arbitrary, capricious or irrational. The adoption of such a loose, flexible, uncontrolled standard for holding laws unconstitutional, if ever it is finally achieved, will amount to a great unconstitutional shift of power to the courts which I believe and am constrained to say will be bad for the courts and worse for the country. . . .

I realize that many good and able men have eloquently spoken and written, sometimes in rhapsodical strains, about the duty of this Court to keep the Constitution in tune with the times. The idea is that the Constitution must be changed from time to time and that this Court is charged with a duty to make those changes. For myself, I must with all deference reject that philosophy. The Constitution makers knew the need for change and provided for it. Amendments suggested by the people's elected representatives can be submitted to the people or their selected agents for ratification. That method of change was good for our Fathers, and being somewhat old-fashioned I must add it is good enough for me. And so, I cannot rely on the Due Process Clause or the Ninth Amendment or any mysterious and uncertain natural law concept as a reason for striking down this state law. . . .

Mr. Justice Stewart, whom Mr. Justice Black joins, dissenting.

Since 1879 Connecticut has had on its books a law which forbids the use of contraceptives by anyone. I think this is an uncommonly silly law. . . . But we are not asked in this case to say whether we think this law is unwise, or even asinine. We are asked to hold that it violates the United States Constitution. And that I cannot do.

In the course of its opinion the Court refers to no less than six Amendments to the Constitution: the First, the Third, the Fourth, the Fifth, the Ninth, and the Fourteenth. But the Court does not say which of these Amendments, if any, it thinks is infringed by this Connecticut law.

We *are* told that the Due Process Clause of the Fourteenth Amendment is not, as such, the "guide" in this case. With that much I agree. . . .

As to the First, Third, Fourth, and Fifth Amendments, I can find nothing in any of them to invalidate this Connecticut law, even assuming that all those Amendments are fully applicable against the States. . . .

The Court also quotes the Ninth Amendment, and my Brother Goldberg's concurring opinion relies heavily upon it. But to say that the Ninth Amendment has anything to do with this case is to turn somersaults with history. . . .

B. Dissent of Justice Harlan in Poe v. Ullman, 367 U.S. 497 (U.S. Supreme Court 1961)

[This was an earlier challenge to the Connecticut birth control law. The majority dismissed the appeal on justiciability grounds. Justice Harlan dissented.]

. . . Precisely what is involved here is this: the State is asserting the right to enforce its moral judgment by intruding upon the most intimate details of the marital relation with the full power of the criminal law. Potentially, this could allow the deployment of all the incidental machinery of the criminal law, arrests, searches and seizures; inevitably, it must mean at the very least the lodging of criminal charges, a public trial, and testimony as to the *corpus delicti.* Nor could any imaginable elaboration of presumptions, testimonial privileges, or other safeguards, alleviate the necessity for testimony as to the mode and manner of the married couples' sexual relations, or at least the opportunity for the accused to make denial of the charges. In sum, the statute allows the State to enquire into, prove and punish married people for the private use of their marital intimacy. . . .

The statute must pass a more rigorous Constitutional test than that going merely to the plausibility of its underlying rationale. . . . This enactment involves what, by common understanding throughout the English-speaking world, must be granted to be a most fundamental aspect of "liberty," the privacy of the home in its most basic sense, and it is this which requires that the statute be subjected to "strict scrutiny." . . .

Of course . . . there are countervailing considerations. It would be an absurdity to suggest either that offenses may not be committed in the bosom of the family or that the home can be made a sanctuary for crime. The right of privacy most manifestly is not an absolute. Thus, I would not suggest that adultery, homosexuality, fornication and incest are immune from criminal enquiry, however privately practiced. So much has been explicitly recognized in acknowledging the State's rightful concern for its people's moral welfare. . . .

But not to discriminate between what is involved in this case and either the traditional offenses against good morals or crimes which, though they may be committed anywhere, happen to have been committed or concealed in the home, would entirely misconceive the argument that is being made.

Adultery, homosexuality and the like are sexual intimacies which the State forbids altogether, but the intimacy of husband and wife is necessarily an essential and accepted feature of the institution of marriage, an institution which the State not only must allow, but which always and in every age it has fostered and protected. It is one thing when the State exerts its power either to forbid extra-marital sexuality altogether, or to say who may marry, but it is quite another when, having acknowledged a marriage and the intimacies inherent in it, it undertakes to regulate by means of the criminal law the details of that intimacy. . . .

C. Commentary and Issues

1. Sources of the Right of Privacy

As the richness and diversity of the opinions in the *Griswold* case indicates, there is little agreement about the source of the right of privacy. Justice Douglas found the right in "penumbras" around or "emanations" from specific rights contained in the Bill of Rights. The "penumbras-emanations" theory has been the subject of considerable critical commentary by constitutional scholars.[19] Is there, in fact, a "right of privacy older than the Bill of Rights?" Even if there exists such a right, is it inferrable from the specific guarantees of the First, Third, Fourth, Fifth, and Ninth Amendments? Does the use of a "penumbras-emanations" rationale logically imply a "freewheeling, flexible, uncontrolled judiciary" as charged by Justice Black? Justice Goldberg's emphasis on the genesis of the right of privacy in the Ninth Amendment remains controversial and has never gathered much judicial support. Justices Harlan and White took a more traditional view that the right of privacy is located in the due process clause of the Fourteenth Amendment. However, this approach raises the issue of "substantive due process," discussed p. 47, *supra,* recalling a period of active Supreme Court intervention in economic affairs generally repudiated by modern jurists and scholars. Notwithstanding some bitter and embarrassing recollections of what are now considered excesses of the Supreme Court, recent decisions have distinguished economic from personal rights and have located the right of privacy within the due process clause of the Fourteenth Amendment.[20]

Justices Black and Stewart argued that no constitutional rights exist unless specifically mentioned in the Constitution. Does this viewpoint create an inflexible, static view of the Constitution, unre-

[19]Volume 64 of the MICHIGAN LAW REVIEW 197–288 (1965) contains a symposium which analyzes the *Griswold* decision. *See particularly* the careful exegises of each of the opinions in the case by P. Kauper, *Penumbras, Peripheries, Emanations, Things Fundamental and Things Forgotten: The Griswold Case, id.* at 235, and T. Emerson, *Nine Justices in Search of a Doctrine, id.* at 219. Justice Black's argument has historical roots in a major constitutional debate about whether the due process clause made all of the first eight amendments applicable to the states or only those deemed "fundamental." The Supreme Court finally settled on a theory of "selective incorporation" but found that the Fourteenth Amendment incorporated virtually all of the rights specified in the first eight amendments. *See* Duncan v. Louisiana, 391 U.S. 145 (1968).

[20]*See* Roe v. Wade, p. 70, *infra*.

sponsive to change, or does it merely recognize the limits of the judiciary inherent in the United States constitutional system?

To a large extent, the disagreement between the majority and minority opinions mirrors the divergent philosophies of judicial activism versus judicial restraint. Both Justices Black and Stewart observed that the legislature, as the elected representatives of the people, not the courts, should be the branch of government to change the Connecticut birth control statute. Justices Douglas' and Goldberg's opinions made the case for a much more active judiciary, involved in major social issues of the day. The jurisprudential literature on whether decisions such as those made in *Griswold* should be within the province of the legislature or the judiciary is abundant.[21] The issue surfaces throughout the cases examined in the next four chapters.

2. Fundamental Rights

As noted on pp. 47–49, *supra*, courts will generally uphold legislation—indeed, presume it to be constitutional—if it bears a reasonable relationship to a permissible state objective. However, where the state's police power comes into conflict with a *fundamental* right, they will require the more exacting standard of *compelling interest.* But what are fundamental rights? How do courts recognize them? How are they distinguished from non-fundamental rights? A classic definition talked in terms of "the basic values implicit in the concept of ordered liberty." *Palko v. Connecticut,* 302 U.S. 319 (1937). Justice Harlan's dissent in *Poe v. Ullman* refers to enactments which "by common understanding throughout the English-speaking world must be granted to be a most fundamental aspect of 'liberty'." How much guidance do these phrases provide in distinguishing a fundamental from a non-fundamental right? Do these definitions avoid the problem raised by Justice Black's dissent that judges' "personal and private notions" can affect their decision-

[21] *See* A. Cox, THE ROLE OF THE SUPREME COURT IN AMERICAN LIFE (Oxford, 1976); A. BICKEL, THE LEAST DANGEROUS BRANCH: THE SUPREME COURT AT THE BAR OF POLITICS (Bobbs-Merrill, 1962); H. Wechsler, *Toward Neutral Principles of Constitutional Law,* 73 HARV.L. REV. 1 (1959); R. McCloskey, THE MODERN SUPREME COURT (1972); J. Wright, *Professor Bickel, The Scholarly Tradition, and the Supreme Court,* 84 HARV. L. REV. 769 (1971); R. Bork, *Neutral Principles and Some First Amendment Problems,* 47 IND. L.J. 1 (1971). The competing positions are ably reviewed in M. Perry, *The Abortion Funding Cases: A Comment of the Supreme Court's Role in American Government,* 66 GEO. L.J. 1191 (1978).

making? How satisfactory is Justice Goldberg's response that "judges . . . must look to the traditions and collective conscience of our people" to determine whether a principle is "rooted" or whether a right "is of such a character that it cannot be denied without violating those fundamental principles of liberty and justice which lie at the base of all our civil and political institutions?"

As Justice Douglas noted in *Griswold*, courts will not "sit as a super-legislature" where economic or commercial rights are concerned, but will carefully scrutinize enactments that violate individual rights. Are there grounds to distinguish the special protection that was given to property and contractual rights in the 1920's from the special protection of individual liberties in *Griswold* and other cases? Are personal rights somehow more "fundamental" than economic rights? Emerson explains the difference as follows:

> In the [personal liberty] type of case, the legislation touches upon fundamental individual and personal rights essential to maintaining the independence, integrity, and private development of a citizen in a highly organized, yet democratic society. In the [economic liberty] situation, the legislation deals with economic regulation of commercial and property rights, essential to maintaining the public interest in controlling a highly complex, industrialized society. The distinction is thus basic. . . .[22]

During the years of the Warren Court, the scope of fundamental personal rights was expanded significantly. In addition to incorporating guarantees of fair criminal procedures, the Court used the Fourteenth Amendment to apply First Amendment and voting rights to the states. At one time it appeared the Fourteenth Amendment might be used to guarantee certain basic rights of minimum welfare, but later Supreme Court decisions have made it clear that there is no constitutional right to education, public welfare, and, by extension, health care.[23]

3. Scope of the Privacy Right

a. Components of the Privacy Right. Although *Griswold* concerned the *use* of *contraceptives* by *married* couples in their *home,*

[22]T. Emerson, *supra* n. 19 at 224.

[23]San Antonio Independent School Dist. v. Rodriguez, 411 U.S. 1 (1973); Dandridge v. Williams, 397 U.S. 471 (1970).

the implications of the case obviously go well beyond the specific fact situation. The scope of the right of privacy, in both the reproductive and other areas, is still being determined on a case-by-case basis and is considered, at least with regard to fertility control, in the next four chapters.

The right of privacy established in *Griswold* appeared to be based on the sanctity of marriage and the home. Is this all there is, or should be, to the right? Is the right of privacy, as suggested by Justice Brandeis (quoted in Justice Goldberg's concurrence), the "right to be let alone"? Can this view be reconciled with *Jacobson v. Massachusetts,* pp. 36–40, *supra*.? Compare Justice Douglas' listing of the components of the privacy right in his concurrance to *Doe v. Bolton,* 410 U.S. 179, 211–213 (1973):

> *First is the autonomous control over the development and expression of one's intellect, interest, tastes, and personality.*
>
> These are rights protected by the First Amendment and, in my view, they are absolute, permitting of no exceptions. . . .
>
> *Second is freedom of choice in the basic decisions of one's life respecting marriage, divorce, procreation, contraception, and the education and upbringing of children.*
>
> These rights, unlike those protected by the First Amendment, are subject to some control by the police power. . . . These rights are "fundamental," and we have held that in order to support legislative action the statute must be narrowly and precisely drawn and that a "compelling state interest" must be shown in support of the limitation. . . .
>
> *Third is the freedom to care for one's health and person, freedom from bodily restraint or compulsion, freedom to walk, stroll, or loaf.*
>
> These rights, though fundamental, are likewise subject to regulation on a showing of "compelling state interest". . . .

b. Privacy and Autonomy. Supreme Court decisions after *Griswold* have expanded the concept of privacy to include what Henkin has termed, "autonomy," *i.e.,* the right to make important personal decisions without government interference.[24] Thus, an abortion

[24]L. Henkin, *Privacy and Autonomy,* 74 COLUM. L. REV. 1410 (1974). *See* Whalen v. Roe, 429 U.S. 589, 598–600 (1977) where the Supreme Court said, "The cases sometimes characterized as protecting 'privacy' have in fact involved at least two different kinds of interests. One is the individual interest in avoiding disclosure of personal matters and another is the interest in independence in making certain kinds of important decisions."

could come within the zone of privacy since it is an intimately personal decision, even though there is nothing "private," as that term is used in ordinary conversation, about an abortion procedure. In this regard, the use of the term "privacy" is something of a misnomer.

But how can a person know whether an action comes within the constitutionally protected zone of privacy? Certainly not all personal decisions merit designation as fundamental privacy rights. The Supreme Court has not provided any conceptual guidelines, preferring to consider each case as it arises and to catalogue specific areas where the right of privacy applies. For example, in *Paris Adult Theatre I v. Slaton* the Court noted that the privacy right "encompasses and protects the personal intimacies of the home, the family, marriage, motherhood, procreation, and child rearing."[25] Some commentators have attempted to piece together an underlying rationale of the privacy right from the clues dropped by the Court in *Griswold* and its progeny. Consider in the light of the materials in the next four chapters the list of factors that apparently influence the Court to recognize a fundamental privacy right:

> Impact of denial of privacy protection on the life of the individual claimant;
>
> Whether a personal (*e.g.*, husband-wife) or confidential (*e.g.*, doctor-patient) relationship is involved;
>
> Special concern for family life and particularly the institution of marriage;
>
> Acceptability of an activity within traditional or "contemporary" morality;
>
> Locus of activity in the home.[26]

c. Privacy and Marriage. How important was it that the defendants in *Griswold* were married? The Supreme Court reached this question in the 1972 case of *Eisenstadt v. Baird,* 405 U.S. 438. In that case the Court held that Massachusetts statutes prohibiting the distribution of contraceptives, except where prescribed by a physician for a married person, violated the equal protection clause of the Fourteenth Amendment. After finding the statutes could not be

[25]Paris Adult Theatre I v. Slaton, *supra* n. 10 at 65.

[26]Excerpted from Note, *Roe and Paris: Does Privacy Have a Principle?*, 26 STAN. L.REV. 1161, 1173–1189 (1974).

justified as a deterrant to fornication or as a health measure, Justice Brennan, writing for the four-person plurality, stated:

> If under *Griswold* the distribution of contraceptives to married persons cannot be prohibited, a ban on distribution to unmarried persons would be equally impermissable. It is true that in *Griswold* the right of privacy in question inhered in the marital relationship. Yet the marital couple is not an independent entity with a mind and heart of its own, but an association of two individuals each with a separate intellectual and emotional make-up. If the right of privacy means anything, it is the right of the *individual*, married or single, to be free from unwarranted governmental intrusion into matters as fundamentally affecting a person as the decision whether to bear or beget a child. . . . We hold that by providing dissimilar treatment for married and unmarried persons who are similarly situated, [the statutes] violate the Equal Protection Clause.

d. Privacy and the Home. How significant is it that the activity in *Griswold* took place in the home? Does that imply that a person can read an obscene book in his home? The Supreme Court said "Yes" in *Stanley v. Georgia,* 394 U.S. 557 (1969), although later cases have effectively cordoned off the home, holding that a person has no right to carry obscene materials in his personal luggage, even if it can be demonstrated that the materials are for private use in the home.[27] Is *Griswold* authority for the proposition that unorthodox sexual behavior between consenting adults will be protected in the home? The Court of Appeals for the Fourth Circuit recently held, in a closely-divided decision, that although oral-genital relations between a married couple in its home was constitutionally protected, the right of privacy was waived if these relations were carried out in the presence of a third person.[28]

e. The Limits of the Right of Privacy. What is the significance of *Griswold* and later privacy cases for private sexual behavior?[29]

[27] *See, e.g.*, United States v. 37 Photographs, 402 U.S. 363, 376 (1971).

[28] Lovisi v. Slayton, 539 F. 2d 349 (1976), *cert. denied* 429 U.S. 977 (1976). For commentary on this case, *see* C. Taber, *Consent, Not Morality, as the Proper Limitation on Sexual Privacy,* 4 HASTINGS CON. L. Q. 637 (1977).

[29] The implications of the right of privacy for alternative lifestyles and sexual behavior are comprehensively explored in J. Wilkinson III & G. White, *Constitutional Protection for Personal Lifestyles,* 62 CORNELL L. REV. 563 (1977) and Note, *On Privacy: Constitutional Protection for Personal Liberty,* 48 N.Y.U. L. REV. 670 (1973).

Does it imply that private homosexual behavior between consenting adults is constitutionally protected? In *Doe v. Commonwealth's Attorney,*[30] the United States Supreme Court summarily affirmed (*i.e.*, affirmed without a written opinion) a decision of a three-judge federal court upholding a Virginia statute making criminal sexual relations between consenting homosexuals. Although this is considered an adjudication on the merits, the case was not argued before the Court, no reasons for the decision were given, and the case provides little guidance for the future.

Does it imply constitutional protection for unusual heterosexual behavior between married couples or between unmarried consenting couples? Commenting on this, one analyst recently noted:

> In the wake of *Griswold*, the overwhelming majority of reported cases in which the marital privacy defense was discussed have ruled that criminal sanctions cannot be imposed on married couples for deviate sexual conduct, at least where such conduct takes place outside the public gaze. . . . However, it is not yet clear whether the right of sexual privacy recognized in *Griswold* is broader than the confines of the marriage relationship.[31]

The Supreme Court has never delineated the outermost extremes of the right of privacy and has shown little inclination to do so. In a footnote to the plurality opinion in *Carey v. P.S.I.,* 431 U.S. 678, n. 17 (1977), Justice Brennan noted:

> Appellees argue that . . . the right to privacy comprehends a right . . . to engage in private consensual sexual behavior. We observe that the Court has not definitively answered the difficult question whether and to what extent the Constitution prohibits state statutes regulating such behavior among adults.

[30]425 U.S. 901 (1976), *aff'g* Doe v. Commonwealth's Attorney, 403 F. Supp. 1199 (E.D. Va. 1975). For commentary on this case, *see* Comment, *Doe v. Commonwealth's Attorney: Closing the Door to a Fundamental Right of Sexual Privacy,* 53 DENVER L.J. 553 (1976); Comment, *Doe v. Commonwealth's Attorney: A Set-Back for the Right of Privacy,* 65 KY.L.J. 748 (1977).

[31]Note, *The Constitutionality of Sodomy Statutes,* 45 FORDHAM L. REV. 553, 574 (1976). *See also* Note, *The Right of Privacy: A Renewed Challenge to Laws Regulating Private Consensual Behavior,* 25 WAYNE L. REV. 1067 (1979) which examines *State v. Saunders,* 75 N.J. 200, 381 A. 2d 333 (1977) in which the New Jersey Supreme Court struck down the state's fornication statute as a violation of the right of privacy.

On a different level, does existence of the right of privacy mean that long hair and bizarre dress merit constitutional protection?[32]

Does it mean that a terminally ill patient has a "right to die?" The latter question is being litigated with increasing frequency. In *In re Quinlan* the New Jersey Supreme Court held that the father of Karen Quinlan, a young woman living in a comatose, vegetative state, could assert her right of privacy to terminate her life by natural forces and discontinue the use of life-support apparatus.[33] In *Superintendent of Belchertown v. Saikewicz,* the Supreme Judicial Court of Massachusetts held that a guardian *ad litem* could assert the right of a mentally-retarded 67-year-old man suffering from leukemia to refuse the administration of life-prolonging treatment, in this case chemotherapy.[34]

[32]*See* Kelley v. Johnson, 425 U.S. 238 (1976), upholding a police department regulation limiting the length of an officer's hair.

[33]70 N.J. 10, 355 A. 2d 647, *cert. denied* 429 U.S. 922 (1976). For analysis of the *Quinlan* decision and its implications, *see In re Quinlan, A Symposium,* 30 RUTGERS L. REV. 243–328 (1977).

[34]1977 Mass. Adv. Sh. 2461, 370 N.E. 2d. 417 (1977). For commentary on the right of a terminally-ill patient to refuse treatment, *see* A. Relman, *The Saikewicz Decision: A Medical Viewpoint,* 4 AM. J. L. & MED. 233 (1978); G. Annas, *Reconciling Quinlan and Saikewicz: Decision Making for the Terminally Ill Incompetent,* 4 AM. J. L. & MED. 367 (1979); A. Buchanan, *Medical Paternalism or Legal Imperialism: Not the Only Alternatives for Handling Saikewitz-type Cases,* 5 AM. J. L. & MED. 97 (1979).

Appendix: The Bill of Rights and the Fourteenth Amendment

AMENDMENT I

Congress shall make no law respecting an establishment of religion, or prohibiting the free exercise thereof; or abridging the freedom of speech, or of the press, or the right of the people peaceably to assemble, and to petition the Government for a redress of grievances.

AMENDMENT II

A well regulated Militia, being necessary to the security of a free State, the right of the people to keep and bear Arms, shall not be infringed.

AMENDMENT III

No Soldier shall, in time of peace, be quartered in any house, without the consent of the Owner, nor in time of war, but in a manner to be prescribed by law.

AMENDMENT IV

The right of the people to be secure in their persons, houses, papers, and effects, against unreasonable searches and seizures, shall not be violated, and no Warrants shall issue, but upon probable cause, supported by Oath or affirmation, and particularly describing the place to be searched, and the persons or things to be seized.

AMENDMENT V

No person shall be held to answer for a capital, or otherwise infamous crime, unless on a presentment or indictment of a Grand Jury, except in cases arising in the land or naval forces, or in the Militia, when in actual service in time of War or public danger; nor shall any person be subject for the same offense to be twice put in jeopardy of life or limb; nor shall be compelled in any criminal case to be a witness against himself, nor be deprived of life, liberty, or property, without due process of law; nor shall private property be taken for public use, without just compensation.

AMENDMENT VI

In all criminal prosecutions, the accused shall enjoy the right to a speedy and public trial, by an impartial jury of the State and district wherein the crime shall have been committed, which district shall have been previously ascertained by law, and to be informed of the nature and cause of the accusation; to be confronted with the witnesses against him; to have compulsory process for obtaining Witnesses in his favor, and to have the Assistance of Counsel for his defense.

AMENDMENT VII

In Suits at common law, where the value in controversy shall exceed twenty dollars, the right of trial by jury shall be preserved, and no fact tried by a jury, shall be otherwise re-examined in any Court of the United States, than according to the rules of the common law.

AMENDMENT VIII

Excessive bail shall not be required, nor excessive fines imposed, nor cruel and unusual punishments inflicted.

AMENDMENT IX

The enumeration in the Constitution, of certain rights, shall not be construed to deny or disparage others retained by the people.

AMENDMENT X

The powers not delegated to the United States by the Constitution, nor prohibited by it to the States, are reserved to the States respectively, or to the people.

AMENDMENT XIV

SECTION 1. All persons born or naturalized in the United States and subject to the jurisdiction thereof, are citizens of the United States and of the State wherein they reside. No State shall make or enforce any law which shall abridge the privileges or immunities of citizens of the United States; nor shall any State deprive any person of life, liberty, or property, without due process of law; nor deny to any person within its jurisdiction the equal protection of the laws.

CHAPTER 3

ABORTION

I. THE UNITED STATES

A. The Situation Prior to Roe v. Wade

Laws regulating abortion in the United States are of relatively recent vintage, products by and large of the second half of the nineteenth century. In 1800 not one state had enacted a statute on the subject of abortion, and abortion, at least prior to "quickening" (the first perception of fetal movement), was considered legal. By 1900 virtually every state had adopted a law making abortion a criminal offense and sharply restricting its practice.[1] On the eve of the United States Supreme Court landmark decision in *Roe v. Wade* (January, 1973), 30 states still had statutes prohibiting abortions without exception or with the single exception of saving the life of the woman. Fourteen states had recently passed legislation based on the American Law Institute's Model Penal Code, which permitted abortions under specified indications, such as substantial risk that continuance

[1]For a historical study of abortion in the United States, *see* J. MOHR, ABORTION IN AMERICA: THE ORIGINS AND EVOLUTION OF NATIONAL POLICY, 1800–1900 (Oxford, 1978).

of the pregnancy would impair the physical or mental health of the mother, that the child would be born physically or mentally defective, or that the pregnancy resulted from rape or incest. Four states —New York, Washington, Alaska, and Hawaii—had removed nearly all restrictions on abortion. The New York law, for example, permitted abortion on request during the first 24 weeks of pregnancy and thereafter to save the life of the mother.

Many of the more restrictive abortion laws were challenged in court—some successfully, others unsuccessfully. In 1971 the U.S. Supreme Court, in *United States v. Vuitch,* 402 U.S. 62, considered a challenge to the District of Columbia's abortion statute. The Court held that the statute, which prohibited abortion except "as necessary for the preservation of the mother's life or health," was not unconstitutionally vague. Other challenges to state abortion laws were made at the state or lower federal court levels. For example, in 1972 courts in Kentucky, Missouri, South Dakota, and Indiana upheld restrictive abortion legislation, while courts in Connecticut, New Jersey, and Vermont struck down similar laws.

Although the diversity of state laws created a chaotic situation, one where illegal abortion was rampant and where women would travel long distances to obtain an abortion in a state with a "liberal" abortion law, the existence of a few states which permitted relatively easy access to abortion enabled investigators to study the health-related effects of abortion. New York City was singled out for intensive study and provided evidence of the low mortality and morbidity associated with first-trimester abortion.[2]

B. Roe v. Wade, 410 U.S. 113 (U.S. Supreme Court 1973)

Mr. Justice Blackmun delivered the opinion of the Court.

> . . . The Texas statutes that concern us here are Arts. 1191–1194 and 1196 of the State's Penal Code. These make it a crime to "procure an abortion," as therein defined, or to attempt one, except with respect to "an abortion procured or attempted by medical advice for the purpose of saving the life of the mother." Similar statutes are in existence in a majority of the States. . . .

[2] *See, e.g.,* C. Tietze & S. Lewit, *A National Medical Experience: The Joint Program for the Study of Abortion,* in THE ABORTION EXPERIENCE: PSYCHOLOGICAL AND MEDICAL IMPACT 1 (H. Osofsky & J. Osofsky, eds., Harper & Row, 1973); J. Pakter, D. O'Hare, F. Nelson & M. Svigir, *A Review of Two Years' Experience in New York City with the Liberalized Abortion Law, id.* at 47.

Jane Roe, a single woman who was residing in Dallas County, Texas, instituted this federal action in March 1970 against the District Attorney of the county. She sought a declaratory judgment that the Texas criminal abortion statutes were unconstitutional on their face, and an injunction restraining the defendant from enforcing the statutes.

Roe alleged that she was unmarried and pregnant; that she wished to terminate her pregnancy by an abortion "performed by a competent, licensed physician, under safe, clinical conditions"; that she was unable to get a "legal" abortion in Texas because her life did not appear to be threatened by the continuation of her pregnancy; and that she could not afford to travel to another jurisdiction in order to secure a legal abortion under safe conditions. She claimed that the Texas statutes were unconstitutionally vague and that they abridged her right of personal privacy, protected by the First, Fourth, Fifth, Ninth, and Fourteenth Amendments. By an amendment to her complaint, Roe purported to sue "on behalf of herself and all other women" similarly situated. . . .

[Omitted are parts of the Court's opinion dealing with issues of standing, justiciability, and judicial abstention. Also omitted is a long and erudite dissertation tracing laws regarding and attitudes towards abortion from ancient times through the present.]

VII

Three reasons have been advanced to explain historically the enactment of criminal abortion laws in the 19th century, and to justify their continued existence.

It has been argued occasionally that these laws were the product of a Victorian social concern to discourage illicit sexual conduct. Texas, however, does not advance this justification in the present case. . . .

A second reason is concerned with abortion as a medical procedure. When most criminal abortion laws were first enacted, the procedure was a hazardous one for the woman. This was particularly true prior to the development of antisepsis. Antiseptic techniques, of course, were based on discoveries by Lister, Pasteur, and others first announced in 1867, but were not generally accepted and employed until about the turn of the century. Abortion mortality was high. Even after 1900, and perhaps until as late as the development of antibiotics in the 1940's, standard modern techniques such as dilation and curettage were not nearly so safe as they are today. Thus it has been argued that a State's real concern in enacting a criminal abortion law was to protect the pregnant woman, that is, to restrain her from submitting to a procedure that placed her life in serious jeopardy.

Modern medical techniques have altered this situation . . .

The third reason is the State's interest—some phrase it in terms of duty—in protecting prenatal life. Some of the argument for this justification rests on the theory that a new human life is present from the moment of conception. The State's interest and general obligation to protect life then extends, it is argued, to prenatal life. Only when the life of the pregnant mother herself is at stake, balanced against the life she carries within her, should the interest of the embryo or fetus not prevail. Logically, of course, a legitimate state interest in this area need not stand or fall on acceptance of the belief that life begins at conception or at some other point prior to live birth. In assessing the State's interest, recognition may be given to the less rigid claim that as long as at least *potential* life is involved, the State may assert interests beyond the protection of the pregnant woman alone. . . .

VIII

It is with these interests, and the weight to be attached to them, that this case is concerned. . . .

The Constitution does not explicitly mention any right of privacy. In a line of decisions, however, going back perhaps as far as *Union Pacific R. Co. v. Botsford,* 141 U.S. 250, 251 (1891), the Court has recognized that a right of personal privacy, or a guarantee of certain areas or zones of privacy, does exist under the Constitution. . . . These decisions make it clear that only personal rights that can be deemed "fundamental" or "implicit in the concept of ordered liberty," *Palko v. Connecticut,* 302 U.S. 319, 325 (1937), are included in this guarantee of personal privacy. They also make it clear that the right has some extension to activities relating to marriage . . . contraception . . . procreation . . . family relationships . . . and child rearing and education. . . .

This right of privacy, whether it be founded in the Fourteenth Amendment's concept of personal liberty and restrictions upon state action, as we feel it is, or, as the District Court determined, in the Ninth Amendment's reservation of rights to the people, is broad enough to encompass a woman's decision whether or not to terminate her pregnancy. The detriment that the State would impose upon the pregnant woman by denying this choice altogether is apparent. Specific and direct harm medically diagnosable even in early pregnancy may be involved. Maternity, or additional offspring, may force upon the woman a distressful life and future. Psychological harm may be imminent. Mental and physical health may be taxed by child care. There is also the distress, for all concerned, associated with the unwanted child, and there is the problem of bringing a child into a family already unable, psychologically and otherwise, to care for it. In other cases, as in this one, the additional difficulties and continuing stigma of unwed motherhood may be involved. All these are factors the woman and her responsible physician necessarily will consider in consultation.

On the basis of elements such as these, appellant and some *amici* argue that the woman's right is absolute and that she is entitled to terminate her pregnancy at whatever time, in whatever way, and for whatever reason she alone chooses. With this we do not agree. Appellants' arguments that Texas either has no valid interest at all in regulating the abortion decision, or no interest strong enough to support any limitation upon the woman's sole determination, are unpersuasive. The Court's decisions recognizing a right of privacy also acknowledge that some state regulation in areas protected by that right is appropriate. As noted above, a state may properly assert important interests in safeguarding health, in maintaining medical standards, and in protecting potential life. At some point in pregnancy, these respective interests become sufficiently compelling to sustain regulation of the factors that govern the abortion decision. The privacy right involved, therefore, cannot be said to be absolute. In fact, it is not clear to us that the claim asserted by some *amici* that one has an unlimited right to do with one's body as one pleases bears a close relationship to the right of privacy previously articulated in the Court's decisions. The Court has refused to recognize an unlimited right of this kind in the past. *Jacobson v. Massachusetts,* 197 U.S. 11 (1905) (vaccination); *Buck v. Bell,* 274 U.S. 200 (1927) (sterilization).

We therefore conclude that the right of personal privacy includes the abortion decision, but that this right is not unqualified and must be considered against important state interests in regulation. . . .

IX

The District Court held that the appellee failed to meet his burden of demonstrating that the Texas statute's infringement upon Roe's rights was necessary to support a compelling state interest, and that, although the appellee presented "several compelling justifications for state presence in the area of abortions," the statutes outstripped these justifications and swept "far beyond any areas of compelling state interest." . . . Appellant and appellee both contest that holding. Appellant, as has been indicated, claims an absolute right that bars any state imposition of criminal penalties in the area. Appellee argues that the State's determination to recognize and protect prenatal life from and after conception constitutes a compelling state interest. As noted above, we do not agree fully with either formulation.

A. The appellee and certain *amici* argue that the fetus is a "person" within the language and meaning of the Fourteenth Amendment. In support of this they outline at length and in detail the well-known facts of fetal development. If this suggestion of personhood is established, the appellant's case, of course, collapses, for the fetus' right to life would then be guaranteed specifically by the Amendment. The appellant conceded as much on reargument. On the other hand, the appellee conceded on reargument that no case could be cited that holds that a fetus is a person within the meaning of the Fourteenth Amendment. . . .

This, together with our observation, *supra,* that throughout the major portion of the 19th century prevailing legal abortion practices were far freer than they are today, persuades us that the word "person," as used in the Fourteenth Amendment, does not include the unborn. . . .

This conclusion, however, does not of itself fully answer the contentions raised by Texas, and we pass on to other considerations.

B. The pregnant woman cannot be isolated in her privacy. She carries an embryo and, later, a fetus, if one accepts the medical definitions of the developing young in the human uterus. . . . The situation therefore is inherently different from marital intimacy, or bedroom possession of obscene material, or marriage, or procreation, or education with which [earlier cases] were concerned. As we have intimated above, it is reasonable and appropriate for a State to decide that at some point in time another interest, that of health of the mother or that of potential human life, becomes significantly involved. The woman's privacy is no longer sole and any right of privacy she possesses must be measured accordingly.

Texas urges that, apart from the Fourteenth Amendment, life begins at conception and is present throughout pregnancy, and that, therefore, the State has a compelling interest in protecting that life from and after conception. We need not resolve the difficult question of when life begins. When those trained in the respective disciplines of medicine, philosophy, and theology are unable to arrive at any consensus, the judiciary, at this point in the development of man's knowledge, is not in a position to speculate as to the answer.

It should be sufficient to note briefly the wide divergence of thinking on this most sensitive and difficult question. There has always been strong support for the view that life does not begin until live birth.

This was the belief of the Stoics. It appears to be the predominant, though not the unanimous, attitude of the Jewish faith. It may be taken to represent also the position of a large segment of the Protestant community, insofar as that can be ascertained; organized groups that have taken a formal position on the abortion issue have generally regarded abortion as a matter for the conscience of the individual and her family. As we have noted, the common law found greater significance in quickening. Physicians and their scientific colleagues have regarded that event with less interest and have tended to focus either upon conception, upon live birth, or upon the interim point at which the fetus becomes "viable," that is, potentially able to live outside the mother's womb, albeit with artificial aid. Viability is usually placed at about seven months (28 weeks) but may occur earlier, even at 24 weeks. The Aristotelian theory of "mediate animation," that held sway throughout the Middle Ages and the Renaissance in Europe, continued to be official Roman Catholic dogma until the 19th century, despite opposition to this "ensoulment" theory from those in the Church who would recognize the existence of life from the moment of conception. The latter is now, of course, the official belief of the Catholic Church. As one brief *amicus* discloses, this is a view strongly held by many non-Catholics as well, and by many physicians. Substantial problems for precise definition of this view are posed, however, by new embryological data that purport to indicate that conception is a "process" over time, rather than an event, and by new medical techniques such as menstrual extraction, the "morning-after" pill, implantation of embryos, artificial insemination, and even artificial wombs.

In areas other than criminal abortion, the law has been reluctant to endorse any theory that life, as we recognize it, begins before live birth or to accord legal rights to the unborn except in narrowly defined situations and except when the rights are contingent upon live birth. For example, the traditional rule of tort law denied recovery for prenatal injuries even though the child was born alive. That rule has been changed in almost every jurisdiction. In most States, recovery is said to be permitted only if the fetus was viable, or at least quick, when the injuries were sustained, though few courts have squarely so held. In a recent development, generally opposed by the commentators, some States permit the parents of a stillborn child to maintain an action for wrongful death because of prenatal injuries. Such an action, however, would appear to be one to vindicate the parents' interest and is thus consistent with the view that the fetus, at most, represents only the potentiality of life. Similarly, unborn children have been recognized as acquiring rights or interests by way of inheritance or other devolution of property, and have been represented by guardians *ad litem.* Perfection of the interests involved, again, has generally been contingent upon live birth. In short, the unborn have never been recognized in the law as persons in the whole sense. . . .

X

In view of all this, we do not agree that, by adopting one theory of life, Texas may override the rights of the pregnant woman that are at stake. We repeat, however, that the State does have an important and legitimate interest in preserving and protecting the health of the pregnant woman, whether she be a resident of the State or a nonresident who seeks medical consultation and treatment there, and that it has still *another* important and legitimate interest in protecting the potentiality of human life. These interests are separate and distinct. Each grows in substantiality as the woman approaches term and, at a point during pregnancy, each becomes "compelling."

With respect to the State's important and legitimate interest in the health of the mother, the "compelling" point, in the light of present medical knowledge, is at approximately the end of the first trimester. This is so because of the now-established medical fact, referred to above, that until the end of the first trimester mortality in abortion may be less than mortality in normal childbirth. It follows that, from and after this point, a State may regulate the abortion procedure to the extent that the regulation reasonably relates to the preservation and protection of maternal health. Examples of permissible state regulation in this area are requirements as to the qualifications of the person who is to perform the abortion; as to the licensure of that person; as to the facility in which the procedure is to be performed, that is, whether it must be a hospital or may be a clinic or some other place of less-than-hospital status; as to the licensing of the facility; and the like.

This means, on the other hand, that, for the period of pregnancy prior to this "compelling" point, the attending physician, in consultation with his patient, is free to determine, without regulation by the State, that in his medical judgment, the patient's pregnancy should be terminated. If that decision is reached, the judgment may be effectuated by an abortion free of interference by the State.

With respect to the State's important and legitimate interest in potential life, the "compelling" point is at viability. This is so because the fetus then presumably has the capability of meaningful life outside the mother's womb. State regulation protective of fetal life after viability thus has both logical and biological justifications. If the State is interested in protecting fetal life after viability, it may go so far as to proscribe abortion during that period, except when it is necessary to preserve the life or health of the mother.

Measured against these standards, Art. 1196 of the Texas Penal Code, in restricting legal abortions to those "procured or attempted by medical advice for the purpose of saving the life of the mother," sweeps too broadly. The statute makes no distinction between abortions performed early in pregnancy and those performed later, and it limits to a single reason, "saving" the mother's life, the legal justification for the procedure. The statute, therefore, cannot survive the constitutional attack made upon it here. . . .

XI

To summarize and to repeat:

A state criminal abortion statute of the current Texas type, that excepts from criminality only a *life-saving* procedure on behalf of the mother, without regard to pregnancy stage and without recognition of the other interests involved, is violative of the Due Process Clause of the Fourteenth Amendment.

(a) For the stage prior to approximately the end of the first trimester, the abortion decision and its effectuation must be left to the medical judgment of the pregnant woman's attending physician.

(b) For the stage subsequent to approximately the end of the first trimester, the State, in promoting its interest in the health of the mother, may, if it chooses, regulate the abortion procedure in ways that are reasonably related to maternal health.

(c) For the stage subsequent to viability, the State in promoting its interest in the potentiality of human life may, if it chooses, regulate, and even proscribe, abortion except where it is necessary, in appropriate medical judgment, for the preservation of the life or health of the mother.

The State may define the term "physician," as it has been employed in the preceding paragraphs of this Part XI of this opinion, to mean only a physician currently licensed by the State, and may proscribe any abortion by a person who is not a physician as so defined. . . .

[The concurring opinions of Chief Justice Burger and Justices Douglas and Stewart are omitted.]

Mr. Justice White, with whom Mr. Justice Rehnquist joins, dissenting.

At the heart of the controversy in these cases are those recurring pregnancies that pose no danger whatsoever to the life or health of the mother but are, nevertheless, unwanted for any one or more of a variety of reasons—convenience, family planning, economics, dislike of children, the embarrassment of illegitimacy, etc. The common claim before us is that for any one of such reasons, or for no reason at all, and without asserting or claiming any threat to life or health, any woman is entitled to an abortion at her request if she is able to find a medical advisor willing to undertake the procedure. . . .

With all due respect, I dissent. I find nothing in the language or history of the Constitution to support the Court's judgment. The Court simply fashions and announces a new constitutional right for pregnant mothers and, with scarcely any reason or authority for its action, invests that right with sufficient substance to override most existing state abortion statutes. The upshot is that the people and the legislatures of the 50 States are constitutionally disentitled to weigh the relative importance of the continued existence and development of the fetus, on the one hand, against a spectrum of possible impacts on the mother, on the other hand. As an exercise of raw judicial power, the Court perhaps has authority to do what it does today; but in my view its judgment is an improvident and extravagant exercise of the power of judicial review which the Constitution extends to this Court. . . .

Mr. Justice Rehnquist, dissenting.

The Court's opinion brings to the decision of this troubling question both extensive historical fact and a wealth of legal scholarship. While the opinion thus commands my respect, I find myself nonetheless in fundamental disagreement with those parts of it that invalidate the Texas statute in question, and therefore dissent. . . .

Even if there were a plaintiff in this case capable of litigating the issue which the Court decides, I would reach a conclusion opposite to that reached by the Court. I have difficulty in concluding, as the Court does, that the right of "privacy" is involved in this case. Texas, by the statute here challenged, bars the performance of a medical abortion by a licensed physician on a plaintiff such as Roe. A transaction resulting in an operation such as this is not "private" in the ordinary usage of that word. Nor is the "privacy" which the Court finds here even a distant relative of the freedom from searches and seizures protected by the Fourth Amendment to the Constitution, which the Court has referred to as embodying a right to privacy.

If the Court means by the term "privacy" no more than that the claim of a person to be free from unwanted state regulation of consensual transactions may be a form of "liberty" protected by the Fourteenth Amendment, there is no doubt that similar claims have been upheld in our earlier decisions on the basis of that liberty. . . . The test traditionally applied in the area of social and economic legislation is whether or not a law such as that challenged has a rational relation to a valid state objective. *Williamson v. Lee Optical Co.,* 348 U.S. 483, 491 (1955). The Due Process Clause of the Fourteenth Amendment undoubtedly does place a limit, albeit a broad one, on legislative power to enact laws such as this. If the Texas statute were to prohibit an abortion even where the mother's life is in jeopardy, I have little doubt that such a statute would lack a rational relation to a valid state objective under the test stated in *Williamson, supra.* But the Court's sweeping invalidation of any restrictions on abortion during the first trimester is impossible to justify under that standard, and the conscious weighing of competing factors which the Court's opinion apparently substitutes for the established test is far more appropriate to a legislative judgment than to a judicial one.

The Court eschews the history of the Fourteenth Amendment in its reliance on the "compelling state interest" test . . . But the Court adds a new wrinkle to this test by transposing it from the legal considerations associated with the Equal Protection Clause of the Fourteenth Amendment to this case arising under the Due Process Clause of the Fourteenth Amendment. Unless I misapprehend the consequences of this transplanting of the "compelling state interest test," the Court's opinion will accomplish the seemingly impossible feat of leaving this area of the law more confused than it found it. . . .

The adoption of the compelling state interest standard will inevitably require this Court to examine the legislative policies and pass on the wisdom of these policies in the very process of deciding whether a particular state interest put forward may or may not be "compelling." The decision here to break pregnancy into three distinct terms and to outline the permissible restrictions the State may impose in each one, for example, partakes more of judicial legislation than it does of a determination of the intent of the drafters of the Fourteenth Amendment.

The fact that a majority of the States reflecting, after all, the majority sentiment in those States, have had restrictions on abortions for at least a century is a strong indication, it seems to me, that the asserted right to an abortion is not "so rooted in the traditions and conscience of our people as to be ranked as fundamental . . ."

Even if one were to agree that the case that the Court decides were here, and that the enunciation of the substantive constitutional law in the Court's opinion were proper, the actual disposition of the case by the Court is still difficult to justify. The Texas statute is struck down *in toto,* even though the Court apparently concedes that at later

> periods of pregnancy Texas might impose these selfsame statutory limitations on abortion. My understanding of past practice is that a statute found to be invalid as applied to a particular plaintiff, but not unconstitutional as a whole, is not simply "struck down" but is, instead, declared unconstitutional as applied to the fact situation before the Court.

C. DOE v. BOLTON, 410 U.S. 179 (1973)

This case is the companion to *Roe* v. *Wade,* handed down on the same day. Based on its reasoning in the *Roe* case, the Court held a Georgia abortion statute, a more "modern" law than the Texas one, based on provisions of the Model Penal Code, to be unconstitutional. In *Doe,* an indigent married woman in Georgia was denied a first trimester abortion because she did not meet the requirements set forth in the Georgia abortion statute. The decision dealt particularly with procedural obstacles that the state had established,* specifically requirements that

Abortions performed in a hospital accredited by the Joint Commission on Accreditation of Hospitals (JCAH):

> We hold that the JCAH-accreditation requirement does not withstand constitutional scrutiny in the present context. It is a requirement that simply is not "based on differences that are reasonably related to the purposes of the Act in which it is found." [citations]
>
> This is not to say that Georgia may not or should not, from and after the end of the first trimester, adopt standards for licensing all facilities where abortions may be performed so long as those standards are legitimately related to the objective the State seeks to accomplish.

The procedure be approved by the hospital staff abortion committee:

> Viewing the Georgia statute as a whole, we see no constitutionally justifiable pertinence in the structure for the advance approval by the

*The opinion also considered issues of standing and justiciability, vagueness (the statutory language proscribing abortion except when "based upon [the physician's] best clinical judgment that an abortion is necessary" was held not to be unconstitutionally vague), and a residency requirement (held to violate the "Privileges and Immunities" clause of the Constitution). The concurring opinions of Chief Justice Burger and Justice Douglas, and the dissenting opinion of Justice White, applied to both *Roe v. Wade* and *Doe v. Bolton.* Justice Rehnquist wrote a separate dissenting opinion for *Doe v. Bolton.*—Ed.

abortion committee. With regard to the protection of potential life, the medical judgment is already completed prior to the committee stage, and review by a committee once removed from diagnosis is basically redundant. We are not cited to any other surgical procedure made subject to committee approval as a matter of state criminal law.

The performing physician's judgment be confirmed by the independent examinations of the patient by two other physicians:

It should be manifest that our rejection of the accredited hospital requirement and, more important, of the abortion committee's advance approval eliminates the major grounds of the attack based on the system's delay and the lack of facilities. There remains, however, the required confirmation by two Georgia-licensed physicians in addition to the recommendation of the pregnant woman's own consultant (making under the statute, a total of six physicians involved, including the three on the hospital's abortion committee). We conclude that this provision, too, must fall.

The statute's emphasis, as has been repetitively noted, is on the attending physician's "best clinical judgment that an abortion is necessary." That should be sufficient.

D. Challenges to the Supreme Court Abortion Decisions: The Scope of Roe v. Wade

As might be expected of a case taking such a definite stand in a controversial area of public policy, *Roe v. Wade* provoked both great popular reaction and intense scholarly debate.[3] *Roe* required every state to revise its abortion laws. Many of the revised statutes were in direct defiance of the *Roe* standards, and almost all were

[3]For scholarly commentary on Roe v. Wade, *pro* and *con, see* J. Ely, *The Wages of Crying Wolf: A Comment on Roe v. Wade,* 82 YALE L. J. 920 (1973); L. Tribe, *Forward: Toward a Model of Roles in the Due Process of Life and Law,* 87 HARV. L. REV. 1 (1973); R. Byrn, *An American Tragedy: The Supreme Court on Abortion,* 41 FORDHAM L. REV. 807 (1973); P. Heymann & D. Barzelay, *The Forest and the Trees: Roe v. Wade and Its Critics,* 53 B. U. L. REV. 765 (1973); M. Perry, *Abortion, the Public Morals, and the Police Power: The Ethical Function of Substantive Due Process,* 23 U.C.L.A. L. REV. 689 (1976); J. Dellapenna, *Nor Piety Nor Wit: The Supreme Court on Abortion,* 6 COLUM. HUM. RTS. L. REV. 379 (1974-75); D. Regan, *Rewriting Roe v. Wade,* 77 MICH. L. REV. 1569 (1979); T. NOONAN, A PRIVATE CHOICE: ABORTION IN AMERICA IN THE SEVENTIES (Free Press, 1979).

struck down immediately by the courts.[4] For example, Rhode Island enacted a law which declared that life begins at the moment of conception and that such life is a "person" for purposes of the Fourteenth Amendment. This was held unconstitutional.[5] In general, the challenges to *Roe* can be classified into the areas listed below. Many issues raised by these challenges are still being adjudicated while others have been settled or partially settled by the U.S. Supreme Court decisions reprinted *infra.*

1. Constitutional Amendments

Article V of the Constitution provides two methods of amending the Constitution: either two-thirds of each house of Congress can propose an amendment, or the legislatures of two-thirds of the states can call for a Constitutional convention. In either case, a Constitutional amendment must be ratified by three-fourths of the states—either by the state legislature or by a state convention.[6]

An initial reaction to *Roe v. Wade* came in the form of a call from numerous Congressmen for a constitutional amendment. The proposed amendments were of two kinds: "right to life" amendments, guaranteeing the fetus a right to life or similar constitutional protection from the moment of conception or fertilization, and "states rights" amendments which would leave states the discretion to regulate abortions. A sampling of constitutional amendments that have been introduced in Congress include:

> With respect to the right to life guaranteed in this Constitution, every human being, subject to the jurisdiction of the United States, or of any State, shall be deemed, from the moment of fertilization, to be a person and entitled to the right of life.
>
> Neither the United States nor any State shall deprive any human being, from conception, of life without due process of law; nor deny to any human being, from conception, within its jurisdiction the equal protection of the law.

[4]The early challenges to Roe v. Wade are reviewed in Note, *Implications of the Abortion Decisions: Post Roe and Doe Litigation and Legislation,* 74 COLUM. L. REV. 237 (1974), and M. Bryant, *State Legislation on Abortion after Roe v. Wade: Selected Constitutional Issues,* 2 AM. J. LAW & MED. 101 (1976).

[5]Doe v. Israel, 482 F. 2d 156 (1st. Cir. 1973), *cert. denied* 416 U.S. 993 (1974).

[6]*See* Note, *The Process of Constitutional Amendment,* 79 COLUM. L. REV. 106 (1979).

With respect to the right to life, the word person as used in this article and in the Fifth and Fourteenth Articles of Amendment to the Constitution of the United States applies to all human beings irrespective of age, health, function, or condition of dependency, including their unborn offspring at every stage of their biological development.

Nothing in this Constitution shall bar any State or territory or the District of Columbia, with regard to any area over which it has jurisdiction, from allowing, regulating, or prohibiting the practice of abortion.[7]

So far, no proposed amendment has succeeded in getting the number of votes in Congress needed to send it to the states for ratification.

With the failure to win approval of a Congressionally-sponsored amendment, supporters of a constitutional amendment turned to the other road open to them, a constitutional convention. As of February, 1981, 19 states (of 34 needed to propose an amendment) had passed resolutions requesting a convention to pass a right to life amendment. There has never been a convention called to amend the Constitution.[8] Although the views of constitutional scholars differ, some feel that a convention could not be restricted to considering the abortion issue alone but might, if it decided, consider other matters such as the guarantees of individual freedom found in the Bill of Rights.[9] Additionally, there are questions about how a constitutional convention would work, how long it would stay in existence, under what rules it would function, etc.[10] On a parallel line, the possibility exists that a constitutional convention called to balance the federal budget might also propose an anti-abortion amendment.

[7]These amendments, introduced by Congressmen Snyder, Erlenborn, Oberstar, and Whitehurst, respectively, have been excerpted from H. Pilpel, *The Collateral Consequences of a Constitutional Convention,* 5 FAM. PLAN./POP. Rep. 45 (1976). *See also* C. Rice, *Overruling Roe v. Wade: An Analysis of the Proposed Constitutional Amendments,* 15 B. C. INDUS. & COMMER. L. REV. 307 (1973).

[8]However, in 1967, 32 states had passed legislation calling for a constitutional convention to overturn the Supreme Court's one man-one vote decisions.

[9]*See* L. Wohl, *Are We 25 Votes Away from Losing the Bill of Rights . . . and the Rest of the Constitution,* MS., Feb. 1978 at 46.

[10]*See* Note, *Proposed Legislation on the Convention Method of Amending the United States Constitution,* 85 HARV. L. REV. 1612 (1972) and the legislation proposed by Senator Ervin to provide procedures for a convention to amend the Constitution. S. 2307, 90th Cong., 1st Sess. (1967). The bill passed in the Senate but died in the House.

2. Consent of the Spouse

The issue of consent (both spousal and parental) was one of the most frequently litigated in the years following *Roe v. Wade.* Three years after *Roe* the Supreme Court held, in *Planned Parenthood of Central Missouri v. Danforth,*[11] that a husband cannot be delegated veto power over his wife's abortion. Justice Blackmun, writing for the majority, wrote:

> *The spouse's consent* . . . We now hold that the State may not constitutionally require the consent of the spouse, as is specified under § 3(3) of the Missouri Act, as a condition for abortion during the first 12 weeks of pregnancy. We thus agree with the dissenting judge in the present case, and with the courts whose decisions are cited above, that the State cannot "delegate to a spouse a veto power which the state itself is absolutely and totally prohibited from exercising during the first trimester of pregnancy." . . . Clearly, since the State cannot regulate or proscribe abortion during the first stage, when the physician and his patient make that decision, the State cannot delegate authority to any particular person, even the spouse, to prevent abortion during that same period.
>
> We are not unaware of the deep and proper concern and interest that a devoted and protective husband has in his wife's pregnancy and in the growth and development of the fetus she is carrying. Neither has this Court failed to appreciate the importance of the marital relationship in our society. Moreover, we recognize that the decision whether to undergo or to forego an abortion may have profound effects on the future of any marriage, effects that are both physical and mental, and possibly deleterious. Notwithstanding these factors, we cannot hold that the State has the constitutional authority to give the spouse unilaterally the ability to prohibit the wife from terminating her pregnancy, when the State itself lacks that right. . . .
>
> We recognize, of course, that when a woman, with the approval of her physician but without the approval of her husband, decides to terminate her pregnancy, it could be said that she is acting unilaterally. The obvious fact is that when the wife and the husband disagree on this decision, the view of only one of the two marriage partners can prevail. Inasmuch as it is the woman who physically bears the child and who is the more directly and immediately affected by the pregnancy, as between the two, the balance weighs in her favor.[12]

[11]428 U.S. 52 (1976).

[12]For a review critical of the Court's reasoning in this part of the *Danforth* decision, *see* Note, *Third Party Consent to Abortions Before and After Danforth: A Theoretical Analysis,* 15 J. FAM. L. 508 (1976–77).

3. Informed Consent of the Woman

Section 3(2) of the statute challenged in *Planned Parenthood of Central Missouri v. Danforth* required that, during the first twelve weeks of pregnancy, a woman must certify, in writing, her consent to the procedure. This was challenged as a violation of *Roe v. Wade,* imposing an extra layer and burden of regulation on the abortion decision. In its *Danforth* decision, the Court upheld the constitutionality of this consent requirement, stating:

> . . . It is true that *Doe* and *Roe* clearly establish that the State may not restrict the decision of the patient and her physician regarding abortion during the first stage of pregnancy. Despite the fact that apparently no other Missouri statute . . . requires a patient's prior written consent to a surgical procedure, the imposition by § 3(2) of such a requirement for termination of pregnancy even during the first stage, in our view, is not in itself an unconstitutional requirement. The decision to abort, indeed, is an important, and often a stressful one, and it is desirable and imperative that it be made with full knowledge of its nature and consequences. The woman is the one primarily concerned, and her awareness of the decision and its significance may be assured, constitutionally, by the State to the extent of requiring her prior written consent.
>
> We could not say that a requirement imposed by the State that a prior written consent for any surgery would be unconstitutional. As a consequence, we see no constitutional defect in requiring it only for some types of surgery as, for example, an intracardiac procedure, or where the surgical risk is elevated above a specified mortality level, or, for that matter, for abortions.

Does the "important and stressful nature" of abortion and the requirement that "it be made with full knowledge of its nature and consequences" open an area of potential state regulation, even during the first trimester? Could a state, for example, constitutionally require that all women seeking abortions receive professional counseling prior to the procedure?[13] Could it constitutionally impose a day's waiting period during the first trimester? Such a waiting period was upheld in *Wolfe v. Schroering,* 541 F. 2d 523 (6th Cir. 1976) and *Akron Center for Reproductive Health v. Akron,* 479 F. Supp. 1171 (N.D. Ohio, 1979) and was struck down in *Margaret S. v. Edwards,*

[13]The constitutional ramifications of mandatory counseling are explored in M. Wood & W. Durham, Jr., *Counseling, Consulting, and Consent: Abortion and the Doctor-Patient Relationship,* 1978 B.Y.U. L. REV. 783, 830–845 (1978).

C.A. No. 78-2765 (E.D. La., 1980). To what extent do the constitutional considerations change if a longer waiting period, say 48 hours, is required?[14] If the waiting period is imposed during the second or third trimester?

How much leeway do states or communities have in determining the detail and accuracy of the information given to a woman requesting abortion? Consider for example, the ordinance passed by the Akron, Ohio, City Council:[15]

> . . .In order to insure that the consent for an abortion is truly informed consent, an abortion shall be performed or induced upon a pregnant woman only after she, and one of her parents or her legal guardian whose consent is required in accordance with Section 1870.05 (B) of this Chapter, have been orally informed by her attending physician of the following facts, and have signed a consent form acknowledging that she, and the parent or legal guardian where applicable, have been informed as follows:
>
> (1) That according to the best judgment of her attending physician she is pregnant.
>
> (2) The number of weeks elapsed from the probable time of the conception of her unborn child, based upon the information provided by her as to the time of her last menstrual period or after a history and physical examination and appropriate laboratory tests.
>
> (3) That the unborn child is a human life from the moment of conception and that there has been described in detail the anatomical and physiological characteristics of the particular unborn child at the gestational point of development at which time the abortion is to be performed, including, but not limited to, appearance, mobility, tactile sensitivity, including pain, perception or response, brain and heart function, the presence of internal organs and the presence of external members.
>
> (4) That her unborn child may be viable, and thus capable of surviving outside of her womb, if more than twenty-two (22) weeks have elapsed from the time of conception, and that her attending physician has a legal obligation to take all reasonable steps to preserve the life and health of her viable unborn child during the abortion.
>
> (5) That abortion is a major surgical procedure which can result in serious complications, including hemorrhage, perforated uterus, infection, menstrual disturbances, sterility and miscarriage and

[14] *See* Planned Parenthood of Kansas City, Missouri v. Ashcroft, 438 F. Supp. 679 (W.D. Mo., 1980) observing that the increased risk to a pregnant woman's health of a 48-hour waiting period is substantial.

[15] Ordinance No. 160-1978, passed by the City Council of Akron, Ohio, Feb. 28, 1978.

prematurity in subsequent pregnancies; and that abortion may leave essentially unaffected or may worsen any existing psychological problems she may have, and can result in severe emotional disturbances.

(6) That numerous public and private agencies and services are available to provide her with birth control information, and that her physician will provide her with a list of such agencies and the services available if she so requests.

(7) That numerous public and private agencies and services are available to assist her during pregnancy and after the birth of her child, if she chooses not to have the abortion, whether she wishes to keep her child or place him or her for adoption, and that her physician will provide her with a list of such agencies and the services available if she so requests.

Prior to any medical procedure, the informed consent of the patient must be obtained.[16] However, the content of informed consent provisions may be subject to judicial scrutiny. In the *Danforth* case, the Supreme Court noted:

> One might well wonder, offhand, just what "informed consent" of a patient is. The three Missouri federal judges who composed the . . . District Court, however, were not concerned, and we are content to accept, as the meaning, the giving of information to the patient as to just what would be done and as to its consequences. To ascribe more meaning than this might well confine the attending physician in an undesired and uncomfortable straitjacket in the practice of his profession.[17]

Citing this language, a federal district court in Ohio held the Akron informed consent provisions an unconstitutional infringement of a woman's right to consult a physician free from state interference.[18] Striking down similar legislation in Louisiana, a federal district noted that, in addition to leaving the physician without discretion about what to communicate with a patient, the consent provision forced a physician to communicate questionable factual information.[19]

[16]See *infra* pp. 156–157 for discussion of informed consent.

[17]428 U.S. at 67, n.8.

[18]Akron Center for Reproductive Health v. Akron, 479 F. Supp. 1172 (N.D. Ohio, 1979).

[19]In particular, the court noted that abortion is now considered a minor, not a major, procedure. Margaret S. v. Edwards, C.A. No. 78-2765 (E.D. La., 1980).

4. Parental Consent

This topic is explored in Chapter 6, *Minors.*

5. Medicaid and Other Restrictions on Abortion Funding

a. Introductory Note. Medicaid was enacted in 1965 as Title XIX of the Social Security Act.[20] Under Title XIX the federal government reimburses providers for part of the cost of medical care delivered to indigent recipients.[21] The state provides financing of the part not covered by federal funds. Each state administers its own Medicaid program. No state is compelled to participate in Medicaid, but those that do participate (which includes every state but Arizona) must comply with federal guidelines and submit for federal approval plans which specify coverage, services provided, and minimum standards for health care providers. Thus, Medicaid requires funding by both state and federal governments, and challenges to abortion under it took place at both levels.

After *Roe v. Wade,* many states enacted legislation that restricted Medicaid funding of elective abortions, *i.e.,* those abortions not necessary to save the life or protect the health of the woman. These laws were challenged in court, where many were struck down as a violation of the equal protection clause of the Fourteenth Amendment.[22]

At the same time, Congress was showing a concern with allocation of federal funds to Medicaid that could be used for abortion. In 1976, Congress passed the "Hyde amendment" to the appropriations

[20]Social Security Act §§ 1901–1911, 42 U.S.C. §§ 1396–1396j (1976).

[21]Under Medicaid, the state must provide medical services to the "categorically needy," which includes welfare recipients, and may provide services to the "medically needy," which includes poor people with incomes too high to qualify for welfare. Participating states must provide financial assistance in five general categories of medical care:

inpatient hospital services;
outpatient hospital services;
laboratory and x-ray services;
nursing facility services for people over 21, early and periodic screening and diagnosis, and family planning services and supplies;
physician's services.

[22]For a comprehensive review of these cases, *see* P. Butler, *The Right to Medicaid Payment for Abortion,* 28 HASTINGS. L. J. 931 (1977).

bill funding HEW and the Labor Departments for fiscal year 1977. The Hyde amendment stated:

> None of the funds contained in this Act shall be used to perform abortion except where the life of the mother would be endangered if the fetus were carried to term.[23]

The Hyde amendment was promptly challenged and its enforcement by HEW enjoined by a federal district court.[24]

In 1977, the United States Supreme Court, in the *Beal* and *Maher* decisions excerpted below, ruled on the state's obligation to pay for elective (i.e., not medically necessary) abortions. The *Beal* case dealt with statutory considerations, the *Maher* case with constitutional aspects.

b. Beal v. Doe, 432 U.S. 438 (U.S. Supreme Court 1977)

Mr. Justice Powell delivered the opinion of the Court.

The issue in this case is whether Title XIX of the Social Security Act . . . requires States that participate in the Medical Assistance (Medicaid) program to fund the cost of nontherapeutic abortions. . . .

The only question before us is one of statutory construction: whether Title XIX requires Pennsylvania to fund under its Medicaid program the cost of *all* abortions that are permissible under state law . . . Title XIX makes no reference to abortions, or, for that matter, to any other particular medical procedure. Instead, the statute is cast in terms that require participating States to provide financial assistance with respect to five broad categories of medical treatment. But nothing in the statute suggests that participating States are required to fund every medical procedure that falls within the delineated categories of medical care. Indeed, the statute expressly provides:

> "A State plan for medical assistance must . . . include reasonable standards . . . for determining eligibility for and the extent of medical assistance under the plan which . . . are consistent with the objectives of this [Title] . . ."42 U.S.C. § 1396(a)(17).

This language confers broad discretion on the States to adopt stan-

[23]Depts. of Labor and HEW, Approp. Act, 1977, Pub. L. No. 94-439, § 209, 90 Stat. 1434 (1976). For an analysis of the political aspects, see M. Vinovskis, *The Politics of Abortion in the House of Representatives in 1976,* 77 MICH. L. REV. 1790 (1979).

[24]McRae v. Mathews, 421 F. Supp. 533 (E.D.N.Y. 1976). The injunction was vacated after the *Beal* and *Maher* decisions. Califano v. McRae, 433 U.S. 916 (1977). The *McRae* litigation culminated in Harris v. McRae, *infra* pp. 100–109.

dards for determining the extent of medical assistance, requiring only that such standards be "reasonable" and "consistent with the objectives" of the Act.

Pennsylvania's regulation comports fully with Title XIX's broadly stated primary objective to enable each State, as far as practicable, to furnish medical assistance to individuals whose income and resources are insufficient to meet the costs of necessary medical services. Although serious statutory questions might be presented if a state Medicaid plan excluded necessary medical treatment from its coverage, it is hardly inconsistent with the objectives of the Act for a State to refuse to fund *unnecessary*—though perhaps desirable—medical services. . . .

We therefore hold that Pennsylvania's refusal to extend Medicaid coverage to nontherapeutic abortions is not inconsistent with Title XIX. We make clear, however, that the federal statute leaves a State free to provide such coverage if it so desires. . . .

Mr. Justice Brennan, with whom Mr. Justice Marshall and Mr. Justice Blackmun join, dissenting.

The Court holds that the "necessary medical services" which Pennsylvania must fund for individuals eligible for Medicaid do not include services connected with elective abortions. I dissent. . . . Title XIX, in my view, read fairly in light of the principle of avoidance of unnecessary constitutional decisions, requires agreement with the Court of Appeals that the legislative history of Title XIX and our abortion cases compel the conclusion that elective abortions constitute medically necessary treatment for the condition of pregnancy. I would therefore find that Title XIX requires that Pennsylvania pay the costs of elective abortions for women who are eligible participants in the Medicaid program. . . .

c. Maher v. Roe, 432 U.S. 464 (U.S. Supreme Court 1977)

Mr. Justice Powell delivered the opinion of the Court.

In *Beal v. Doe,* we hold today that Title XIX of the Social Security Act does not require the funding of nontherapueutic abortions as a condition of participation in the joint federal-state Medicaid program established by that statute. In this case, as a result of our decision in *Beal,* we must decide whether the Constitution requires a participating State to pay for nontherapeutic abortions when it pays for childbirth.

I

A regulation of the Connecticut Welfare Department limits state Medicaid benefits for first trimester abortions to those that are "medically necessary," a term defined to include psychiatric necessity. . . . Connecticut enforces this limitation through a system of prior authorization from its Department of Social Services. In order to obtain authorization for a first trimester abortion, the hospital or clinic where the abortion is to be performed must submit, among other things, a certificate from the patient's attending physician stating that the abortion is medically necessary.

This attack on the validity of the Connecticut regulation was brought against Appellant Maher, the Commissioner of Social Services, by appellees Poe and Roe, two indigent women who were unable to obtain a physician's certificate of medical necessity. . . .

Although it found no independent constitutional right to a state-financed abortion, the District Court held that the Equal Protection Clause forbids the exclusion of nontherapeutic abortions from a state welfare program that generally subsidizes the medical expenses incident to pregnancy and childbirth. The court found implicit in *Roe v. Wade* and *Doe v. Bolton* the view that "abortion and childbirth, when stripped of the sensitive moral arguments surrounding the abortion controversy, are simply two alternative medical methods of dealing with pregnancy. . . ."

II

The Constitution imposes no obligation on the States to pay the pregnancy-related medical expenses of indigent women, or indeed to pay any of the medical expenses of indigents. But when a State decides to alleviate some of the hardships of poverty by providing medical care, the manner in which it dispenses benefits is subject to constitutional limitations. Appellees' claim is that Connecticut must accord equal treatment to both abortion and childbirth, and may not evidence a policy preference by funding only the medical expenses incident to childbirth. This challenge to the classifications established by the Connecticut regulation presents a question arising under the Equal Protection Clause of the Fourteenth Amendment. The basic framework of analysis of such a claim is well settled:

> We must decide, first, whether [state legislation] operates to the disadvantage of some suspect class or impinges upon a fundamental right explicitly or implicitly protected by the Constitution, thereby requiring strict judicial scrutiny. . . . If not, the [legislative] scheme must still be examined to determine whether it rationally furthers some legitimate, articulated state purpose

> and therefore does not constitute an invidious discrimination . . . *San Antonio School Dist. v. Rodriguez,* 411 U.S. 1, 17 (1973). . . .

Applying this analysis here, we think the District Court erred in holding that the Connecticut regulation violated the Equal Protection Clause of the Fourteenth Amendment.

A

This case involves no discrimination against a suspect class. An indigent woman desiring an abortion does not come within the limited category of disadvantaged classes so recognized by our cases. Nor does the fact that the impact of the regulation falls upon those who cannot pay lead to a different conclusion . . . This Court has never held that financial need alone identifies a suspect class for purposes of equal protection analysis. . . . Accordingly, the central question in this case is whether the regulation "impinges upon a fundamental right explicitly or implicitly protected by the Constitution". . . .

B

The Texas statute [in *Roe v. Wade*] imposed severe criminal sanctions on the physicians and other medical personnel who performed abortions, thus drastically limiting the availability and safety of the desired service. . . . We held that only a compelling state interest would justify such a sweeping restriction on a constitutionally protected interest, and we found no such state interest during the first trimester. Even when judged against this demanding standard, however, the State's dual interest in the health of the pregnant woman and the potential life of the fetus were deemed sufficient to justify substantial regulation of abortions in the second and third trimesters. . . .

The Texas law in *Roe* was a stark example of impermissible interference with the pregnant woman's decision to terminate her pregnancy. In subsequent cases, we have invalidated other types of restrictions, different in form but similar in effect, on the woman's freedom of choice. Thus, in *Planned Parenthood of Central Missouri v. Danforth* we held that Missouri's requirement of spousal consent was unconstitutional because it "granted [the husband] the right to prevent unilaterally, and for whatever reason, the effectuation of his wife's and her physician's decision to terminate her pregnancy." Missouri had interposed an *"absolute obstacle* to a woman's decision that *Roe* held to be constitutionally protected from such interference." (Emphasis added.) Although a state-created obstacle need not be absolute to be impermissible, see *Doe v. Bolton and Carey v. Population Services International,* we have held that a requirement for a lawful abortion "is not constitutional unless it unduly burdens the right to seek an abortion." *Bellotti v. Baird* (1976). We recognized in *Bellotti* that "not all distinction between abortion and other procedures is forbidden" and that "the constitutionality of such distinction will depend upon its degree and the justification for it." . . .

These cases recognize a constitutionally protected interest "in making certain kinds of important decisions" free from governmental compulsion. *Whalen v. Roe* 429 U.S. 589 (1976). As *Whalen* makes clear, the right in *Roe v. Wade* can be understood only by considering both the woman's interest and the nature of the State's interference with it. *Roe* did not declare an unqualified "constitutional right to an abortion," as the District Court seemed to think. Rather, the right protects the woman from unduly burdensome interference with her freedom to decide whether to terminate her pregnancy. It implies no limitation on the authority of a State to make a value judgment favoring childbirth over abortion, and to implement that judgment by the allocation of public funds.

The Connecticut regulation before us is different in kind from the laws invalidated in our previous abortion decisions. The Connecticut regulation places no obstacles—absolute or otherwise—in the pregnant woman's path to an abortion. An indigent woman who desires an abortion suffers no disadvantage as a consequence of Connecticut's decision to fund childbirth; she continues as before to be dependent on private sources for the service she desires. The State may have made childbirth a more attractive alternative, thereby influencing the woman's decision, but it has imposed no restriction on access to abortions that was not already there. The indigency that may make it difficult—and in some cases, perhaps, impossible—for some women to have abortions is neither created nor in any way affected by the Connecticut regulation. We conclude that the Connecticut regulation does not impinge upon the fundamental right recognized in *Roe.*

C

Our conclusion signals no retreat from *Roe* or the cases applying it. There is a basic difference between direct state interference with a protected activity and state encouragement of an alternative activity consonant with legislative policy. Constitutional concerns are greatest when the State attempts to impose its will by force of law; the State's power to encourage actions deemed to be in the public interest is necessarily far broader. . . .

. . . We think it abundantly clear that a State is not required to show a compelling interest for its policy choice to favor normal childbirth any more than a State must so justify its election to fund public but not private education.

D

The question remains whether Connecticut's regulation can be sustained under the less demanding test of rationality that applies in the absence of a suspect classification or the impingement of a fundamental right. This test requires that the distinction drawn between childbirth and nontherapeutic abortion by the regulation be "rationally related" to a "constitutionally permissible" purpose . . . We hold that the Connecticut funding scheme satisfies this standard.

Roe itself explicitly acknowledged the State's strong interest in protecting the potential life of the fetus. That interest exists throughout the pregnancy, "grow[ing] in substantiality as the woman approaches term." *Roe v. Wade.* Because the pregnant woman carries a potential human being, she "cannot be isolated in her privacy. . . . [Her] privacy is no longer sole and any right of privacy she possesses must be measured accordingly." . . . The State unquestionably has a "strong and legitimate interest in encouraging normal childbirth," *Beal v. Doe,* an interest honored over the centuries.* Nor can there be any question that the Connecticut regulation rationally furthers that interest. . . .

In conclusion, we emphasize that our decision today does not proscribe government funding of nontherapeutic abortions. It is open to Congress to require provision of Medicaid benefits for such abortions as a condition of state participation in the Medicaid program. Also, under Title XIX as construed in *Beal v. Doe,* Connecticut is free—through normal democratic processes—to decide that such benefits should be provided. We hold only that the Constitution does not require a judicially imposed resolution of these difficult issues. . . .

Mr. Chief Justice Burger, concurring.

. . . The Court's holdings in *Roe v. Wade* and *Doe v. Bolton* simply require that a State not create an absolute barrier to a woman's decision to have an abortion. These precedents do not suggest that the State is constitutionally required to assist her in procuring it.

From time to time, every state legislature determines that, as a matter of sound public policy, the government ought to provide certain health and social services to its citizens. Encouragement of childbirth and child care is not a novel undertaking in this regard. Various governments, both in this country and in others, have made such a

*In addition to the direct interest in protecting the fetus, a State may have legitimate demographic concerns about its rate of population growth. Such concerns are basic to the future of the State and in some circumstances could constitute a substantial reason for departure from a position of neutrality between abortion and childbirth.—Footnote of the Supreme Court.

determination for centuries. In recent times, they have similarly provided educational services. The decision to provide any one of these services—or not to provide them—is not required by the Federal Constitution. Nor does the providing of a particular service require, as a matter of federal constitutional law, the provision of another. . . .

Mr. Justice Brennan, with whom Mr. Justice Marshall and Mr. Justice Blackmun join, dissenting.

. . . A distressing insensitivity to the plight of impoverished pregnant women is inherent in the Court's analysis. The stark reality for too many, not just "some," indigent pregnant women is that indigency makes access to competent licensed physicians not merely "difficult" but "impossible." . . . This disparity in funding by the State clearly operates to coerce indigent pregnant women to bear children they would not otherwise choose to have, and just as clearly, this coercion can only operate upon the poor, who are uniquely the victims of this form of financial pressure. Mr. Justice Frankfurter's words are apt:

> "To sanction such a ruthless consequence, inevitably resulting from a money hurdle erected by the State, would justify a latter-day Anatole France to add one more item to his ironic comments on the 'majestic equality' of the law. 'The law, in its majestic equality, forbids the rich as well as the poor to sleep under bridges, to beg in the streets, and to steal bread' . . .

Roe v. Wade and cases following it hold that an area of privacy invulnerable to the State's intrusion surrounds the decision of a pregnant woman whether or not to carry her pregnancy to term. The Connecticut scheme clearly impinges upon that area of privacy by bringing financial pressures on indigent women that force them to bear children they would not otherwise have. That is an obvious impairment of the fundamental right established by *Roe v. Wade* . . .

Until today, I had not thought the nature of the fundamental right established in *Roe* was open to question, let alone susceptible to the interpretation advanced by the Court. The fact that the Connecticut scheme may not operate as an absolute bar preventing all indigent women from having abortions is not critical. What is critical is that the State has inhibited their fundamental right to make that choice free from state interference. . . .

Mr. Justice Blackmun, with whom Mr. Justice Brennan and Mr. Justice Marshall join, dissenting.*

*Justice Blackmun's dissent encompasses the *Maher, Beal,* and *Poelker* cases, all of which were decided on the same day.—Ed.

The Court today, by its decisions in these cases, allows the States, and such municipalities as choose to do so, to accomplish indirectly what the Court in *Roe v. Wade* and *Doe v. Bolton*—by a substantial majority and with some emphasis, I had thought—said they could not do directly. The Court concedes the existence of a constitutional right but denies the realization and enjoyment of that right on the ground that existence and realization are separate and distinct. For the individual woman concerned, indigent and financially helpless, as the Court's opinions in the three cases concede her to be, the result is punitive and tragic. Implicit in the Court's holdings is the condescension that she may go elsewhere for her abortion. I find that disingenuous and alarming, almost reminiscent of: "Let them eat cake." . . .

There is another world "out there," the existence of which the Court, I suspect, either chooses to ignore or fears to recognize. And so the cancer of poverty will continue to grow. This is a sad day for those who regard the Constitution as a force that would serve justice to all evenhandedly and, in so doing, would better the lot of the poorest among us.

Mr. Justice Marshall, dissenting.*

It is all too obvious that the governmental actions in these cases, ostensibly taken to "encourage" women to carry pregnancies to term, are in reality intended to impose a moral viewpoint that no State may constitutionally enforce. *Roe v. Wade; Doe v. Bolton.* Since efforts to overturn those decisions have been unsuccessful, the opponents of abortion have attempted every imaginable means to circumvent the commands of the Constitution and impose their moral choices upon the rest of society. . . . The present cases involve the most vicious attacks yet devised. . . . I am appalled at the ethical bankruptcy of those who preach a "right to life" that means, under present social policies, a bare existence in utter misery for so many poor women and their children.

I

The Court's insensitivity to the human dimension of these decisions is particularly obvious in its cursory discussion of appellees' equal protection claims in *Maher v. Roe.* That case points up once again the need for this Court to repudiate its outdated and intellectually disingenuous "two-tier" equal protection analysis. As I have suggested

*Justice Marshall's dissent encompasses the *Maher, Beal,* and *Poelker* cases. —Ed.

before, this "model's two fixed modes of analysis, strict scrutiny and mere rationality, simply do not describe the inquiry the Court has undertaken—or should undertake—in equal protection cases." . . . In the present case, in its evident desire to avoid strict scrutiny—or indeed any meaningful scrutiny—of the challenged legislation, which would almost surely result in its invalidation, the Court pulls from thin air a distinction between laws that absolutely prevent exercise of the fundamental right to abortion and those that "merely" make its exercise difficult for some people. . . .

As I have argued before, an equal protection analysis far more in keeping with the actions rather than the words of the Court, carefully weighs three factors—"the importance of the governmental benefits denied, the character of the class, and the asserted state interests." . . . Application of this standard would invalidate the challenged regulations.

The governmental benefits at issue here, while perhaps not representing large amounts of money for any individual, are nevertheless of absolutely vital importance in the lives of the recipients. The right of every woman to choose whether to bear a child is, as *Roe v. Wade* held, of fundamental importance. . . .

I have already adverted to some of the characteristics of the class burdened by these regulations. While poverty alone does not entitle a class to claim government benefits, it is surely a relevant factor in the present inquiry. . . .

It is no less disturbing that the effect of the challenged regulations will fall with great disparity upon women of minority races. Nonwhite women now obtain abortions at nearly twice the rate of whites, and it appears that almost 40 percent of minority women—more than five times the proportion of whites—are dependent upon Medicaid for their health care. Even if this strongly disparate racial impact does not alone violate the Equal Protection Clause, "at some point a showing that state action has a devastating impact on the lives of minority racial groups must be relevant." . . .

Against the brutal effect that the challenged laws will have must be weighed the asserted state interest. The Court describes this as a "strong interest in protecting the potential life of the fetus." Yet, in *Doe v. Bolton,* the Court expressly held that any state interest during the first trimester of pregnancy, when 88 percent of all abortions occur, was wholly insufficient to justify state interference with the right to abortion. If a State's interest in potential human life before the point of viability is insufficient to justify requiring several physicians' concurrence for an abortion, I cannot comprehend how it magically becomes adequate to allow the present infringement on rights of disfavored classes. . . .

d. Commentary on Public Funding of Abortion between Maher and Harris v. McRae. The Medicaid decisions touched off a rash of controversy about the apparent Supreme Court retreat from the principles enunciated in *Roe v. Wade* and the effect of the decisions on poor women in need of abortions.[25] On the federal level, after acrimonious debate, Congress passed in 1977, and repassed in 1978, a somewhat less restrictive version of the Hyde Amendment permitting funding of abortions in cases of threat to the life of the woman, promptly reported rape or incest, and "severe and long-lasting physical damage" to the woman as certified by two physicians.[26] The last-mentioned condition was dropped from the 1979 version of the Hyde Amendment.[27]

With the Hyde Amendments having tightened the conditions for federal reimbursement of abortion and the Supreme Court having ruled that states were not required to fund elective abortions, many states restricted their own funding of Medicaid abortions.[28] Since there is no national reporting system on Medicaid and since state reporting systems are not necessarily compatible, it is difficult to ascertain how many women have been affected by restrictive Medicaid funding. The Alan Guttmacher Institute estimated that 295,000 Medicaid-financed abortions were performed during fiscal year 1977, the year before the first Hyde Amendment was enacted.[29] Gold and Cates found that "during the first 11 months after the expanded DHEW guidelines were in effect, 2,421 abortions qualified for federal

[25] *See, e.g.,* M. Perry, *The Abortion Funding Cases: A Comment on the Supreme Court's Role in American Government,* 66 GEO. L. J. 1191 (1978); Note, *The Effect of Recent Medicaid Decisions on a Constitutional Right: Abortions Only for the Rich?,* 6 FORDHAM. URB. L. J. 687 (1978); Note, *Medicaid Funding for Abortions: The Medicaid Statute and the Equal Protection Clause,* 6 HOFSTRA L. REV. 421 (1978); R. Lincoln, B. Döring-Bradley, B. Lindheim & M. Cotterill, *The Court, the Congress and the President: Turning Back the Clock on the Pregnant Poor,* 9 FAM. PLAN. PERSPECTIVES 207 (1977).

[26] Continuing Appropriations, 1978, Pub. L. No. 95-205, § 101, 91 Stat. 1460 (1977) and Depts. of Labor and HEW Approp. Act, 1979, Pub. L. 95-480, § 210, 92 Stat. 1586 (1978).

[27] Continuing Appropriations, 1980, Pub. L. No. 96-123, § 109, 93 Stat. 926 (1979).

[28] For example, at the beginning of 1979, 18 states had adopted the federal (Hyde Amendment) standard, 16 states funded abortion only to save the life of the woman, 10 states and the District of Columbia funded medically-necessary abortions, and the remainder financed abortion under varying conditions. ALAN GUTTMACHER INST., ABORTIONS AND THE POOR: PRIVATE MORALITY, PUBLIC RESPONSIBILITY 22 (1979).

[29] *Id.* at 13.

matching funds; thus, the restrictive legislation markedly reduced the number of abortions to Medicaid-eligible women for which federal monies were spent—to less than 1 percent of the pre-restriction level."[30] However, they also found that even in states that had passed restrictive legislation, "most low-income women were able to obtain legally induced abortions primarily with a combination of personal funds and reduced clinic fees although these abortions may have been obtained at later gestations than would have been expected."[31]

Both state laws restricting Medicaid-funded abortions and the federal Hyde amendment have been challenged in court. Lower courts had found restrictive state legislation to violate either the language of the Medicaid act, which refers to an obligation to fund "medically necessary" procedures,[32] or the constitutional guarantees of due process and equal protection.[33] In February, 1980, a federal district court in New York held the Hyde Amendment violated the equal protection component of the Fifth Amendment's due process clause and the free exercise of religion clause of the First Amendment and ordered the federal government to resume funding medi-

[30]J. Gold & W. Cates, Jr., *Restriction of Federal Funds for Abortion: 18 Months Later,* 69 AM. J. PUB. HLTH. 929 (1979).

[31]*Id.* at 930. *See also* W. Cates, Jr., A. Kimball, J. Gold, G. Rubin, J. Smith, R. Rochat & C. Tyler, *The Health Impact of Restricting Public Funds for Abortion October 10, 1977–June 10, 1978,* 69 AM. J. PUB. HLTH. 945 (1979) and J. Trussell, J. Menken, B. Lindheim & B. Vaughan, *The Impact of Restricting Medicaid Financing for Abortion,* 12 FAM. PLAN. PERSPECTIVES 120 (1980).

[32]The Medicaid statute, 42 U.S.C. § 1396 (1976), states:

> For the purpose of enabling each State . . . to furnish (1) medical assistance on behalf of families with dependent children and of aged, blind and disabled individuals, whose income and resources are insufficient to meet the costs of *necessary medical* services . . . there is hereby authorized to be appropriated . . ."(emphasis added)

HEW regulations issued pursuant to Title XIX state that "the medicaid agency may not arbitrarily deny or reduce the amount, duration, or scope of a required service . . . to an otherwise eligible recipient solely because of the diagnosis, type of illness, or condition." 42 C.F.R. § 440.230 (1979). Cases that held restrictive state legislation a violation of Title XIX include: Prete Emma G. v. Edwards, *supra* n. 19; Doe v. Kenley, 584 F. 2d 1362 (4th Cir. 1978); Roe v. Casey, 464 F. Supp. 487 (E.D. Pa. 1978). For a review of litigation on state restriction of Medicaid abortion, *see* Note, *Limiting Public Funds for Abortions: State Response to Congressional Action,* 13 SUFFOLK L. REV. 923 (1979).

[33]*See* Zbaraz v. Quern, 469 F. Supp. 1212 (N.D. Ill. 1979), *rev'd sub. nom* Williams v. Zbaraz, 100 Sup Ct. 2694 (1980).

cally necessary abortions under the Medicaid program. *McRae v. Califano,* 491 F. Supp. 630 (E.D.N.Y. 1980). The decision was appealed to the United States Supreme Court, which issued a decision in June, 1980, reversing the lower court and holding the Hyde Amendment constitutional. That decision, *Harris v. McRae,* is excerpted below, as is *Williams v. Zbaraz,* a companion case that held state restrictions on Medicaid funding to be constitutional.

e. Harris v. McRae, 100 Sup. Ct. 2671 (1980)

Mr. Justice Stewart delivered the opinion of the Court.

This case presents statutory and constitutional questions concerning the public funding of abortions under Title XIX of the Social Security Act, commonly known as the "Medicaid" Act, and recent annual appropriations acts containing the so-called "Hyde Amendment." The statutory question is whether Title XIX requires a State that participates in the Medicaid program to fund the cost of medically necessary abortions for which federal reimbursement is unavailable under the Hyde Amendment. The constitutional question, which arises only if Title XIX imposes no such requirement, is whether the Hyde Amendment, by denying public funding for certain medically necessary abortions, contravenes the liberty or equal protection guarantees of the Due Process Clause of the Fifth Amendment, or either of the Religion Clauses of the First Amendment.

[Section I, which recounts the history of the *McRae* litigation, has been omitted]

II

... We turn first to the question whether Title XIX requires a State that participates in the Medicaid program to continue to fund those medically necessary abortions for which federal reimbursement is unavailable under the Hyde Amendment. If a participating State is under such an obligation, the constitutionality of the Hyde Amendment need not be drawn into question in the present case, for the availability of medically necessary abortions under Medicaid would continue, with the participating State shouldering the total cost of funding such abortions. . . .

... The Medicaid program created by Title XIX is a cooperative endeavor in which the Federal Government provides financial assistance to participating States to aid them in furnishing health care to needy persons ... Nothing in Title XIX as originally enacted, or in its legislative history, suggests that Congress intended to require a participating State to assume the full costs of providing any health services in its Medicaid plan. . .

Since the Congress that enacted Title XIX did not intend a participating State to assume a unilateral funding obligation for any health service in an approved Medicaid plan, it follows that Title XIX does not require a participating State to include in its plan any services for which a subsequent Congress has withheld federal funding. Title XIX was designed as a cooperative program of shared financial responsibility, not as a device for the Federal Government to compel a State to provide services that Congress itself is unwilling to fund . . .

III

Having determined that Title XIX does not obligate a participating State to pay for those medically necessary abortions for which Congress has withheld federal funding, we must consider the constitutional validity of the Hyde Amendment. . . .

A

We address first the appellees' [Cora McRae, a Medicaid recipient in the first trimester of a pregnancy she wished to terminate, and the New York Health and Hospitals Corporation, among others] argument that the Hyde Amendment, by restricting the availability of certain medically necessary abortions under Medicaid, impinges on the "liberty" protected by the Due Process Clause as recognized in *Roe v. Wade* and its progeny. . . .

The present case does differ factually from *Maher* insofar as that case involved a failure to fund nontherapeutic abortions, whereas the Hyde amendment withholds funding of certain medically necessary abortions. Accordingly, the appellees argue that because the Hyde Amendment affects a significant interest not present or asserted in *Maher*—the interest of a woman in protecting her health during pregnancy—and because that interest lies at the core of the personal constitutional freedom recognized in *Wade,* the present case is constitutionally different from *Maher.* It is the appellees' view that to the extent that the Hyde Amendment withholds funding for certain medically necessary abortions, it clearly impinges on the constitutional principle recognized in *Wade*. . .

Regardless of whether the freedom of a woman to choose to terminate her pregnancy for health reasons lies at the core or the periphery of the due process liberty recognized in *Wade,* it simply does not follow that a woman's freedom of choice carries with it a constitutional entitlement to the financial resources to avail herself of the full range of protected choices. The reason why was explained in *Maher:* although government may not place obstacles in the path of a woman's exercise of her freedom of choice, it need not remove those not of its own creation. Indigency falls in the latter category. The financial constraints that restrict an indigent woman's ability to enjoy the full range of constitutionally protected freedom of choice are the product not of governmental restrictions on access to abortions, but rather of her indigency . . .

Although the liberty protected by the Due Process Clause affords protection against unwarranted government interference with freedom of choice in the context of certain personal decisions, it does not confer an entitlement to such funds as may be necessary to realize all the advantages of that freedom . . . It cannot be that because government may not prohibit the use of contraceptives, *Griswold v. Connecticut,* or prevent parents from sending their child to a private school, government, therefore, has an affirmative constitutional obligation to ensure that all persons have the financial resources to obtain contraceptives or send their children to private schools. To translate the limitation on governmental power implicit in the Due Process Clause into an affirmative funding obligation would require Congress to subsidize the medically necessary abortion of an indigent woman even if Congress had not enacted a Medicaid program to subsidize other medically necessary services. Nothing in the Due Process Clause supports such an extraordinary result. Whether freedom of choice that is constitutionally protected warrants federal subsidization is a question for Congress to answer, not a matter of constitutional entitlement. . . .

B

The appellees also argue that the Hyde Amendment contravenes rights secured by the Religion Clauses of the First Amendment. It is the appellees' view that the Hyde Amendment violates the Establishment Clause because it incorporates into law the doctrines of the Roman Catholic Church concerning the sinfulness of abortion and the time at which life commences. Moreover, insofar as a woman's decision to seek a medically necessary abortion may be a product of her religious beliefs under certain Protestant and Jewish tenets, the appellees assert that the funding limitations of the Hyde Amendment impinge on the freedom of religion guaranteed by the Free Exercise Clause.

1

. . . Although neither a State nor the Federal Government can constitutionally "pass laws which aid one religion, aid all religions, or prefer one religion over another," . . . it does not follow that a statute violates the Establishment Clause because it "happens to coincide or harmonize with the tenets of some or all religions." . . . That the Judaeo-Christian religions oppose stealing does not mean that a State or the Federal Government may not, consistent with the Establishment Clause, enact laws prohibiting larceny. The Hyde Amendment, as the District Court noted, is as much a reflection of "traditionalist" values toward abortion, as it is an embodiment of the views of any particular religion. In sum, we are convinced that the fact that the funding restrictions in the Hyde Amendment may coincide with the religious tenets of the Roman Catholic Church does not, without more, contravene the Establishment Clause.

2

We need not address the merits of the appellees' arguments concerning the Free Exercise Clause, because the appellees lack standing to raise a free exercise challenge to the Hyde Amendment. . . .

C

It remains to be determined whether the Hyde Amendment violates the equal protection component of the Fifth Amendment. This challenge is premised on the fact that, although federal reimbursement is available under Medicaid for medically necessary services generally, the Hyde Amendment does not permit federal reimbursement of all medically necessary abortions. . . .

1

For the reasons stated above, we have already concluded that the Hyde Amendment violates no constitutionally protected substantive rights. We now conclude as well that it is not predicated on a constitutionally suspect classification. In reaching this conclusion, we again draw guidance from the Court's decision in *Maher v. Roe*. . . .

It is our view that the present case is indistinguishable from *Maher* in this respect [that no suspect classification is involved]. Here, as in *Maher,* the principal impact of the Hyde Amendment falls on the indigent. But that fact does not itself render the funding restriction constitutionally invalid, for this Court has held repeatedly that poverty, standing alone, is not a suspect classification. . . .

2

The remaining question then is whether the Hyde Amendment is rationally related to a legitimate governmental objective . . .

In *Wade,* the Court recognized that the State has "an important and legitimate interest in protecting the potentiality of human life." That interest was found to exist throughout a pregnancy, "grow[ing] in substantiality as the woman approaches term." Moreover, in *Maher,* the Court held that Connecticut's decision to fund the costs associated with childbirth but not those associated with non-therapeutic abortions was a rational means of advancing the legitimate state interest in protecting potential life by encouraging childbirth.

It follows that the Hyde Amendment, by encouraging childbirth except in the most urgent circumstances, is rationally related to the legitimate governmental objective of protecting potential life. By subsidizing the medical expenses of indigent women who carry their pregnancies to term while not subsidizing the comparable expenses of women who undergo abortions (except those whose lives are threatened), Congress has established incentives that make childbirth a more attractive alternative than abortion for persons eligible for Medicaid. These incentives bear a direct relationship to the legitimate congressional interest in protecting potential life. Nor is it irrational that Congress has authorized federal reimbursement for medically necessary services generally, but not for certain medically necessary abortions. Abortion is inherently different from other medical procedures, because no other procedure involves the purposeful termination of a potential life. . . .

Where, as here, the Congress has neither invaded a substantive constitutional right or freedom, nor enacted legislation that purposefully operates to the detriment of a suspect class, the only requirement of equal protection is that congressional action be rationally related to a legitimate governmental interest. The Hyde Amendment satisfies that standard. It is not the mission of this Court or any other to decide whether the balance of competing interests reflected in the Hyde Amendment is wise social policy. If that were our mission, not every Justice who has subscribed to the judgment of the Court today could have done so. But we cannot, in the name of the Constitution, overturn duly enacted statutes simply "because they may be unwise, improvident, or out of harmony with a particular school of thought." . . .

Mr. Justice White, concurring.

. . . The constitutional right recognized in *Roe* v. *Wade* was the right to choose to undergo an abortion without coercive interference by the government. As the Court points out, *Roe* v. *Wade* did not purport to adjudicate a right to have abortions funded by the government, but only to be free from unreasonable official interference with private choice. . . .

Roe v. *Wade* thus dealt with the circumstances in which the governmental interest in potential life would justify official interference with the abortion choices of pregnant women. There is no such calculus involved here. The government does not seek to interfere with or to impose any coercive restraint on the choice of any woman to have an abortion. The woman's choice remains unfettered, the government is not attempting to use its interest in life to justify a coercive restraint, and hence in disbursing its Medicaid funds it is free to implement rationally what *Roe* v. *Wade* recognized to be its legitimate interest in a potential life by covering the medical costs of childbirth but denying funds for abortions. Neither *Roe* v. *Wade* nor any of the cases decided in its wake invalidates this legislative preference. . . .

Mr. Justice Brennan, with whom Mr. Justice Marshall and Mr. Justice Blackmun join, dissenting.*

. . . I write separately to express my continuing disagreement with the Court's mischaracterization of the nature of the fundamental right recognized in *Roe v. Wade,* and its misconception of the manner in which that right is infringed by federal and state legislation withdrawing all funding for medically necessary abortions. . . .

. . .*Roe* and its progeny established that the pregnant woman has a right to be free from state interference with her choice to have an abortion—a right which, at least prior to the end of the first trimester, absolutely prohibits any governmental regulation of that highly personal decision. The proposition for which these cases stand thus is not that the State is under an affirmative obligation to ensure access to abortions for all who may desire them; it is that the State must refrain from wielding its enormous power and influence in a manner that might burden the pregnant woman's freedom to choose whether to have an abortion. The Hyde Amendment's denial of public funds for medically necessary abortions plainly intrudes upon this constitutionally protected decision, for both by design and in effect it serves to coerce indigent pregnant women to bear children that they would otherwise elect not to have. . . .

. . .The Hyde Amendment is a transparent attempt by the Legislative Branch to impose the political majority's judgment of the morally acceptable and socially desirable preference on a sensitive and intimate decision that the Constitution entrusts to the individual. Worse yet, the Hyde Amendment does not foist that majoritarian viewpoint with equal measure upon everyone in our Nation, rich and poor alike;

*Justices Brennan, Marshall, Blackmun, and Stevens wrote single dissents to *Harris v. McRae* and *Williams v. Zbaraz.—Ed.*

rather, it imposes that viewpoint only upon that segment of our society which, because of its position of political powerlessness, is least able to defend its privacy rights from the encroachments of state-mandated morality. The instant legislation thus calls for more exacting judicial review than in most other cases. . . .

. . .It is clear that the Hyde Amendment not only was designed to inhibit, but does in fact inhibit the woman's freedom to choose abortion over childbirth. "Pregnancy is unquestionably a condition requiring medical services . . . Treatment for the condition may involve medical procedures for its termination, or medical procedures to bring the pregnancy to term, resulting in a live birth" . . . In every pregnancy, one of these two courses of treatment is medically necessary, and the poverty-stricken woman depends on the Medicaid Act to pay for the expenses associated with that procedure. But under the Hyde Amendment, the Government will fund only those procedures incidental to childbirth. By thus injecting coercive financial incentives favoring childbirth into a decision that is constitutionally guaranteed to be free from governmental intrusion, the Hyde Amendment deprives the indigent woman of her freedom to choose abortion over maternity, thereby impinging on the due process liberty right recognized in *Roe v. Wade*. . . .

The fundamental flaw in the Court's due process analysis, then, is its failure to acknowledge that the discriminatory distribution of the benefits of governmental largesse can discourage the exercise of fundamental liberties just as effectively as can an outright denial of those rights through criminal and regulatory sanctions. . . .

Mr. Justice Marshall, dissenting.

. . .The Court's decision today marks a retreat from *Roe v. Wade* and represents a cruel blow to the most powerless members of our society. I dissent.

I

. . . The impact of the Hyde Amendment on indigent women falls into four major categories. First, the Hyde Amendment prohibits federal funding for abortions that are necessary in order to protect the health and sometimes the life of the mother. Numerous conditions—such as cancer, rheumatic fever, diabetes, malnutrition, phlebitis, sickle cell anemia, and heart disease—substantially increase the risks associated with pregnancy or are themselves aggravated by pregnancy. Such conditions may make an abortion medically necessary in the judgment of a physician, but cannot be funded under the Hyde Amendment. . . .

Second, federal funding is denied in cases in which severe mental disturbances will be created by unwanted pregnancies. The result of such psychological disturbances may be suicide, attempts at self-abortion, or child abuse. The Hyde Amendment makes no provision for funding in such cases.

Third, the Hyde Amendment denies funding for the majority of women whose pregnancies have been caused by rape or incest. The prerequisite of a report within 60 days serves to exclude those who are afraid of recounting what has happened or are in fear of unsympathetic treatment by the authorities. Such a requirement is, of course, especially burdensome for the indigent. . . .

Finally, federal funding is unavailable in cases in which it is known that the fetus itself will be unable to survive. . . .

II

The Court resolves the equal protection issue in this case through a relentlessly formalistic catechism. Adhering to its "two-tiered" approach to equal protection, the Court first decides that so-called strict scrutiny is not required because the Hyde Amendment does not violate the Due Process Clause and is not predicated on a constitutionally suspect classification. . . . I continue to believe that the rigid "two-tiered" approach is inappropriate and that the Constitution requires a more exacting standard of review than mere rationality in cases such as this one. Further, in my judgment the Hyde Amendment cannot pass constitutional muster even under the rational-basis standard of review. . . .

C

. . . The Court treats this case as though it were controlled by *Maher*. To the contrary, this case is the mirror image of *Maher*. The result in *Maher* turned on the fact that the legislation there under consideration discouraged only nontherapeutic, or medically unnecessary, abortions. . . . Thus the plaintiffs were seeking benefits which were not available to others similarly situated. I continue to believe that *Maher* was wrongly decided. But it is apparent that while the plaintiffs in *Maher* were seeking a benefit not available to others similarly situated, respondents are protesting their exclusion from a benefit that is available to all others similarly situated. This, it need hardly be said, is a crucial difference for equal protection purposes.

Under Title XIX and the Hyde Amendment, funding is available for essentially all necessary medical treatment for the poor. Respondents have met the statutory requirements for eligibility, but they are excluded because the treatment that is medically necessary involves the exercise of a fundamental right, the right to choose an abortion.

In short, respondents have been deprived of a governmental benefit for which they are otherwise eligible, solely because they have attempted to exercise a constitutional right. . . .

[The dissenting opinion of Justice Blackmun has been omitted.]

Mr. Justice Stevens, dissenting.

. . .This case involves the pool of benefits that Congress created by enacting Title XIX of the Social Security Act in 1965. Individuals who satisfy two neutral statutory criteria—financial need and medical need—are entitled to equal access to that pool. The question is whether certain persons who satisfy those criteria may be denied access to benefits solely because they must exercise the constitutional right to have an abortion in order to obtain the medical care they need. Our prior cases plainly dictate the answer to that question.

A fundamentally different question was decided in *Maher v. Roe.* Unlike these plaintiffs, the plaintiffs in *Maher* did not satisfy the neutral criterion of medical need; they sought a subsidy for nontherapeutic abortions—medical procedures which by definition they did not need. . . . Nontherapeutic abortions were simply outside the ambit of the medical benefits program. Thus, in *Maher,* the plaintiffs' desire to exercise a constitutional right gave rise to neither special access nor special exclusion from the pool of benefits created by Title XIX.

This case involves a special exclusion of women who, by definition, are confronted with a choice between two serious harms: serious health damage to themselves on the one hand and abortion on the other. The competing interests are the interest in maternal health and the interest in protecting potential human life. It is now part of our law that the pregnant woman's decision as to which of these conflicting interests shall prevail is entitled to constitutional protection.

In *Roe* v. *Wade* and *Doe* v. *Bolton* the Court recognized that the States have a legitimate and protectible interest in potential human life. But the Court explicitly held that prior to fetal viability that interest may not justify any governmental burden on the woman's choice to have an abortion nor even any regulation of abortion except in furtherance of the State's interest in the woman's health. In effect, the Court held that a woman's freedom to elect to have an abortion prior to viability has absolute constitutional protection, subject only to valid health regulations. Indeed, in *Roe* v. *Wade* the Court held that even after fetal viability, a State may "regulate, and even proscribe, abortion *except where it is necessary, in appropriate medical judgment, for the preservation of the life or health of the mother.*" 410 U. S., at 165 (emphasis added). We have a duty to respect that holding. The Court simply shirks that duty in this case.

If a woman has a constitutional right to place a higher value on avoiding either serious harm to her own health or perhaps an abnormal childbirth than on protecting potential life, the exercise of that right cannot provide the basis for the denial of a benefit to which she would otherwise be entitled. The Court's sterile equal protection analysis evades this critical though simple point. The Court focuses exclusively on the "legitimate interest in protecting the potential life of the fetus." It concludes that since the Hyde Amendments further that interest, the exclusion they create is rational and therefore constitutional. But it is misleading to speak of the Government's legitimate interest in the fetus without reference to the context in which that interest was held to be legitimate. For *Roe v. Wade* squarely held that the States may not protect that interest when a conflict with the interest in a pregnant woman's health exists. It is thus perfectly clear that neither the Federal Government nor the States may exclude a woman from medical benefits to which she would otherwise be entitled solely to further an interest in potential life when a physician, "in appropriate medical judgment," certifies that an abortion is necessary "for the preservation of the life or health of the mother." *Roe* v. *Wade.* The Court totally fails to explain why this reasoning is not dispositive here. . . .

Nor can it be argued that the exclusion of this type of medically necessary treatment of the indigent can be justified on fiscal grounds. There are some especially costly forms of treatment that may reasonably be excluded from the program in order to preserve the assets in the pool and extend its benefits to the maximum number of needy persons. . . . The records in both *McRae* and *Zbaraz* demonstrate that the cost of an abortion is only a small fraction of the costs associated with childbirth. . . .

f. Williams v. Zbaraz, 100 Sup. Ct. 2694 (1980)

Appellees, two physicians who perform medically necessary abortions for indigent women, a welfare rights organization, and an indigent pregnant woman, challenged an Illinois statute that prohibited state medical assistance for all abortions except those necessary to preserve the life of the woman. After extensive litigation, a federal district court held the statute unconstitutional. *Zbaraz v. Quern,* 469 F. Supp. 1212 (N.D. Ill. 1979). On appeal, the Supreme Court, with Justice Stewart writing for the five-person majority, reversed the lower court decision, using the language quoted below.

. . .The appellees argue that (1) Title XIX requires Illinois to provide coverage in its state Medicaid plan for all medically necessary abortions, whether or not the life of the pregnant woman is endangered, and (2) the funding by Illinois of medically necessary services gener-

> ally, but not of certain medically necessary abortions, violates the Equal Protection Clause of the Fourteenth Amendment. Both arguments are foreclosed by our decision today in *Harris v. McRae*. As to the appellees' statutory argument, we have concluded in *McRae* that a participating State is not obligated under Title XIX to pay for those medically necessary abortions for which federal reimbursement is unavailable under the Hyde Amendment. As to their constitutional argument, we have concluded in *McRae* that the Hyde Amendment does not violate the equal protection component of the Fifth Amendment by withholding public funding for certain medically necessary abortions, while providing funding for other medically necessary health services. It follows, for the same reasons, that the comparable funding restrictions in the Illinois statute do not violate the Equal Protection Clause of the Fourteenth Amendment.

g. Other Restrictions on Abortion Funding. In addition to restrictions on Medicaid, legislation has been passed at both federal and local levels restricting other sources of funding abortions. For example, Congress has forbidden the use of federal funds for abortions of Peace Corps volunteers[34] and military personnel[35] and their dependents and for abortion as a method of family planning in both the foreign aid program[36] and the domestic family planning program.[37] Moreover, federal legislation prohibits Legal Services lawyers from litigating cases concerned with elective abortion and forbids the United States Civil Rights Commission from conducting studies on abortion.

6. Public Hospitals and Institutional Conscience Clauses

a. Poelker v. Doe, 432 U.S. 519 (U.S. Supreme Court 1977). *Poelker v. Doe* was decided on the same day as the *Beal* and *Maher* cases and presents another aspect of the same issue, in this situation whether a hospital or other institution can refuse to provide abor-

[34]Foreign Assistance and Related Programs Approp. Act, 1979, Pub. L. No. 95-481, Title III, 92 Stat. 1597 (1978).

[35]Dept. of Def. Approp. Act, 1980, Pub. L. No. 96-154, § 762, 93 Stat. 1162 (1979).

[36]Foreign Assistance Act of 1973, Pub. L. No. 93-189, § 114, 87 Stat. 716 (1973).

[37]Fam. Plan. Serv. and Pop. Res. Act, Pub. L. No. 91-572, § 1008, 84 Stat. 1508 (1970).

tions if abortion violates the moral principles or conscience of the institution.[38]

Per Curiam.

Respondent Jane Doe, an indigent, sought unsuccessfully to obtain a nontherapeutic abortion at Starkloff Hospital, one of two city-owned public hospitals in St. Louis, Mo. She subsequently brought this class action under 42 U.S.C. § 1983 against the Mayor of St. Louis and the Director of Health and Hospitals, alleging that the refusal by Starkloff Hospital to provide the desired abortion violated her constitutional rights. Although the District Court ruled against Doe following a trial, the Court of Appeals for the Eighth Circuit reversed in an opinion that accepted both her factual and legal arguments. . . .

The Court of Appeals concluded that Doe's inability to obtain an abortion resulted from a combination of a policy directive by the Mayor and a longstanding staffing practice at Starkloff Hospital. The directive, communicated to the Director of Health and Hospitals by the Mayor, prohibited the performance of abortions in the city hospitals except when there was a threat of grave physiological injury or death to the mother. Under the staffing practice, the doctors and medical students at the obstetrics-gynecology clinic at the hospital are drawn from the faculty and students at the St. Louis University School of Medicine, a Jesuit-operated institution opposed to abortion. Relying on our decision in *Roe v. Wade* and *Doe v. Bolton,* the Court of Appeals held that the city's policy and the hospital's staffing practice denied the "constitutional rights of indigent pregnant women . . . long after those rights had been clearly enunciated" in *Roe* and *Doe.* The court cast the issue in an equal protection mold, finding that the provision of publicly financed hospital services for childbirth but not for elective abortions constituted invidious discrimination. . . .

We agree that the constitutional question presented here is identical in principle with that presented by a State's refusal to provide Medicaid benefits for abortions while providing them for childbirth. This was the issue before us in *Maher v. Roe.* For the reasons set forth in our opinion in that case, we find no constitutional violation by the city of St. Louis in electing, as a policy choice, to provide publicly financed hospital services for childbirth without providing corresponding services for nontherapeutic abortions.

In the decision of the Court of Appeals and in the briefs supporting that decision, emphasis is placed on Mayor Poelker's personal opposi-

[38] A distinction should be made between following the dictates of the conscience of an individual and an institution. Generally, it is agreed that individuals have the right to refuse to participate in procedures which violate their moral principles. The issue herein is whether institutions have the same right.—Ed.

tion to abortion, characterized as "a wanton, callous disregard" for the constitutional rights of indigent women. Although the Mayor's personal position on abortion is irrelevant to our decision, we note that he is an elected official responsible to the people of St. Louis. His policy of denying city funds for abortions such as that desired by Doe is subject to public debate and approval or disapproval at the polls. We merely hold, for the reasons stated in *Maher,* that the Constitution does not forbid a State or city, pursuant to democratic processes, from expressing a preference for normal childbirth as St. Louis has done.

. . . Mr. Justice Brennan, with whom Mr. Justice Marshall and Mr. Justice Blackmun join, dissenting.*

. . .The fundamental right of a woman freely to choose to terminate her pregnancy has been infringed by the city of St. Louis through a deliberate policy based on opposition to elective abortions on moral grounds by city officials. While it may still be possible for some indigent women to obtain abortions in clinics or private hospitals, it is clear that the city policy is a significant, and in some cases insurmountable, obstacle to indigent pregnant women who cannot pay for abortions in those private facilities. Nor is the closing of St. Louis, public hospitals an isolated instance with little practical significance. The importance of today's decision is greatly magnified by the fact that during 1975 and the first quarter of 1976 only about 18% of all public hospitals in the country provided abortion services, and in 10 States there were no public hospitals providing such services.

A number of difficulties lie beneath the surface of the Court's holding. Public hospitals that do not permit the performance of elective abortions will frequently have physicians on their staffs who would willingly perform them. This may operate in some communities significantly to reduce the number of physicians who are both willing and able to perform abortions in a hospital setting. It is not a complete answer that many abortions may safely be performed in clinics, for some physicians will not be affiliated with those clinics, and some abortions may pose unacceptable risks if performed outside a hospital. Indeed, such an answer would be ironic, for if the result is to force some abortions to be performed in a clinic that properly should be performed in a hospital, the city policy will have operated to increase rather than reduce health risks associated with abortions; and in *Roe v. Wade* the Court permitted regulation by the State solely to *protect* maternal health.

*Justices Marshall and Blackmun wrote single dissents in the *Poelker, Maher,* and *Beal* cases, which were all decided the same day. Their dissents in these cases are found on pp. 95–97, *supra.*—Ed.

> The Court's holding will also pose difficulties in small communities where the public hospital is the only nearby health care facility. If such a public hospital is closed to abortions, any woman—rich or poor—will be seriously inconvenienced; and for some women—particularly poor women—the unavailability of abortions in the public hospital will be an insuperable obstacle. Indeed, a recent survey suggests that the decision in this case will be felt most strongly in rural areas, where the public hospital will in all likelihood be closed to elective abortions, and where there will not be sufficient demand to support a separate abortion clinic. . . .

b. Commentary on Institutional Conscience Clauses. The *Poelker* decision resolved, in part at least, one of the major challenges to *Roe v. Wade,* whether a hospital or other institution could refuse to provide abortions based on the moral principles or conscience of the institution. There are two different considerations, which sometimes tended to intertwine.

The first is whether *public* hospitals are required under the Constitution to provide abortion services. Prior to *Poelker,* many courts had followed the reasoning of *Hathaway v. City of Worcester Hospital,* 475 F. 2d 701 (1st Cir. 1973), which held that a public hospital that offered similar services could not constitutionally refuse to provide the services of voluntary sterilizations. *Poelker* makes it clear, however, that a public hospital can refuse to provide elective abortions.

The second is whether a *private* hospital that receives governmental assistance becomes, in effect, an arm of the state and if so, whether it can invoke an institutional conscience clause. This is essentially a jurisdictional question. Since the Fourteenth Amendment applies only to governmental action and does not reach purely private conduct, courts will determine whether the state is involved to such an extent (*e.g.,* by providing government funds and tax benefits) that the private conduct has become "clothed" in state action. If there is no state action, then a court does not have the jurisdiction to adjudicate the case. If, on the other hand, state action is involved, then a court can determine whether the Fourteenth Amendment has been violated.[39]

In 1973 Senator Church introduced legislation which attempted to exclude hospitals which received federal funds from having to

[39]For a comprehensive examination of the complex question of what constitutes "state action," *see* Note, *State Action: Theories for Applying Constitutional Restrictions to Private Activities,* 74 COLUM. L. REV. 656 (1974).

provide abortions or sterilizations if these violated the entity's religious beliefs or moral convictions.[40] However, it has been questioned whether an act of Congress could relieve an institution considered public of its duty to obey the Constitution. Commenting on the Church Amendment and other institutional conscience clauses, Pilpel and Patton state:[41]

> What then is the purpose and effect of the entity conscience clauses? They are superfluous with respect to private entities whose action would not be considered "state action" anyway. In the absence of a sufficient number of public indicators of state action, such entities may follow their "religious belief" and "moral conviction" as they see fit free of constitutional constraint—and they do not need the entity conscience clauses to do so. But if, on the other hand, public entities or private entities whose action would otherwise be considered state action are involved, an institutional conscience clause cannot transform their action into nonstate action. . . .The conclusion is plain: the receipt of federal funds cannot be made the basis for insulating any entity receiving them from otherwise applicable constitutional guarantees.

7. Viability, Standard of Care, and Fetal Protection

***a. Planned Parenthood of Central Missouri v. Danforth,* 428 U.S. 52 (U.S. Supreme Court 1976).** In *Planned Parenthood of Central Missouri v. Danforth,* the Supreme Court ruled on those portions of the Missouri statute defining viability and establishing standards of care for a fetus which emerges "alive." The relevant parts of Justice Blackmun's opinion are excerpted below:

> *The definition of viability.* Section 2(2) of the Act defines "viability" as "that stage of fetal development when the life of the unborn child may be continued indefinitely outside the womb by natural or artificial life-supportive systems." Appellants claim that this definition violates and conflicts with the discussion of viability in our opinion in *Roe.* In particular, appellants object to the failure of the definition to contain any reference to a gestational time period, to its failure to

[40] Health Programs Extension Act of 1973, Pub. L. No. 93-45 §401(b) (c), 42 U.S.C. § 300a-7 (1976).

[41] H. Pilpel & D. Patton, *Abortion, Conscience and the Constitution: An Examination of Federal Institutional Conscience Clauses,* 6 COLUM. HUM. RTS. L. REV. 279, 304-305 (1974–75).

incorporate and reflect the three stages of pregnancy, to the presence of the word "indefinitely," and to the extra burden of regulation imposed. . . .

In *Roe,* we used the term "viable," properly we thought, to signify the point at which the fetus is "potentially able to live outside the mother's womb, albeit with artifical aid," and presumably capable of "meaningful life outside the mother's womb." We noted that this point "is usually placed" at about seven months or 28 weeks, but may occur earlier. . . .

. . .We agree with the District Court that it is not the proper function of the legislature or the courts to place viability, which essentially is a medical concept, at a specific point in the gestation period. The time when viability is achieved may vary with each pregnancy, and the determination of whether a particular fetus is viable is, and must be, a matter for the judgment of the responsible attending physician. The definition of viability in § 2(2) merely reflects this fact. . . .

We thus do not accept appellants' contention that a specified number of weeks in pregnancy must be fixed by statute as the point of viability . . .

Standard of care. Appellee Danforth . . . appeals from the unanimous decision of the District Court that § 6(1) of the Act is unconstitutional. That section provides:

> "No person who performs or induces an abortion shall fail to exercise that degree of professional skill, care and diligence to preserve the life and health of the fetus which such person would be required to exercise in order to preserve the life and health of any fetus intended to be born and not aborted. Any physician or person assisting in the abortion who shall fail to take such measures to encourage or to sustain the life of the child, and the death of the child results, shall be deemed guilty of manslaughter. . . . Further, such physician or other person shall be liable in an action for damages."

. . . Section 6(1) requires the physician to exercise the prescribed skill, care, and diligence to preserve the life and health of the *fetus.* It does not specify that such care need to be taken only after the stage of viability has been reached. As the provision now reads, it impermissibly requires the physician to preserve the life and health of the fetus, whatever the stage of pregnancy. The fact that the second sentence of § 6(1) refers to a criminal penalty where the physician fails "to take such measures to encourage or to sustain the life of the *child,* and the death of the *child* results" (emphasis supplied), simply does not modify the duty imposed by the previous sentence or limit that duty to pregnancies that have reached the stage of viability.

b. Colautti v. Franklin, 439 U.S. 379 (U.S. Supreme Court 1979). The Court, in this 6–3 decision, elaborated on the concepts of viability and standard of care:

Mr. Justice Blackmun delivered the opinion of the Court.

At issue here is the constitutionality of subsection (a) of § 5 of the Pennsylvania Abortion Control Act. . . . This statute subjects a physician who performs an abortion to potential criminal liability if he fails to utilize a statutorily prescribed technique when the fetus "is viable" or when there is "sufficient reason to believe that the fetus may be viable". . . .

Section 5(a) requires every person who performs or induces an abortion to make a determination, "based on his experience, judgment or professional competence," that the fetus is not viable. If such person determines that the fetus is viable, or if "there is sufficient reason to believe that the fetus may be viable," then he must adhere to the prescribed standard of care. This requirement contains a double ambiguity. First, it is unclear whether the statute imports a purely subjective standard, or whether it imposes a mixed subjective and objective standard. Second, it is uncertain whether the phrase "may be viable" simply refers to viability, as that term has been defined in *Roe* and in *Planned Parenthood,* or whether it refers to an undefined penumbral or "gray" area prior to the stage of viability.

The statute requires the physician to conform to the prescribed standard of care if one of two conditions is satisfied: if he determines that the fetus "is viable," or "if there is sufficient reason to believe that the fetus may be viable." Apparently, the determination of whether the fetus "is viable" is to be based on the attending physician's experience, judgment or professional competence," a subjective point of reference. But it is unclear whether the same phrase applies to the second triggering condition, that is, to "sufficient reason to believe that the fetus may be viable." In other words, it is ambiguous whether there must be "sufficient reason" from the perspective of the judgment, skill, and training of the attending physician, or "sufficient reason" from the perspective of a cross-section of the medical community or a panel of experts. The latter, obviously, portends not an inconsequential hazard for the typical private practitioner who may not have the skills and technology that are readily available at a teaching hospital or large medical center.

The intended distinction between the phrases "is viable" and "may be viable" is even more elusive. Appellants argue that no difference is intended, and that the use of the "may be viable" words "simply incorporates the acknowledged medical fact that a fetus is 'viable' if it has that statistical 'chance' of survival recognized by the medical community." The statute, however, does not support the contention that "may be viable" is synonymous with, or merely intended to explicate the meaning of, "viable."

Section 5(a) requires the physician to observe the prescribed standard of care if he determines "that the fetus is viable *or* if there is sufficient reason to believe that the fetus may be viable" (emphasis supplied). The syntax clearly implies that there are two distinct conditions under which the physician must conform to the standard of care. Appellants' argument that "may be viable" is synonymous with "viable" would make either the first or the second condition redundant or largely superfluous, in violation of the elementary canon of construction that a statute should be interpreted so as not to render one part inoperative. . . .

The vagueness of the viability determination requirement of § 5(a) is compounded by the fact that the Act subjects the physician to potential criminal liability without regard to fault. Under § 5(d), a physician who fails to abide by the standard of care when there is sufficient reason to believe that the fetus "may be viable" is subject "to such civil or criminal liability as would pertain to him had the fetus been a child who was intended to be born and not aborted." . . .

The perils of strict criminal liability are particularly acute here because of the uncertainty of the viability determination itself. As the record in this case indicates, a physician determines whether or not a fetus is viable after considering a number of variables: the gestational age of the fetus, derived from the reported menstrual history of the woman; fetal weight, based on an inexact estimate of the size and condition of the uterus; the woman's general health and nutrition; the quality of the available medical facilities; and other factors. Because of the number and the imprecision of these variables, the probability of any particular fetus' obtaining meaningful life outside the womb can be determined only with difficulty. Moreover, the record indicates that even if agreement may be reached on the probability of survival, different physicians equate viability with different probabilities of survival, and some physicians refuse to equate viability with any numerical probability at all. In the face of these uncertainties, it is not unlikely that experts will disagree over whether a particular fetus in the second trimester has advanced to the stage of viability. The prospect of such disagreement, in conjunction with a statute imposing strict civil and criminal liability for an erroneous determination of viability, could have a profound chilling effect on the willingness of physicians to perform abortions near the point of viability in the manner indicated by their best medical judgment.

Because we hold that the viability determination provision of § 5 (a) is void on its face, we need not now decide whether, under a properly drafted statute, a finding of bad faith or some other type of scienter would be required before a physician could be held criminally responsible for an erroneous determination of viability. We reaffirm, however, that "the determination of whether a particular fetus is viable is, and must be, a matter for the judgment of the responsible attending physician." *Planned Parenthood of Central Missouri v. Danforth*. State regulation that impinges upon this determination, if it is to be constitutional, must allow the attending physician "the room he needs to make his best medical judgment." *Doe v. Bolton.*

c. Issues and Commentary. The Supreme Court in *Colautti* reemphasized the importance of the physician's judgment in determining viability. Does *Colautti* mean that the physician's judgment about viability is conclusive? After *Colautti,* could a physician who in good faith determined a fetus to be viable be prosecuted for performing a late abortion?[42] After *Danforth* and *Colautti,* could a state, for the sake of certainty, arbitrarily designate a specific point (say the 24th week) as that of viability? Could it require that emergency medical care be made available for all fetuses aborted after a certain number of weeks? To what extent does the right to abort a nonviable fetus imply the right to withhold lifesaving measures?[43] What effect will the invention of new machinery to keep infants artificially alive at increasingly earlier periods have on the standard of care provision of *Danforth* and *Colautti?* On the underlying rationale for *Roe v. Wade?* Beyond these legal consequences, what are the implications for fetal research?[44]

[42]Anders v. Floyd, 440 U.S. 445 (1979), appears to leave open some possibility of prosecution for criminal abortion or homicide of a fetus aborted in the 25th week. The Supreme Court said, "The District Court enjoined the prosecution, concluding that under *Roe v. Wade,* there was no possibility of obtaining a constitutionally binding conviction of the appellee. Because the District Court may have reached this conclusion on the basis of an erroneous concept of "viability," which refers to potential, rather than actual, survival of the fetus outside the womb, *Colautti v. Franklin,* the judgment is vacated and the case is remanded . . . for further consideration in light of *Colautti.*"

[43]The sensitive moral and legal issues related to this issue are discussed in short articles by S. Bok, B. Nathanson, D. Nathan & L. Walters, *The Unwanted Child: Caring for the Fetus Born Alive After an Abortion,* HASTINGS CENTER REPORT vol. 6, no. 5, pp. 10–15 (1976). *See also* Commonwealth v. Edelin, 359 N.E. 2d 4 (Mass. 1976).

[44]For a review of federal policy toward fetal research, *see* J. Friedman, *The Federal Fetal Experimentation Regulations: An Establishment Clause Analysis,* 61 MINN. L.REV. 961, 962–975 (1977).

8. Restrictions on Second and Third Trimester Abortions

a. Methods of Inducing Abortion. To what extent can a state require a specific method of performing abortions? The Supreme Court's *Danforth* decision, 428 U.S. 52 (1976), dealt in part with this issue in the context of a prohibition on the use of saline amniocentesis:

> . . . The State, through § 9, would prohibit the use of a method which the record shows is the one most commonly used nationally by physicians after the first trimester and which is safer, with respect to maternal mortality, than even continuation of the pregnancy until normal childbirth. Moreover, as a practical matter, it forces a woman and her physician to terminate her pregnancy by methods more dangerous to her health than the method outlawed.
>
> As so viewed, particularly in the light of the present unavailability—as demonstrated by the record—of the prostaglandin technique, the outright legislative proscription of saline fails as a reasonable regulation for the protection of maternal health. It comes into focus, instead, as an unreasonable or arbitrary regulation designed to inhibit, and having the effect of inhibiting, the vast majority of abortions after the first 12 weeks. As such, it does not withstand constitutional challenge.

In *Colautti v. Franklin,* 439 U.S. 379 (1979), the court also dealt with a statute that regulated second and third trimester abortions:

> We also conclude that the standard-of-care provision of § 5(a) is impermissibly vague. The standard-of-care provision, when it applies, requires the physician to
>
> > "exercise that degree of professional skill, care and diligence to preserve the life and health of the fetus which such person would be required to exercise in order to preserve the life and health of any fetus intended to be born and not aborted and the abortion technique employed shall be that which would provide the best opportunity for the fetus to be aborted alive so long as a different technique would not be necessary in order to preserve the life or health of the mother."
>
> Plaintiffs-appellees focus their attack on the second part of the standard, requiring the physician to employ the abortion technique offering the greatest possibility of fetal survival, provided some other technique would not be necessary in order to preserve the life or health of the mother. . . .

The parties acknowledge that there is disagreement among medical authorities about the relative merits and the safety of different abortion procedures that may be used during the second trimester. The appellants submit, however, that the only legally relevant considerations are that alternatives exist among abortifacients, "and that the physician, mindful of the state's interest in protecting viable life, must make a competent and good faith medical judgment on the feasibility of protecting the fetus' chance of survival in a manner consistent with the life and health of the pregnant woman." We read § 5(a), however, to be much more problematical.

The statute does not clearly specify, as appellants imply, that the woman's life and health must always prevail over the fetus' life and health when they conflict. The woman's life and health are not mentioned in the first part of the stated standard of care, which sets forth the general duty to the viable fetus; they are mentioned only in the second part which deals with the choice of abortion procedures. Moreover, the second part of the standard directs the physician to employ the abortion technique best suited to fetal survival "so long as a different technique would not be *necessary* in order to preserve the life or health of the mother" (emphasis supplied). In this context, the word "necessary" suggests that a particular technique must be indispensable to the woman's life or health—not merely desirable—before it may be adopted. And "the life or health of the mother," as used in § 5 (a), has not been construed by the courts of the Commonwealth, nor does it necessarily imply, that all factors relevant to the welfare of the woman may be taken into account by the physician in making his decision. . . .

Consequently, it is uncertain whether the statute permits the physician to consider his duty to the patient to be paramount to his duty to the fetus, or whether it requires the physician to make a "trade-off" between the woman's health and additional percentage points of fetal survival. Serious ethical and constitutional difficulties, that we do not address, lurk behind this ambiguity. We hold only that where conflicting duties of this magnitude are involved, the State, at the least, must proceed with greater precision before it may subject a physician to possible criminal sanctions . . . The choice of an appropriate abortion technique, as the record in this case so amply demonstrates, is a complex medical judgment about which experts can—and do—disagree. The lack of any scienter requirement exacerbates the uncertainty of the statute. We conclude that the standard-of-care provision, like the viability determination requirement, is void for vagueness. . . .

b. Other Restrictions on Second Trimester Abortions. The Supreme Court dealt with committee review, concurring physicians' opinions, and JCAH accreditation during the first trimester in *Doe v. Bolton, supra* pp. 80–81 Would these requirements be reasonably related to maternal health for second and third trimester abortions? What about requirements that second trimester abortions be performed only in hospitals?[45] Or that facilities have immediate hospital backup, or be equipped with expensive emergency equipment?

c. Restrictions on Third Trimester Abortions. *Roe v. Wade* held that after viability states could prohibit abortion except where necessary to protect the life or health of the woman. Does preserving the life mean that a woman must be in imminent danger of death? Can long-term danger to life from the effects of childbirth be considered in a physician's determination? Could a state require verification by a second physician that a woman's life, or health, is in danger? Similarly, does "health" refer only to physical health or does it refer to emotional or psychological health as well? In *United States v. Vuitch,* 402 U.S. 62 (1971), the Supreme Court found the word "health" in an abortion statute not unconstitutionally vague, since it was commonly understood to encompass both physical and mental health. *Vuitch* was cited approvingly in *Doe v. Bolton*, 410 U.S. 179 (1973), where the Court, interpreting the meaning of the sentence prohibiting abortion except where it is "based upon his (the physician's) best clinical judgment that an abortion is necessary," stated:

> We agree with the District Court that the medical judgment may be exercised in the light of all factors—physical, emotional, psychological, familial, and the woman's age—relevant to the well-being of the patient. All these factors may relate to health.

9. Information and Advertising

Restrictions on advertising and publicizing abortion services run into two constitutionally protected rights: those of privacy and free speech.[46] Thus, within boundaries of "good taste," it appears

[45]The United States Supreme Court, in *Sendak v. Arnold,* 429 U.S. 968 (1977), held unconstitutional a requirement that first trimester abortions be performed only in hospitals. For a requirement that second trimester abortions be performed in hospitals, *see* Virginia v. Simopoulos, CR-30906 (Va. Cir. Ct., Fairfax County, 1980) as reported in 9 FAM. PLAN./POP. REP. 40 (1980).

[46]*See* Bigelow v. Virginia, 421 U.S. 809 (1975); Carey v. Population Services International, 431 U.S. 678 (1977).

that abortion clinics cannot constitutionally be prohibited from advertising their services, at least in the print media.

10. Recordkeeping

After *Roe v. Wade,* several states enacted elaborate, even onerous, reporting requirements. It was argued in the *Danforth* case, 428 U.S. 52 (1976), that Missouri's reporting requirements were so elaborate as to hinder a woman's right to abortion. The court found:

> . . . Recordkeeping and reporting requirements that are reasonably directed to the preservation of maternal health and that properly respect a patient's confidentiality and privacy are permissible. This surely is so for the period after the first stage of pregnancy, for then the State may enact substantive as well as recordkeeping regulations that are reasonable means of protecting maternal health. As to the first stage, one may argue forcefully, as the appellants do, that the State should not be able to impose any recordkeeping requirements that are significantly different from those imposed with respect to other, and comparable, medical or surgical procedures. We conclude, however, that the provisions of § § 10 and 11, while perhaps approaching impermissible limits, are not constitutionally offensive in themselves. Recordkeeping of this kind, if not abused or overdone, can be useful to the State's interest in protecting the health of its female citizens, and may be a resource that is relevant to decisions involving medical experience and judgment. The added requirements for confidentiality, with the sole exception for public health officers, and for retention for seven years, a period not unreasonable in length, assist and persuade us in our determination of the constitutional limits. . . .

Based on *Danforth,* it appears that courts will tend to uphold reporting requirements if they can be related to reasonable health recordkeeping needs.

11. Other Challenges

As opposition to abortion has become more vocal and the right-to-life movement has grown more strident, the legal and political challenges to abortion have increased. Many of the barriers to abortion have been struck down by the courts, although decisions depend on the specific facts presented. Some of the obstacles to abortion that have been litigated are ordinances that abortion facilities meet stringent licensing requirements,[47] that abortion facilities have immediate hospital backup or extensive safety and health equipment,[48] and enactment of restrictive zoning codes to block establishment of abortion clinics.[49] Recently, opponents of abortion have succeeded in obtaining the passage of omnibus antiabortion ordinances at the state or local level which contain many restrictive provisions[50] and have even resorted to violence against abortion clinics as a last resort.[51]

E. Abortion Services Since Roe v. Wade

1. J. Forrest, E. Sullivan & C. Tietze, "Abortion in the United States," 1977–1978, 11 *Family Planning Perspectives* 329 (1979)*

There were 1.32 million legal abortions in the United States in 1977 and a projected 1.37 million in 1978, an increase of four percent between 1977 and 1978 compared with one of 12 percent between 1976 and 1977.

In 1978, 29 percent of pregnant women chose to terminate their pregnancies by abortion.

Almost three percent of U.S. women of reproductive age obtained an abortion in 1978.

From 1967 through 1978, approximately six million women obtained almost eight million legal abortions; about one in eight U.S. women of reproductive age has had a legal abortion.

The number of hospitals reporting that they provided abortion services dropped slightly from 1,695 in 1976 to 1,661 in 1977, but the

[47] *See, e.g., Word v. Poelker,* 495 F.2d 1349 (8th Cir. 1974); *Friendship Medical Center, Ltd. v. Chicago Board of Health,* 505 F.2d 1141 (7th Cir. 1974); *People v. Dobbs Ferry Medical Pavillion,* 33 N.Y. 2d 584 (1973).

[48] *See, e.g.,* Friendship Medical Center, Ltd. v. Chicago Board of Health, *supra* n. 47; Fla. Women's Medical Clinic v. Smith, 478 F.Supp. 233 (S.D. Fla. 1979); Westchester Women's Health Org. v. Whalen, 475 F.Supp. 734 (S.D.N.Y. 1979).

[49] *See, e.g.,* Framingham Clinic v. Board of Selectmen of Southborough, 367 N.E.2d 606 (Mass. 1977); West Side Women's Services v. Cleveland, 582 F.2d 1281 (6th Cir 1978.), *cert. denied* 99 Sup. Ct. 572 (1978).

[50] *See, e.g.,* the Akron, Ohio, ordinance, *supra* n. 15 and the Louisiana statute, LA. REV. STAT. ANN. §§40.1299.35.1 *et seq.* (West Supp. 1979), both held unconstitutional in large part, *supra* nn. 18–19.

[51] *See* NEWSWEEK cover story, *Abortion Under Attack,* June 5, 1978.

*Reprinted with permission from *Family Planning Perspectives,* vol. 11, no. 6 (1979).

number of nonhospital abortion clinics increased from 448 to 522, and the number of physicians who reported performing abortions in their offices grew from 424 to 533.

Between 1976 and 1977, the average number of abortions per hospital facility decreased from 246 to 237, while the average number per nonhospital provider increased from 875 to 879.

The percentage of abortions performed in hospitals declined from 35 in 1976 to 30 in 1977, while the percentage reported by freestanding clinics increased from 61 to 66; the percentage performed in physicians' offices remained at four.

Ninety-five percent of abortions in 1977 occurred in metropolitan areas, where 75 percent of the women in need of abortion services live.

In 1977, there were identified abortion providers in only 23 percent of U.S. counties.

Nine percent (more than 118,000) of the women who obtained abortions in 1977 had to travel to another state for services, and many traveled to other, often distant, counties in their home states.

One in three abortions in 1977 were obtained by teenagers, and three in four were obtained by unmarried women.

Twenty-eight percent of the women estimated to be in need of abortion services in 1977, and 26 percent in 1978, were unable to obtain them . . .

Ten states and the District of Columbia have official policies to pay for most abortions for poor women. In addition, 12 states do so under court order . . .

2. S. Seims, "Abortion Availability in the United States," 12 *Family Planning Perspectives 88* (1980).

Seven years after the Supreme Court decisions legalizing abortion in the United States, many women are still unable to obtain abortions or experience great difficulty in doing so—because either there are no abortion providers in the counties in which they live, or the services that do exist are minimal or public laws and policies restrict their access. More than three-quarters of 3,105 counties in the country have no abortion providers—and an estimated 481,000 women in need of abortion services live in these counties. In two-thirds of the 718 counties that do have providers, fewer than half of the women estimated to need abortion services are able to obtain them. More than one million women were unable to obtain abortions in their home counties in 1977 . . . more than one-half million women each year are not able to obtain the abortions they want and need in their own or any other community . . .

II. INTERNATIONAL PERSPECTIVE

A. Abortion Legislation Worldwide

1. C. Tietze, "Abortion Laws and Policies," *Induced Abortion: 1979, Third Edition,* 7–14 (Population Council, 1979)*

. . . The situation as of mid-1978 can be summarized as follows: Nine percent of the world's population lived in countries where abortion was prohibited without exception, and 11 percent lived in countries where it was permitted only to save the life of the pregnant woman. Around 14 percent lived under statutes authorizing abortion on broader medical grounds, that is, to avert a threat to the woman's health rather than to her life (with mental health specifically mentioned in several countries), and sometimes on eugenic, or fetal, indication (known genetic or other impairment of the fetus or increased risk of such impairment) and/or juridical indication (rape, incest, etc.) as well. Twenty-five percent of the world's population resided in countries in which social factors, such as inadequate income, substandard housing, unmarried status, and the like, could be taken into consideration in the evaluation of the threat to the woman's health (social-medical indication) or in which adverse social conditions alone, without reference to health, could justify termination of pregnancy. Countries allowing abortion on request without specifying reasons for at least some categories of women—generally defined in terms of age, number of children, and/or duration of pregnancy—accounted for 39 percent. In the latter group of countries, abortions on medical grounds were generally permitted beyond the gestational limit prescribed for elective abortion. No information is available for the remaining 2 percent of the world's people; it would appear, however, that most of them lived in areas with restrictive abortion laws. . . .

The Americas

United States and Canada [omitted]

Latin America

Abortion laws in Latin America are generally restrictive. Among the 22 independent countries with more than one million inhabitants,

*Reprinted with the permission of the Population Council from Christopher Tietze, "Abortion laws and policies," *Induced Abortion: 1979, Third Edition.* (New York: 1979): pp. 7–14.

seven forbid abortion under all circumstances, six permit it only to avert a threat to the pregnant woman's life, while nine countries recognize broader medical indications. It is worth noting that at least seven countries allow termination of pregnancy in cases of rape and/or incest. In one country (Uruguay) penalties may be waived if the abortion is performed during the first three months of pregnancy for reasons of serious economic stress . . .

Europe

The Nordic Countries

The first definitive steps toward the liberalization of abortion laws were taken by three of the five Nordic countries: Iceland (1935), Sweden (1937), and Denmark (1938). After World War II, Sweden and Denmark further liberalized their laws, and new statutes were enacted in Finland and Norway. The range of acceptable grounds for abortion was roughly the same in each of these countries and included medical and social-medical, eugenic, and juridical indications. The more recent statutes extended the traditional eugenic indications, covering the hereditary transmission of mental disease, mental retardation, and other severe maladies and defects, to include any damage acquired during intrauterine life, such as the effects of maternal rubella or thalidomide ingestion during the early weeks of pregnancy. A Danish law of 1970 authorized termination of pregnancy on request during the first 12 weeks of pregnancy for all women over age 38 domiciled in Denmark and for those with four or more living children. A similar statute, with age 40 as a cutoff point for elective abortion, was also enacted in Finland.

The most recent Danish statute, which came into force on 1 October 1973, authorizes abortion on request during the first trimester for all women. At later stages of pregnancy, abortion may be performed on any of the grounds listed in the 1970 statute. A new Swedish law, implemented on 1 January 1975, goes even further by specifically recognizing the woman's right, in the absence of medical contraindications, to have her pregnancy terminated up to the end of the eighteenth week of gestation. Beyond that point, abortion can be approved in exceptional cases by the National Board of Health and Welfare. Iceland and Norway also liberalized their abortion laws in 1975, stopping just short of authorizing abortion at the request of the pregnant woman on the Danish and Swedish model. Three years later, in June 1978, Norway legalized abortion on request during the first 12 weeks of gestation. The new law took effect on 1 January 1979.

United Kingdom

. . . The Offenses Against the Person Act of 1861 made "unlawfully" induced abortion a felony regardless of the duration of the pregnancy. The Act did not define "unlawfully" and made no provision for the termination of pregnancy on medical grounds. However, in 1938, in *Rex v. Bourne,* the judge ruled that abortion need not be unlawful if done in good faith to preserve the mother's life. The jury was further instructed that: "If the doctor is of the opinion . . . that the probable consequences . . . will be to make the woman a physical and mental wreck, the jury is quite entitled to take the view that the doctor . . . is operating for the purpose of preserving the life of the mother." Bourne, who had performed an abortion on a young woman who had been raped by several men, was acquitted and a legal precedent was set.

Almost 30 years later, in October 1967, after a long and bitter legislative struggle, Parliament enacted a liberalized abortion statute authorizing abortions if two physicians

> . . . are of the opinion, formed in good faith: that the continuance of the pregnancy would involve risk to the life of the pregnant woman or of injury to the physical or mental health of the pregnant woman or any existing children of her family, greater than if the pregnancy were terminated; or that there is a substantial risk that if the child were born it would suffer from such physical or mental abormalities as to be seriously handicapped.

The Act provides further that in determining whether or not there is such risk of injury to health, "account may be taken of the pregnant woman's actual or reasonably foreseeable environment." Abortions may be performed in National Health Service (NHS) hospitals or in facilities approved by the Minister of Health. The latter category includes mainly private nursing homes. The Act, which came into force on 27 April 1968, applies to England, Wales, and Scotland, but not to Northern Ireland. . . .

Other Countries in Western Europe

All countries in western Europe, with the exception of the Nordic countries and Great Britain, had restrictive abortion laws until 1 January 1975, when an Austrian law, passed in the preceding year, came into force, permitting elective abortion during the first trimester. A few days later France authorized (for a period of five years) abortion on request during the first ten weeks of pregnancy, subject to a number of provisions, which include the following: (1) after applying for an abortion the pregnant woman must receive counseling at an approved social service agency; (2) after this consultation, a waiting period of one week must be observed; and (3) the number of elective abortions in any institution must not exceed one-fourth of all obstetrical and surgical procedures. Strong opposition to these new abortion laws has been expressed by many members of the medical profession in both Austria and France, and availability of abortion services remains uneven in both countries.

The German Federal Republic also passed a new abortion law in 1974, authorizing abortion on request during the first trimester. This law, however, was struck down by the Constitutional Court. Following guidelines set by the Court, revised legislation was adopted by the Federal Legislature in May 1976. The new law permits abortion if, "according to medical findings, a pregnancy termination is indicated, taking account of the present and future living conditions of the pregnant woman, in order to avert a risk to the life or a risk of serious damage to the physical or mental state of health of the pregnant woman, and such risk cannot be averted by any other means that the woman can be expected to accept." Abortion may also be performed until 22 weeks "from conception" if, according to medical opinion, "imperative grounds exist for presuming that, as a consequence of a hereditary predisposition or harmful influences prior to birth, the child would suffer from irremediable injury to its state of health of such gravity that the pregnant woman cannot be required to continue the pregnancy to term"; until 12 weeks from conception in cases of rape and other forms of sexual abuse, and if "a pregnancy termination is otherwise indicated in order to prevent the pregnant woman from being exposed to the risk of serious consequences which: (a) are of such gravity that the pregnant woman cannot be expected to continue the pregnancy to term; and (b) cannot be averted by any other means that the woman can be expected to accept." It is clear that this last provision gives considerable latitude to the physician. The use of the words "from conception" implies upper gestational limits of 24 or 14 weeks from the woman's last menstrual period, depending on which indication is applicable.

For all abortions other than those performed to avert a risk to life or health "deriving from a somatic disease or physical injury," the German law requires that the woman be counseled concerning "public and private assistance available to pregnant women, mothers, and children" and that she wait three days after such counseling before the abortion is performed. The physician authorizing the abortion is not allowed to carry out the procedure. An interesting feature of the law is a provision exempting any "procedures that take effect before nidation of the fertilized ovum in the uterus has occurred."

According to early reports, the implementation of the new law varies greatly among the component states of the Federal Republic, legal abortion being more accessible in the northern, predominantly Protestant regions, than in the southern, predominantly Roman Catholic, regions.

In May 1978, Italy liberalized its abortion law. Women over age 18 may obtain an abortion in the first trimester for medical, economic, social, family, or psychological reasons, or if there is a risk of defect in the fetus, provided they seek consultation. In any case, the woman has the right to obtain an abortion after a seven-day waiting period. Abortions after the first trimester are permitted if continued pregnancy endangers the health of the woman or if there are grounds for believing the fetus is defective. Abortions for women under 18 years of age require parental consent. The text of the law leaves unanswered many questions regarding its implementation. Strong opposition by the Roman Catholic Church and the medical profession has been reported.

In the Netherlands, a bill authorizing abortion on request of the pregnant woman was passed in the lower house of the national legislative body in 1976 but was defeated in the upper chamber. This left the Netherlands with a restrictive law and liberal practice (15 nonprofit clinics openly performing about 100,000 abortions per year, with about 80 percent being obtained by nonresidents). In Switzerland, similar propositions were rejected by two popular referenda. The current law permitting abortion on medical grounds is narrowly interpreted in some cantons and very liberally in others, notably in Geneva. Belgium, the Republic of Ireland, Malta, and Portugal remain the only countries in the region prohibiting abortion under all circumstances.

Eastern Europe, Including USSR

In the socialist countries of eastern Europe, abortion policies have undergone several major changes since 1920, when the USSR became the first country to legalize abortion on request. This nonrestrictive policy was reversed in 1936 by limiting legal abortion to a list of specified medical and eugenic indications but was reinstituted in 1955, when the decree of 1936 was repealed. In the words of the preamble to the 1955 Soviet decree, its aims were "the limitation of harm caused to the health of women by abortions carried out outside of hospitals" and to give "women the possibility of deciding themselves the question of motherhood."

Following the example of the USSR, the socialist countries of eastern Europe, with the exception of the German Democratic Republic and Albania, liberalized their abortion laws in 1956–57. The new statutes permitted abortion on request or on broadly interpreted social indications during the first trimester (in Hungary up to 18 weeks in the case of minors). Otherwise, abortions in the second trimester were permitted on medical indications only. In several countries, abortion was not allowed if the pregnant woman had obtained an induced abortion within the previous six months.

In recent years, some of the countries of eastern Europe have enacted more restrictive laws, doubtless in response to concern about low birth rates. The change was most drastic in Romania, where a statute permitting elective abortions enacted in 1957 was reversed in

October 1966 by a decree restricting abortion to women over age 45 (lowered to age 40 in 1972) and to women supporting four or more living children, in addition to the usual medical, eugenic, and juridical indications.

In Bulgaria, abortion on request was available from 1956 to 1968. Instructions by the Ministry of Public Health in February 1968 and again in April 1973 (modified in 1974) have limited access to elective abortions to married women with two or more living children, unmarried women without regard to age, and married women over 40 with one living child. In addition, the maximum duration of pregnancy at which abortion may be performed was reduced from 12 to 10 weeks.

In Czechoslovakia, applications for abortion were adjudicated by commissions throughout the period of the liberalized law enacted in 1957. While some of the provisions of that law were tightened up in 1962, virtually all abortions on medical indication and most of those requested for other reasons continued to be approved. A new directive, issued in 1973, restricted to exceptional cases the approval of applications for abortion on social grounds made by married women without living children or with only one living child. Abortion on medical indication is regulated by a list of approved diagnoses that appears to limit consideration of mental health to severe disorders, such as reactive depression with suicidal tendencies confirmed by hospitalization; the previous list referred to possible suicidal tendencies without mention of hospitalization.

In Hungary, too, abortion committees had been maintained throughout the period of abortion on request (1956–73), but their function was purely advisory since applications had to be approved if the woman persisted. Since 1 January 1974, access to abortion has been significantly restricted. Termination of pregnancy on request is still available to single, divorced, separated, and widowed women over age 40 (until 31 December 1978, the age limit was 35); and to married women who have at least three living children, or have experienced three deliveries, or have two living children and have, in addition, undergone at least one "obstetrical event." This term includes live births, stillbirths, ectopic pregnancies, spontaneous abortions, and induced abortions. The latter may be taken into account only if they occurred after the woman's second delivery. Women who do not meet these requirements may obtain abortions on medical, eugenic, and juridical grounds; the only social indication that makes approval mandatory is lack of adequate housing, defined as a separate dwelling unit.

The German Democratic Republic did not participate in the general liberalization of abortion laws during the 1950s. After World War II, the harsh restrictions of the Third Reich were replaced by state laws under which legal abortions could be performed on medical, eugenic, and juridical indications and, to some extent, on social and economic grounds. These statutes were superseded in 1950 by a new law that permitted abortion on medical and eugenic indications only. In 1965 an extension of the medical indication was administratively authorized, taking into account the woman's social environment, and in 1972 legislation was enacted permitting abortion on request during the first trimester and on medical grounds thereafter.

Yugoslavia is the only country in eastern Europe where a woman's right to "free decision on childbirth" is anchored in its Federal Constitution adopted in 1974. Implementation of this provision by the several republics and autonomous provinces is in process. . . .

Asia, Africa, and Oceania

China

In the People's Republic of China, abortion on the request of the pregnant woman was legalized in 1957 by a directive from the Ministry of Health to the effect that henceforth requests for abortion "must be granted without restrictions in regard to the age of the applicant or the number of her children and without the requirement of special approval procedures." However, elective abortion was limited to the first ten weeks of gestation and could not be performed on the same woman more than once a year. . . . In 1972 abortion was reported to be freely available, usually performed during the first 12 weeks of pregnancy by nurses and, at least in some rural communes, by trained "barefoot doctors" or midwives.

In Taiwan, abortion is categorically prohibited, without exception, but apparently is readily available from medical practitioners throughout the island.

Japan

In Japan, Article 14 of the Eugenic Protection Law of 1948 permits termination of pregnancy for a woman "whose health may be affected seriously by continuation of pregnancy or by delivery from the physical or economic viewpoint." The interpretation of this paragraph by the medical profession and by the authorities has been tantamount to making abortion available on request. . . . In 1976 the upper limit of the gestational period during which abortion may be performed was reduced from 28 to 24 weeks.

Korea

. . . In 1973 legislation was adopted authorizing termination of pregnancy on medical, eugenic, and juridical indications. The wording of the new law is far more restrictive than actual practice has been during recent years. The law is not enforced, however, and the government subsidizes abortions in the private sector if they are combined with surgical sterilization or if the pregnancy resulted from IUD failure.

Information on the legal status of abortion in North Korea was not located.

Other Countries of East and Southeast Asia

Abortion on request has been available in North Vietnam at least since 1971 and in the entire country since its unification in 1975. Previously, only narrowly interpreted medical indications were acceptable in South Vietnam.

In Hong Kong, abortion on medical indication, as defined in the British Abortion Act of 1967, was authorized in 1972 for a period of two years. The ordinance was extended for two additional years in 1974 and made permanent in 1976. However, the clauses of the British Act concerning the health of existing children and the risk of physical or mental abnormalities in the child to be born do not apply in Hong Kong.

Singapore liberalized its abortion law in 1969, permitting termination of pregnancy on medical and social grounds. Abortion on request was legalized for all residents in 1974 and is permitted up to 24 weeks gestation. Abortions must be performed in hospitals, and certain restrictions as to the qualifications of the physician apply after 16 weeks.

South-Central Asia

In India, legalization of abortion has been a matter of governmental concern for more than a decade. In 1971 an abortion statute patterned after the British Abortion Act of 1967 was adopted, with the important additions that a pregnancy alleged by the woman to be caused by rape and, in the case of a married woman, a pregnancy resulting from contraceptive failure "may be presumed to constitute a grave injury to the mental health of the woman." Rules formulated by the Department of Family Planning of the Ministry of Health in February 1972 include the following: (1) only adequately trained physicians may induce an abortion; (2) such physicians must apply for and receive a certificate qualifying the holder to terminate a pregnancy; (3) the physician who is to perform the abortion is to constitute a committee of one to approve the abortion if the gestation period is under 12 weeks, or be one of a committee of two if the gestation is further advanced; and (4) the facilities where abortions are performed must meet specific requirements.

In Bangladesh, Pakistan, and Sri Lanka, restrictive legislation remains in effect . . .

Southwest Asia and Northern Africa

In most of the countries of southwest Asia and northern Africa, abortion is illegal or restricted to the termination of pregnancies on medical indication. The only exceptions are Tunisia, Cyprus, Iran, and Israel. In Tunisia elective abortion has been available since 1965 to women with five or more living children. In September 1973, Tunisia authorized elective abortion for all women during the first trimester of pregnancy if performed by a physician in a hospital or clinic. After the third month, termination of pregnancy is permitted on medical, including psychiatric, and eugenic indications.

Cyprus revised its penal code in 1974, authorizing abortions on medical and eugenic indications as well as in cases of rape.

In Iran, Parliament had in 1974 enacted revisions to the penal code providing that decisions on abortion be left to the person concerned and a qualified medical practitioner. Regulations implementing the revised code were not issued until October 1976. According to these regulations, first-trimester abortion is authorized if the reasons presented "by the couple" are considered sufficient and satisfactory by the physician; according to another clause the unmarried woman's request is sufficient, which makes the meaning of "couple" somewhat obscure. Performance of abortions in nonhospital clinics is specifically authorized. No reports on the implementation of this law have been located.

In Israel, the British Offenses Against the Person Act of 1861 remained in force until 1977; however, in 1952 the District Court of Haifa ruled that abortion openly performed on bona fide medical grounds was permissible. In practice, the law was not enforced and abortions were freely obtainable from medical practitioners. In 1977 a modest liberalization was legislated permitting abortion to avert "grave harm to the woman or her children owing to difficult family or social circumstances." . . .

Africa South of the Sahara

In Africa south of the Sahara, restrictive codes introduced during the period of European colonial rule are still in force in all of the newly independent countries with the exception of Zambia, where a law virtually identical to the British Abortion Act of 1967 was passed in 1972. The Republic of South Africa permits abortion on medical, eugenic, and juridical indications.

Oceania

In Australia, the regulation of abortion falls within the jurisdiction of the several states. One of these, South Australia, liberalized its abortion law in 1969, following the pattern of the British Abortion Act of 1967, but omitting the clause concerning the health of existing children, and prescribing performance of the abortion in a hospital. A similar statute was enacted in the Northern Territory in 1974. Abortion on social-medical grounds has been legalized by court decisions in two other states, New South Wales and Victoria. . . .

Some liberalization of abortion statutes was achieved in Fiji and New Zealand in 1976 by judicial decision. In the following year, however, New Zealand enacted legislation narrowing the indications for abortion and establishing extremely cumbersome procedural requirements.

2. Commentary on Abortion Law Reform

Two aspects of Tietze's review of abortion laws are particularly noteworthy. First, that almost 80 percent of the world lives in countries where, as the law is written, abortion is available on comparatively permissive grounds. Put differently, only 20 percent of the world's population lives in countries where abortion is either completely prohibited or available only to save the life of the woman. Table 3–1 on p. 135 presents the legal status of abortion.[52]

The second noteworthy factor is the remarkable trend toward liberalization of the world's abortion laws. Cook and Dickens, in a comprehensive review of changes in the world's abortion laws, noted that in 42 jurisdictions which modified their abortion laws between 1976 and 1977, 39 extended the grounds for abortion and only three, all in Eastern Europe, have narrowed them.[53]

The primary way in which abortion laws are changed is modification of the grounds, if any, under which abortion may be performed legally. These generally are:

Prohibited completely
Risk to the life of the woman
Risk to the physical health of the woman
Risk to the mental or emotional health of the woman
Risk of fetal deformity
Rape or incest
Contraceptive failure
Social or economic hardship
On simple request

Additionally, a legislature or court can adjust the time during which abortions are legal, prescribe the qualifications of practitioners, regu-

[52]Source: Pop. Crisis. Comm., *World Abortion Trends,* Briefing Paper on Issues of National and International Importance in the Population Field No. 9 (1979).

[53]R. Cook & B. Dickens, *A Decade of International Change in Abortion Law: 1967–1977,* 68 AM. J. PUB. HLTH. 637 (1978).

Table 3–1 Legal Status of Abortion Worldwide

	On request or for social indications	*Conditional (includes eugenic, rape, incest and/or broad health indications)*	*Only life-threatening circumstances*	*Illegal (no exceptions)*
Total Population Covered (in millions)	2,568.3	614.1	449.6	369.2
Total Number of Countries Represented	27	36	30	15
Percentage of World Population	61%	15%	11%	9%
Major Countries	Austria	Argentina	Algeria	Belgium
	Bulgaria	Australia	Bangladesh	Burma
	Czechoslovakia	Brazil	Cambodia	Colombia
	Denmark	Cameroon	Guatemala	Dominican Republic
	France	Canada	Iraq	Egypt
	German Democratic Republic	Chile	Ivory Coast	Indonesia
	German Federal Republic	Cuba	Madagascar	Philippines
	Hungary	Ecuador	Malawi	Portugal
	India	Ethiopia	Malaysia	Taiwan
	Italy	Ghana	Netherlands	Zaire
	Japan	Greece	Nigeria	
	People's Republic of China	Kenya	Pakistan	
	Poland	Mexico	Senegal	
	Romania	Morocco	Spain	
	Sweden	Nepal	Sri Lanka	
	Tunisia	Peru	Sudan	
	United Kingdom	Republic of Korea	Upper Volta	
	U.S.A.	Rhodesia	Venezuela	
	U.S.S.R.	South Africa		
	Yugoslavia	Switzerland		
	Zambia	Syria		
		Thailand		
		Turkey		
		Uganda		

late the institutions in which abortions can be performed, require approvals or committee review, and establish parental or spousal consent requirements.[54]

B. Enforcement of Abortion Laws

Abortion is an area in which laws are honored more in the breach than the observance. In countries with restrictive legislation, the strictness of the abortion laws as written is relieved by their virtual non-enforcement in practice. The reasons are easy to understand. Almost all abortions are provoked at the request of the pregnant woman. Except in cases of death or serious injury, there is nobody to bring a complaint. Even if the state chose to prosecute, the woman might not be willing to testify and few witnesses exist. Finally, if serious efforts were made to bring to trial a significant number of those who perform abortions, the courts would be clogged, the jails would be filled, and a disproportionate percentage of the nation's resources would be devoted to combatting this offense.

Although there is little reliable data on the extent to which the laws are enforced, studies in Latin America have shown that restrictive abortion laws are not generally enforced and that criminal proceedings are generally initiated only when a woman dies or a practitioner is shown to be grossly incompetent.[55] A study of abortion in the British Commonwealth reached similar conclusions:[56]

> The dearth of prosecutions for offenses against abortion laws have shown them to be almost completely unenforced. The overwhelming majority of jurisdictions have no recorded instance in their recent or longer-term history, or indeed ever, of a prosecution of an illegal abortionist or of a woman employing his services, or performing a procedure upon herself.

The issue, however, is whether occasional prosecution of abortion practitioners is a sufficient threat to deter physicians from performing abortions. The widespread recourse to abortion indicates

[54] Indications for abortion are discussed in B. Dickens & R. Cook, *Development of Commonwealth Abortion Laws,* 28 INTL. & COMP. L. Q. 424 (1979).

[55] *See* S. Isaacs & H. Sanhueza, *Law and the Practice of Abortion in Latin America,* paper presented at the Third World Conference on Medical Law (1973).

[56] R. Cook & B. Dickens, *A Survey of Abortion Laws in Commonwealth Countries,* in *COMMONWEALTH SECRETARIAT, THREE STUDIES OF ABORTION LAWS IN THE COMMONWEALTH 39 (1977).*

that restrictive laws do not deter women from seeking abortions, either from reputable physicians or back-alley abortionists.[57]

Permissive abortion laws are not well implemented. Tietze, Jaffe, Weinstock, and Dryfoos wrote in 1976 "the response of hospitals to the legalization of abortion (in the United States) continued to be so limited, two years after the Supreme Court [abortion] decisions as to be tantamount to no response."[58] A 1977 report of the Badgely Commission in Canada concluded that the law for obtaining therapeutic abortions was operating unfairly, with the burden falling on poorer, less educated, rural women. The problems of implementation mentioned in the Badgely Report included: unnecessary requirements established by provincial governments, medical custom, or hospital administrations; failure of most hospitals to establish abortion review committees; delay by physicians ("on the average, women took 2.8 weeks after they first suspected they had become pregnant to visit a physician. After this contact had been made there was an average interval of 8.0 weeks until the operation was done."), and, despite nation-wide health insurance, levying of additional charges on women seeking abortions.[59]

C. Demographic Consequences of Abortion

Many questions remain unanswered about the demographic effects of abortion laws. Is the law a significant determinant of the number of abortions in a country? Does a permissive law merely shift abortions from illegal to legal? Does a restrictive law deter induced abortion? Does awareness of a permissive abortion law undermine contraceptive practice? Potts, Diggory, and Peel, after examining the demographic consequences of abortion laws throughout the world, concluded:[60]

> . . . The law does not appear to be a major determinant of the total number of induced abortions occurring in a community. . . . There is

[57]C. Tietze & S. Lewit, *Legal Abortion,* 236 SCIENTIFIC AMERICAN 21 (1977) estimated that between 30 and 55 million abortions are induced worldwide every year.

[58]C. TIETZE, F. JAFFE, E. WEINSTOCK & J. DRYFOOS, ABORTION 1974–1975: NEEDS & SERVICES IN THE UNITED STATES, EACH STATE & METROPOLITAN AREA 13 (Alan Guttmacher Inst., 1976).

[59]R. Badgely, *Report of the Committee on the Operation of the Abortion Law* (1977).

[60]M. POTTS, P. DIGGORY & J. PEEL, ABORTION 132 (Cambridge, 1977). [hereinafter cited as M. Potts et al.]

> considerable evidence that the major effect of a liberal abortion law is to transfer illegal operations to the legal sector, without any great alteration in the total rate.

Nevertheless, liberalized abortion laws are considered responsible for having brought down the birth rate in post World War II Japan[61] and in Eastern Europe.[62] The experience of Romania is particularly instructive in this regard. There, birth rates dropped sharply after passage of a liberal abortion in 1957, rose dramatically after a more restrictive law was passed in 1966, and then gradually declined again.[63]

D. Health Consequences of Abortion

The health consequences of liberalized abortion law are discussed in C. Tietze, *Induced Abortion: 1979, Third Edition,* 83–84 (Population Council, 1979):*

> The earliest data on mortality following legal abortion originated in Sweden and Denmark, where the first steps toward the liberalization of abortion laws were taken in the 1930s. The longest continuous series of data, that for Sweden, indicates a dramatic decline in mortality over three decades, from 250 per 100,000 legal abortions in 1946–48 to 18 per 100,000 in 1964–68 and none since. A comparable series of statistics for Denmark, extending over a longer period but with three breaks in continuity, also shows a marked decline in mortality from 195 per 100,000 in 1940–50 to 33 per 100,000 in 1961–66 and no deaths since 1969.
>
> In eastern Europe, Czechoslovakia and Hungary provide the most reliable national statistics on mortality following legal abortion. Lev-

[61] *See* M. Muramatsu, *Abortion in Japan* in ABORTION IN A CHANGING WORLD vol. 1, 260 (R. Hall, ed., Columbia, 1970).

[62] *See* H. DAVID, FAMILY PLANNING AND ABORTION IN THE SOCIALIST COUNTRIES OF CENTRAL AND EASTERN EUROPE (Pop. Council, 1970).

[63] There is some debate about the fertility effects of Romania's abortion laws. M. Teitlebaum, *Fertility Effects of the Abolition of Legal Abortion in Romania,* 26 POP. STUDIES 405 (1972) concluded that the effects of a restrictive law on fertility would probably be transitory. B. Berelson, *Romania's 1966 Anti-Abortion Decree: The Demographic Experience of the First Decade,* 33 POP. STUDIES 209 (1979) found that the birthrate had leveled off at the point desired by Romanian population policy and that the restrictive abortion legislation had a major demographic impact.

els of mortality during the late 1950s and early 1960s in these countries were far lower than those reported from northern Europe, but even these low ratios have declined further in recent years. The low levels of mortality reflect the fact that virtually all legal abortions in eastern Europe are performed in the first trimester. While initially viewed with disbelief by some western observers, these low levels have been confirmed by later experience in Britain and the United States.

Mortality associated with legal abortion in England and Wales in 1968–69, following the implementation of the Abortion Act, was on a level comparable to that achieved in Denmark and Sweden a few years earlier. By 1973–76, it had declined substantially.

In the United States, as elsewhere, high levels of mortality from legal abortion prevailed during the period of restrictive legislation, when a significant proportion of the women undergoing abortion suffered from preexisting complications that made them poor risks for any type of surgery. By 1973–75, with abortion more easily available, the mortality ratio had declined to about 3 per 100,000 legal terminations. The precipitous drop to less than 1 per 100,000 in 1976 may represent a random fluctuation of mortality.

One of the main factors responsible for the differences among countries in mortality associated with legal abortion is the period of gestation at which pregnancies are terminated. In the United States during 1972–76, the mortality ratio ranged from 0.5 per 100,000 legal abortions at eight weeks or less to 25 per 100,000 for abortions at 21 weeks or more. Mortality increases by almost two-fifths with *each week* of gestation, more rapidly than major complications. . . .

Abortion-related mortality may be compared appropriately with the risk to life associated with carrying a pregnancy to term. In the United States, maternal mortality attributed to complications of pregnancy and childbirth, *excluding* abortion and ectopic gestation, has declined to 12.2 deaths per 100,000 live births in 1972–76. Most of these deaths occurred late in pregnancy, during labor, or during the puerperal period. Adjusting to the age distribution of women obtaining legal abortions raises the maternal mortality ratio to about 15 per 100,000. The corresponding ratios for England and Wales in 1968–73 were 14 and 18, respectively, and those for Great Britain, marginally higher. It would appear, then, that, in both countries, mortality was substantially lower with first-trimester abortion without sterilization than with childbirth. Mortality following late second-trimester abortion, even without sterilization, was higher than maternal mortality associated with childbirth.

The major causes of death following legal abortion, as recorded in the United States during 1972–75, were infection (27 percent), embolism (26 percent), complications of general or local anesthesia (15 percent), and hemorrhage (10 percent). . . .

> It is generally recognized that mortality is much higher following abortions that are self-induced or induced by untrained persons than after those legally performed in hospitals and clinics. It is impossible, however, to quantify these higher risks, since mortality reflects not only the skill of the persons performing or initiating the illegal abortion but also the availability, utilization, and quality of subsequent medical and hospital services in the event life-threatening complications develop.
>
> In some communities where illegal abortions are performed by untrained persons under unsanitary conditions and where medical facilities are inadequate or shunned because women are afraid of being denounced to law enforcement agencies, mortality ratios may reach or exceed 1,000 per 100,000 illegal abortions . . .

As this excerpt makes clear, one result of abortion law reform, given the growing recognition that early abortions are safer and less traumatic than later ones, is the availability of safer alternatives for a woman faced with an unwanted pregnancy. In the United States, legally induced abortion prior to 12 weeks' gestation carries a risk of death similar to that of routine intramuscular penicillin for treatment of infection.[64] Similarly, the risk of complications is greatly reduced where abortion is performed early in pregnancy; according to Tietze and Lewit, the rate of serious early complications is only about .05 percent for abortions performed in the first trimester and about two percent thereafter.[65]

E. Abortion and Contraception

The widespread use of abortion to reduce fertility in Japan and Eastern Europe has led some observers to question whether abortion would replace contraception as the preferred means of fertility regulation where both are generally available and, beyond that, to inquire about the relationship between abortion and contraception.[66]

[64]D. Kramer, *Public Health Aspects of Legal Abortion,* paper presented at the Regional Council Meeting of the International Planned Parenthood Federation/ Western Hemisphere Region (1980). Kramer points out that 90 percent of abortions in the United States are done during the first trimester.

[65]Tietze & Lewit, *supra* n. 57 at 24.

[66]Contraceptives were not widely available in Japan until recently so that people did not have a choice between contraceptives and abortion. In fact, contraception has only recently replaced abortion as the primary means of fertility control in Japan. M. Muramatsu & J. van der Tak, *From Abortion to Contraception —The Japanese Experience,* in ABORTION IN PSYCHOSOCIAL PERSPECTIVE: TRENDS IN TRANSNATIONAL RESEARCH 145 (H. David, H. Friedman, J. van der Tak & M. Sevilla, eds., Springer, 1978).

According to Potts, Diggory, and Peel:[67]

> Sociological observation suggests that contraception and induced abortion are used to complement one another in the difficult task of controlling human fertility. Given a reasonable availability of contraceptives, there is no evidence that induced abortion and contraceptive practice compete.

Abortion and contraception are intertwined in their use. Experience has demonstrated that, in many communities, when there has been a background of neither contraception nor abortion, fertility control follows a two-stage evolution. The first phase corresponds to recognition of the need to limit family size and is accompanied by some use of contraception together with an increased number of abortions. The rise in the number of abortions may reflect increased demand for services before family planning methods are readily available, ignorance of how to use the methods, or failure of the methods. In the second phase, contraception becomes the primary means of regulating family size.[68]

Another link between abortion and contraception concerns the risk associated with the two methods of fertility control. Tietze has analyzed the risk to life of various methods of fertility control, set forth in table 3–2 on the following page.[69]

The salient findings from the table are: (1) among women under 30 years of age, with exception of pill takers who smoke, the total risk to life associated with each of the major methods of fertility regulation is about equal and quite low; (2) beyond the age of 30, the risk to life increases rapidly for pill users, especially those who smoke; (3) at all ages, the lowest level of mortality is by far achieved by a combined regimen, that is, use of barrier contraceptives with recourse to early abortion in case of failure.[70]

Finally, Tietze and Bongaarts, using a computer simulation model, concluded that levels of fertility required for population stabilization were unlikely to be achieved by the use of contraception

[67]M. Potts et al., *supra* n. 60 at 496–497.

[68]See S. Isaacs & H. Sanhueza, *Induced Abortion in Latin America: The Legal Perspective,* in EPIDEMIOLOGY OF ABORTION AND PRACTICES OF FERTILITY REGULATION IN LATIN AMERICA: SELECTED REPORTS 39, PAHO Scientific Publication No. 306 (1975).

[69]Source: C. TIETZE, INDUCED ABORTION: 1979 (3d Ed., Pop. Council, 1979) at 90.

[70]*Id.* at 89–90.

Table 3–2 Birth-Related, Method-Related, and Total Deaths per 100,000 Women per Year, by Regimen of Control and Age of Woman

Regimen and type of deaths	*Age (years)*					
	15–19	*20–24*	*25–29*	*30–34*	*35–39*	*40–44*
No control						
Birth-related	5.3	5.8	7.2	12.7	20.8	21.6
Abortion only						
Method-related	1.0	1.9	2.4	2.3	2.9	1.7
Pills only/nonsmokers						
Birth-related	0.1	0.2	0.2	0.4	0.6	0.4
Method-related	0.6	1.1	1.6	3.0	9.1	17.7
Total deaths	0.7	1.3	1.8	3.4	9.7	18.1
Pills only/smokers						
Birth-related	0.1	0.2	0.2	0.4	0.6	0.4
Method-related	2.1	4.2	6.1	11.8	31.3	60.9
Total deaths	2.2	4.4	6.3	12.2	31.9	61.3
IUDs only						
Birth-related	0.1	0.2	0.2	0.4	0.6	0.4
Method-related	0.8	0.8	1.0	1.0	1.4	1.4
Total deaths	0.9	1.0	1.2	1.4	2.0	1.8
Barrier methods only						
Birth-related	1.1	1.5	1.9	3.3	5.0	4.0
Barrier methods, plus abortion						
Method related	0.1	0.3	0.4	0.4	0.4	0.2

alone; to reach these levels would require the use of both contraception and induced abortion.[71]

F. Menstrual Regulation

The development of early menstrual extraction, either by prostaglandins, or, more commonly, by a simple, hand-held uterine suction device, has placed "menstrual regulation" in a legal gray area. Since menstrual regulation can be used within fourteen days after a missed menstrual period, it is difficult, if not impossible, to determine whether the woman was pregnant. And since menstrual regulation can be used either to induce menstruation or to abort a pregnancy, motivation is difficult to prove. In effect, menstrual regulation can be

[71]C. Tietze & J. Bongaarts, *Fertility Rates and Abortion Rates: Simulations of Family Limitation,* 6 STUDIES IN FAM. PLAN. 114 (1975).

analogized to abortion on the one hand or to delayed-action contraceptives (such as IUDs or "morning after pills") on the other.

Menstrual regulation is an area in which technology has outstripped law. It raises questions whether criminal abortion statutes are applicable, whether proof of pregnancy is required for conviction, how important intention or motivation is, and who carries the burden of proof.

In countries where abortion is legal, menstrual regulation would also be legal; for example, the United States Supreme Court, in *Roe v. Wade*, mentioned menstrual extraction as a form of first-trimester abortion. Where abortion is prohibited, two different approaches can be followed according to Lee and Paxman:[72]

> Some countries make the intent to interrupt pregnancy a crime, whether or not the woman was actually pregnant. However, it might be difficult to prove a woman had intended to abort, given that the device can be used to induce a period or treat an incomplete spontaneous abortion;
>
> Other countries require definite proof of pregnancy. Argentine, Brazilian, and Mexican judges have found that, if pregnancy has not been proven, no crime has been committed regardless of intent.

G. Bibliographic Note

It is something of an understatement to note that the literature on international aspects of abortion is voluminous. Probably the most comprehensive single volume, covering legal, medical, sociological, psychological, and ethical considerations, is D. Callahan, *Abortion: Law, Choice and Morality* (Macmillan, 1970). C. Tietze, *Induced Abortion,* provides an excellent analysis of legal, epidemiological, and demographic facets; published by the Population Council, it is revised and made current every two years. H. David, "Abortion Policies," in *Techniques of Abortion and Sterilization* (J. Hodgson, ed., Academic, forthcoming) provides an analysis of current laws and policies. M. Potts, P. Diggory & J. Peel, *Abortion* (Cambridge, 1977) covers the topic comprehensively. The *Population Reports* series, initially published by George Washington University and later by Johns Hopkins University, periodically reviews abortion

[72]L. Lee & J. Paxman, *Legal Aspects of Menstrual Regulation,* 8 STUDIES IN FAM. PLAN. 273 (1977).

law and practice. The most recent monograph on abortion is Series E., No. 3 (1976). Finally, the World Health Organization, *International Digest of Health Legislation,* reprints abortion laws, and the *Law File,* a monthly publication of the International Planned Parenthood Federation, serves as a clearinghouse for abortion law and policy developments.

CHAPTER 4

STERILIZATION

I. INTRODUCTION

Sterilization has become one of the world's most popular methods of controlling fertility with more than an estimated 90 million couples using it to prevent unwanted births.[1] In the United States alone, it is the most popular method of birth control for couples over thirty and it rivals the pill as the most utilized method for all couples.[2] In countries as diverse as China, Thailand, Sri Lanka, and El Salvador, sterilization is a popular method of controlling fertility.[3] Studies have shown that one-third of the women of fertile age in

[1]L. Landman, *Fourth International Conference on Voluntary Sterilization,* 11 FAM. PLAN. PERSPECTIVES 241 (1979). *See also,* C. Green, *Voluntary Sterilization: World's Leading Contraceptive Method,* POPULATION REPORTS, series M, no. 2 (George Washington Univ., 1978).

[2]C. Westoff & E. Jones, *Contraception and Sterilization in the United States, 1965–75,* 9 FAM. PLAN. PERSPECTIVES 153 (1977).

[3]R. Ravenholt, *World Epidemiology and Potential Fertility Impact of Voluntary Sterilization Services,* in NEW ADVANCES IN STERILIZATION: PROCEEDINGS OF THE THIRD INTERNATIONAL CONFERENCE ON VOLUNTARY STERILIZATION 23–33 (M. Schima & I. Lubell, eds., AVS, 1976). [Hereafter cited as M. Schima & I. Lubell, eds.]

Puerto Rico used sterilization to control their fertility,[4] and the sterilization camps in India, discussed on pp. 316–318 *infra,* have attracted millions of men.

The sterilization boom, if it can be termed that, is a relatively recent phenomenon. According to the Office of Population of the Agency for International Development, the number of couples using sterilization as their means of fertility control rose from 5 million in 1960 to 15 million in 1970 and jumped to 65 million in 1975.[5] How can this extraordinary rise be explained? What are the advantages of sterilization? The problems associated with it?

Sterilization has recently become a comparatively safe and simple operation. New techniques, such as laparoscopy, mini-laporotomy, and culdoscopy, have transformed female sterilization from a major procedure requiring several days hospitalization into a quick outpatient procedure that can be done under local anesthesia. The development of these new procedures has enabled women to obtain a sterilization while not pregnant (interval sterilization) instead of, as was previously the case, only at the time of childbirth (postpartum sterilization). The male procedure, vasectomy, is a 15-minute operation performed under local anesthesia.[6] Also, sterilization is considered irreversible, commending it to older couples who want to end childbearing (as contrasted with spacing of children). As the risks of oral contraception to women over 35 become more widely appreciated, so do the comparative advantages of sterilization for people of this age group. Both male and female sterilization have the lowest failure rates—0.15 percent and 0.04 percent respectively—of all contraceptive methods.[7] Finally, the risks to life and health of sterilization are minimal.[8]

Both internationally and in the United States, sterilization has become increasingly recognized as an accepted method of fertility control, one which should be made widely available. At the same

[4]H. Presser, *Sterilization and Fertility Decline in Puerto Rico,* University of California/Berkeley International Population and Urban Research Monograph No. 13 (1973).

[5]R. Ravenholt, *supra* n. 3 at 27.

[6]For discussion of sterilization techniques, see POPULATION REPORTS *Series C (female sterilization)* and *Series D (male sterilization)*, published by George Washington University through July, 1978, and by Johns Hopkins University thereafter.

[7]I. Lubell & R. Frischer, *Sterilization Demand Exceeds Facilities,* Draper World Population Fund Report No. 3 (1976).

[8]M. Potts, *The International Sterilization Revolution,* in M. Schima and I. Lubell, ed. *supra* n. 3, at 17.

time, sterilization should be truly voluntary and people should not be coerced or tricked into undergoing the procedure. There is a tension between the policy of making sterilizations freely available (which improves access while increasing the potential for abuse) and that of establishing legal and administrative obstacles to sterilization (which reduces the potential for coercion but can also frustrate people who genuinely want sterilizations). The legal issues raised by these tensions domestically are explored in section II of this chapter, particularly (1) voluntary sterilization as a "fundamental right," and the implications in terms of service delivery and governmental funding (section II.A.) and (2) coercion, and the restrictions that have been established to eliminate or reduce it (section II.B.); this is followed, in section II.C., by an analysis of those situations where sterilization is not truly voluntary, involving special problems of consent, especially for the mentally retarded and minors. Section III explores sterilization internationally, first by reviewing the legal status of voluntary sterilization worldwide (section III.A.) and then by examining the experience of India, the only country where compulsory sterilization has been seriously considered as a means of population control (section III.B.).

II. VOLUNTARY STERILIZATION IN THE UNITED STATES

A. The Right of an Individual to Be Sterilized and the State's Duty to Provide the Service

The United States Supreme Court has not considered directly the question whether voluntary sterilization is a fundamental right. Certainly the logic of the Court's fertility regulation decisions and its language in *Skinner v. Oklahoma,* p. 167, *infra,* that "Marriage and procreation are fundamental to the very existence and survival of the race . . . he [whom the law touches] is forever deprived of a basic liberty." lead towards the view that voluntary sterilization would be considered an element of the constitutionally protected right of privacy. If voluntary sterilization is in fact a fundamental right, what are the constitutional implications for impediments to the procedure?[9] These have included:

[9]For a review of the barriers to sterilization, see Comment, *A Constitutional Evaluation of Statutory and Administrative Impediments to Voluntary Sterilization,* 14 J. FAM. LAW 67 (1975).

Spousal consent[10]
Age or parity requirements or both[11]
Concurrence of other physicians or a hospital committee
Stricter standards for one sex

Would requirements such as these be able to withstand constitutional scrutiny if challenged on the grounds of violating the right of privacy? Equal protection of the laws? What arguments could a state muster in support of these kinds of impediments?

A related issue is the state's duty to pay for or provide voluntary sterilization. At this point, re-read the cases of *Maher v. Roe, supra* p. 90, *Poelker v. Doe, supra* p. 110, and *Harris v. McRae, supra* p. 100. Is *Maher* authority for the proposition that states could refuse to use Medicaid funds for elective sterilizations? Is *McRae* authority for the principle that states could refuse Medicaid funds for sterilizations that were even medically necessary? Regarding these questions, how much weight should be given to the requirement in the Medicaid legislation that states must provide family planning services? Should sterilization, in this context, be considered as just another method of fertility control or as an analogue to abortion? In light of *Poelker* and *McRae,* what duty does a public hospital have to provide voluntary sterilizations? Medically necessary sterilizations?[12]

B. Coercion and State Restrictions on Access to Sterilization

1. The Potential for Abuse

The dramatic rise in the popularity of sterilization, coupled with reports of abuse, has led to grave concern that many individuals are

[10]On this point *see* Note, *Sterilization: Who Says No?* 29 MERCER L. REV. 821 (1978) and Note, *A Spouse's Right to Marital Dissolution Predicated on the Partner's Contraceptive Surgery,* 23 N.Y.L.S. L. REV. 99 (1977). The HEW Guidelines, p. 200, *infra,* do not require spousal consent for federally-funded sterilizations.

[11]Probably the most common obstacle was the old "120 rule," whereby sterilizations were prohibited unless the number of living children times the woman's age totaled at least 120. Under this rule, a 35-year-old woman with three living children would not be eligible to have a sterilization performed, whereas a 31-year-old woman with four living children would be eligible. Although the 120 rule has largely been abandoned, its vestiges remain in some places.

[12]*See Hathaway v. City of Worcester Hospital,* 475 F. 2d 701 (1st Cir. 1973), the leading pre-*Poelker* decision, which held that a public hospital must provide voluntary sterilizations if it offerred similar medical services. The case involved a request for a therapeutic sterilization.

being sterilized under duress or without understanding the nature and consequence of the procedure. While there is little hard statistical evidence on the extent of sterilization abuse, reports from several sources[13,14] have documented large numbers of sterilizations performed without proper consent procedures being utilized. Coercion is said to fall hardest on those people least in a position to defend themselves: poor black or Hispanic women. Notwithstanding the paucity of hard data on sterilization abuse, there is agreement that the potential for coercion exists and that monitoring of instances of sterilization abuse to date has been weak. Perhaps the best example of the nature of sterilization abuse and the difficulties in controlling it is the history of the Relf sisters litigation and the Department of Health, Education, and Welfare guidelines which followed it.

2. The Relf Sisters Case

In 1973 the case of the Relf sisters attracted national atention. The case inolved two black women who, at the ages of 12 and 14 respectively, were sterilized through a federally-funded family planning program in Montgomery, Alabama, allegedly without either their consent or that of their parents. Attention was also focused on welfare recipients in Aiken, South Carolina, whose doctor refused to deliver their children unless they agreed to be sterilized. The national outcry led the Department of Health, Education, and Welfare (HEW) to propose regulations restricting the circumstances under which federally-funded sterilizations could be performed. These regulations were struck down by the Federal District Court for the District of Columbia in *Relf v. Weinberger,* 372 F. Supp. 1196 (D.C., 1974), excerpted below:

> Gesell, District Judge
>
> These two related cases, which have been consolidated with the consent of all parties, challenge the statutory authorization and constitutionality of regulations of the Department of Health, Education and Welfare (HEW) governing human sterilizations under programs and

[13]COMPTROLLER GENERAL, LETTER REPORT B-164031(5), INFORMATION CONCERNING CERTAIN ACTIVITIES OF THE INDIAN HEALTH SERVICE, (1976).

[14]PUBLIC CITIZEN'S HEALTH RESEARCH GROUP, STERILIZATION WITHOUT CONSENT: TEACHING HOSPITAL VIOLATIONS OF HEW REGULATIONS, (1975) AND SURGICAL STERILIZATION: PRESENT ABUSES AND PROPOSED REGULATIONS, (1973).

projects funded by the Department's Public Health Service and its Social and Rehabilitation Service. . . .

Although Congress has been insistent that all family planning programs function on a purely voluntary basis, there is uncontroverted evidence in the record that minors and other incompetents have been sterilized with federal funds and that an indefinite number of poor people have been improperly coerced into accepting a sterilization operation under the threat that various federally supported welfare benefits would be withdrawn unless they submitted to irreversible sterilization. Patients receiving Medicaid assistance at childbirth are evidently the most frequent targets of this pressure, as the experiences of plaintiffs Waters and Walker illustrate. Mrs. Waters was actually refused medical assistance by her attending physician unless she submitted to a tubal ligation after the birth. Other examples were documented.

When such deplorable incidents began to receive nationwide public attention due to the experience of the Relf sisters in Alabama, the Secretary took steps to restrict the circumstances under which recipients of federal family planning funds could conduct sterilization operations. On August 3, 1973, the Department published in the Federal Register a notice of Guidelines for Sterilization Procedures under HEW Supported Programs. . . .

Plaintiffs do not oppose the voluntary sterilization of poor persons under federally funded programs. However, they contend that these regulations are both illegal and arbitrary because they authorize *involuntary* sterilizations, without statutory or constitutional justification. They argue forcefully that sterilization of minors or mental incompetents is necessarily involuntary in the nature of things. Further, they claim that sterilization of competent adults under these regulations can be undertaken without insuring that the request for sterilization is in actuality voluntary. . . .

[The Court first disposed of the issues of standing and justiciability.]

The court must therefore proceed to the merits. While plaintiffs invoke both statutory and constitutional principles, relying on the Fourth, Fifth, Sixth, Eighth and Ninth Amendments to the Constitution in support of their position, the issues tendered may be readily resolved simply by resort to the underlying statutes. Accordingly, no occasion exists to consider the related constitutional claims.

For the reasons developed below, the Court finds that the Secretary has no statutory authority . . . to fund the sterilization of any person incompetent under state law to consent to such an operation, whether because of minority or of mental deficiency. It also finds that the challenged regulations are arbitrary and unreasonable in that they fail to implement the congressional command that federal family planning funds not be used to coerce indigent patients into submitting to sterilization. . . .

Although the term "voluntary" is nowhere defined in the statutes under consideration, it is frequently encountered in the law. Even its dictionary definition assumes an exercise of free will and clearly precludes the existence of coercion or force. . . . And its use . . . at least when important human rights are at stake, entails a requirement that the individual have at his disposal the information necessary to make his decision and the mental competence to appreciate the significance of that information . . .

No person who is mentally incompetent can meet these standards, nor can the consent of a representative, however sufficient under state law, impute voluntariness to the individual actually undergoing irreversible sterilization. Minors would also appear to lack the knowledge, maturity and judgment to satisfy these standards with regard to such an important issue, whatever may be their competence to rely on devices or medication that temporarily frustrates procreation. . . .

The regulations also fail to provide the procedural safeguards necessary to insure that even competent adults voluntarily request sterilization. . . . Even a fully informed individual cannot make a "voluntary" decision concerning sterilization if he has been subjected to coercion from doctors or project officers. . . .

In order to prevent express or implied threats, which would obviate the Secretary's entire framework of procedural safeguards, and to insure compliance with the statutory language, the Court concludes that the regulations must also be amended to require that individuals seeking sterilization be orally informed at the very outset that no federal benefits can be withdrawn because of a failure to accept sterilization. This guarantee must also appear prominently at the top of the consent document already required by the regulations. To permit sterilization without this essential safeguard is an unreasonable and arbitrary interpretation of the congressional mandate. . . .

Surely the Federal Government must move cautiously in this area [birth control] under well-defined policies determined by Congress after full consideration of constitutional and far-reaching social implications. The dividing line between family planning and eugenics is murky. And yet the Secretary, through the regulations at issue, seeks to sanction one of the most drastic methods of population control—the involuntary irreversible sterilization of men and women—without any legislative guidance. Whatever might be the merits of limiting irresponsible reproduction, which each year places increasing numbers of unwanted or mentally defective children into tax-supported institutions, it is for Congress and not individual social workers and physicians to determine the manner in which federal funds should be used to support such a program. We should not drift into a policy which has unfathomed implications and which permanently deprives unwilling or immature citizens of their ability to procreate without adequate legal safeguards and a legislative determination of the appropriate standards in light of the general welfare and of individual rights.

As a result of the *Relf* decision, the Department of Health, Education, and Welfare promulgated new regulations applicable to sterilization procedures in federally-funded programs. These established requirements for informed consent, such as an assurance that federal benefits would not be withheld if the person changed his or her mind, and instituted a 72-hour waiting period between the giving of informed consent and the performance of the operation. In 1975, HEW proposed modifications of the 1974 regulations, which would have lowered the age of consent for sterilization from 21 to 18 and permitted sterilization of mental incompetents under certain conditions. These modifications were rejected by Judge Gesell as insufficient to prevent abuse.[15]

Toward the end of 1977, HEW proposed new regulations which completely overhauled the existing ones. These were issued in final form in November 1978.[16] Excerpts from the text of the final HEW regulations and commentary on them are found below:

3. The HEW Regulations on Sterilizations*

§ 50.203 Sterilization of a mentally competent individual aged 21 or older. Programs or projects to which this subpart applies shall perform or arrange for the performance of sterilization of an individual only if the following requirements have been met:

(a) The individual is at least 21 years old at the time consent is obtained.

(b) The individual is not a mentally incompetent individual.

(c) The individual has voluntarily given his or her informed consent in accordance with the procedures of § 50.204 of this subpart.

(d) At least 30 days but not more than 180 days have passed between the date of informed consent and the date of the sterilization,

[15] *Relf v. Mathews,* 403 F. Supp. 1235 (D.C., 1975).

[16] 42 C.F.R. § 50.201 *et seq.* (1979).

*In 1978 the Department of Health, Education, and Welfare (HEW) was divided into a Department of Education and a Department of Health and Human Services (HHS). Since the regulations were issued while HEW still existed, they are referred to in this section as the HEW regulations. HHS is now responsible for their enforcement.—Ed.

except in the case of premature delivery or emergency abdominal surgery. An individual may consent to be sterilized at the time of premature delivery or emergency abdominal surgery, if at least 72 hours have passed after he or she gave informed consent to sterilization. In the case of premature delivery, the informed consent must have been given at least 30 days before the expected date of delivery.

§ 50.204 Informed consent requirement. Informed consent does not exist unless a consent form is completed voluntarily and in accordance with all the requirements of this section and § 50.205 of this subpart.

(a) A person who obtains informed consent for a sterilization procedure must offer to answer any questions the individual to be sterilized may have concerning the procedure, provide a copy of the consent form, and provide orally all of the following information or advice to the individual who is to be sterilized:

(1) Advice that the individual is free to withhold or withdraw consent to the procedure any time before the sterilization without affecting his or her right to future care or treatment and without loss or withdrawal of any federally funded program benefits to which the individual might be otherwise entitled:

(2) A description of available alternative methods of family planning and birth control;

(3) Advice that the sterilization procedure is considered to be irreversible;

(4) A thorough explanation of the specific sterilization procedure to be performed;

(5) A full description of the discomforts and risks that may accompany or follow the performing of the procedure, including an explanation of the type and possible effects of any anesthetic to be used;

(6) A full descritption of the benefits or advantages that may be expected as a result of the sterilization; and

(7) Advice that the sterilization will not be performed for at least 30 days except under the circumstances specified in § 50.203(d) of this subpart.

(b) An interpreter must be provided to assist the individual to be sterilized if he or she does not understand the language used on the consent form or the language used by the person obtaining the consent.

(c) Suitable arrangements must be made to insure that the information specified in paragraph (a) of this section is effectively communicated to any individual to be sterilized who is blind, deaf or otherwise handicapped.

(d) A witness chosen by the individual to be sterilized may be present when consent is obtained.

(e) Informed consent may not be obtained while the individual to be sterilized is:

(1) In labor or childbirth;

(2) Seeking to obtain or obtaining an abortion; or

(3) Under the influence of alcohol or other substances that affect the individual's state of awareness.

(f) Any requirement of State and local law for obtaining consent, except one of spousal consent, must be followed.

§ 50.205 Consent form requirements.

(a) *Required consent form.* The consent form appended to this subpart or another consent form approved by the Secretary must be used.

(b) *Required signatures.* The consent form must be signed and dated by:

(1) The individual to be sterilized; and

(2) The interpreter, if one is provided; and

(3) The person who obtains the consent; and

(4) The physician who will perform the sterilization procedure.

(c) *Required certifications.* (1) The person obtaining the consent must certify by signing the consent form that: (i) before the individual to be sterilized signed the consent form, he or she advised the individual to be sterilized that no Federal benefits may be withdrawn because of the decision not to be sterilized, (ii) he or she explained orally the requirements for informed consent as set forth on the consent form, and (iii) to the best of his or her knowledge and belief, the individual to be sterilized appeared mentally competent and knowingly and voluntarily consented to be sterilized.

(2) The physician performing the sterilization must certify by signing the consent form, that: (i) shortly before the performance of the sterilization, he or she advised the individual to be sterilized that no Federal benefits may be withdrawn because of the decision not to be sterilized, (ii) he or she explained orally the requirements for informed consent as set forth on the consent form, and (iii) to the best of his or her knowledge and belief, the individual to be sterilized appeared mentally competent and knowingly and voluntarily consented to be sterilized. Except in the case of premature delivery or emergency abdominal surgery, the physician must further certify that at least 30 days have passed between the date of the individual's signature on the consent form and the date upon which the sterilization was performed. If premature delivery occurs or emergency abdominal surgery is required within the 30-day period, the physician must certify that the sterilization was performed less than 30 days but not less than 72 hours after the date of the individual's signature on the consent

form because of premature delivery or emergency abdominal surgery, as applicable. In the case of premature delivery, the physician must also state the expected date of delivery. In the case of emergency abdominal surgery, the physician must describe the emergency.

(3) If an interpreter is provided, the interpreter must certify that he or she translated the information and advice presented orally, read the consent form and explained its contents, and to the best of the interpreter's knowledge and belief, the individual to be sterilized understood what the interpreter told him or her.

§ 50.206 Sterilization of a mentally incompetent individual or of an institutionalized individual. Programs or projects to which this subpart applies shall not perform or arrange for the performance of a sterilization of any mentally incompetent individual or institutionalized individual.

§ 50.207 Sterilization by hysterectomy.

(a) Programs or projects to which this subpart applies shall not perform or arrange for the performance of any hysterectomy solely for the purpose of rendering an individual permanently incapable of reproducing or where, if there is more than one purpose to the procedure, the hysterectomy would not be performed but for the purpose of rendering the individual permanently incapable of reproducing.

(b) Programs or projects to which this subpart applies may perform or arrange for the performance of a hysterectomy not covered by paragraph (a) of this section only if:

(1) The person who secures the authorization to perform the hysterectomy has informed the individual and her representative, if any, orally and in writing, that the hysterectomy will render her permanently incapable of reproducing; and

(2) The individual or her representative, if any, has signed a written acknowledgment of receipt of that information. . . .

§ 50.209 Use of Federal financial assistance.

(a) Federal financial assistance adminstered by the Public Health Service may not be used for expenditures for sterilization procedures unless the consent form appended to this section or another form approved by the Secretary is used.

(b) A program or project shall not use Federal financial assistance for any sterilization or hysterectomy without first receiving documentation showing that the requirements of this subpart have been met. Documentation includes consent forms, and acknowledgments of receipt of hysterectomy information.

§ 50.210 Review of regulation. The Secretary will request public comment on the operation of the provisions of this subpart not later than 3 years after their effective date.

4. Issues And Commentary

a. The 30-Day Waiting Period. The 30-day waiting period generated more controversy than any other part of the HEW Guidelines. Opponents argued it would discriminate against the poor and against disadvantaged groups such as migrant workers and rural inhabitants. They also argued that 30 days was arbitrary, would not prevent abuse, and constituted excessive regulation of medical practice. It was further suggested that the waiting period should not apply to men or nonpregnant women since they were not subject to the most common forms of coercion associated with hospitalized childbirth or abortion. Supporters responded that 30 days gave a person sufficient time to reflect and to consult with friends and family, that it allowed a person sufficient time out of an intimidating hospital environment, and that few instances of hardship had been found in New York City, which had previously enacted a 30-day waiting period. In many ways, the 30-day waiting period was felt to be the key to reducing sterilization abuse. In its decision to establish a 30-day waiting period, with exceptions for premature delivery or emergency abdominal surgery, HEW recognized that it might be a hardship for rural inhabitants and migrant workers, but found that provisions for waiver of the 30-day rule would be hard to monitor and would be susceptible of abuse.

b. Informed Consent. Before any medical procedure can be performed, the informed consent of the patient must be obtained. Informed consent is usually defined in terms of "understanding the nature and consequences of the procedure to be performed." Specifically, informed consent comprises three elements: first, the person must have the capacity to consent; second, the consent must be voluntary, *i.e.,* uncoerced and unpressured, and third, the person must be given sufficient information to weigh the alternatives and to make the decision.

With respect to informed consent generally, the trend in the United States is toward giving patients more rather than less information. A physician who fails to obtain informed consent can be sued by the patient either for battery (an unlawful touching) or, more commonly today, for negligence. The traditional rule for determining how much information a doctor was required to give a patient was *standard medical practice.* In many states, including New York and California, the traditional rule has given way to what is called an *objective standard, i.e.,* an individual must be informed of the *material risks* of the procedure and it is for a jury to determine whether a reasonable person would have felt that the risk in question was material.[17]

With respect to sterilization, how well do the federal guidelines meet three criteria listed above? Note that to assure that consent is voluntary, under the HEW regulations a person cannot consent to sterilization while in labor or when obtaining an abortion, the two circumstances which have been considered as most coercive. Note also that HEW places considerable reliance on the consent form and the detailed information which must be provided to the individual as means of preventing abuse. Is this information sufficient to give an individual an understanding of the nature and consequences of sterilization? Is it too much information? Does the potential for sterilization abuse justify imposing consent requirements more stringent than those required for other procedures?

c. Capacity to Consent to Sterilization.

(1) Minimum Age Limit The HEW regulations prohibit the sterilization of people under 21 years of age. This raises a number of issues. Since the age of majority in most states is now 18, what is the justification for establishing a 21-year limit in the case of sterilizations? Does the permanence of sterilization justify an age limit three years in excess of the norm? Would determination of an age limitation better have been left to each state? Are there extraordinary

[17]For examination of informed consent generally *see* D. Seidelson, *Medical Malpractice: Informed Consent in "Full-Disclosure" Jurisdictions,* 14 DUQUESNE L. REV. 309 (1976); J. Waltz and T. Scheuneman, *Informed Consent to Immunization: The Risks and Benefits of Individual Autonomy,* 65 CALIF. L. REV. 1286 (1977); A. SOUTHWICK, THE LAW OF HOSPITAL AND HEALTH CARE ADMINISTRATION 203 *et seq.* (Health Admin. Press 1978) and G. ANNAS, L. GLANTZ & B. KATZ, INFORMED CONSENT TO HUMAN EXPERIMENTATION: THE SUBJECT'S DILEMMA 27–62 (Ballinger, 1977) [hereafter cited as G. Annas et al.]. The seminal case is *Canterbury v. Spence,* 464 F. 2d 772 (D.C. 1972); *c.f., Cobbs v. Grant,* 8 Cal. 3d 229 (1972). Informed consent in the context of fertility regulation is examined in E. Paul & G. Scofield, *Informed Consent for Fertility Control Services,* 11 FAM. PLAN. PERSPECTIVES 159 (1979).

circumstances under which people under 21 should be allowed to be sterilized? For example, where an individual has a condition which makes pregnancy life threatening, regardless of age, or where pregnancy is inadvisable because of a high probability of producing children with a serious genetic disease. Despite these considerations, which surfaced in the comments to the draft regulations, HEW decided to retain the 21-year-old age minimum, partly because younger people who were sterilized had higher regret rates and partly because monitoring exceptions to a minimum age limit is difficult.

(2) Other Limitations on Capacity to Consent The regulations also prohibit the sterilization of individuals who are either institutionalized or have been declared mentally incompetent (unless having been declared competent for purposes including the ability to consent to sterilizations). Sterilization of the mentally incompetent is examined in section IIC., *infra.* pp. 161–185.

d. Monitoring the Regulations. The guidelines affect sterilizations only where federal funding is involved. This includes Title XIX (Medicaid) and Title XX (Social Services) of the Social Security Act, Title X of the Public Health Services Act, and other programs administered by HHS.[18] The need for effective enforcement was the leitmotif of the hearings on the draft regulations. The two most significant mechanisms for enforcing the guidelines are (a) occasional government audits and (b) reimbursement of Medicaid (or other federal financing) only of those claims where the proper consent forms have been signed. As enforcement mechanisms, how effective are these? What other mechanisms to monitor compliance with the guidelines could be envisioned? What remedies, outside of non-payment of Medicaid, might deter sterilization abuse?

Of course, an individual who has been coerced into being sterilized can bring a battery or negligence suit against the physician or hospital. Such a suit might be difficult to win, however, since a signed consent form imputes a presumption of voluntariness.[19] Similarly, a suit against a physician for violating the civil and constitutional rights of women coerced into having sterilizations might be difficult

[18] The state of California and the city of New York have adopted regulations similar to those of the federal government to regulate sterilizations performed within their jurisdictions. CALIF. WELF.-INST. CODE §§ 14190-14194; N.Y.C. ADMIN. CODE C-22-1.0 to 9.0.

[19] *See* Madrigal v. Quilligan, CA No. 75.2057 (C.D. Calif. 1978), as reported in 7 FAM. PLAN./POP. REP 77 *See also* A. (1978). SOUTHWICK, *supra* n. 17 at 225.

to maintain. In *Walker v. Pierce,*[20] the Court of Appeals for the Fourth Circuit held that a physician who refused to deliver the children of pregnant women on Medicaid unless they agree to be sterilized was not acting as an agent of the state. Since no state action was involved, he could not be held liable for violating the civil rights of the women.

e. Access v. Abuse. How well do the HEW regulations maintain a balance between access to sterilization and protection against abuse? Do the rules interfere with women's rights to reproductive freedom? Do they create a double standard by limiting access to sterilization for poor women? Noting the difficulty in balancing the competing policy interests of access and abuse, HEW wrote:[21]

> . . . These rules reflect what is hoped to be a workable balance between them [the competing policy interests], in which no one consideration is given so much weight that another is not achieved, and in which the overall goal of providing federally funded sterilizations to those who voluntarily choose this service is realized.
>
> The final rules resolve the competing considerations of insuring access to sterilization and insuring that this access does not lead to involuntary sterilizations in two ways. They limit the access of those individuals least able to give an informed consent or those least able to understand the consequences of a permanent and irreversible sterilization. In addition, they establish procedures to insure that those individuals who have access to federally funded sterilizations are provided an opportunity to make an informed and voluntary choice. This must be accomplished without burdensome administrative procedures or excessive paperwork.
>
> These approaches have been developed in light of the third consideration guiding the Department's decision making—the need to ensure the enforceability of the rules. The Department's enforcement record was criticized repeatedly at the public hearings and in many of the written comments. Therefore, in designing these rules the Department had to consider not only its need to develop effective safeguards against abuse but also its need to enforce them. This has dictated the adoption of policies that minimize exceptions, that do not make subtle or individual distinctions, and that are susceptible to verification or documentation. . . .

[20] 560 F. 2d 609 (4th Cir. 1977).
[21] 43 Fed. Reg., 52147 (1978).

5. Liability of Physicians for Voluntary Sterilization

What is the potential liability of a physician for performing a sterilization on an adult who has given informed consent?[22] Insofar as criminal liability, the chances of a successful prosecution are almost negligible. The two traditional grounds are mayhem and assault and battery. Mayhem, which originally had to do with so maiming a person that he could not fight for the King, is now a statutory crime and in most states requires malicious intent; consent is a bar to an assault and battery prosecution.[23]

With regard to civil liability, courts have been reluctant to grant relief to patients suing on grounds of misrepresentation or breach of warranty—both of which involve proving that the physician made assurances that the procedure would be successful. Physicians can be found liable where the procedure was negligently performed; negligence could be found in the procedure itself or in the follow-up. However, failure of the operation itself, or regeneration of the organs involved, do not, by themselves, establish negligence.

Even if a physician is found to have performed negligently, the question of assessing damages is rather tricky. The traditional view held that since having children is a blessing, public policy does not allow damages for the birth of a child, even an unwanted one. This has been changing, and many jurisdictions now assess damages for a negligent sterilization leading to the birth of an unwanted child. But should a negligent physician have to pay all costs related to rearing the child through adulthood, or only those related to childbirth? Should the benefits of childrearing be offset against the financial burdens? Should damages be mitigated by an injured party's failure to get an abortion or to put the child up for adoption? These issues have not been fully litigated and courts have differed in their conclusions.[24]

[22]Potential liability of physicians for failing to obtain informed consent is discussed in the text at pp. 156–157, *infra.*

[23]*See* Note, *Contraceptive Sterilization: The Doctor, the Patient, and the United States Constitution,* 25 FLA. L. REV. 327 (1973) and P. Tierney, *Voluntary Sterilization: A Necessary Alternative?* 4 FAM. L.Q. 373 (1970).

[24]For examinations of these issues, *see* H. Clark, Jr., *Wrongful Conception: A New Kind of Medical Malpractice?* 12 FAM. L. Q. 259 (1979); Note, *Wrongful Conception: Who Pays for Bringing Up Baby?* 47 FORDHAM L. REV. 418 (1978); G. Robertson, *Civil Liability Arising from "Wrongful Birth" Following an Unsuccessful Sterilization Operation,* 4 AM. J. LAW MED. 131 (1978); Comment, *Liability for Failure of Birth Control Methods,* 76 COLUM. L. REV. 1187 (1976).

C. Involuntary Sterilization of the Mentally Retarded—The Special Problems of Informed Consent

1. Eugenic Sterilization—A Brief Historical Overview

Beginning early in the twentieth century, many states enacted laws permitting involuntary sterilization of the mentally retarded and others considered to possess inheritable undesirable traits. The legislative history of involuntary sterilization began in 1897 when a bill to authorize the procedure was introduced in the Michigan legislature and defeated.[25] In 1905 the Pennsylvania legislature passed an "Act for the Prevention of Idiocy," which permitted the sterilization of mentally retarded people in institutions by "such operation for the prevention of procreation as shall be decided safest and most effective." The Act was vetoed by Governor Samuel Pennybacker with the following message:

> This bill has what may be called with propriety an attractive title. If idiocy could be prevented by an Act of Assembly, we may be quite sure that such an act would have long been passed and approved in this state. . . . What is the nature of the operation is not described, but it is such an operation as they shall decide to be "safest and most effective." It is plain that the safest and most effective method of preventing procreation would be to cut the heads off the inmates, and such authority is given by the bill to this staff of scientific experts. . . .[26]

Indiana passed the first compulsory sterilization law in 1907 and by 1930 the number of states with similar statutes had risen to thirty.[27]

Some of the early sterilization laws were clearly punitive, providing for sterilization of habitual criminals, moral degenerates, or

[25]According to E. Ferster, *Eliminating the Unfit—Is Sterilization the Answer?* 27 OHIO STATE L.J. 591 (1966), some proponents of eugenic sterilization were so eager that they began sterilizing people even before state legislatures authorized the procedure. For example, in the 1890's, F. Hoyt Pilcher, Superintendent of the Winfield, Kansas, State Home for the Feeble-minded, castrated forty-four boys and fourteen girls, and Dr. Harry Sharp, who originated the vasectomy procedure, is said to have sterilized 600 or 700 boys at the Indiana Reformatory before the Indiana legislature had passed a sterilization statute.

[26]Quoted in E. Ferster, *supra* n. 25 at 593.

[27]As of 1979, at least 14 states still had laws authorizing sterilization of mentally retarded people. Note, *Addressing the Consent Issue Involved in the Sterilization of Mentally Incompetent Females,* 43 ALB. L. REV. 322, 324 (1979).

sexual perverts. In Oklahoma, for example, two convictions for chicken stealing would have been grounds for involuntary sterilization. Most statutes authorizing sterilization as a penalty for criminals were held unconstitutional as "cruel and unusual punishment."[28] Today, punitive sterilization has been excised from state laws, or, in those cases where it is still written into law, is not enforced. It is doubtful that any such statute could withstand constitutional scrutiny.

Most of the early, and some of the current, laws are based on eugenic considerations, *i.e.,* improving the race by eliminating undesirable traits that are thought to be inheritable.[29] Under this rationale, compulsory sterilization has been applied to the mentally retarded, the insane, the feeble minded, and to epileptics. The scientific basis for eugenic sterilization, an amalgam of genetics and social Darwinism, has been summarized by Bligh:[30]

> . . . The real impetus for the eugenics movement began with Francis Galton, a follower and relative of Charles Darwin, who coined the word "eugenics." Galton assumed that certain types of persons are socially more desirable than others and proposed to increase the desirable types by decreasing the rate of propagation of the inferior individuals and increasing that of the superior types. But even from early times, we can find reference to race betterment. Plato expressed this idea, saying, ". . . The principle has been already laid down that the best of either sex should be united with the best as often, and the inferior with the inferior, as seldom as possible; and that they should rear the offspring of the one sort of union, but not of the other, if the flock is to be maintained in first-rate condition." In 1516, Sir Thomas More also referred to the advisability of a physical examination of

[28]This was not, however, unanimous. In 1912 the state of Washington upheld sterilization as a penalty for a child rapist. State v. Feilen, 126 Pac. 75 (1912). The early sterilization cases are reviewed in Note, *Compulsory Sterilization: Weeding Mendel's Garden,* 22 DRAKE L. REV. 355 (1973).

[29]The development of eugenic sterilization laws is reviewed in E. Ferster, *supra* n.25; J. Paul, *State Eugenic Sterilization History: A Brief Overview, in EUGENIC STERILIZATION* 25 (J. Robitscher, ed., Charles Thomas, 1973) [hereafter cited as J. Robitscher, ed.]; Comment *Eugenic Sterilization Statutes: A Constitutional Re-Evaluation,* 14 J. FAM. L. 280 (1975); Note, *Sterilization of Mental Defectives,* 3 CUM-SAN. L. REV. 458 (1972); Comment, *Compulsory Eugenic Sterilization: For Whom Does the Bell Toll?* 6 DUQUESNE L. REV. 145 (1967–1968). *See also,* A. CHASE, THE LEGACY OF MALTHUS (Knopf, 1977).

[30]R. Bligh, *Sterilization and Mental Retardation,* 51 A.B.A.J. 1059 (1965). According to Bligh, almost 70,000 people were sterilized through January 1964, under eugenic sterilization laws.

partners before marriage as a customary procedure in that imaginary community, Utopia. Philosophical and ideal as these ideas appear, it was not, however, until Gregor Mendel announced his "unit particle" rule in 1900 [sic] that the eugenists had a scientific basis for their hypothesis. The Mendelian theory, based on experimentation with plants and insects, maintained that unit characters that are either dominant or recessive are transmitted from each parent to the offspring, and that the recurrence of these characters in succeeding generations follows a definite mathematical formula from which the characteristics of the offspring can be determined.

At about the same time that Mendel announced his rule, several genealogical studies were made available. In 1874, R. L. Dugdale, a penologist, was deputed by the Prison Association of New York to visit and report on the county jails and state prisons. His survey of the Jukes family made no special reference to mental deficiency. However, in 1915, Arthur H. Estabrook of the Department of Experimental Evolution of the Carnegie Institution made a follow-up investigation of the Jukes, concluding that "one-half of the Jukes were and are feeble-minded." Similar sweeping results of "decaying stock" were reported in 1891 by the Rev. O. C. M'Culloch in his presentation of the tribe of Ishmael, a family plagued by pauperism. The Nam family showed a similar strain of degenerate and defective progeny. In 1912, Henry Goddard published his study of the Kallikak family, again asserting that mental deficiency was a transmitted defect passed on generation to generation. Such studies seem to substantiate the proponents of the Mendelian law as applied to human beings. In 1917, Edgar A. Doll observed:

> In approximately two-thirds of the cases investigated, feeble-mindedness has been traced to biological inheritance of defective germ-plasm. . . . Recent studies, notably those of Goddard, seem to prove that this inheritance follows Mendel's Law of unit characters. For the hereditary feeble-minded, we might therefore establish the criterion of ancestral transmissibility. According to this criterion, mental defectives of known feeble-minded ancestry must, upon mating, transmit their defect according to the Mendelian Law.
>
> Charles B. Davenport, a leader in the international eugenics movement, declared categorically that "Two mentally defective parents will produce only mentally defective offspring. This is the first law of inheritance of mental ability. . . ."*

Time and advances in genetic knowledge have eroded much of the strength of the eugenics movement. Scientific opinion now seems

*Reprinted with permission from the American Bar Association Journal.

agreed that the causes of mental retardation—with the exception of a few diseases that can be genetically pinpointed—are too complex and unpredictable to justify eugenic sterilization.[31] While the eugenists framed their arguments in terms of heredity alone, the more modern view holds that heredity and environment interact. On the interaction, Tarjan has written:[32]

> I must also raise the question as to whether our increased knowledge in genetics, biological engineering and euphenics rendered many of our historical notions on eugenics anachronistic. At one time it was customary and reasonable to speak about the *nature-nurture controversy.* Scientific evidence of those days suggested that innate characteristics were not readily influenced by external forces. Today, we have sufficient evidence to realize that the two seemingly independent realms constantly interact and affect one another. . . . It is more proper, therefore, to speak about *nature-nurture interaction.* In this context, many traditional eugenic concepts may well be based on a one-sided approach to a two-sided issue.*

Perhaps as a result of this, some current laws justify compulsory sterilization on the grounds that a person would not be "fit" for parenthood.

2. Eugenic Sterilization Decisions in the United States Supreme Court

a. Buck v. Bell 274 U.S. 200 (U.S. Supreme Court 1927)

Mr. Justice Holmes delivered the opinion of the Court.

This is a writ of error to review a judgment of the Supreme Court of Appeals of the State of Virginia, affirming a judgment of the Circuit

[31]P. Moorhead, *Views of a Geneticist on Eugenic Sterilization,* in J. Robitscher, ed., *supra* n. 29 at 113–115 and M. Bass, *Voluntary Eugenic Sterilization,* in J. Robitscher, ed., *supra* n. 29 at 94. *See also* A. Myerson, *Certain Medical and Legal Phases of Eugenic Sterilization,* 52 YALE L.J. 618 (1943). Opinion is by no means unanimous, however. E. REED & S. REED, MENTAL RETARDATION: A FAMILY STUDY (Saunders, 1965) and T. Kemp, *Genetic-Hygienic Experiences in Denmark in Recent Years,* 49 EUGENICS REVIEW 11 (1957) concluded that the incidence of mental retardation could be substantially decreased by sterilization of mentally retarded people.

[32]G. Tarjan, *Some Thoughts on Eugenic Sterilization,* in J. Robitscher, *supra* n. 29 at 23. *See also* the thorough review of the scientific and legal literature in W. Vukowich, *The Dawning of the Brave New World—Legal, Ethical, and Social Issues of Eugenics,* 1971 LAW FORUM 189 (1971).

*Reprinted with permission from Jonas Robitscher, J.D., M.D.

Court of Amherst County, by which the defendant in error, the superintendent of the State Colony for Epileptics and Feeble-Minded, was ordered to perform the operation of salpingectomy upon Carrie Buck, the plaintiff in error, for the purpose of making her sterile. 143 Va. 310. The case comes here upon the contention that the statute authorizing the judgment is void under the Fourteenth Amendment as denying to the plaintiff in error due process of law and the equal protection of the laws.

Carrie Buck is a feeble minded white woman who was committed to the State Colony above mentioned in due form. She is the daughter of a feeble minded mother in the same institution, and the mother of an illegitimate feeble minded child. She was eighteen years old at the time of the trial of her case in the Circuit Court, in the latter part of 1924. An Act of Virginia, approved March 20, 1924, recites that the health of the patient and the welfare of society may be promoted in certain cases by the sterilization of mental defectives, under careful safeguard, &c.; that the sterilization may be effected in males by vasectomy and in females by salpingectomy, without serious pain or substantial danger to life; that the Commonwealth is supporting in various institutions many defective persons who if now discharged would become a menace but if incapable of procreating might be discharged with safety and become self-supporting with benefit to themselves and to society; and that experience has shown that heredity plays an important part in the transmission of insanity, imbecility, &c. The statute then enacts that whenever the superintendent of certain institutions including the above named State Colony shall be of opinion that it is for the best interests of the patients and of society that an inmate under his care should be sexually sterilized, he may have the operation performed upon any patient afflicted with hereditary forms of insanity, imbecility, & c., on complying with the very careful provisions by which the act protects the patients from possible abuse. . . .

The attack is not upon the procedure but upon the substantive law. It seems to be contended that in no circumstances could such an order be justified. It certainly is contended that the order cannot be justified upon the existing grounds. The judgment finds the facts that have been recited and that Carrie Buck "is the probable potential parent of socially inadequate offspring, likewise afflicted, that she may be sexually sterilized without detriment to her general health and that her welfare and that of society will be promoted by her sterilization," and thereupon makes the order. In view of the general declarations of the legislature and the specific findings of the Court, obviously we cannot say as matter of law that the grounds do not exist, and if they exist they justify the result. We have seen more than once that the public welfare may call upon the best citizens for their lives. It would be strange if it could not call upon those who already sap the strength of the State for these lesser sacrifices, often not felt to be such by those concerned, in order to prevent our being swamped with incompetence. It is better for all the world, if instead of waiting to execute degenerate offspring for crime, or to let them starve for their imbecility, society can prevent those who are manifestly unfit from continuing their kind. The principle that sustains compulsory vaccination is broad enough to cover cutting the Fallopian tubes. *Jacobson v. Massachusetts,* 197 U.S. 11. Three generations of imbeciles are enough.

But, it is said, however it might be if this reasoning were applied generally, it fails when it is confined to the small number who are in the institutions named and is not applied to the multitudes outside. It is the usual last resort of constitutional arguments to point out shortcomings of this sort. But the answer is that the law does all that is needed when it does all that it can, indicates a policy, applies it to all within the lines, and seeks to bring within the lines all similarly situated so far and so fast as its means allow. Of course so far as the operations enable those who otherwise must be kept confined to be returned to the world, and thus open the asylum to others, the equality aimed at will be more nearly reached.

Judgment affirmed.

Buck v. Bell is the only case in which the Supreme Court considered a direct challenge to the constitutionality of a state sterilization statute. Although subject to considerable criticism,[33] it is still relied upon by decisions upholding state sterilization statutes.[34]

As a historical footnote, the facts of the *Buck* case subsequently became the center of some dispute. It has been said that Carrie Buck was a moron and not an imbecile,[35] that her daughter (the "third generation of imbeciles") was only one month old when adjudged an imbecile by a Red Cross nurse, and that this daughter who died in 1932 of the measles, after completing the second grade, was reportedly very bright.[36]

[33]For an example of a recent criticism, see R. Burgdorf, Jr. and M. Burgdorf, *The Wicked Witch Is Almost Dead: Buck v. Bell and the Sterilization of Handicapped Persons,* 50 TEMPLE L. Q. 995 (1977).

[34]*See, e. g., In re* Moore, 289 N.C. 95, 221 S.E. 2d. 307 (1976), upholding a recently enacted sterilization law in North Carolina.

[35]According to the Stanford Revision of the Binet-Simon intelligence test, an imbecile is a person with an I.Q. of between 25 and 49, a moron a person with an I.Q. of between 50 and 69. A. ANASTASI, PSYCHOLOGICAL TESTING 208 as cited in Comment, *Eugenic Sterilization Statutes: A Constitutional Re-Evaluation, supra* n. 29 at 296. The use of terms such as "moron" and "imbecile" has been replaced, in modern parlance, by distinctions between grades of mental retardation.

[36]As reported in E. Ferster, *supra* n. 25.

b. Skinner v. Oklahoma 316 U.S. 535 (U.S. Supreme Court 1942)

The only sterilization law considered by the United States Supreme Court after *Buck v. Bell* was an Oklahoma statute which provided for the sterilization of habitual criminals convicted of crimes involving moral turpitude but excluding felonies such as embezzlement. In this case, *Skinner v. Oklahoma,* the Court held the statute unconstitutional as a violation of the equal protection clause of the Fourteenth Amendment. Justice Douglas wrote:

> We are dealing here with legislation which involves one of the basic civil rights of man. Marriage and procreation are fundamental to the very existence and survival of the race. . . . There is no redemption for the individual whom the law touches. Any experiment which the State conducts is to his irreparable injury. He is forever deprived of a basic liberty. We mention these matters not to reexamine the scope of the police power of the States. We advert to them merely in emphasis of our view that strict scrutiny of the classification which a State makes in a sterilization law is essential, lest unwittingly, or otherwise, invidious discriminations are made against groups or types of individuals in violation of the constitutional guaranty of just and equal laws. . . . Sterilization of those who have thrice committed grand larceny, with immunity for those who are embezzlers, is a clear, pointed, unmistakable discrimination . . .

3. Current Issues: In re Cavitt, 182 Neb. 712, 157 N.W. 2d 171 (Nebraska Supreme Court 1968)

Although the number of sterilizations of mentally handicapped people has been diminishing, the subject raises many important issues. Many of the contemporary issues regarding sterilization are found in the Nebraska case of *In re Cavitt.* * The case is excerpted below and is followed by a discussion of the major issues.

> Carter, J.
>
> This is an appeal by the State of Nebraska from a judgment of the district court for Gage County reversing an order of the Board of

* *Cavitt* is an unusual case in that even though four out of seven judges of the Nebraska Supreme Court found the law in question to be unconstitutional, it remained on the books since Nebraska requires a majority of five judges to hold a law unconstitutional. After the *Cavitt* decision, the Nebraska legislature repealed the law and an appeal to the U.S. Supreme Court was vacated. 396 U.S. 996 (1970).—Ed.

Examiners of Mental Deficient directing the sterilization of Gloria Cavitt. . . .

The primary question before this court is the constitutionality of sections 83–501 to 83–508, R.R.S. 1943, particularly section 83–504, R.R.S. 1943, which states: "It shall be the duty of the board of examiners to make a psychiatric and physical examination of these patients and, if after a careful examination, such board of examiners finds that such patient is mentally deficient, in the opinion of the board of examiners, is apparently capable of bearing or begetting offspring and, based on their psychiatric and medical findings as a result of this examination, it is the opinion of the board of examiners that such patient should be sterilized, as a condition prerequisite to the parole or discharge, then such patient shall not be paroled or discharged, as the case may be, unless said patient be made sterile, and that such operation be performed for the prevention of procreation as in the judgment of the board of examiners would be most appropriate to each individual case." . . .

It can hardly be disputed that the right of a woman to bear and the right of a man to beget children is a natural and constitutional right, nor can it be successfully disputed that no citizen has any rights that are superior to the common welfare. Acting for the public good, the state, in the exercise of its police power, may impose reasonable restrictions upon the natural and constitutional rights of its citizens. Measured by its injurious effect upon society, the state may limit a class of citizens in its right to bear or beget children with an inherited tendency to mental deficiency, including feeblemindedness, idiocy, or imbecility. It is the function of the legislature, and its duty as well, to enact appropriate legislation to protect the public and preserve the race from the known effects of the procreation of mentally deficient children by the mentally deficient. . . .

Gloria was 35 years of age at the time of trial in the district court and had been a patient in the Beatrice State Home since October 10, 1962. That she is mentally deficient is not disputed. The cause of her mental deficiency is not known. Before entering the home she had lived with one William Cavitt for some 14 years in what she called a common law relationship. After breaking up her relationship with Cavitt, she had much difficulty in caring for her eight children resulting from this association and after her commitment they were cared for by her parents. She came from a low social and economic group. Both she and the children were provided for largely by public aid. Four of the doctors on the board who heard the petition of the superintendent of the home to determine if she should be sterilized as a condition precedent to her release from the home testified at the hearing in district court. None of these doctors had investigated the mental condition of her parents or of her children.

The testimony of the two psychiatrists, the psychologist, and the general medical practitioner, all members of the board, can be summarized as follows: Gloria has an I.Q. of 71 and is in the lower two or three percent of the population in intelligence. All agreed that she was mentally deficient and probably capable of bearing children. After a review of Gloria's record and the observation of her, plus the I.Q. test, it was determined that she lacked the mental stability to handle social adjustment problems. Her attitude and personal feelings were considered. Consideration was given to the probable effect upon her of having more children, her minimal capacity to handle the responsibilities of parenthood, the possibility of producing mentally defective children, and the probability that added responsibilities of parenthood would in all likelihood handicap her potential rehabilitation.

The legislative authorization for the sterilization of mental defectives is a proper exercise of the police power, if constitutional requirements are met. . . . The fact that the sterilization statute is limited to mental defectives in the Beatrice State Home, the only state institution of its kind in the state, does not deny the equal protection of the law as class legislation. . . .

It is contended that the words "mentally deficient" when applied to persons is so vague and indefinite as to make the sterilization statutes unconstitutional. The terms mentally deficient and mentally retarded are generally considered as synonymous terms having a generally accepted meaning. A statutory definition can be drawn from section 83–219, R.R.S. 1943, which meets all constitutional requirements. . . .

It is contended here that the standards and guidelines under which the professional board of physicians is to act do not meet constitutional requirements. Two findings are essential before the board may act, a finding of mental deficiency of the patient and that in its opinion the patient is capable of bearing children. The statute then provides that if, in its opinion, on its psychiatric and medical findings, such patient should be sterilized as a condition for release, the board has authority to make such an order. But it is here contended that the statue is deficient in not requiring a finding that any children born to the patient would inherit a tendency to mental deficiency. Many of the earlier cases on the subject seem to have adopted that theory. But the advances in medical science have dispelled the theory that all mental defectives produce mental defectives and all normal persons do not. Such is not the case for unexplainable reasons which has brought about a change of thinking in the medical profession. . . . Heredity is not always the cause of mental deficiency. Environment is a factor that must be considered. It is an established fact that mental deficiency accelerates sexual impulses and any tendencies toward crime to a harmful degree. Many states have sterilization laws which have been upheld that are applied to certain types of crimes such as rape and incest. They have been applied to habitual criminals. They have been applied to mental defectives where transmission of mental weakness to offspring is not possible. The effect of mental deficiency upon the patient, children born to him, the community, and the general welfare, as well as the conditions leading to his commitment, are pertinent considerations in the area of sterilization. The question is a legislative one which is valid if constitutional due process is afforded and the rights of the patient protected. We point out that the sterilization statute before us is compulsory only when required before release from the Beatrice State Home. It is not compulsory in the sense that the patient is to be sterilized under all circumstances, since it is applicable only as a prerequisite to discharge or parole from the home. Remaining in the home makes the statute inapplicable. The fundamental issue is the reasonableness of the statute as an exercise of the police power. We think it reasonable . . .

Sterilization is a much misunderstood subject when applied to the mentally deficient. The public has a natural revulsion of feeling against sterilization of mental defectives even when it is clear that the public welfare requires it. Mental deficiency with its alarming results presents a social and economic problem of grave importance which gives rise to the exercise of the police power by the Legislature. The Beatrice State Home is full to overflowing with these unfortunates as is evidenced by the fact that Gloria was compelled to wait 10 days after commitment before being admitted to the home because of a lack of room. Thus far we have been endeavoring to demonstrate that the statute under consideration, measured by the purpose for which it was enacted and the conditions which warranted it, and justified by the findings of experts in biological science, is a proper and reasonable exercise of the police power. The opposition to such a statute as we have before us is largely based on the assumption that the operation is inhuman, unreasonable, and oppressive. The surgical operation of vasectomy on mentally defective males and of salpingectomy on mentally defective females is a simple operation without pain or discomfort to the patient. It does not reduce his sex impulses nor limit his capacity to engage in sexual relations. It does no harm to the patient other than to eliminate his capacity to procreate.

We limit our holding to the facts of this case and the statute we have before us. We have here a case where the patient has not been cured, but who is eligible for release from the home if she is sterilized. She can remain in the home without being sterilized. Sterilization is only a condition for parole or discharge. It is compulsory only if she insists upon her release. We fail to see how the statute is in any manner unconstitutional on any grounds under these precise circumstances. It constitutes a reasonable invocation of the police power for the public welfare. . . .

Justice Smith, dissenting:

The critical issue is whether the sterilization law denies substantitive due process of law guaranteed by the Constitution of Nebraska. I too believe that the right of man to procreate is not absolute, that a balance must be struck between the private right and the police power. Two considerations are the statutory interpretation made by the court and the strength of reliable scientific opinion about involuntary sterilization.

The law applies, according to the court, to voluntary sterilizations alone—an interpretation with which I do not concur. The court supplies, however, little guidance to anyone in solving problems of effective consent by the mentally retarded and of substitute consent. More important, the coercive feature is hardly masked by the fictive option of sterilization or life imprisonment.

The factual approach to constitutionality begins with the record. The board members concluded that heredity, environment, or both produce mental retardation, and their conclusion is obviously undeniable. Some also found a probability that future offspring of Gloria would be mentally retarded, but nothing in the record shows the competence of anyone to make that judgment . . .

The State itself cites an article that reads: ". . . Dr. Leo Kanner has written, 'In my 20 years of psychiatric work with thousands of children and their parents, I have seen percentually at least as many "intelligent" adults unfit to rear their offspring as I have seen such "feebleminded" adults. I have—and many others have—come to the conclusion that, to a large extent independent of the I.Q., fitness for parenthood is determined by emotional involvements and relationships.' Kanner, A Miniature Textbook of Feeble-Mindedness, p.5."

The scientific arguments against sterilization were ably summarized in 1960 by Dr. Bernard L. Diamond when he served as a special consultant to the American Psychiatric Association for its report on mental health legislation in British Columbia: ". . . In short, the present state of our scientific knowledge does not justify the widespread use of the sterilization procedures in mentally ill or mentally deficient persons". . . .

Reviewing genetic aspects of intelligent behavior, Irving G. Gottesman warned: "The issues involved in eugenics are only partly based on a knowledge of genetics, the others being social, axiological, moral, economic, and political. . . . [T]he preservation and improvement of these genetic attributes of man that have resulted in his favored evolutionary position are important but . . . premature attempts to apply our fragmentary knowledge in any dogmatic fashion would be extremely complex." Ellis (Ed.), Handbook of Mental Deficiency, p. 291. . . .

> In determining the reasonableness of the sterilization law, we consider private deprivation, societal benefits, and possibilities of the state realizing those benefits at a lower cost. Appraisal of goals and remedies is difficult at best and impossible without identification of the environmental elements. I cannot imagine a causality vaguer than that of heredity, environment, or both; and that very vagueness warns of menacing power over bodily integrity. Judicial review is an empty safeguard when legislative, administrative, and judicial standards of protection are as deficient as those in this case. The sterilization law denies substantive due process of law guaranteed by the Constitution of Nebraska. . . .

a. Substantive Due Process. Justice Smith's dissent observes that the key issue is whether the statute in *Cavitt* violates substantive due process, *i.e.,* is the procedure repugnant to accepted standards of fairness and decency? Using a more contemporary mode of analysis, the appropriate question would be whether involuntary sterilization violates a person's right of privacy. Since the right to procreate has been declared *fundamental* in *Skinner v. Oklahoma, supra,* any state interest infringing that right must be *compelling* in order to be constitutional. This issue arose in the context of challenges to a North Carolina sterilization statute. A federal district court found the state interest of preventing the birth of a defective child or the birth of a nondefective child that cannot be cared for by its parent to be both legitimate and compelling.[37] A state court, relying on the precedent of *Buck v. Bell,* stated:

> Our research does not disclose any case which holds that a state does not have the right to sterilize an insane or a retarded person if notice and hearing are provided, if it is applied equally to all persons, and if it is not prescribed as a punishment for a crime.[38]

On the other hand, commentators have suggested that state sterilization statutes are an unconstitutional violation of the right of privacy, with no state interest strong enough to be considered compelling.[39]

[37]North Carolina Assn. for the Mentally Retarded v. North Carolina, 420 F. Supp. 451 (M.D.N.C. 1976). For a criticism of this opinion, *see* R. Burgdorf, Jr. & M. Burgdorf, *supra* n. 33.

[38]*In re* Moore, *supra* n. 34 at 309.

[39]E. Paul, *The Sterilization of Mentally Retarded Persons: The Issues and Conflicts* 3 FAM. PLAN./POP. REP. 96 (1974); C. Murdock, *Sterilization of the Retarded: A Problem or a Solution?* 62 CALIF. L. REV. 917 (1974).

b. Informed Consent. The issues concerning informed consent of mentally incompetent persons, particularly substituted consent, *i.e.*, consent given by a person such as a guardian, parent, or superintendent of an institution, are as delicate as any considered in this chapter. Recall the traditional definition of informed consent as "understanding the nature and consequences of the procedure."[40] The difficult problem is how to apply consent procedures to persons who are not considered to have the capacity to understand sterilization or to make the decision for themselves.[41] In other words, who can consent to a sterilization for a mentally retarded person? Should it be a parent? the person him or herself? a guardian *ad litem*? the superintendent of a mental institution? nobody? Should consent be subject to review by a court or impartial committee? Allied to this is the question of what procedural safeguards a mentally retarded person should have before a sterilization based on third-party consent is performed.

(1) Consent of the Person to Be Sterilized. Whether a mentally retarded person is capable of providing consent for a sterilization depends on his or her ability to understand the nature and consequences of the procedure. Capacity to consent varies from state-to-state and may depend on the nature of the illness or the degree of retardation. However, mental retardation does not necessarily prevent a person

[40]See text at pp. 156–157.

[41]Although the terms "competence" and "capacity" are sometimes used interchangeably, they refer to separate legal concepts. A person is said to lack competence when he or she has been adjudicated incompetent pursuant to a judicial proceeding. A person may be held to lack competence over some affairs, but not others. "Capacity" refers to the ability to understand the nature and consequences of a procedure. A mentally retarded person may have been declared incompetent by a court, pursuant to a commitment proceeding, yet still have the mental capacity to appreciate the responsibilities of parenthood and the implications of sterilization. G. Neuwirth, P. Heisler & K. Goldrich, *Capacity, Competence, Consent: Voluntary Sterilization of the Mentally Retarded,* 6 COLUM. HUM. RTS. L. REV. 447, 488 (1974–75) [hereafter cited as G. Neuwirth *et al.*].

With respect to the mentally retarded, there are four distinct situations that can arise:

Person declared incompetent and lacks capacity to consent;
Person declared incompetent and has capacity to consent;
Person not declared incompetent and lacks capacity to consent;
Person not declared incompetent and has capacity to consent.

These four situations can be complicated by the person's being a minor or being institutionalized.

from consenting to a sterilization. Given the irreversibility of sterilization as well as the potential for coercion, should the consent of a mentally retarded person (or a minor) ever be considered sufficient? Should there be, in all such cases, review by a court or committee?[42]

Note that the HEW regulations specifically prohibit federal funding of sterilizations of people who have been declared mentally incompetent by a court unless they have been "declared competent for purposes which include the ability to consent to sterilization."[43]

(2) Substituted Consent of a Parent, Guardian, or Other Third Party. Under many statutes and the rulings of some courts, sterilization may be carried out without the consent of the patient if a third party has consented to the procedure.[44] That third person is usually a parent, the superintendent of a mental institution, or a court-appointed guardian.

(a) Parental Consent for a Child's Sterilization. Generally, a parent or guardian can consent to medical treatment for a minor child. However, this authority is not unlimited, and a parent or guardian cannot consent to a risky or unusual procedure which is not clearly for the benefit of the child. In the case of sterilization of a retarded child, however, it has been questioned whether the interests of the parent and child coincide. Is it not likely that the interests of parent and child would, in fact, clash? If so, should additional authorization, or at least verification that the procedure is in the retarded child's best

[42]C. Baron, *Voluntary Sterilization of the Mentally Retarded,* in GENETICS AND THE LAW (A. Milunsky & G. Annas, eds., Plenum, 1976) argues that consent of a mentally retarded person should, in all cases, be reviewed.

[43]42 CFR §§ 50.202 and 50.203 (1979).

[44]Consent of a third person is often considered to have made the procedure "voluntary" rather than "involuntary." The fiction of substituted consent has been criticized by Price and Burt in the following terms:

> The most flexible technique disguising the deprivation of rights is the doctrine of consent and voluntariness. And the most peculiar aspect of the doctrine of consent . . . is third-party consent, where the state is permitted to intervene because a person other than the subject has given approval . . . By characterizing the transaction as voluntary rather than involuntary, constitutional, ethical, and moral questions are bypassed and the violation of taboos is avoided. Third-party consent is a miraculous creation of the law, adroit and flexible, capable of covering unseemly realities with the patina of cooperation.

M. Price & R. Burt, *Nonconsensual Medical Procedures and the Right to Privacy,* in THE MENTALLY RETARDED CITIZEN AND THE LAW 94–95 (M. Kindred, ed., Free Press, 1976).

interest, be required?[45] Neuwirth *et al.* recommend that a parent's consent to authorize a sterilization for a mentally retarded child should be supplemented by a court order, granted on the basis of committee recommendation, following a hearing in which the child is represented by legal counsel.[46] In fact, many of the requests for sterilization coming before courts are made by parents of retarded daughters. The judge in a recent Connecticut case, involving three families with severely retarded and physically handicapped daughters, characterized the parents' request for sterilization as an "unmistakably . . . poignant cry for help."[47]

(b) Substituted Consent Pursuant to Statute. Where there is an applicable statute, it will define who can give consent, on what grounds sterilization can be obtained by substituted consent, and what procedural requirements are to be followed. A taste of the considerable variety can be gathered from the review of state sterilization statutes excerpted below:

> . . . All the sterilization laws provide for sterilization of institutionalized persons, but only nine of the statutes deal with the non-institutionalized mentally deficient as well. Sterilization proceedings may be initiated by application of the superintendent of the institution in which the incompetent is confined, by report from a member of a eugenics board or on the petition of a physician, guardian, relative or public agency. Grounds for a sterilization order vary from state to state, but typically they are vague. . . .
>
> The consent mechanism takes various forms in different states; in Minnesota, the Commissioner of Public Welfare, as the "legal guardian" of feebleminded persons, may give his consent to a sterilization if no spouse or close relative of the patient can be found. Connecticut law permits consent by the trustees of the institution where the mental patient is confined if the patient has no next of kin or guardian. In Georgia, mental incompetents may be sterilized after an adjudication that the individual's condition is "irreversible and incurable" with the written consent of parents or a court-appointed guardian ad litem and

[45]A much-cited analogue is the case of *Strunk v. Strunk,* 445 S.W. 2d 145 (Ky. App., 1969) where the court authorized a kidney transplant from a retarded brother to his normal sibling based upon the petition of the boys' mother who had been appointed guardian *ad litem. Strunk* has not necessarily been followed in other jurisdictions where similar cases have arisen. *See* In re Richardson, 284 S. 2d 1981 (La. App. 1973) and discussion in G. Annas *et al., supra* n. 17 at 80–93.

[46]G. Neuwirth *et al., supra* n. 41 at 455.

[47]Ruby v. Massey, 452 F. Supp. 361 at 367 (D. Conn, 1978).

approval by a committee of the hospital where the operation is to be performed.[48]

(c) Substituted Consent Pursuant to Court Order. Where no statute expressly covers the situation, courts have been asked to authorize sterilizations based on the application of a third party. Although decisions have been divided, the prevailing view appears to be that courts will not take such authority absent a specific legislative authorization.[49] The arguments pro and con can be seen in the cases excerpted below:

Tully v. Tulley, 146 Cal. Reptr. 266 (Calif. Ct. of App. 1978)

. . .The record showed that Dianne was suffering from cerebral palsy with brain damage. At age 20 she had the intelligence and comprehension of a three-year-old child. As a consequence, she was not only unable to comprehend the normal bodily function of the menstrual cycle, but was also incapable of attending to its attendant sanitary needs.

The medical testimony ruled out the probability that the severe retardation would change to any extent in the future. It was further established that although Dianne was capable of engaging in sexual intercourse, the potential pregnancy resulting therefrom would cause psychiatric harm. Based upon these facts, the medical experts concluded that a hysterectomy operation, which would remove the uterus without "unsexing" the patient, would be the right step to take and would also be in the best interest of the ward. While agreeing that the proposed sterilization would be justified both medically and socially and would serve the best interest of Dianne as well, the trial court felt compelled to deny the petition on the ground that the court was not authorized to approve or order the involuntary sterilization of an incompetent person who is unable to give her consent. . . .

To begin with, it has been widely recognized that sterilization (even if medically and socially indicated) is an extreme remedy which irreversibly denies a human being the fundamental right to bear and beget a child. Accordingly, the overwhelming majority of courts hold that

[48]G. Neuwirth *et al., supra* n. 41, at 459–461; *c.f.,* the discussion of state statutes in Comment, *Eugenic Sterilization Statutes: A Constitutional Re-Evaluation, supra* n. 29.

[49]*See, for example, In re* D.D., 90 Misc. 2d 236, 394, N.Y.S. 2d 139 (Sur. Ct. 1977), *aff'd on other grounds,* 64 A.D. 2d 898, 408 N.Y.S. 2d 104 (1978); *In re* S.C.E., 378 A.2d 144 (Del. Ch. Ct. 1977); Ruby v. Massey, *supra* n. 47; Holmes v. Powers, 439 S.W.2d 579 (Ky. 1968). *Contra, In re* Sallmaier, 85 Misc. 2d 295, 378 N.Y.S. 2d 989 (Sup. Ct. 1976).

the jurisdiction to exercise such awesome power may not be inferred from the general principles of common law, but rather must derive from specific legislative authorization. The position of case law is thus clear that in the absence of specific statutory authority the courts may not order the sterilization of a mentally defective person. . . .

The general proposition of law that in the absence of a specific statute the courts may not order the sterilization of incompetent persons, is not predicated on the eventuality whether the tribunal proceeds as a probate court or a court of general jurisdiction. As mentioned before, the underlying rationale of the general rule is the obvious concern that the awesome power to deprive a human being of his or her fundamental right to bear or beget offspring must be founded on the explicit authorization of the Legislature rather than a mere inference deduced from the general principles of common law or the canons of equity jurisprudence . . .

In re Simpson, 180 N.E. 2d 206 (Probate Court of Zanesville, Ohio, 1962)

. . . This matter arises upon an affidavit filed by Rosa Lee Simpson, mother of Nora Ann Simpson, alleging that said Nora Ann Simpson is feeble-minded. Upon hearing medical testimony, and in addition testimony of a psychologist as to the results of psychological tests which show Nora Ann has an I.Q. of 36, the court finds that Nora Ann Simpson is a feeble-minded person within the definition set out in Section 5125.24 of the Revised Code. . . .

It has also been the observation of this court that the institutions for the feeble-minded, due to overcrowding and the constant pressure of new admissions, have been forced to return to the community some feeble-minded persons who were not yet capable of caring for themselves. . . .

Nora Ann Simpson is a physically attractive young woman, aged 18. She has already given birth to one illegitimate child, and according to the testimony of her mother, and her own admission, has been sexually promiscuous with a number of young men since the birth of the child. Nora Ann is unable to give her child proper care, and it is being cared for by her mother. A portion of the medical testimony stated: "Because of the combination of normal physical appearance and serious mental limitations, this girl is likely to become pregnant repeatedly and produce children for whom she cannot provide even the rudiments of maternal care." There is the further probability that such offspring will also be mentally deficient and become a public charge for most of their lives. Application has been made to the Muskingum County Welfare Department for Aid for Dependent Children payments for the child already born. To permit Nora Ann

> to have further children would result in additional burdens upon the county and state welfare departments, which have already been compelled to reduce payments because of shortage of funds, and have consistently importuned the General Assembly for additional appropriations.
>
> The authority granted this court by the statutes is extremely broad, and should be construed, so as to provide for the best possible care and maintenance of the parties before the court, as well as for the benefit of society as a whole. It is the opinion of the court that the welfare of both Nora Ann Simpson and society would best be served by having an operation performed which would prevent further pregnancies. Such an operation, termed medically "salpingectomy," can be safely performed by any qualified surgeon. To deny Nora Ann such an operation would be to condemn her to a lifetime of frustration and drudgery, as she continued to bring children into the world for whom she is not capable, either physically or mentally, of providing proper care. . . .

Does the refusal of courts to authorize sterilization based upon a parent's petition frustrate the legitimate desires of parents who want to improve the chances of their child's living happily? How much weight should be given to the argument made in *Simpson* that denial of the petition would "condemn her to a lifetime of frustration and drudgery"? In determining whether a court should authorize sterilization based upon substituted consent, should it make a difference whether the person to be sterilized is profoundly or mildly retarded? Some commentators have suggested that mildly retarded persons, those who could understand the nature and consequences of sterilization, should be sterilized if they consented or *assented*, but the seriously retarded, who were not capable of consenting, should not be sterilized.[50] Is it not paradoxical that the most seriously retarded, *i.e.,* precisely those people with the least possibility of integrating into the community and raising children effectively, are the people who could not understand the nature and consequences of sterilization and could not be sterilized under these criteria?[51]

In 1978, the United States Supreme Court held that a judge could not be sued for having authorized the sterilization, upon request of the mother, of a "somewhat retarded" 15-year-old girl who

[50]*See* discussion in the proposed HEW Sterilization Guidelines, 42 Fed. Reg. 62718, Part III (1977).

[51]This issue is discussed in D. Hart, *A National Sterilization Policy: No Consensus, Especially for the Mentally Incompetent,* 7 FAM. PLAN./POP. REP. 45 (1978).

apparently had been having sexual relations with older youths. The girl was sterilized unbeknownst to her, having been told she was being admitted to the hospital for an appendectomy. Several years later, when she learned the truth, the women sued her mother, the doctor, and the judge who authorized the procedure. Reversing the lower court decision, the Supreme Court held that the judge had been acting in a judicial capacity and was therefore immune from suit.[52]

c. Grounds for Sterilizing the Mentally Retarded. The grounds for sterilizing the mentally retarded fall into two classifications: transmission of inherited defects and lack of capacity to raise children. The statutes generally require that the court or body authorizing the sterilizations find that the procedure is in the "best interests" of the person or of society based upon one or both of these grounds.

(1) Transmission of Inherited Tendencies. Statutory language authorizing sterilization of the mentally retarded is often vague and includes wording such as the following:

> According to the law of heredity the subject is the potential parent of socially inadequate children who would be likewise afflicted;
>
> Procreation of the subject is deemed inadvisable;
>
> Procreation would produce children with an inherited tendency to certain named conditions or that the physical and/or mental condition of the patient would be improved by the operation;
>
> The subject is afflicted with a mental disease which is likely to be inherited.[53]

The issue of whether involuntary sterilization could produce a better breed of people was squarely joined in the *Cavitt* case. Note Justice Smith's careful marshalling of the scientific literature and contrast it with Justice Carter's assertion of the old saw that "it is an established fact that mental deficiency accelerates sexual impulses and impulses towards crime to a harmful degree." In a recent challenge to the North Carolina sterilization statute, a federal district court, after noting that the nature of retardation and its causes are not susceptible to facile generalizations, observed:

[52]Stump v. Sparkman, 435 U.S. 349 (1978).
[53]G. Neuwirth *et al., supra* n. 41 at 459–60.

> Mental retardation in some cases has as its cause an identifiable genetic defect. Under some circumstances it is within the capability of modern medical and genetical science to establish that the genetic defect is inheritable and that there is a significant probability or substantial likelihood that the offspring of a mentally defective parent would also be retarded.[54]

The court went on to say that before a mentally retarded person in North Carolina could be sterilized, a petitioner must provide "clear, strong, and convincing" evidence that the retarded person, unless sterilized, would be likely to produce a mentally retarded child or would be unable to care for the child.[55]

(2) Capability to Raise Children. Another argument to justify sterilization of the mentally retarded is that they cannot properly care for their children or that the children would grow up in a deprived home.[56] Can reasonable classifications be drawn to require sterilization of unfit parents? What criteria might be used? Would such criteria be likely to discriminate against the poor? If potentially unfit parents can be the subjects of sterilization, should parents known to be unfit, such as child abusers, also be sterilized? To what extent does use of child neglect statutes provide a less restrictive approach to the same problem? Almost every state statute is broad enough to authorize compulsory removal of a child from a parent who is determined to be incapable of childrearing because of mental deficiency.[57]

d. Procedural Due Process. Assuming the requirements for informed consent are met, what procedural safeguards must a state provide if a sterilization statute is to comply with procedural due

[54]North Carolina Assn. for the Mentally Retarded v. North Carolina, *supra* n. 37 at 454.

[55]Id at p. 458.

[56]*See e.g.,* North Carolina General Statutes § 35–39; Cook v. State, 9 Ore. App. 224, 495 P. 2d 768 (1972). There is little empirical evidence to support the generalization that mentally retarded people necessarily make unfit parents. The meager literature on the subject provides no consensus on whether childrearing is beneficial for the retarded individual. *See, e.g.,* L. Floor D. Baxter, M. Rosen & L. Zisfein *A Survey of Marriages Among Previously Institutionalized Retardates,* MENTAL RETARDATION, vol. 13, no. 2, p. 33 (1975); M. ROSEN, HABILITATION OF THE HANDICAPPED 254–258 (U. Park Press, 1977).

[57]The pros and cons of using child neglect laws are discussed in M. Price & R. Burt, *supra* n. 44 at 106–107. For a comprehensive survey of American laws, *see* S. Katz, R. Howe & M. McGrath, *Child Neglect Laws in America,* 9 FAM. L.Q.I (1975).

process requirements? Litigation regarding the 1973 revision of North Carolina's sterilization law is instructive. A federal district court, ruling on the constitutionality of the statute, described the procedural protection due a mentally retarded person against whom sterilization proceedings are brought. The court noted the following procedural requirements:

> The petition filed with the district court must contain the results of psychological or psychiatric testing;
>
> The retarded person and his guardian must be given 20 days notice prior to the hearing;
>
> A hearing on the petition must be held in the district court. The retarded person has the right to call witnesses, to present evidence in his own behalf, and to cross-examine witnesses supporting the petition;
>
> If dissatisfied with the outcome, the retarded person has the right to appeal; The retarded person has the right to counsel, provided by the state in case of indigency;
>
> The evidence must be "clear, strong and convincing" before a sterilization order can be entered.[58]

Compare the procedural safeguards, which stress the role of a review committee, handed down by a federal district court in Alabama.[59]

> . . . No resident shall be sterilized unless such resident has consented in writing to such sterilization. Except as set forth below, such consent must be informed, in that it is (a) based upon an understanding of the nature and consequences of sterilization, (b) given by a person competent to make such a decision, and (c) wholly voluntary and free from any coercion, express or implied. . . .
>
> The Director [of the Partlow State School, the Alabama state mental institution] shall prepare a report evaluating the resident's understanding of the proposed sterilization and describing the steps taken to inform the resident of the nature and consequences of sterilization. If the resident has been determined by a court of competent jurisdiction to be legally incompetent, or if the Director cannot certify without reservation that the resident understands the nature and consequences of sterilization, the sterilization shall not be performed

[58]North Carolina Assn. for the Mentally Retarded v. North Carolina, *supra* n. 37 at 456.

[59]Wyatt v. Aderholt, 368 F. Supp. 1383 (M.D. Ala. 1974).

unless (a) the Director sets forth reasonable grounds for believing that such sterilization is in the best interest of the resident; (b) the Review Committee described below approves such sterilization; and (c) it is determined by a court of competent jurisdiction that such sterilization is in the best interest of the resident.

No sterilization shall be performed without prior approval of a Review Committee formed in accordance with this paragraph. The Review Committee shall consist of five members, and shall be selected by the Partlow Human Rights Committee and approved by the Court. The members shall be so selected that the Committee will be competent to deal with the medical, legal, social and ethical issues involved in sterilization; to this end, at least one member shall be a licensed physician, at least one shall be a licensed attorney, at least two shall be women, at least two shall be minority group members, and at least one shall be a resident of the Partlow State School (the foregoing categories are not mutually exclusive). No member shall be an officer, employee, or agent of the Partlow State School, nor may any member be otherwise involved in the proposed sterilization.

Any fees or costs incurred by reason of services performed by the Review Committee, including reasonable fees for the physician and the attorney, shall be paid by the Alabama Department of Mental Health upon a certification of reasonableness by the Partlow Human Rights Committee.

Prior to approving the proposed sterilization of any resident, the Review Committee shall:

> Review appropriate medical, social, and psychological information concerning the resident, including the report of the Director prepared pursuant to paragraph 4;
>
> Interview the resident to be sterilized;
>
> Interview concerned individuals, relatives, and others who in its judgment will contribute pertinent information;
>
> Determine whether the resident has given his or her informed consent to the sterilization, or, if the resident is legally incompetent or the Director cannot certify without reservation that the resident understands the nature and consequences of sterilization, whether the resident has formed, without coercion, a genuine desire to be sterilized. . . .
>
> Determine whether the proposed sterilization is in the best interest of the resident.

If the Review Committee does not reach an affirmative determination as to the matters set forth in [the] paragraphs [above] it shall not approve the proposed sterilization. Any doubts as to such matters shall be resolved against proceeding with sterilization.

Residents shall be represented throughout all the procedures described above by legal counsel. . . .

As the court notes, the composition of a review committee is crucial to its effectiveness. Suggestions have been made that at least one person from the same ethnic group as the patient be included as a committee member and that a patient advocate be appointed to represent the patient and see that his or her best interests are served.

e. Sterilization of Institutionalized Persons. Several states have enacted laws which establish criteria and procedural requirements for sterilizing people in mental institutions while remaining silent on sterilization of noninstitutionalized mentally retarded persons. These statutes raise a number of provocative issues which are being settled on a case-by-case basis. Do such laws deny equal protection to the institutionalized mentally retarded by authorizing their sterilization only? Do these laws unfairly deny the non-institutionalized the opportunity to be sterilized? Is sterilization of the institutionalized so inherently coercive that informed consent can never really be obtained?

The contention that the existence of rules for sterilizing the institutionalized but not the non-institutionalized mentally retarded unfairly penalizes those in mental institutions and therefore violates the equal protection clause of the Fourteenth Amendment was summarily dismissed by Justice Holmes in *Buck v. Bell*[60] and has never gained judicial acceptance.[61] The issue arose recently in a different context in Connecticut where parents of severely retarded and deaf children sought a court order authorizing their sterilization. A federal district court judge ruled that the parents of these non-institutionalized retarded children must be given the same opportunity to seek authorization for the sterilization of their children that is available under Connecticut law to parents or guardians of institutionalized children. The judge noted, "If the state may rationally decide to sterilize some individuals to avoid incomprehensible pregnancy, it makes shamefully limited sense to contend that the same right should be denied to others in the same situation."[62]

[60] *See supra* p. 164.

[61] *See, e.g., In re* Moore, *supra* n. 34 at 313.

[62] Ruby v. Massey, *supra* n. 47 at 368.

In the context of sterilization, courts have not ruled that an institutional setting, or for that matter that release from an institutional setting conditioned upon sterilization, is inherently coercive. However, in a parallel situation, that of human experimentation, at least one court has held that an inmate in a mental institution could not give informed consent to experimental psychosurgery because "the very nature of his incarceration diminishes the capacity to consent."[63] And, as noted earlier, the HEW Regulations prohibit the use of federal funds to sterilize institutionalized people.[64]

f. Sterilization as a Condition for Granting or Withholding a Benefit. In the *Cavitt* decision, Justice Carter concluded that it was not coercive for the state to require sterilization as a condition of release from a mental institution. Does forcing an inmate to choose the lesser of two evils—sterilization or institutionalization—take the voluntary aspect out of the consent?

Conditioning release from an institution upon sterilization of the inmate has been justified as a way of helping the mentally retarded better adjust to community life. The recent trend in retardation treatment is away from custodial institutions and towards "mainstreaming" retarded people into the community. Would rearing children make it more difficult for a mentally retarded person to adjust to community living? Is this a decision that should be made by an outside person or should it be reserved to the inmate? As the trend toward placing mentally retarded people in the community grows, so will the issue of conditioned release from institutions.

Several years ago, a number of states introduced legislation to require sterilization of mothers of illegitimate children as a condition to receiving welfare.[65] Arguments supportive of these laws were couched in economic terms (rising cost of welfare) or moral terms (alarming rise of illegitimacy). Although none of these proposals passed, similar ones are introduced from time to time in state legislatures.

g. Contraception and Abortion as Alternatives. Burgdorf and Burgdorf argue that under the legal doctrine of the "least restrictive

[63]Kaimowitz v. Wayne County, Dept. of Pub. Health, Civ. No. 73-19434-AW (Cir. Ct. Mich. 1973) discussed in G. Annas *et al. supra* n. 17 at 103–138 and 148–151.

[64]42 CFR § 50.206 (1979).

[65]For an examination of this issue, *see* J. Paul, *The Return of Punitive Sterilization Proposals: Current Attacks on Illegitimacy and the AFDC Program,* 3 LAW & SOC. REV. 77 (1968).

alternative," "before resorting to sterilization, the state . . . should be required to demonstrate that it has made available genetic and sex counseling and voluntary means of birth control, that it has explored the feasibility of temporary involuntary birth control methods, and that none of these alternatives to sterilization is workable."[66] With regard to "temporary involuntary methods," although it is more palatable, is the right of privacy less infringed if the procedure is insertion of an IUD rather than a tubal ligation? What about substituted consent for abortion as an alternative to third-party consent for sterilization? Is involuntary abortion easier to justify than involuntary sterilization? Are the state interests different? What guidelines could be drafted for aborting the fetus of a retarded person?[67] Looking at the future, Price and Burt predict that "involuntary abortion will become increasingly common for persons who are mentally retarded, who formerly would have been institutionalized or sterilized, and who are now in the community."[68]

III. INTERNATIONAL PERSPECTIVE

A. Voluntary Sterilization

1. Major Issues: H. Pilpel, "Voluntary Sterilization and the Law," in *Voluntary Sterilization: A Decade of Achievement* 142–149 (M. Schima & I. Lubell, eds., AVS, 1980).*

Many of the issues explored in relation to sterilization domestically also appear internationally. Pilpel discusses these in the excerpt below:

> Voluntary sterilization is becoming an evermore popular method of family planning, particularly when desired family size has been reached. Recent studies assert that more people desiring to limit their fertility today have used sterilization than any other single method of contraception. Yet the law on the subject has not developed with

[66] R. Burgdorf, Jr. & M. Burgdorf, *supra* n. 33 at 1032.

[67] *See* J. Schukoske, *Abortion for the Severely Retarded: A Search for Authorization,* 1 MENTAL DISABILITY L. REP. 485 (1977) for a discussion of this point.

[68] M. Price and R. Burt, *supra* n. 44 at 106.

*Reprinted with permission of the Association for Voluntary Sterilization and the author. The paper was based in part on John Paxman, ed., Law and Planned Parenthood (IPPF, 1980).

anything like the same speed or prevalence and the legal status of sterilization remains unclear in many countries. The law 1) may say nothing about voluntary sterilization; 2) may specifically prohibit voluntary sterilization; 3) may be thought to prohibit voluntary sterilization by reason of general provisions of the criminal law, *e.g.* those against intentional infliction of bodily harm; or 4) may expressly permit voluntary sterilization, in which case it usually also regulates the provision of voluntary sterilization services.

Where There Is No Law Specifically Prohibiting or Authorizing Sterilization

Since the use of voluntary sterilization for purely contraceptive purposes is a relatively new phenomenon, most countries do not have laws which specifically regulate the procedure. This is a mixed blessing. The lack of laws on the subject may encourage those interested in providing the services to do so. But equally it may make them reluctant to do so. In the large number of countries without any statute specifically authorizing or prohibiting voluntary sterilization, the operation is probably legal. In these settings the availability of voluntary sterilization would, like other medical procedures, only be subject to the laws on medical practice in general, and surgery in particular.

Where there is no *specific* provision in the law concerning the legality or illegality of voluntary sterilization, the doctrine, *nullum crimen, nulla poena sine lege* would seem to apply. Loosely translated, it means that an act is considered "criminal" only when it is specifically stated to be so in the criminal law. This precept of criminal law, common to virtually all legal systems of the world, can be applied with advantage to voluntary sterilization, so that voluntary sterilization is in all likelihood legal in those countries whose laws do not expressly forbid it.

The Criminal Law and Voluntary Sterilization

In some countries the law specifically prohibits voluntary sterilization under any circumstances as it did in Italy until the recent change in the law. Section 552 of the Penal Code, which dated from October 19, 1930, provided:

> whoever performs acts on persons of either sex, with their consent, intended to render them incapable of procreating, will be punished by imprisonment from six months to two years and with a fine from eight to forty thousand lira. Whoever gives consent to those acts being performed on himself shall suffer the same punishment.

However, relatively few countries specifically prohibit voluntary sterilization. In most the criminal law neither specifically prohibits nor permits voluntary sterilization. Despite the general precept already referred to, that what is not prohibited by law is permitted, there is considerable uncertainty on the part of family planners in many countries as to whether various *general* provisions of the criminal law could be applied to make the procedure illegal. Rather than risk possible criminal penalties, those who run family planning programs may abstain from offering voluntary sterilization services. The fear is that sterilization may be considered a form of intentional infliction of "grievous bodily harm," "assault," or "mayhem," as expressed in Common Law systems, or of "coups et blessures volontaires" (internal wounds and injuries), as expressed in Civil Law codes. Such apprehensions have a chilling effect on sterilization services.

Where Voluntary Sterilization Is Expressly Permitted

In many countries, legal uncertainties about voluntary sterilization have been resolved by specific statutes. In Singapore, for example, the Voluntary Sterilization Act of 1974 provides that "sexual sterilization by a registered medical practitioner (under the Act) shall not constitute a 'grievous hurt' within the meaning of the Penal Code." Article 262 of the Revised Penal Code of the Philippines imposes penalties "upon any person who shall intentionally mutilate another by depriving him, either totally or partially, of some organ essential for reproduction." But in an opinion dated September 17, 1973, Secretary of Justice, Vicente Abad Santos, stated that several methods of sterilization (tubal ligation and vasectomy) "do not involve lopping or clipping off the organs of reproduction of both sexes," as may be the case with castration, but "are effected by the closing of a pair of small tubes in either the man or the woman so that the sperm and ovum cannot meet," they should not be regarded as "mutilation within the contemplation of Article 262." Similar interpretations have been handed down in other countries.

The Effect of Consent

Clearly voluntary sterilization must be voluntary, *i.e.* the person sterilized must consent to it of his own free will. This necessity for voluntarism is another important consideration in determining whether sterilization can fall under the general ban of the criminal law. It offers another way of overcoming potential legal barriers. Under the criminal law in many countries, if the so-called "victim" consents, the person inflicting the so-called "injury" cannot be held criminally responsible. Accordingly, surgical procedures may be performed without fear of penal sanctions. For example, Article 24 of the Penal Code of South Korea provides:

> Conduct which infringes a legal interest shall not be punishable, except as otherwise provided by law, where the consent of someone who is authorized to dispose of such an interest is obtained."

Similar provisions are found in the penal codes of Ethiopia and Greece, as well as those of India, Pakistan, Sri Lanka, Burma, Malaysia and Uruguay, to name just a few.

On the other hand, in France, Belgium and some other Civil Law countries, the consent of the "victim" of "grave bodily injury" does not appear to free the surgeon performing the sterilization from criminal liability. . . .

The degree of confusion which exists in many countries is indicated by the fact that the general criminal laws which it is feared may be applicable to voluntary sterilization are the criminal laws on assault and severe bodily injury. If so applied, they would equate the work of a skilled physician on a willing patient under clinical conditions with a brutal assault. Such a view is clearly absurd and has been rejected in many countries. A more reasonable approach is to be seen in some African countries with an English Common Law heritage (Ghana, Nigeria, Tanzania and Zambia for example). There, voluntary sterilization is simply considered "a surgical operation," which, if done in good faith for the intended benefit of the patient, is not the subject of criminal penalties. This is a sensible way to resolve any confusion which exists in many countries as to whether the criminal law applies to voluntary sterilization.

It should be noted, not to overstate the case, that where voluntary sterilization is prohibited, either specifically or by reason of the criminal law generally applicable to the infliction of "grievous bodily harm," the actual prosecution or conviction of the doctors or patients is rare (the last known case in France occurred in 1937, and that in Austria in 1934) or unknown (Chile, Indonesia, Costa Rica, and Colombia). . . .

Trends in Laws on Voluntary Sterilization

On the whole, there is a general trend towards liberalizing the laws affecting the availability of voluntary sterilization. In many instances changes in the law apply to the whole range of sterilization services, therapeutic as well as contraceptive, either through a re-interpretation or by the enactment of new statutes.

Where laws specifically authorize voluntary sterilization, they generally prescribe certain pre-conditions to the performance of the operation. The following are examples of typical legal requirements. Most of them are designed to assure voluntarism.

Waiting Period: . . . The "waiting period" has generated much discussion in the United States of late, where regulations governing federally-funded voluntary sterilization programmes and all sterilizations performed in the City of New York now call for a 30-day waiting period. . . . Some countries have provided for shorter waiting periods. A 1972 amendment of the Singapore Voluntary Sterilization Act of 1969 reduced the waiting period from thirty to seven days. In the 1974 Act the requirement was eliminated altogether. On the other side, Denmark requires that the operation not be performed later than six months after its authorization. This is meant to insure relatively speedy delivery of the service and to avoid possible changes of circumstances. In some countries the request for sterilization is isolated from childbirth or abortion even where there is no evidence of coercion, so that the patient may have to travel far from home for both procedures and often cannot undertake two lengthy absences.

Minimum Age: The imposition of a minimum age requirement on applicants for voluntary sterilization is designed to protect individuals from reaching a rash decision with irreversible consequences, only to regret it later in life. The requirement affects the ability to consent to the operation, but it may also relate to the circumstances under which sterilization is available. In Denmark sterilization is available "on request" at age 25. Between the ages of 18 and 25 careful screening is required and sterilization is permitted, among other reasons, where pregnancy would risk the life or deteriorate the physical or mental health. Sterilization of anyone under 18 is not done unless there are "very special reasons" for doing so. In the United Kingdom in theory the age at which a minor can be sterilized is 16. In Singapore, the age requirement has been eliminated for some individuals, but is 21 if the person is not married. In countries without specific laws the age of majority would probably be the minimum age of consent. . . .

Minimum Number of Living Children: Some laws, and many government policies, require that before an applicant can be given authorization for voluntary sterilization, evidence must be shown that he or she has already a certain number of living children—5 in Panama, 4 (or 3 if the woman concerned is over 35 years of age) in Czechoslovakia, and 3 in India. . . . In many countries this serves as some sort of guarantee that the couple will enjoy the benefits of surviving offspring. Yet by the same standard it may prevent many from exercising a choice when they want to.

Spousal or Parental Consent: Since the number of children is arguably a matter of concern to both of the spouses, some laws require that prior to voluntary sterilization, evidence must be submitted showing that the spouse consents to the operation. Such laws exist in Denmark, Japan and several predominantly Moslem countries. Japan also requires a form of spousal consent whenever the person though "not legally married, possesses marital status" with the applicant. . . .

Parental or guardian consent comes into play where the individual is under age or incompetent to consent. The requirement was not designed with voluntary sterilization for family planning purposes in mind and in the past has most often been associated with eugenic or therapeutic sterilization. The question of the rules which should apply to the sterilization of incompetents and minors has been the focal point of heated discussions in some countries. While the parental or guardian consent requirements are designed as protections, courts in a few countries have adopted the view that parental consent is insufficient as a means of protecting the interests of the young or incompetent and that something more is necessary. In England courts have allowed others to intercede to stop the sterilization of minors. . . .

Facilities: Several laws specifically require that voluntary sterilization operations be performed only in hospitals or sites managed, supervised or authorized by the government. . . .

Authorization by an Official Board: Several countries require the establishment of an official board to receive, review and decide on applications for voluntary sterilization, in all or selected (*e.g.* if the applicant is under age) cases. There is no unanimity, however, with respect to the size or professional composition of the board, or the method for reaching a decision (by majority or unanimity). . . .

2. Note on Voluntary Sterilization

As Pilpel observes, the worldwide trend is toward liberalization of voluntary sterilization laws and practices. An important expression of this liberalization is the 1975 resolution of the Committee of Ministers of the Council of Europe, which states:

The Committee of Ministers . . . recommends member Governments . . . take the following legislation and administrative measures:

Sterilization

1. To ensure that persons who desire sterilization are made fully aware that in the present state of knowledge the operation is generally irreversible.
2. To make sterilization by surgical procedure available as a medical service.[69]

[69]Resolution (75) 29 adopted by the Committee of Ministers of the Council of Europe (1975) as reported in UNFPA, SURVEY OF LAWS ON FERTILITY CONTROL 98 (1979).

Much of the ambiguity regarding the legal status of voluntary sterilization is being resolved in favor of the procedure. As in the United States, it is considered as an acceptable means of fertility regulation. And as in the United States, issues respecting informed consent and sterilization practice are being resolved on a case-by-case basis.

In their comprehensive review of the world's laws on sterilization, Stepan and Kellogg observed that a key issue in many countries is whether the consent of the patient constitutes a defense to an action for assault and battery.[70] It is, of course, informed consent of the patient that makes the procedure voluntary. But how can it be assured that the consent is freely given and the person truly understands the nature and consequences of the procedure? Does it make a difference whether the person to be sterilized is literate or illiterate? A member of a minority religious, ethnic, or philosophical group? To what extent should the HEW guidelines be followed in sterilization programs funded by organizations having United States government financial support? How well does the resolution of the International Planned Parenthood Federation,[71] reprinted below, satisfy the requirements of informed consent:

1. Sterilization as a method of limiting family size is a matter for individual choice which should be made in full knowledge of alternative methods of contraception and the risks and benefits to health and welfare associated with sterilization.
2. The relative simplicity of present sterilization technology and the known minimal side effects following sterilization make it an appropriate procedure for those who have attained their desired family size and wish to choose this method.
3. In the light of current medical technology, it is recommended that male and female sterilization procedures should be regarded as irreversible at the time of choice of the procedure. However, in order to provide for unforeseen events which occasionally induce a client to seek a reversal

[70]J. Stepan & E. Kellogg, *Changes in the World's Laws on Voluntary Sterilization in the 1970's: An Update and Review,* in VOLUNTARY STERILIZATION: A DECADE OF ACHIEVEMENT 245 (M. Schima & I. Lubell, eds., AVS, 1980).

[71]Resolution of the IPPF Management and Planning Committee, adopted May, 1977.

of a sterilization procedure, such techniques should be used as to give the greatest chance of reversibility.

4. It is the individual's right to choose a method of fertility regulation without coercion. No sterilization procedure should be performed unless the person concerned has given voluntary unpressured informed consent. A counselling service and follow-up care should be an integral part of a sterilization programme.
5. With respect to incentives and disincentives in connection with sterilization, IPPF notes the following recommendations adopted by the individual participants at the Symposium on Law and Population, held in Tunis, 21st/24th June 1974:
   a. Any benefits or services provided or withheld as incentives or disincentives should take into account the value system and mores prevailing in any given society . . .;
   b. Governments adopting programmes of incentives relating to family planning should ensure that any benefits or services provided as incentives to family planning be in addition to the benefits and services to which all persons are entitled as basic human rights; and
   c. Governments should ensure that any benefits or services withheld or withdrawn as disincentives in the context of family planning do not conflict with the enjoyment of basic human rights.
6. Family Planning Associations therefore have the responsibility to promote educational activities and services intended to achieve the foregoing objectives. Wherever possible, Member Associations should include sterilization services in their Work Programmes, or secure access to other clinical facilities for such services.
7. Well-established operative procedures, accepted by the medical profession, should be used in cases of sterilization. Remuneration should be designed to attain quality care services and not be linked solely to the number of cases handled. Provision for access to facilities where reversal of the procedure can be attempted would be desirable.
8. In order to keep under review the utilization of this method of family planning, appropriate systems of evaluating sterilization services through the collection and analysis of data should be maintained or established.

An issue that has importance in some developing countries is what classes of people are or should be authorized to perform sterilizations. The growing simplicity of sterilization lends itself to being performed by practitioners trained less fully than physicians. In Bangladesh, paramedics trained for six months are doing minilaparotomies. Their work has been demonstrated to be as effective as that of physicians.[72] Wider use of paramedics to perform sterilizations raises a number of legal issues that have not yet been adequately explored. What legal and administrative changes must be made to permit paramedics to participate more fully? What classes of paramedics should be authorized to perform sterilizations and how much training should they receive? Who has responsibility to make these determinations? What are the supervisory responsibilities of physicians? What should be the liability of paramedics in case of death or serious injury resulting from a sterilization—should they be held to a standard of care of physicians or of paramedics?

B. Compulsory Sterilization for Demographic Reasons: The Example of India

Compulsory sterilization was never put into effect by the Indian government.[73] A law passed by the state government of Maharashtra was awaiting ratification by the central government when the administration of Indira Gandhi was defeated. Many commentators have criticized India's willingness to utilize involuntary sterilization as a means of population control, and it is credited, at least in part, with having brought down the Gandhi government.[74] The arguments for and against compulsory sterilization are examined in the article by Lee that follows:

[72]S. Chowdhury & Z. Chowdhury, *Medical Highlights—The Role of Midwives and Paramedics in Voluntary Sterilization Programs,* in M. Schima and I. Lubell, eds., *supra* n. 3 at 204.

[73]Sterilization as part of India's overall population policy is examined *infra* pp. 405–406. The Indian experience with mass sterilization camps is examined *infra* pp. 316–325.

[74]For analyses of India's sterilization policy, *see* D. Gwatkin, *Political Will and Family Planning: The Implications of India's Emergency Experience,* 5 POP. & DEV. REV. 29 (1979); L. Landman, *Birth Control in India: The Carrot and the Rod,* 9 FAM. PLAN. PERSPECTIVES 101 (1977); M. Minkler, *"Thinking the Unthinkable:" The Prospect of Compulsory Sterilization in India,* 7 INTL. J. HLTH. SERV. 237 (1977); *see also* Civilized Pressure but not Coercion, an Interview with Dr. Karan Singh in PEOPLE vol. 3, no. 4, p. 4 (1976).

1. L. Lee, "Compulsory Sterilization and Human Rights," *Populi,* Vol. 3, no. 4, p. 2. (1976)*

In a statement on 16 April 1976, Dr. Karan Singh, Minister of Health and Family Planning, announced the following policy on compulsory sterilization for India:

> The question of compulsory sterilization has been the subject of lively public debate over the last few months. It is clear that public opinion is now ready to accept much more stringent measures for family planning than before. However, the administrative and medical infrastructure in many parts of the country is still not adequate to cope with the vast implications of nationwide compulsory sterilization. We do not, therefore, intend to bring in central legislation for this purpose, at least for the time being. Some States feel that the facilities available with them are adequate to meet the requirements of compulsory sterilization. We are of the view that where a State legislature, in the exercise of its own powers, decides that the time is ripe and it is necessary to pass legislation for compulsory sterilization, it may do so. . . .

On 21 July 1976, the Maharashtra legislature passed the Maharashtra Family (Restriction on Size) Act, 1976, which provides:

> . . . it shall be the responsibility of every person after the appointed date to restrict the size of family to not more than three and in the case of a person having either all three male or all three female children to restrict the size of family to not more than four children and of every person who on that date has three or more children to ensure that such number of children is not exceeded, and for that purpose, every eligible person shall get himself sterilized at an approved institute. . . .

The law would, upon approval by the Union Government, apply to males under the age of 55 and females under the age of 45. Violation of the law would entail an imprisonment of six months to two years or a fine of Rs. 100 to 500. An estimated 2.2 million couples will be covered by the measure. Similar attempts to limit births through compulsory sterilization have been reported in the States of Punjab and West Bengal. . . .

But are these draconian measures compatible with human rights? Did the World Population Conference not recommend that "no coercive measures be used in family planning programs"? This paper seeks to clarify some of the issues presented by resort to compulsory sterilization, in particular its compatibility with human rights. . . .

a. Arguments for Compulsory Sterilization

(1) Coercion and Human Rights

. . . It is necessary to put coercive measures in perspective. Coercion is a means to influence behaviour. As such, it may be an integral part of a legal order making certain behaviour or conduct compulsory for the benefit of all. Since human rights are of a legal character they, too, imply or sometimes even explicitly invoke the use of coercion or compulsion to achieve certain ends. Thus, the "right" to education includes also a coercive element to help ensure that the "right" is enjoyed. . . . Coercive measures are resorted to not only in education, but also in health. Thus, from the very beginning of WHO's existence, compulsory treatment of certain diseases has played an important role in its programmes. . . . Coercion may also be implied in any specification of a minimum age requirement for marriage or child labour. . . .

. . . In the face of population explosion, and absent the types of abuse feared by Justice Douglas [in *Skinner v. Oklahoma*], can it not be argued that "in allowing children that are born to live a higher quality of life" compulsory sterilization may be considered as "reaffirming an individual's fundamental right to procreate"?

The American cases of *Jacobson v. Massachusetts* and *Buck v. Bell* are instructive. . . .

It would appear that compulsory sterilization for purposes of population control may now also be analogized to compulsory vaccination on the ground that a lack of restraint on individual fertility choice would result in a proliferation of children in a society with limited resources, which in turn would infringe upon the collective rights of other couples to ensure that their children enjoy a fair share of the society's resources. . . .

Based on the foregoing discussion, the following observations may be made with respect to the use of coercive measures to further human rights:

a. The use of coercive measures to further human rights is not necessarily incompatible with human rights principles.

b. Resort to coercive measures to further human rights must take into account the viable alternatives as well as the costs and benefits involved.

c. Coercive measures must not result in discrimination on grounds of race, sex, language, religion, property or income.

(2) Birth Quotas

Can a society limit the number of children each family can have without violating human rights? The magnitude of this problem assumes increasing proportions as our finite world is rapidly filled with people. Any long-term planning must face this problem squarely if the world is to avoid the devastating consequences envisaged by Malthus.

Since the laws of practically all countries restrict the number of spouses one can have at any one time, may laws also restrict the number of children a couple can have? What human rights considerations justifying the restriction of the number of spouses are inapplicable to the restriction of the number of children?

There are, to be sure, religious injunctions as to the number of spouses one can have at any given time, *e.g.,* monogamy for the Christians, polygamy up to four wives for the Moslems, polyandry for some Tibetans and Nepalese, and celibacy for certain religious orders. With such injunctions, however, we are not concerned in view of the human right to freedom of religion.

As for nonreligious grounds, one searches in vain for any sociological, ethical, economic or other reasons for legal restrictions on the number of spouses which cannot apply equally to legal restrictions on the number of children. The conclusion is inescapable that either both types of restrictions are incompatible with human rights or both are compatible with human rights. . . .

To be sure, there are arguments against restrictions on the number of children based on the difficulty of enforcement.

But these enforcement problems exist also with regard to laws against bigamy. The wisdom of jailing a bigamist who thus cannot support his wives and children has also been called into question. . . .

b. *Arguments Against Compulsory Sterilization*

. . . The use of coercion in the specific case of sterilization is not justifiable simply because there is precedent for and acceptance of the use of compulsion in certain education, health and marriage laws. A decision to implement a coercive policy in response to the threat posed by population growth requires a balancing process rather than discussion of the means alone. For example, it is possible to envision coercive family planning policies that would be preferred over other measures which allowed individual freedom of choice. Voluntary infanticide and perhaps even voluntary abortion would be viewed by many human rights advocates as less desirable than some compulsory family planning measures. Failure to assess the values to be protected [ends] and the full range of protective measures consistent with those values [means] produces muddled thinking and irresponsible decisions.

Coercion has been used in health and education with much restraint and then only where other means were not available. . . . Apparently, the balancing process between the desire for universal literacy and freedom of choice has resulted in a compromise compelling education of children but not of adults. In the case of compulsory treatment of communicable disease, compulsory health care has been acceptable where there is no other way to prevent or control the spread of that disease. To resort to coercion in the case of family planning, it would have to be argued that all other measures had been found wanting. This is not cogent in light of the success of voluntary family planning in some countries.

(1) Invasion of the Person

Compulsion need not necessarily be in a form that can be described as cruel and unusual punishment before it can be rejected as a violation of human rights. Sterilization can after all be performed with a minimum of physical discomfort for the patient and the psychological trauma that may result from sterilization, even compulsory sterilization, might abate as long as there were no other adverse side effects such as impotence or physical discomfort. Any comparison of sterilization with physical torture and degrading treatment entirely misses the point that the sterilization operation literally invades a person's self. If this invasion is permitted when alternative means of achieving the same goal are available, then governmental intervention will have become a greater threat than the possible consequences of population growth.

(2) Administration

Even if compulsory sterilization were acceptable on a theoretical basis, administration of such a policy would present several serious problems . . .

Balancing in the area of population policy could involve more effective sex education and increased availability of contraceptives as long as the consequences of population growth were not of disastrous proportions. In the event of a crisis, measures ranging along a continuum from absolute freedom of choice to absence of all choice would have to be considered in order to maintain the balance between the right to live and the right to choose to give life. Unless the threat were very real, however, compulsory sterilization would only be an abridgement of the right to choose, especially since sterilization is still *de facto* irreversible.

2. Note on Sterilization in India

The Lee article raises a number of provocative points. Is compulsory sterilization conceptually analogous to laws prohibiting bigamy? How relevant are compulsory education and health measures to sterilization? How serious does the population problem have to be before draconian measures such as compulsory sterilization are justified? Do noncoercive measures have to be exhausted before compulsion can be invoked? In this regard, note that only in 1974 did the Indian government permit oral contraceptives to be distributed at even a limited number of government health stations. How important is it that the government could not administer the law?[75]

[75]This is a crucial point in M. Henry's criticism, *Compulsory Sterilization in India: Is Coercion the Only Alternative to Chaos?*, HASTINGS CENTER REPORT, vol. 6, no. 3, p. 14 (1976).

CHAPTER 5

CONTRACEPTION

I. INTRODUCTION

It is an interesting coincidence that recognition of the problems caused by excessive population growth coincided with development of effective contraceptive methods. Of course, people have been controlling their fertility from time immemorial. We know, for example, that the ancient Egyptians recommended crocodile dung, honey, and a gum-like substance to prevent conception.[1] But it is only with the relatively recent development of oral contraceptives in the 1950's and effective intrauterine devices in the 1960's that control of fertility on a world scale became practicable. It is estimated that at least 170 million couples were using non-permanent contraception at the end of 1977: 55 million oral contraception; 35 million condoms; 15 million IUDs; and 65 million others.[2]

[1] N. HIMES, MEDICAL HISTORY OF CONTRACEPTION 61 (Williams & Wilkins 1936, reissued by Schocken, 1970).

[2] B. Stokes, *Filling Family Planning Gaps,* POPULATION REPORTS, series J, no. 20 (Johns Hopkins Univ., 1978).

Potts has described the arsenal of contraceptives currently available in the following terms:[3]

Coitus Interruptus (Withdrawal).

This remains the most frequently used technique for much of continental Europe. It is significant in Latin America, the Philippines and most Moslem countries, but seems genuinely less common in Hindu and Oriental societies. Many couples achieve low pregnancy rates with its use. In historical terms it has been a significant variable in demographic change.

Prolonged Lactation.

Calculations from at least one developing country show that more people are protected against pregnancy by lactation than by the very extensive family planning programme. While lactation does have an inherent contraceptive effect, and is often prolonged for this reason, it is difficult to predict when the first ovulation will occur. The woman is generally vulnerable if she uses no other method towards the expected end of lactation.

The Rhythm Method (Periodic Abstinence).

Like oral contraceptives and intrauterine devices, there are several varieties of the rhythm method. Those varieties which attempt to identify when ovulation has occurred and restrict coitus to the days following proven ovulation can achieve a high degree of effectiveness. However, a significant number of women have menstrual cycles of such irregularity that many versions of the method are unsatisfactory. It is also difficult to use during lactation and near puberty and the menopause.

Condoms.

Consistently used, condoms are an effective method of contraception and have the added advantage of not requiring medical supervision. Their use is increasing rapidly, especially in the developing world, to the extent that demand is outstripping present production.

Spermicides.

A variety of spermicides are available, including tablets, jellies, creams, foams and water soluble plastic films. Some are used alone,

[3]M. Potts, *Laws Regulating the Manufacture and Distribution of Contraceptives,* in THE SYMPOSIUM ON LAW AND POPULATION 82 (UNFPA, 1975). For detailed reports on, and literature reviews of, the various kinds of contraceptives, *see* the POPULATION REPORTS series of George Washington University (pre-July 1978) and Johns Hopkins University (July 1978 and after). Among the relevant topic headings are "oral contraceptives," "intrauterine devices," "barrier methods," "periodic abstinence," "family planning programs," and "injectables and implants."

others in combination with a mechanical barrier, such as the *diaphragm* or *cervical cap,* which acts as a vehicle to hold the spermicide in relation to the cervix.

Intrauterine Devices.

There are two principal types: inert plastic devices and those which have an active chemical or metallic addition to them. They all require a trained person to insert them. Therefore, in addition to any regulation of distribution, they raise issues relating to medico-legal responsibility.

Steroidal Contraceptives.

A variety of hormone agents will control fertility. They are mostly given by mouth, but some are available as injections, and experiments are taking place to test the effectiveness of subcutaneous contraceptive implants.

The orally effective agents mostly consist of combinations of oestrogens and progestins, but some progestin only preparations ("minipills") have been developed. The combined pills, properly taken, have the lowest failure rate of any of the reversible contraceptives. Both oestrogen and progestins, in isolation, can prevent embryonic development and implantation when given post-coitally.*

Research is now underway on such new forms of contraception as vaccines, implants, long-acting oral contraceptives, vaginal rings, and steroidal contraception for men.[4] Most of these are modifications of current contraceptives rather than development of new methods. Commenting on the potential for a breakthrough in contraceptive technology, the House of Representatives' Select Committee on Population wrote, "There is a general consensus that no truly new contraceptives will become available for at least five—and more likely ten to fifteen—years."[5]

*Reprinted with permission from the United Nations Fund for Population Activities.

[4]*See* S. Segal and O. Nordberg, *Fertility Regulation Technology: Status Report and Prospects,* POPULATION BULLETIN vol. 31, no. 6 (Pop. Ref. Bur., 1977); W.H.O., SPECIAL PROGRAMME OF RESEARCH, DEVELOPMENT AND RESEARCH TRAINING IN HUMAN REPRODUCTION: SEVENTH ANNUAL REPORT (1978).

[5]FERTILITY AND CONTRACEPTION IN THE UNITED STATES, REPORT PREPARED BY THE SELECT COMMITTEE ON POPULATION, U.S. House of Representatives, 95th Congress (1978), at 118. A report sponsored by the Ford Foundation found governmental funding of research on contraceptive technology to be woefully inadequate, noting that an adequate effort would have required \$361 million in 1976 and nearly \$500 million in 1980, most of this coming from the federal government. Less than \$120 million was spent in 1976 and 1977. *See* R.

This chapter is concerned only with reversible methods that act before implantation of the fertilized egg. This includes the IUD, which may act to inhibit implantation, and DES, the so-called "morning after pill," but excludes menstrual regulation, which is discussed in Chapter 3.

There is an extensive literature on contraceptive effectiveness.[6] The Boston Women's Health Book Collective, after reviewing the literature, provided the table appearing on p. 203.[7]

Looking at the list, it appears that an inverse relationship exists between contraceptive effectiveness and medical problems.[8] The most effective contraceptive, the pill, increases the risk of death from cardiovascular disease, particularly in older women or women who smoke, and is associated with side effects such as nausea and weight gain.[9] IUDs, another very effective contraceptive, have several drawbacks: they can lead to bleeding, cramping, or infection, which leads to voluntary removal, or they can be expelled spontaneously.[10]

GREEP, M. KOBLINSKY & F. JAFFE, REPRODUCTION AND HUMAN WELFARE: A CHALLENGE TO RESEARCH (MIT, 1976) and the testimony of Oscar Harkavy before the House Select Committee on Population in *Fertility and Contraception in America: Contraceptive Technology and Development, Hearings before the Select Committee on Population,* 95th Congress, vol. III (1978), at 570–571.

[6] *See, e.g.,* R. HATCHER, G. STEWART, F. STEWART, F. GUEST, D. SCHWARTZ & S. JONES, CONTRACEPTIVE TECHNOLOGY, 1980–1981, (10th ed. Irvington, 1980); N. Ryder, *Contraceptive Failure in the United States,* 5 FAM. PLAN. PERSPECTIVES 133 (1973); B. Vaughan, J. Trussell, J. Menken & E. Jones, *Contraceptive Failure Among Married Women in the United States,* 1970–1973, 9 FAM. PLAN. PERSPECTIVES 251 (1977).

[7] BOSTON WOMEN'S HEALTH BOOK COLLECTIVE, OUR BODIES, OURSELVES 185 (2d Ed., Simon & Schuster, 1976).

[8] The risks and benefits of the pill and IUD are comprehensively examined in A. Rosenfield, *Oral and Intrauterine Contraception: A 1978 Risk Assessment,* 132 AM. J. OB. & GYN. 92 (1978). The BOSTON WOMEN'S HEALTH BOOK COLLECTIVE, *supra* n. 7, and HATCHER, *supra* n. 6, also analyze the safety of contraceptives.

[9] For analysis and extensive literature reviews on the pill, *see* H. Ory, A. Rosenfield, & L. Landman, *The Pill at 20: An Assessment,* 6 INTL. FAM. PLAN. PERSPECTIVES 125 (1980); and W. Rinehart & P. Piotrow, *OC's: Update on Usage, Safety, and Side Effects,* POPULATION REPORTS, series A, no. 5 (Johns Hopkins, 1979). Recent studies suggest that the relationship between oral contraception and cardiovascular disease is unclear; *see* M. Belsey, Y. Russell & K. Kinnear, *Cardiovascular Disease and Oral Contraceptives: A Reappraisal of Vital Statistics Data,* 11 FAM. PLAN. PERSPECTIVES 84 (1979), and C. Tietze, *The Pill and Mortality from Cardiovascular Disease: Another Look,* 11 FAM. PLAN. PERSPECTIVES 80 (1979).

[10] *See* A. Rosenfield, *supra* n. 8; *see also,* P. Piotrow, W. Rinehart & J. Schmidt, *IUDs—Update on Safety, Effectiveness, and Research,* POPULATION REPORTS, series B, no. 3 (Johns Hopkins, 1979).

Table 5–1 Failure Rates of Contraceptives Based on Pregnancies per 100 Women Years

Contraceptive	*Theoretical failure rate*	*Actual use failure rate*
Oral contraceptives	less than 1	2–5
I.M. long-acting progestin	less than 1	5–10
Condom + spermicidal agent	1	5
Low-dose oral progestin	1–4	5–10
IUD	1–5	6
Condom	3	15–20
Diaphragm	3	20–25
Spermicidal foam	3	30
Coitus interruptus	15	20–25
Rhythm	15	35
Lactation for 12 months	15	40
Chance (sexually active)	80	80

On the other hand, the rhythm method, which produces no medical complications, has a comparatively high failure rate. Measuring the mortality risks of the methods currently available, Tietze, Bongaarts, and Schearer concluded that the safest course is use of a traditional method (condom, diaphragm, foam or jelly) backed up by first-trimester abortion in case of failure.[11]

II. CONTRACEPTION IN THE UNITED STATES

A. THE COMSTOCK LAWS AND THE GROWTH OF THE AMERICAN BIRTH CONTROL MOVEMENT

1. The European Heritage—The Growth of the International Birth Control Movement:[12] J. Noonan, Contraception: A History of Its Treatment by the Catholic Theologians and Canonists, 406–407 (Harvard, 1965).*

In the 1860's a Malthusian League had been founded in England by George Drysdale, the author of *The Elements of Social Science: Or*

[11]C. Tietze, J. Bongaarts & B. Schearer, *Mortality Associated with the Control of Fertility,* 8 FAM. PLAN. PERSPECTIVES 6 (1976).

[12]For a lively account of the origins of the birth control movement, *see* P. FRYER, THE BIRTH CONTROLLERS (Stein and Day, 1965). *See also,* N. Himes, *supra* n. 1, the progenitor of the chronicles of the birth control movement. For the history of the International Planned Parenthood Federation, *see* B. SUITTERS, BE BRAVE AND ANGRY: CHRONICLES OF THE INTERNATIONAL PLANNED PARENTHOOD FEDERATION (1973).

Physical, Sexual, and Natural Religion. This league, designed to foster contraceptive practice, did not flourish. In 1877 the first change in public opinion occurred. The English government prosecuted Annie Besant and Charles Bradlaugh for distributing Charles Knowlton's American text on contraception, *The Fruits of Philosophy.* The prosecution was unsuccessful, and the publicity was immense. In the four years following the trial, the book, which had been selling 1000 copies a year, sold over 200,000 copies. The mass spread of contraceptive information had begun. A new Malthusian League was formed in 1878, and this organization proved viable. It at once began the work of winning a hearing with the English public for contraception as a remedy for miseries attributed to over-population and "over-childbearing." The leaders of the League were also instrumental in spreading abroad the ideal of birth control. English example and influence led to the forming of "Malthusian Leagues" with the purpose of promoting birth control as socially desirable in countries such as these: Germany (1889); Bohemia (1901); Spain (1904); Brazil (1905); Belgium (1906); Cuba (1907); Switzerland (1908); Sweden (1911); Italy (1913).

Next to England, the Netherlands was of particular importance in the birth control movement. In 1875 and 1876 birth control was proposed as a solution for population problems by Greven and Van Houten. George Drysdale's *The Elements of Social Science* was translated into Dutch in 1876. In 1882, with Drysdale's help, a Malthusian League was formed. Aletta Jacobs, the first woman doctor in Holland, was a supporter of the cause. In 1881 she pioneered in a method which was a forerunner of modern birth control clinics: the instruction of midwives so that they could teach contraceptive methods in the home. In France, a Malthusian League started in 1865, but vigorous leadership of the movement did not occur until 1898, when Paul Robin founded "La Ligue de la Régéneration Humaine," a French-Belgian association with both eugenic and contraceptive objectives. Periodicals favoring contraception began to appear in the 1880's.

In the twentieth century the birth control movement became consciously international. International congresses were held in Paris in 1900; in Liège in 1905; in the Hague in 1910; in Dresden in 1911; after the war, in London in 1922; in New York in 1925. In 1927 the proponents of birth control organized a World Conference on Population at Geneva, which gave substantial impetus to the organization of population studies. In 1930 the first international clinic on contraceptive methods was held at Zurich. These international gatherings were milestones in the diffusion of publicity in favor of birth control, in the mobilizing of public opinion for birth control, and in the establishing of birth control as a social objective in the Western world.

Organized promotion of contraception also spread in more countries. In the United States Margaret Sanger in 1913 began the movement which was to lead to the National Birth Control League and then to the American Birth Control League. Sanger brought the message of birth control to Japan in 1921 and to India in 1936. In 1931, birth control societies were formed in Czechoslovakia and Poland. During the 1920's, birth control clinics, dispensing instructions on ways of controlling conception, were established in Great Britain, Germany, Holland, and some American states.

2. The Comstock Laws and Their Enforcement

In 1873, the United States Congress, in what one article has termed a "burst of Puritanical virtue,"[13] passed *An Act for the Suppression of Trade in, and Circulation of Obscene Literature and Articles of Immoral Use,*[14] known forever after as the *Comstock Law* after its chief architect, Anthony Comstock.[15] Section 148 of the Act, managing to mix proscriptions of obscenity and contraception, stated:

> That no obscene, lewd, or lascivious book, pamphlet, picture, paper, print, or other publication of an indecent character, or any article or thing designed or intended for the prevention of conception or procuring of abortion, nor any article or thing intended or adapted for any indecent or immoral use or nature, nor any written or printed card, circular, book, pamphlet, advertisement or notice of any kind giving information, directly or indirectly, where, or how, or of whom, or by what means either of the things before mentioned may be obtained or made, nor any letter upon the envelope of which, or postal-card upon which indecent or scurrilous epithets may be written or printed, shall be carried in the mail, and any person who shall knowingly deposit, or cause to be deposited, for mailing or delivery, any of the hereinbefore-mentioned articles or things, or any notice, or paper containing any advertisement relating to the aforesaid articles or things, and any person who, in pursuance of any plan or scheme for disposing of any of the hereinbefore-mentioned articles or things, shall take, or cause to be taken, from the mail any such letter or package, shall be deemed

[13]H. Abraham and L. Hazlewood, *Comstockery at the Bar of Justice: Birth Control Legislation in the Federal, Connecticut, and Massachusetts Courts,* 4 LAW IN TRANSITION Q. 220 (1967).

[14]17 Stat. Ch. 258, §148 (1873).

[15]The life of this puritanical crusader is described in H. BROUN & M. LEECH, ANTHONY COMSTOCK: ROUNDSMAN OF THE LORD (Albert & Charles Boni, 1927).

> guilty of a misdemeanor, and, on conviction thereof, shall, for every offense, be fined not less than one hundred dollars nor more than five thousand dollars, or imprisoned at hard labor not less than one year nor more than ten years, or both, in the discretion of the judge.

Section 149, written in similar language, prohibited the importation and interstate transportation of contraceptives and obscene matter.

Shortly after passage of the federal law, a number of states, including New York, Massachusetts, and Connecticut, enacted "Little Comstock Acts," similar in their prohibitions to the federal legislation. Connecticut went to the extreme of banning the *use* of contraceptives. Comstock himself was appointed a special agent of the Post Office Department to enforce the federal laws with the help of the various Societies for the Suppression of Vice. According to Dienes[16]

> . . . the tactics of agent provocateur served as his basic means for suppressing the interstate trade in obscene articles. A decoy letter would be sent through the mails by an agent acting under a fictitious name to a suspected offender, pleading for assistance from childbearing. The reply, giving further information on how and where to secure assistance and/or actual contraceptive devices, would then be used to prosecute the offender in the federal courts. Care was taken to assure not only the successful prosecution of the offender, but also the seizure and destruction of the offensive materials. Between 1873 and 1882 Comstock and his associates had been involved in the arrest of over 700 persons (258 under the federal laws); 311 of the cases resulted in convictions and imprisonment; 27,586 pounds of "obscene books" and 64,836 "articles for immoral use" were seized. Comstock would later boast of having convicted "enough persons to fill a passenger train of sixty-one coaches containing sixty passengers each and the sixty-first almost full. . . .
>
> Equally as important as the prosecution of medical practitioners for disseminating contraceptives or birth-control information was the inhibiting effect of the law. Edward B. Foote, Sidney Barrington Eliot, William Josephus Robinson were all required to delete sections dealing with birth-control methods from their medical treatises because of potential criminal prosecution. Robinson, in his book *Fewer and Better Babies* (1915), left two chapters of blank pages with the comment:
>
> > The further discussion of this subject has been completely eliminated by our censorship, which . . . is . . . as real and as terrifying

[16] C. DIENES, LAW, POLITICS, AND BIRTH CONTROL 50-54 (Univ. Ill., 1972).

as any that ever existed in darkest Russia. . . . Our censorship hangs like a Damocles' sword over the head of every honest radical writer. . . . Not only are we not permitted to mention the safe and harmless means, we cannot even discuss the unsafe and injurious means and methods. And this we call Freedom of the Press!

Perhaps the most potent societal impact of the Comstock Act and its state counterparts, then, was not their sensational enforcement, which Comstock himself frequently sought to avoid because of the publicity, but their terrorizing effect on free expression concerning, and experimentation on, devices for family limitation. . . .*

Against this background, the American birth control movement developed. Its rise did not take place in isolation from other social movements. In its early days, it was associated with various reformist and often radical movements, such as the Free Thought and the Free Love Movements.[17] Birth control was espoused by Robert Owens' and Robert Dale Owens' early experiments in communal living, anarchists such as Emma Goldman, and early proponents of the women's rights movement. Margaret Sanger was an intimate of John Reed (author of *Ten Days that Shook the World*), Big Bill Heywood (of "IWW" fame), and Emma Goldman. Many of the early radical leaders saw birth control as an element in an anti-government, anti-religious, anti-marriage war. It was only in the 1920's that the movement became dominated by physicians and became separated from its radical roots.[18]

Margaret Sanger, public health nurse, avowed radical, and fighter against Comstockery, was the originator and leader of the American birth control movement.[19] In 1914, under indictment for

[17]S. DITZION, MARRIAGE, MORALS AND SEX IN AMERICA (Norton, 1969) and L. GORDON, WOMAN'S BODY, WOMAN'S RIGHT: A SOCIAL HISTORY OF BIRTH CONTROL IN AMERICA (Grossman, 1976) examine the birth control movement in the context of other social movements.

[18]The development of the American birth control movement is explored in J. REED, FROM PRIVATE VICE TO PUBLIC VIRTUE: THE BIRTH CONTROL MOVEMENT AND AMERICAN SOCIETY SINCE 1830 (Basic, 1978); L. Gordon, *supra* n. 17 at 249–300 and D. KENNEDY, BIRTH CONTROL IN AMERICA: THE CAREER OF MARGARET SANGER 172–217 (Yale, 1970).

[19]Margaret Sanger's career is chronicled in her own writings, MY FIGHT FOR BIRTH CONTROL (Farrar & Rinehart, 1931) and AN AUTOBIOGRAPHY (Norton, 1938) and numerous biographies, the best of which is D. Kennedy, *supra* n. 18; *c.f.*, L. LADER, THE MARGARET SANGER STORY (Doubleday, 1955); P. FRYER, *supra* n. 12 at 222–243, and J. Reed, *supra* n. 18 at 67–139.

publishing a radical feminist magazine entitled *The Woman Rebel,* Sanger fled to Europe where, under the tutelage of Havelock Ellis, she was able to gain a fuller understanding of birth control techniques and to plan strategies for future action. When she returned a year later, the government dropped the prosecution against her. In 1916, Sanger and her sister, Ethel Byrne, opened America's first birth control clinic in the Brownsville section of Brooklyn. As expected, the police raided the clinic and both sisters were charged with violating the New York penal code for having distributed contraceptives. Ethel Byrne was tried first, convicted, and sentenced to 30 days in prison. Margaret Sanger was also convicted and sentenced to 30 days imprisonment. When her case was appealed to the New York State Court of Appeals, Judge Crane fashioned a judicial exemption into New York's Little Comstock Act. Although upholding the conviction, he interpreted the law as permitting physicians to give out birth control information and supplies:

> This exception in behalf of physicians does not permit . . . promiscuous advice to patients irrespective of their condition, but it is broad enough to protect the physician who in good faith gives such help or advice to a married person to cure or prevent disease.[20]

Although this exemption did not help Margaret Sanger, it did further the birth control movement by providing a legal basis for operating birth control clinics in New York.

B. Judicial Responses to Contraception

Efforts to repeal or amend the federal Comstock law or the Little Comstock Acts in the New York, Massachusetts, and Connecticut legislatures met with failure.[21] It has been speculated that one of the reasons for the failure to achieve some success in the legislatures was the schism that had developed within the birth control movement. One wing, headed by Mary Ware Dennett, advocated repeal of all restrictive laws on contraception, while the other wing, dominated by Margaret Sanger, fought for modifi-

[20] People v. Sanger, 222 N.Y. 192, 194 (1918).

[21] *See* C. Dienes, *supra* n. 16 at 88–108. As a historical footnote, it was not until 1971 that Congress finally repealed the Comstock Act. It did maintain, however, a provision banning the use of the mails for unsolicited contraceptives or contraceptive advertising. Pub. L. No. 91–662 (1971).

cation of the laws to permit doctors to deliver birth control services.[22]

In the late 1920's and the 1930's, the attention of many reformers turned to the courts. Through the 1920's, courts consistently upheld the prohibitions of the Comstock Act, even where the device or information was sent in response to a decoy letter by a Post Office inspector posing as a person in dire need of contraception.[23] During the 1930's, several federal court decisions eased some of the restrictiveness of the Comstock Acts.[24]

1. United States v. One Package, 86 F. 2d 737 (2d. Cir. 1936)

The key federal case in the early fight to permit the distribution of contraceptives was *United States v. One Package,* 86 F.2d 737 (2d. Cir. 1936). In this test case, Dr. Hannah Stone, an obstetrician and leader of the birth control movement, had been convicted of importing a package of pessaries. Although the Comstock Act contained an absolute prohibition on the import of contraceptives, the Court of Appeals for the Second Circuit fashioned a judicial exemption for doctors, saying:

> . . . We are satisfied that this statute . . . embraced only such articles as Congress would have denounced as immoral if it had understood all the conditions under which they were to be used. Its design, in our opinion, was not to prevent the importation, sale, or carriage by mail of things which might intelligently be employed by conscientious and competent physicians for the purpose of saving life or promoting the well being of their patients.[25]

Judge Learned Hand concurred, noting, however, that even though times had changed in the sixty years since the passage of the Comstock Act, Congress, rather than the courts, was the appropriate body to change the law.

[22] *See* J. Reed, *supra* n. 18 at 97–107.

[23] The early cases are reviewed in H. Abraham and L. Hazlewood, *supra* n. 13 at 222–223.

[24] *See* Youngs Rubber Corp. v. C. I. Lee & Co., 45 F. 2d 103 (2d Cir. 1930) and Davis v. United States, 62 F. 2d 473 (6th Cir. 1933). Litigation in the Federal courts and in the courts of New York, Connecticut, and Massachusetts is reviewed in Comment, *The History and Future of the Legal Battle over Birth Control,* 49 CORNELL L.Q. 275 (1964); H. Abraham and L. Hazlewood, *supra* n. 13, and C. Dienes, *supra* n. 16.

[25] 86 F. 2d at 739.

2. Griswold v. Connecticut, 381 U.S. 479 (U.S. Supreme Court 1965)

After several unsuccessful attempts to challenge in the United States Supreme Court the Connecticut statute forbidding the use of contraceptives,[26] a group of plaintiffs, including the Executive Director of the Connecticut Planned Parenthood and the Chairman of Yale Medical School's Obstetrics and Gynecology Department, succeeded in bringing the constitutionality of the Connecticut statute before the Court. In 1965 a divided Supreme Court issued its decision in the *Griswold* case, reprinted on pp. 49–57, *supra,* holding the Connecticut statute unconstitutional. Since *Griswold,* the Supreme Court has decided two major cases that concern access to contraceptives, *Eisenstadt v. Baird* and *Carey v. Population Services International.*

3. Eisenstadt v. Baird, 405 U.S. 438 (U.S. Supreme Court 1972)

Mr. Justice Brennan delivered the opinion of the Court.

Appellee William Baird was convicted at a bench trial in the Massachusetts Superior Court under Massachusetts General Laws Ann., c. 272, § 21, first, for exhibiting contraceptive articles in the course of delivering a lecture on contraception to a group of students at Boston University and, second, for giving a young woman a package of Emko vaginal foam at the close of his address. . . .

Massachusetts General Laws Ann., c. 272, § 21, under which Baird was convicted, provides a maximum five-year term of imprisonment for "whoever . . . gives away . . . any drug, medicine, instrument or article whatever for the prevention of conception," except as authorized in § 21A. Under § 21A, "a registered physician may administer to or prescribe for any married person drugs or articles intended for the prevention of pregnancy or conception. [And a] registered pharmacist actually engaged in the business of pharmacy may furnish such drugs or articles to any married person presenting a prescription from a registered physician." . . .

. . .The question for our determination in this case is whether there is some ground of difference that rationally explains the different

[26]*See* Tileston v. Ullman, 318 U.S. 44 (1943) (appeal dismissed because of lack of standing); Poe v. Ullman, 367 U.S. 497 (1961) (since the Connecticut law was not being enforced, the Court held that no "case or controversy" existed—Justice Harlan's dissent is excerpted *supra* pp. 57–58). *See also* C. Dienes, *supra* n. 16 at 148–193.

treatment accorded married and unmarried persons under Massachusetts General Laws Ann., c. 272 §§ 21 and 21A. For the reasons that follow, we conclude that no such ground exists. . . .

It would be plainly unreasonable to assume that Massachusetts has prescribed pregnancy and the birth of an unwanted child as punishment for fornication. . . . Even on the assumption that the fear of pregnancy operates as a deterrent to fornication, the Massachusetts statute is thus so riddled with exceptions that deterrence of premarital sex cannot reasonably be regarded as its aim. . . . Despite the statute's superficial earmarks as a health measure, health, on the face of the statute, may no more reasonably be regarded as its purpose than the deterrence of premarital sexual relations.

. . . If the Massachusetts statute cannot be upheld as a deterrent to fornication or as a health measure, may it, nevertheless, be sustained simply as a prohibition on contraception? . . . We need not and do not, however, decide that important question in this case because, whatever the rights of the individual to access to contraceptives may be, the rights must be the same for the unmarried and the married alike.

If under *Griswold* the distribution of contraceptives to married persons cannot be prohibited, a ban on distribution to unmarried persons would be equally impermissible. It is true that in *Griswold* the right of privacy in question inhered in the marital relationship. Yet the marital couple is not an independent entity with a mind and heart of its own, but an association of two individuals each with a separate intellectual and emotional makeup. If the right of privacy means anything, it is the right of the *individual,* married or single, to be free from unwarranted governmental intrusion into matters so fundamentally affecting a person as the decision whether to bear or beget a child. [citations]

On the other hand, if *Griswold* is no bar to a prohibition on the distribution of contraceptives, the State could not, consistently with the Equal Protection Clause, outlaw distribution to unmarried but not to married persons. In each case the evil, as perceived by the State, would be identical, and the underinclusion would be invidious. . . . We hold that by providing dissimilar treatment for married and unmarried persons who are similarly situated, Massachusetts General Laws Ann., c. 272, §§ 21 and 21A, violate the Equal Protection Clause. The judgment of the Court of Appeals is

Affirmed.

Mr. Justice Powell and Mr. Justice Rehnquist took no part in the consideration or decision of this case.

Mr. Justice Douglas, concurring.

While I join the opinion of the Court, there is for me a narrower ground for affirming the Court of Appeals. This to me is a simple First Amendment case. . . .

Under no stretch of the law as presently stated could Massachusetts require a license for those who desire to lecture on planned parenthood, contraceptives, the rights of women, birth control, or any allied subject, or place a tax on that privilege. . . . Baird addressed an audience of students and faculty at Boston University on the subject of birth control and overpopulation. . . . At the close of the address Baird invited members of the audience to come to the stage and help themselves to the contraceptive articles. We do not know how many accepted Baird's invitation. We only know that Baird personally handed one woman a package of Emko Vaginal Foam. He was then arrested. . . .

First Amendment rights are not limited to verbal expression. . . . Putting contraceptives on display is certainly an aid to speech and discussion. Handing an article under discussion to a member of the audience is a technique known to all teachers and is commonly used. . . .

I do not see how we can have a Society of the Dialogue, which the First Amendment envisages, if time-honored teaching techniques are barred to those who give educational lectures.

Mr. Justice White, with whom Mr. Justice Blackmun joins, concurring in the result.

. . . Had Baird distributed a supply of the so-called "pill," I would sustain his conviction under this statute. . . . Baird, however, was found guilty of giving away vaginal foam. . . .

Due regard for protecting constitutional rights requires that the record contain evidence that a restriction on distribution of vaginal foam is essential to achieve the statutory purpose, or the relevant facts concerning the product must be such as to fall within the range of judicial notice.

Neither requirement is met here. . . . Given *Griswold v. Connecticut, supra,* and absent proof of the probable hazards of using vaginal foam, we could not sustain appellee's conviction had it been for selling or giving away foam to a married person. Just as in *Griswold,* where the right of married persons to use contraceptives was "diluted or adversely affected" by permitting a conviction for giving advice as to its exercise, so here, to sanction a medical restriction upon distribution of a contraceptive not proved hazardous to health would impair the exercise of the constitutional right.

That Baird could not be convicted for distributing Emko to a married person disposes of this case. . . .

Mr. Chief Justice Burger, dissenting.

. . . It is undisputed that appellee is not a physician or pharmacist and was prohibited under Massachusetts law from dispensing contraceptives to anyone, regardless of marital status. To my mind the validity of this restriction on dispensing medicinal substances is the only issue before the Court. . . .

. . . It is inappropriate for this Court to overrule a legislative classification by relying on the present consensus among leading authorities. The commands of the Constitution cannot fluctuate with the shifting tides of scientific opinion.

Even if it were conclusively established once and for all that the product dispensed by appellee is not actually or potentially dangerous in the somatic sense, I would still be unable to agree that the restriction on dispensing it falls outside the State's power to regulate in the area of health. The choice of a means of birth control, although a highly personal matter, is also a health matter in a very real sense, and I see nothing arbitrary in a requirement of medical supervision. . . .

4. Carey v. Population Services International, 431 U.S. 678 (U.S. Supreme Court 1977).

The case involved a challenge to § 6811(8) of the New York Education law which made it a crime for (a) any person to sell or distribute contraceptives to a minor under the age of 16, (b) anyone other than a licensed pharmacist to distribute contraceptives to persons over 16, and (c) anyone, including licensed pharmacists, to advertise or display contraceptives. The Supreme Court struck down all three provisions as unconstitutional. That portion of the decision dealing with minors is reprinted in Chapter 6.

Justice Brennan delivered the opinion of the Court with regard to the pharmacists' requirement and advertising of contraceptives. Part I of the opinion, which concerns standing, has been omitted.

II

Although "the Constitution does not explicitly mention any right of privacy," the Court has recognized that one aspect of the "liberty" protected by the Due Process Clause of the Fourteenth Amendment is "a right of personal privacy, or a guarantee of certain areas or zones of privacy." *Roe v. Wade.* This right of personal privacy includes "the interest in independence in making certain kinds of important decisions." . . .

The decision whether or not to beget or bear a child is at the very heart of this cluster of constitutionally protected choices. That decision holds a particularly important place in the history of the right of privacy, a right first explicitly recognized in an opinion holding unconstitutional a statute prohibiting the use of contraceptive, *Griswold v. Connecticut,* and most prominently vindicated in recent years in the contexts of contraception, *Griswold v. Connecticut, Eisenstadt v. Baird,* and abortion, *Roe v. Wade, Doe v. Bolton, Planned Parenthood of Central Missouri v. Danforth.* This is understandable, for in a field that by definition concerns the most intimate of human activities and relationships, decisions whether to accomplish or to prevent conception are among the most private and sensitive. . . .

That the constitutionally protected right of privacy extends to an individual's liberty to make choices regarding contraception does not, however, automatically invalidate every state regulation in this area. The business of manufacturing and selling contraceptives may be regulated in ways that do not infringe protected individual choices. And even a burdensome regulation may be validated by a sufficiently compelling state interest. . . . "Compelling" is of course the key word; where a decision as fundamental as that whether to bear or beget a child is involved, regulations imposing a burden on it may be justified only by compelling state interests, and must be narrowly drawn to express only those interests. . . .

With these principles in mind, we turn to the question whether the District Court was correct in holding invalid the provisions of § 6811(8) as applied to the distribution of nonprescription contraceptives.

III

We consider first the wider restriction on access to contraceptives created by § 6811(8)'s prohibition of the distribution of nonmedical contraceptives to adults except through licensed pharmacists.

Appellants argue that this Court has not accorded a "right of access to contraceptives" the status of a fundamental aspect of personal liberty. . . .

The fatal fallacy in this argument is that it overlooks the underlying premise . . . that the Constitution protects "the right of the individual . . . to be free from unwarranted governmental intrusion into . . . the decision whether to bear or beget a child." *Eisenstadt v. Baird. Griswold* did state that by "forbidding the *use* of contraceptives rather than regulating their manufacture or sale," the Connecticut statute there had "a maximum destructive impact" on privacy rights. . . . This intrusion into "the sacred precincts of marital bedrooms" made that statute particularly "repulsive." . . . But subsequent decisions have made clear that the constitutional protection of individual autonomy in matters of childbearing is not dependent on that element. *Eisenstadt v. Baird,* holding that the protection is not limited to married couples, characterized the protected right as the "*decision* whether to bear or beget a child.". . . Similarly, *Roe v. Wade* held that the Constitution protects "a woman's *decision* whether or not to terminate her pregnancy." . . . These decisions put *Griswold* in proper perspective. *Griswold* may no longer be read as holding only that a State may not prohibit a married couple's use of contraceptives. Read in light of its progeny, the teaching of *Griswold* is that the Constitution protects individual decisions in matters of childbearing from unjustified intrusion by the State. 

Restrictions on the distribution of contraceptives clearly burden the freedom to make such decisions. A total prohibition against sale of contraceptives, for example, would intrude upon individual decisions in matters of procreation and contraception as harshly as a direct ban on their use. Indeed, in practice, a prohibition against all sales, since more easily and less offensively enforced, might have an even more devastating effect upon the freedom to choose contraception. . . .

An instructive analogy is found in decisions after *Roe v. Wade,* . . . that held unconstitutional statutes that did not prohibit abortions outright but limited in a variety of ways a woman's access to them. . . . The significance of these cases is that they establish that the same test must be applied to state regulations that burden an individual's right to decide to prevent conception or terminate pregnancy by substantially limiting access to the means of effectuating that decision as is applied to state statutes that prohibit the decision entirely. Both types of regulation "may be justified only by a 'compelling state interest' . . . and . . . must be narrowly drawn to express only the legitimate state interests at stake." . . . This is so not because there is an independent fundamental "right of access to contraceptives," but because such access is essential to exercise of the constitutionally protected right of decision in matters of childbearing that is the underlying foundation of the holdings in *Griswold, Eisenstadt v. Baird,* and *Roe v. Wade.*

Limiting the distribution of nonprescription contraceptives to licensed pharmacists clearly imposes a significant burden on the right of the individuals to use contraceptives if they choose to do so. . . . The burden is of course not as great as that under a total ban on distribution. Nevertheless, the restriction of distribution channels to a small fraction of the total number of possible retail outlets renders contraceptive devices considerably less accessible to the public, reduces the opportunity for privacy of selection and purchase, and lessens the possibility of price competition. . . .

There remains the inquiry whether the provision serves a compelling state interest. Clearly "interests . . . in maintaining medical standards, and in protecting potential life," *Roe v. Wade,* cannot be invoked to justify this statute. Insofar as § 6811(8) applies to nonhazardous contraceptives, it bears no relation to the State's interest in protecting health. . . . Nor is the interest in protecting potential life implicated in state regulation of contraceptives. . . .

Appellants therefore suggest that § 6811(8) furthers other state interests. But none of them is comparable to those the Court has heretofore recognized as compelling. Appellants argue that the limitation of retail sales of nonmedical contraceptives to pharmacists (1) expresses "a proper concern that young people not sell contraceptives"; (2) "allows purchasers to inquire as to the relative qualities of the varying products and prevents anyone from tampering with them"; and (3) facilitates enforcement of the other provisions of the statute. . . . The first hardly can justify the statute's incursion into constitutionally protected rights, and in any event the statute is obviously not substantially related to any goal of preventing young people from selling contraceptives. Nor is the statute designed to serve as a quality control device. Nothing in the record suggests that pharmacists are particularly qualified to give advice on the merits of different nonmedical contraceptives, or that such advice is more necessary to the purchaser of contraceptive products than to consumers of other nonprescription items. Why pharmacists are better able or more inclined than other retailers to prevent tampering with prepackaged products, or, if they are, why contraceptives are singled out for this special protection, is also unexplained. As to ease of enforcement, the prospect of additional administrative inconvenience has not been thought to justify invasion of fundamental constitutional rights. . . .

[Section IV, which concerns access of minors to nonprescriptive contraceptives, is reprinted pp. 258–306, *infra.*]

V

The District Court's holding that the prohibition of any "advertisement or display" of contraceptives is unconstitutional was clearly correct. Only last Term *Virginia Pharmacy Board v. Virginia Citizens Consumer Council,* 425 U.S. 748 (1976), held that a state may not "completely suppress the dissemination of concededly truthful information about entirely lawful activity," even when that information could be categorized as "commercial speech." *Id.,* at 773. Just as in that case, the statute challenged here seeks to suppress completely any information about the availability and price of contraceptives. . . .*

*The prohibition of advertising and display of contraceptives is invalid as to prescription as well as nonprescription contraceptives, at least when the advertising is by persons who are licensed to sell such products. *Virginia Pharmacy Board v. Virginia Citizens Consumer Council,* 425 U.S. 748.(1976)—Footnote of the Court.

Appellants contend that advertisements of contraceptive products would be offensive and embarrassing to those exposed to them, and that permitting them would legitimize sexual activity of young people. But these are classically not justifications validating the suppression of expression protected by the First Amendment. At least where obscenity is not involved, we have consistently held that the fact that protected speech may be offensive to some does not justify its suppression. . . . As for the possible "legitimation" of illicit sexual behavior, whatever might be the case if the advertisements directly incited illicit sexual activity among the young, none of the advertisements in this record can even remotely be characterized as "directed to inciting or producing imminent lawless action and . . . likely to incite or produce such action." . . .

The Chief Justice dissents.

[The concurring opinion of Justice White is omitted.]

Mr. Justice Powell, concurring in part and concurring in the judgment . . .

I

The Court apparently would subject all state regulation affecting adult sexual relations to the strictest standard of judicial review. Under today's decision, such regulation "may be justified only by compelling state interests, and must be narrowly drawn to express only those interests.". . . Even regulation restricting only the sexual activity of the young must now be justified by a "significant state interest," a standard that is "apparently less rigorous" than the standard the Court would otherwise apply. . . . In my view, the extraordinary protection the Court would give to all personal decisions in matters of sex is neither required by the Constitution nor supported by our prior decisions.

A

The cases on which the Court relies for its "compelling interest" standard do not support the sweeping principle it adopts today. Those cases generally involved direct and substantial interference with constitutionally protected rights. . . .

. . . Neither our precedents nor sound principles of constitutional analysis require state legislation to meet the exacting "compelling state interest" standard whenever it implicates sexual freedom. In my view, those cases [*Griswold v. Connecticut, Roe v. Wade, Planned Parenthood of Central Mo. v. Danforth, Doe v. Bolton*] make clear that the standard has been invoked only when the state regulation entirely frustrates or heavily burdens the exercise of constitutional rights in this area. See *Bellotti v. Baird,* 428 U.S. 132 (1976). This is not to say that other state regulation is free from judicial review. But a test so severe that legislation rarely can meet it should be imposed by courts with deliberate restraint in view of the respect that properly should be accorded legislative judgments. . . .

II

With these considerations in mind, I turn to the specific provisions of the New York statute limiting the distribution of contraceptives. . . .

B

New York also makes it a crime for anyone other than a licensed pharmacist to sell or distribute contraceptives to adults and to minors aged 16 or over. The only serious justification offered by the State for this prohibition is that it is necessary to facilitate enforcement of the limitation on distribution to children under 16 years of age. Since the Court invalidates that limitation today, the pharmacy restriction lacks any rational justification. I therefore agree with the Court that § 6811(8)'s limitation on the distribution of nonprescription contraceptives cannot be sustained.

But even if New York were to enact constitutionally permissible limitations on access for children, I doubt that it could justify the present pharmacy restriction as an enforcement measure. Restricting the kinds of retail outlets that may distribute contraceptives may well be justified, but the present statute even prohibits distribution by mail to adults. In this respect, the statute works a significant invasion of the constitutionally protected privacy in decisions concerning sexual relations. By requiring individuals to buy contraceptives over the counter, the statute heavily burdens constitutionally protected freedom.

III

I also agree with the Court that New York cannot lawfully prohibit all "advertisement or display" of contraceptives. But it seems to me that the Court's opinion may be read too broadly. It flatly dismisses, as justifications "classically" irrelevant, the State's contentions that the indiscriminate advertisement of contraceptive products in some settings could be unduly offensive and could be viewed by the young as legitimation of sexual promiscuity. I agree that these justifications cannot support a complete ban on advertising, but I see no reason to cast any doubt on the authority of the State to impose carefully tailored restrictions designed to serve legitimate governmental concerns as to the effect of commercial advertising on the young.

Mr. Justice Stevens, concurring in part and concurring in the judgment.

In Part V of its opinion, the Court holds that New York's total ban on contraceptive advertising is unconstitutional under *Bigelow v. Virginia,* 421 U.S. 809, and *Virginia Pharmacy Board v. Virginia Citizens Consumer Council,* 425 U.S. 748. Specifically, the Court holds that all contraceptive advertising may not be suppressed because *some* advertising of that subject may be offensive and embarrassing to the reader or listener. I also agree with that holding.

The Court properly does not decide whether the State may impose any regulation on the content of contraceptive advertising in order to minimize its offensive character. I have joined Part V of the opinion on the understanding that it does not foreclose such regulation simply because an advertisement is within the zone protected by the First Amendment. . . .

[Justice Rehnquist's dissent is reprinted on pp. 296–297, *infra.*]

5. Note on Current Legal Issues in Contraception

With the Supreme Court decisions in *Griswold, Eisenstadt,* and *Carey*—coupled with decisions on the right of privacy in *Roe v. Wade* and its successor abortion cases (pp. 49–66, *supra*) and a public policy favoring birth control as expressed by the Family Planning Services and Population Research Act (pp. 221–224, *infra*)—there appear to be few legal barriers to the distribution of contraceptives to adults in the United States. Currently, contraceptive distribution to adults is permitted in all states, either in pharmacies or through organized family planning programs. The degree of governmental regulation of contraceptive advertising might become an issue in the future. On a parallel line, the National Association of Broadcasters (NAB) has imposed a ban on radio and television advertising of contraceptives; the prohibition is being reviewed by the NAB. The major remaining legal issues concern the rights of minors to contraceptive services, examined in the next chapter.

C. Federal Family Planning Legislation[27]

1. Introduction

In 1942 the Surgeon General issued a policy statement permitting states to include family planning as part of their maternal-child health services and to pay for them from funds available from Title V of the Social Security Act. This was the sole venture of the U.S. Government in the field of family planning until the mid-1960s.

The first grant to support family planning services domestically was made in 1965 to a Community Action Program in Corpus Cristi, Texas, under the Economic Opportunity Act. In 1967 Congress amended the Economic Opportunity Act to designate family planning as a "special emphasis" program, amended Title V of the Social Security Act to require that states earmark six percent of their Title V funds for family planning, and amended Title IV–A of the same Act to require that states provide family planning to welfare recipients on a voluntary basis. Also in 1967, the Secretary of HEW designated family planning as an eligible service under Medicaid. During that same year, the Agency for International Development removed contraceptives from its list of ineligible commodities.[28] The major legislation in the field, the Family Planning Services and Population Research Act, was enacted in 1970.

Currently, four separate federal sources provide funding for family planning services and information domestically. These are:

[27]For a clear and comprehensive review of federal family planning legislation, *see* J. Rosoff, *Summary and Analysis of Federal Laws and Policies Relating to Family Planning, Contraception, Voluntary Sterilization and Abortion* in DHEW, FAMILY PLANNING, CONTRACEPTION, VOLUNTARY STERILIZATION AND ABORTION: AN ANALYSIS OF LAWS AND POLICIES IN THE UNITED STATES, EACH STATE AND JURISDICTION 3 (DHEW Pub. No. (HSA) 79-5623, 1978). Some of the narrative in this section is adapted from Rosoff's summary. The publication also provides a state-by-state review of applicable laws and policies.

[28]AID's population assistance actually began in 1965. In the years 1965–1967, AID population assistance was about $10 million. By 1978, it had reached a level of $160 million. R. Ravenholt, *Population Program Assistance, U.S. Agency for International Development, 1965–1978,* testimony before the House of Representatives' Select Committee on Population, table 1 (1978); UNFPA, POPULATION PROGRAMMES AND PROJECTS; vol. 1, GUIDE TO SOURCES OF INTERNATIONAL POPULATION ASSISTANCE, 1979 at 147. For a detailed review of United States family planning policy with a focus on foreign aid, *see* P. PIOTROW, WORLD POPULATION CRISIS: THE UNITED STATES RESPONSE (Praeger, 1973).

The Family Planning Services and Population Research Act (Title X of the Public Health Services Act), Medicaid (Title XIX of the Social Security Act), the Maternal and Child Health and Crippled Children's Service's Act (Title V of the Social Security Act), and Social Services (Title XX of the Social Security Act). Table 5–2 detailing some of the major provisions of these laws appears on p. 227, *infra.*

2. The Family Planning Services and Population Research Act (Title X of the Public Health Services Act)[29]

Title X has been the principal source of funding for family planning services and contraceptive research in the United States since its passage in 1970. The controversy surrounding its introduction raised many of the policy issues explored in chapter 8, particularly the effectiveness of family planning programs and whether reproductive control is a public responsibility.[30] Since the mid-1970's, it has been funded at levels averaging approximately $150 million a year, with roughly $100 million earmarked for services and the remainder for research.

[29]Pub. L. No. 91–572. The text quoted is that of the original Act, Pub. L. No. 91–572, passed in 1970. The law was amended in 1975 (Pub. L. No. 95–83) and 1978 (Pub. L. No. 96–613). The 1978 amendments included a provision requiring a broad range of family planning methods and services including natural family planning methods, infertility services, and services for adolescents. 42 U.S.C.A. § 300 (West Supp. 1974–1978).

[30]For a brief review of the political skirmishes preceding passage of U.S. family planning legislation *see* T. LITTLEWOOD, THE POLITICS OF POPULATION CONTROL 44–68 (Notre Dame, 1977). *See also* the detailed examination of the history of domestic family planning legislation in M. Holzer, *Public Policymaking and the Case of Family Planning,* unpublished Ph.D. dissertation (Univ. of Michigan, 1971). A flavor of the controversy surrounding passage of the Act can be gathered from the learned debate that took place in the pages of *Science* magazine. *See* J. Blake, *Population Policy for Americans: Is the Government Being Misled?,* 164 SCIENCE 522 (1969); O. Harkavy, F. Jaffe, S. Wishik, *Family Planning and Public Policy: Who Is Misleading Whom?,* 165 SCIENCE 367 (1969), and J. Blake, *A Reply to Harkavy et al.,* 165 SCIENCE 1203 (1969). A central issue was the existence, or lack thereof, of five million low-income women said to be in need of family planning services. This issue continued on into the 1970s. *See* J. Blake and P. Das Gupta, *The Fallacy of the Five Million Women: A Re-estimate,* 9 DEMOGRAPHY 569 (1972) and J. Dryfoos, *A Formula for the 1970s: Estimating Need for Subsidized Family Planning Services in the United States,* 5 FAM. PLAN. PERSPECTIVES 145 (1973). Another issue was that of genocide, raised by a number of black and other minority leaders; *see* R. WEISBORD, GENOCIDE? BIRTH CONTROL AND THE BLACK AMERICAN (Greenwood, 1975).

Declaration of Purpose

Sec. 2. It is the purpose of this Act—

(1) to assist in making comprehensive voluntary family planning services readily available to all persons desiring such services;

(2) to coordinate domestic population and family planning research with the present and future needs of family planning programs;

(3) to improve administrative and operational supervision of domestic family planning services and of population research programs related to such services;

(4) to enable public and nonprofit private entities to plan and develop comprehensive programs of family planning services;

(5) to develop and make readily available information (including educational materials) on family planning and population growth to all persons desiring such information;

(6) to evaluate and improve the effectiveness of family planning service programs and of population research;

(7) to assist in providing trained manpower needed to effectively carry out programs of population research and family planning services; and

(8) to establish an Office of Population Affairs in the Department of Health, Education, and Welfare as a primary focus within the Federal Government on matters pertaining to population research and family planning, through which the Secretary of Health, Education, and Welfare (hereafter in this Act referred to as the "Secretary") shall carry out the purposes of this Act.

Office of Population Affairs

Sec. 3. (a) There is established within the Department of Health, Education, and Welfare an Office of Population Affairs to be directed by a Deputy Assistant Secretary for Population Affairs under the direct supervision of the Assistant Secretary for Health and Scientific Affairs. The Deputy Assistant Secretary for Population Affairs shall be appointed by the Secretary.

(b) The Secretary is authorized to provide the Office of Population Affairs with such full-time professional and clerical staff and with the services of such consultants as may be necessary for it to carry out its duties and functions. . . .

Project Grants and Contracts for Family Planning Services

Sec. 1001. (a) The Secretary is authorized to make grants and enter into contracts with public or nonprofit private entities to assist in the establishment and operation of voluntary family planning projects.

(b) In making grants and contracts under this section the Secretary shall take into account the number of patients to be served, the extent to which family planning services are needed locally, the relative need of the applicant, and its capacity to make rapid and effective use of such assistance. . . .

Formula Grants to States for Family Planning Services

Sec. 1002. (a) The Secretary is authorized to make grants, from allotments made under subsection (b), to State health authorities to assist in planning, establishing, maintaining, coordinating, and evaluating family planning services. No grant may be made to a State health authority under this section unless such authority has submitted, and had approved by the Secretary, a State plan for a coordinated and comprehensive program of family planning services.

(b) The sums appropriated to carry out the provisions of this section shall be allotted to the States by the Secretary on the basis of the population and the financial need of the respective States.

(c) For the purposes of this section, the term "State" includes the Commonwealth of Puerto Rico, Guam, American Samoa, the Virgin Islands, the District of Columbia, and the Trust Territory of the Pacific Islands. . . .

Training Grants and Contracts

Sec. 1003. (a) The Secretary is authorized to make grants to public or nonprofit private entities and to enter into contracts with public or private entities and individuals to provide the training for personnel to carry out family planning service programs described in section 1001 or 1002. . . .

Research Grants and Contracts

Sec. 1004. (a) In order to promote research in the biomedical, contraceptive development, behavioral, and program implementation fields related to family planning and population, the Secretary is authorized to make grants to public or nonprofit private entities and to enter into contracts with public or private entities and individuals for projects for research and research training in such fields. . . .

Informational and Educational Materials

Sec. 1005. (a) The Secretary is authorized to make grants to public or nonprofit private entities and to enter into contracts with public or private entities and individuals to assist in developing and making available family planning and population growth information (including educational materials) to all persons desiring such information (or materials). . . .

Prohibition of Abortion

Sec. 1008. None of the funds appropriated under this title shall be used in programs where abortion is a method of family planning.

3. Medicaid (Title XIX of the Social Security Act)[31]

Under Medicaid, the federal government provides funds to states for the reimbursement to certified providers for medical services rendered to indigent recipients. Those states that choose to participate in the Medicaid program must provide certain generic classes of medical services[32] to the *categorically needy*[33] and may provide these same services to the *medically needy.*[34] Under the 1972 amendments to the Social Security Act, family planning was named a mandatory service that states must make available to all individuals of childbearing age, including sexually active minors. Family planning services are reimbursed by the federal government at a level of 90 percent.

Reported Medicaid reimbursements for family planning have been termed "grossly unreliable and misleading," since they cover expenditures for sterilization, contraception, and some abortions, without differentiating among them.[35] Reimbursement for family planning in 1976 was estimated variously at $71.6 million (HEW) and $97.3 million (the Alan Guttmacher Institute) of which, at most,

[31]Social Security Act §§ 1901–1911, 42 U.S.C. §§ 1396–1396j (1976).

[32]These include inpatient and outpatient hospital service, laboratory and x-ray services, skilled nursing-home, childhood screening and family planning services, and physicians' services. States may, at their option, offer other listed services as part of their Medicaid program. All states but Arizona participate in Medicaid.

[33]Generally, those people eligible under state requirements to receive welfare.

[34]Generally, needy people (aged, blind, disabled, and families with dependent children) whose income, according to the levels established by the state, makes them ineligible to receive welfare but who cannot pay for medical care.

[35]NATIONAL FAMILY PLANNING FORUM ET AL., PLANNED BIRTHS, THE FUTURE OF THE FAMILY AND THE QUALITY OF AMERICAN LIFE: TOWARDS A COMPREHENSIVE NATIONAL POLICY AND PROGRAM at 16 (1977).

$38 million was directed toward reimbursing either clinics or physicians for contraceptive services.[36]

4. Social Services (Title XX of the Social Security Act) and Aid to Families with Dependent Children (Title IV–A of the Social Security Act)[37]

Title IV–A of the Social Security Act (Aid to Families with Dependent Children) required states to "provide promptly" family planning services to AFDC recipients, including sexually active minors. The federal matching share is 90 percent, and the Act levies a penalty of one percent of the federal share on states failing to provide family planning services.

Social Security legislation was overhauled in 1975. A new title, XX, incorporated the provisions of Title IV–A mandating provision of family planning services for welfare recipients, setting a 90 percent federal matching level, and establishing a one percent penalty for failure to provide family planning services. Under 1976 amendments to Title XX, family planning was declared a *universal* service—*i.e.,* by federal government standards, a request for family planning is, by itself, sufficient evidence of need; however, states remain free to restrict provision of Title XX family planning services to welfare recipients or within prescribed income limitations.

As with Title XIX, expenditure figures under Title XX are considered unreliable. For example, HEW estimated that $52 million was spent on clinical services in 1976 under Title XX while the Alan Guttmacher Institute calculated the amount as $26.8 million.[38]

5. Title V of the Social Security Act, Maternal and Child Health and Crippled Children's Services[39]

The 1967 amendments to the Social Security Act added a requirement that not less than six percent of the appropriations for

[36] J. Dryfoos and B. Döring-Bradley, *The Hundred Million Dollar Misunderstanding,* 10 FAM. PLAN. PERSPECTIVES 144, 146 (1978).

[37] Aid to Families with Dependent Children, Pub. L. No. 90–248, § 240(b), 42 U.S.C. § 601 (1976); Grants to States for Services, Pub. L. No. 94–120 §3, 42 U.S.C. §1397 (1976). The key clause is 42 U.S.C. 602(a)(15).

[38] J. Dryfoos and B. Döring-Bradley, *supra* n. 36 at 145.

[39] Maternal and Child Health and Crippled Children's Sevices, Pub. L. No. 90-248, § 301, 42 U.S.C. 702 (1976).

maternal and child health under Title V be allocated for family planning services. Grants are made to states on the basis of both matching and a formula. The federal government was estimated to have provided $25 million in 1977. Since abortion is excluded under the Act, the money was used for contraception and female sterilization.

6. Family Planning as Part of Federal Benefits

The Indian Health Service Act, the Uniformed Services Act, the Comprehensive Employment and Training Act, and the Migrant Health and Community Health Centers all offer family planning as part of a more comprehensive benefit package. The Health Maintenance Act includes family planning among the services to be furnished by HMOS.[40]

7. Assessment of U.S. Family Planning Programs

a. A. Torres, "Organized Family Planning Services in the United States, 1968–1976," 10 *Family Planning Perspectives* 83 (1978).*

> In 1976, an estimated 4.1 million women were served by the organized family planning program in the United States—more than four times the number served in 1968, when substantial federal funding was initiated ... During the first five years, stimulated by increases in federal project grants, the program grew rapidly; the annual rate of increase in the number of patients served rose steadily, from 24 percent in 1969 to 38 percent in 1972. Since then, the program has continued to grow, although at a diminished rate. By 1976, the rate of growth was down to four percent. . . . Services were provided by an estimated 3,112 hospitals, health departments, Planned Parenthood affiliates and such other agencies as free clinics, neighborhood health centers and community action agencies. . . . The proportion served in hospitals [decreased] from 26 percent of all patients in 1969 to 14 percent of patients in 1976 and [those] that received services from health departments [increased] from 33 percent to 42 percent. Planned Parenthood provided services to 25 percent of all patients in 1969 compared to 27 percent in 1976, and all other agencies served 16 percent in 1969 and 17 percent in the latest year. . . . Nearly nine out of every 10 clinic patients—or 3.6 million—had low or marginal

[40]These are discussed in DHEW, *supra* n. 27.

*Reprinted with permission from FAMILY PLANNING PERSPECTIVES, vol. 10, no. 2 (1978).

Table 5–2 Major U.S. Laws Under Which Family Planning Services and Information Provided*

Law	*Eligibility requirements*	*Funding mechanism and federal matching share*	*Services provided*
Family Planning Services and Population Research. Title X of the Public Health Services Act	Open to "All persons." Priority to low-income individuals.	Generally project grants; some formula grants. Federal matching share can be no less than 90% unless it was less than 90% prior to 1975. In that case, it may continue at that level or be higher.	Medical, social, informational and educational, coordination referral and other services ancillary to the delivery of a "broad range of medically approved methods of family planning including the rhythm method," diagnosis and treatment of infertility. Act specifically excludes abortion.
Maternal and Child Health. Title V of Social Security Act	No income requirements. At states' and programs' option.	One half of the funds appropriated must be matched dollar for dollar (Fund A). The other half (Fund B) is allocated to states on the basis of a formula established by law.	A variety of medically approved methods of family planning, including the rhythm method, surgical procedures for voluntary sterilization, and either service or referral of infertility.
Medicaid. Title XIX of Social Security Act	States must provide to all recipients of federally-aided cash assistance ("categorically needy") including sexually active minors and may provide to others within federal statutory limits ("medically needy").	Reimbursement at 90% level for services defined by states as "family planning." Otherwise, federal government reimburses the states on the basis of a formula under which federal share ranges from 50% to 83%.	Not defined. Under Title XIX, all states pay for all contraceptive services, except Missouri, which excludes drugs and devices.
Social Services. Title XX of Social Security Act	States must provide to recipients of federally-aided, cash assistance, including sexually active minors and may provide to others. A "universal" service with no federal eligibility criteria.	Reimbursement for family planning services at 90% level.	Regulations define services as counseling, educational and medical services. However, some states define family planning as consisting of only education and counseling and assume medical services will be provided under Title XIX.

*Adapted from DHEW, *supra* n. 27.

incomes in 1976, compared to about eight out of 10—or 2.6 million—in 1973. . . . An estimated 600,000 of the low-income women in 1976 were welfare or Medicaid recipients, up 28 percent from 470,000 in 1973.

More patients in organized family planning programs are young and have lower parity than in the early years of the program. The proportion of all patients below age 20 increased from an estimated 20 percent in 1969 to 28 percent in 1976. . . . Among new patients, the proportion below age 20 rose steadily, from 26 percent in 1969 to 40 percent in 1975, at which level it remained in 1976. . . . In both 1972 and 1976 approximately one-half of the new patients had used no method or less effective methods before clinic enrollment; while about four out of five chose the most effective methods after enrollment. The change to more effective methods has been most striking among adolescents—from two-thirds with no previous method or a less effective method to more than four-fifths using the pill or IUD at first visit. . . . The most effective methods continue to be the overwhelming choice of all women in the organized program, although there have been changes in the method mix. Oral contraceptives remain the method of choice—67 percent used pills at their last visit to a clinic during 1976—followed by the IUD, which was chosen by 10 percent. Only two percent obtained sterilizations via the family planning program; however, this small proportion does not reflect the method's actual popularity, since most clinics do not provide sterilizations, but instead refer patients to other services, such as hospitals, and private physicians. Fewer than 15 percent of women chose the less effective methods. Seven percent of clients received no contraceptive method; they were referred elsewhere for sterilization or other services, or were pregnant or trying to become pregnant, or were being assisted with problems of infertility.

The proportion using the pill and IUD has decreased each year since 1972, from 86 percent down to 77 percent. . . . Sterilization, an irreversible surgical method, is more likely to be used for contraception by older women. . . . However, while increasingly more women have obtained sterilizations in organized family planning clinics, they still account for only a negligible proportion of all patients. . . . Between 1972 and 1976, use of diaphragm, foam and condom among clinic patients nearly doubled. Collectively, the three methods accounted for 13 percent of all patients in 1976, compared to seven percent in 1972. . . . The data show a high proportion of new clinic patients in each year (from 49 percent in 1972 to 53 percent in 1976) who had transferred from a private physician or another clinic. An unknown number of clinic patients in each year presumably moved on to a private physician. The data suggest that a principal function of the organized family planning program in recent years has been to maintain continuity of care for a highly mobile family planning target population, as well as to introduce effective medical methods of contraception to women, a growing number of whom are teenagers. A higher proportion of teenagers than of older women use less effective methods or none at all prior to obtaining services from the organized program . . .

An estimated 9.9 million women with family incomes below 200 percent of the federal poverty index were in need of family planning services in 1976; 5.8 million of them (59 percent) were served, 3.6 million (37 percent) by organized programs and an estimated 2.2 million (22 percent) by private physicians. Forty-one percent did not receive services from either source. The question about source or method of contraception among these women remains unanswered. Some may be patients of private physicians and organized clinics who are continuing to use highly effective methods but do not make annual visits to a clinic or private physician. Others may be using drugstore methods effectively. . . .

b. Note on Contraceptive Use and Family Planning Programs in the United States. Fertility in the United States declined dramatically during the 1960's and is now at an all time low—below "replacement level."[41] Westoff, having examined the decline in marital fertility, concluded that it was associated almost entirely with the reduction of unplanned fertility attributable to the wide diffusion of effective birth control technology. He noted that by 1975 nine out of ten women of reproductive age either were using contraception or were pregnant, that three out of four couples using contraception were using an effective mechanism, that the unwanted fertility of black women and white women was tending to converge, and that, except for sterilization, Catholic and non-Catholic birth control practices were very similar.[42]

Cutright and Jaffe have explored the effect of the U.S. family planning program on fertility, concentrating particularly on income and racial variables. They found that independent of other social and

[41]FERTILITY AND CONTRACEPTION IN THE UNITED STATES, *supra* n. 5 at 1.

[42]C. Westoff, *The Decline of Unplanned Births in the United States,* 191 SCIENCE 38 (1976); *The Yield of the Imperfect: The 1970 National Fertility Study,* 12 DEMOGRAPHY 573 (1975);——E. Jones, *Contraception and Sterilization in the United States, 1965–1975,* 9 FAM. PLAN. PERSPECTIVES 153 (1977), ——E. Jones, *The Secularization of U.S. Catholic Birth Control Practices,* 9 FAM. PLAN PERSPECTIVES 203 (1977). *See also* K. Ford, *Contraceptive Use in the United States, 1973–1976,* 10 FAM. PLAN. PERSPECTIVES 264 (1978).

demographic factors, the U.S. family planning program has reduced the fertility of low-income women. They observed that the decline in fertility throughout the entire population has been most pronounced among disadvantaged minorities and low-income groups and suggested that, if all low-income women were enrolled in the program, traditional socioeconomic fertility differences would disappear.[43]

D. Regulation of Contraceptives: The Food and Drug Administration

1. Background

Contraceptive drugs and devices in the United States are regulated by the federal Food and Drug Administration (FDA), the agency charged with administering the Food, Drug, and Cosmetic Act.[44] Originally passed in 1906 as the Pure Food and Drugs Act, the law was substantially amended in 1938, 1962, and 1976. The original Act prohibited the adulteration or misbranding of drugs. After a toxic elixir, marketed without previous testing, had been found to have caused more than 100 deaths, Congress passed the 1938 amendments to the Act. Among other provisions, the 1938 amendments required manufacturers to test new drugs for safety before they could be marketed. In 1962, on the heels of the well-publicized thalidomide tragedy, Congress passed sweeping amendments which, *inter alia,* required manufacturers of new drugs to demonstrate their effectiveness, as well as their safety, to the satisfaction of the FDA. The 1976 amendments gave the FDA considerably expanded authority to regulate the marketing of medical devices, including intrauterine devices.

The FDA can regulate drugs and devices both before they are marketed and after. Before a new hormonal contraceptive can be

[43]P. Cutright & F. Jaffe, *Family Planning Program Effects on the Fertility of Low-income U.S. Women,* 8 FAM. PLAN. PERSPECTIVES 100 (1976). For a comprehensive overview of the program from its inception, *see* J. Dryfoos, *The United States National Family Planning Program, 1968–1974,* 7 STUDIES IN FAM. PLAN. 80 (1976). The administration of Title X is reviewed in D. McFarlane, *The Odyssey of Title X: From Congress to the Clinics* (paper presented at the annual meeting of the APHA, 1979).

[44]21 U.S.C. § 301 *et. seq.* For historical reviews of the Food, Drug, and Cosmetic Act, *see* M. MINTZ, THE THERAPEUTIC NIGHTMARE (Houghton Mifflin, 1965); J. Sadusk, Jr., *Drugs and the Public Safety,* 65 ANNALS OF INTERNAL MEDICINE 849 (1966); W. Janssen, *The U.S. Food and Drug Law: How It Came; How It Works,* 35 FOOD, DRUG, COS. L.J. 132 (1980).

approved for marketing, it must undergo toxicity and efficacy studies in both animals and humans.[45] The manufacturer must first submit to the FDA a "Notice of Claimed Investigational Exemption for a New Drug" (IND). The new drug undergoes 90-day toxicity studies in rats, dogs, and monkeys before initial (phase I) testing on a few human subjects for up to ten days. This is followed by one-year toxicity studies in rats, dogs, and monkeys and then phase II of human testing which, in the case of hormonal contraceptives for women, consists of investigation involving approximately 50 women for three menstrual cycles. Next, two year studies on dogs, rats, and monkeys (measuring fertility and general reproductive performance, teratogenic effects, and perinatal and postnatal effects) are conducted. When these have been completed, and seven-year dog and ten-year monkey studies have been initiated, the final stage (phase III) of human testing can begin. In phase III at least 200 subjects must have completed two years of continuous use. When this clinical investigation is complete and the results are satisfactory to the manufacturer, it may submit a New Drug Application (NDA) for approval to market the drug to the FDA. The FDA reviews the application and, based on a judgment of the risks and benefits, approves or rejects the marketing of the drug. Once a contraceptive has been approved for marketing, the manufacturer must keep records and report to the FDA on its safety and effectiveness. In the case of IUDs, post marketing surveys and reports are required by the FDA.[46] In addition, the FDA monitors the safety and effectiveness of approved contraceptives by means of spontaneous reports, case control or prospective studies, and literature reviews and professional meetings. Review and evaluation are carried out by the FDA staff and consultants, or by advisory committees. The Obstetrics and Gynecology Advisory

[45]Pre-market testing requirements are critically analyzed in C. Djerassi, *Birth Control After 1984,* 169 SCIENCE 941 (1970) and THE POLITICS OF CONTRACEPTION (Norton, 1979). Djerassi estimated a lead time of 17 years before a new hormonal contraceptive could be marketed. The FDA requirements for testing and approval of new contraceptives are more stringent than for other drugs, a policy that has been criticized. *See* R. Greep *et. al., supra* n. 5 at 352–355 and testimony of Syntex president W. N. Hubbard before the U.S. House of Representatives Select Committee on Population, in *Fertility and Contraception in America: Contraceptive Technology and Development, Hearings before the Select Committee on Population, vol.* 3, 486–515 (1978).

[46]FERTILITY AND CONTRACEPTION IN THE UNITED STATES: REPORT PREPARED BY THE 95TH CONGRESS, SELECT COMMITTEE ON POPULATION, U.S. HOUSE OF REPRESENTATIVES 116 (1978).

Committee is active in evaluating safety and effectiveness of contraceptives.[47]

When the FDA needs to take specific action with regard to a contraceptive on the market, various options are available: it may (1) require labeling for consumers (as in the case of oral contraceptives, DES, and IUDs) or (2) remove the product from the market. It may also issue press releases or inform health professionals through its *Drug Bulletin.*[48]

Although the jurisdiction of the FDA encompasses only the United States, its decisions affect foreign countries as well. The U.S. government will not export contraceptive drugs not approved by the FDA for use domestically.[49] This became an issue in the case of the injectable contraceptive, Depo-Provera. Additionally, many countries make decisions about marketing drugs locally based on clinical trials in the United States and determinations of the Food and Drug Administration.

2. The FDA and Contraception

a. Depo-Provera (Medroxyprogesterone acetate). The Food and Drug Administration has followed an ambivalent course with respect to the marketability of Depo-Provera, a long-acting (3-month) injectable. The drug was approved for use in treating endometrial cancer in 1960 and its use as a contraceptive has been under consideration by the FDA since 1963. In September 1974, the FDA, on the recommendation of its Obstetrics and Gynecology Advisory Committee, approved the use of Depo-Provera as a contraceptive. However, because of its potential risks, the FDA limited its use to women provided with a patient insert and recommended its use only for women who had completed childbearing (Depo-Provera is associated with amenorrhea) or who were unable to use other contraceptives.[50] A month later, after Congressman L. H. Fountain, chairman of the House Intergovernmental Relations Subcommittee, ques-

[47]E. Ortiz, *The Role of the Regulatory Agency in Drug Development,* in RISKS, BENEFITS, AND CONTROVERSIES IN FERTILITY CONTROL 12–16 (J. Sciarra, G. Zatuchni, & J. Speidel, eds., Harper & Row, 1978).

[48]*Id.* at 15–16.

[49]This is a policy of the U.S. Agency for International Development. According to the Food, Drug, and Cosmetic Act, drugs and devices not approved for marketing in the United States can be exported under certain conditions. 21 U.S.C. § 381 (d). (1976).

[50]39 Fed. Reg. 32907 (1974).

tioned the safety of the drug, particularly its potential linkage with cervical cancer, this decision was reversed and the FDA agreed to review the matter further. After three and one-half years of study and despite two recommendations to the contrary from its own Obstetrics and Gynecology Advisory Committee, the FDA, in March 1978, turned down the New Drug Application of the Upjohn Company, the manufacturer of Depo-Provera, citing four primary reasons: (a) a possible link with cancer as demonstrated in studies of beagle dogs; (b) a possible risk of congenital malformations of the fetus of women exposed to the drug during pregnancy; (c) an increased risk to health in women given dosages of estrogen, used to counteract irregular bleeding caused by Depo-Provera; and (d) a small population in need of Depo-Provera. The most important of these considerations was the possible link with cancer, a link perhaps also found in ten-year studies of monkeys.[51] In his letter to the Upjohn Company, FDA Commissioner Donald Kennedy emphasized that the decision was based upon United States data and may not be appropriate for other countries. Nonetheless, the U.S. Agency for International Development will not export drugs not approved for use in the United States, and, as a result, has ceased shipping the Depo-Provera overseas, even to countries that had requested it based on their own perception of their needs.

Supporters of the use of Depo-Provera observe that because beagles are especially prone to develop breast tumors, they are not a good model for a human response; that the drug has been extensively utilized around the world in humans, without any deaths being reported from its use; that it is in great demand wherever it has been offered, and that its use-effectiveness is very high.[52] The FDA's rejection of Depo-Provera raises a number of important issues, some of them technical, others more theoretical. How much reliance

[51]The history of the FDA's position regarding Depo-Provera is recounted in D. Maine, *Depo: The Debate Continues,* 10 FAM. PLAN. PERSPECTIVES 342 (1978) and R. Gold & P. Willson, *Depo-Provera: New Developments in a Decade-Old Controversy,* 13 FAM. PLAN. PERSPECTIVES 35 (1981). A WHO Task Force studying the effect of Depo-Provera on monkeys concluded that there was no reason to discontinue the use of Depo-Provera in national family planning programs. WHO, Statement on the Oct. 15–17, 1979, Meeting of the Toxicology Review Panel Task Force on Long-Acting Systemic Agents for Fertility Regulation (1979).

[52]*See e.g.,* A. Rosenfield, *Injectable Long-Acting Protestogen Contraception: A Neglected Modality,* 120 AM. J. OB. GYN. 537 (1974). *See also* Ad Hoc Consultative Panel on Depot Medroxyprogesterone Acetate, *Report to USAID of the Ad Hoc Consultative Panel on Depot Medroxyprogesterone Acetate* (1980).

should be placed on animal studies? How much weight should be given the failure to discover any human deaths caused by Depo-Provera? On what grounds should the FDA reject the advice of its own Ob/Gyn Advisory Committee? Should drugs not approved for use in the United States be exported by the U.S. government? If your answer is "yes," how do you answer the charge that this makes second-class users out of foreign women, particularly since most contraceptives are sent to developing countries? If your answer is "no," how do you respond to the accusation that failure to respond to other countries' requests, often on the basis of studies on their own populations, is a form of U.S. paternalism, or even imperialism?

b. Oral Contraception. The FDA approved marketing of the first oral contraceptive, Enovid, in 1960. Since that time, of course, the Pill has become enormously popular. Because of the widespread use of the drug by healthy women for long periods of time and the popular awareness of the health risks of orals, the FDA has required that each cycle of pills contain a written informational insert ("patient package insert"). The FDA first required a package insert informing women of the nature of the drug and the need for medical supervision in 1970. The regulations were amended in 1975 to include a statement that oral contraception was of no value in preventing or treating venereal disease. In 1979 the federal regulations were again amended, this time to include far more detailed information on the effectiveness, contra-indications, and possible side effects of birth control pills, as well as a comparison of the risks associated with other methods and with pregnancy.[53] The FDA also requires that manufacturers of oral contraception furnish detailed information to physicians, including new medical findings on the Pill.

In addition to its labelling requirements, the FDA also reviews applications for new oral contraceptives and monitors those already on the market. Three manufacturers of "sequential" birth control pills (which contained estrogen alone, as compared with the more common combined estrogen-progestogen-or the progestogen-only "mini-pill") withdrew their products from the market after the FDA found that sequentials posed an unnecessary potential risk in comparison to other birth control pills.[54]

The package inserts required by the FDA raise a number of legal and policy issues. Does it interfere with the doctor-patient

[53]21 C.F.R. 310.501 (1979).
[54]FOOD DRUG COS. L. REP. (CCH) ¶ 41,589 [1976].

relationship, depriving the doctor of the role of prescribing what he or she thinks is best for the patient? Does the widespread use of contraceptives by healthy women, plus the risks of orals, justify singling out contraceptives for package inserts? To what extent does the package insert reduce the possibility of a successful suit against a drug company for serious side effects on the grounds that the user was well-informed and assumed the risk?

c. Intrauterine Devices (IUDs). In 1976, partly as a result of publicity given to a number of deaths associated with the Dalkon Shield IUD,[55] Congress passed the Medical Device Amendment to the Food, Drug, and Cosmetic Act.[56] Before passage of the amendment, the FDA had authority to regulate devices, including IUDs, only after they appeared on the market. It did not have pre-market regulatory authority, as it did in the case of drugs, although, to circumvent this, the FDA classified metal-bearing IUDs, such as the Copper-T, as "drugs" and required pre-market testing.

The 1976 amendments divide devices intended for human use into three classes. Class I, "General Controls," are those devices for which pre-market clearance or specific performance standards are not required to assure their safety and effectiveness, devices whose safety and effectiveness can be assured under the other provisions of the Act, such as those relating to adulteration, misbranding, registration, notification and repair, and good manufacturing practice. Class

[55]At least 14 deaths were associated with septic abortions by women with an IUD *in situ.* In June 1974, the A. H. Robins Company voluntarily withdrew the Dalkon Shield from the market. In December 1974, after review by an *ad hoc* Advisory Committee on Obstetrics and Gynecology, the FDA permitted limited distribution of the Dalkon Shield to carefully controlled and registered women for the purpose of obtaining more information on the device's safety. The Dalkon Shield was subsequently removed from the market. Damage suits against A. H. Robins have largely been consolidated into one action which is still pending. For an examination of the issues in the suits against the A. H. Robins company, *see* J. Van Dyke, *The Dalkon Shield: A "Primer" in IUD Liability,* 6 WEST. ST. UNIV. L. REV. 1 (1978).

[56]Medical Device Amendments of 1976, Pub. L. No. 94–295, 21 U.S.C. §§ 360c–360k (1976). For analysis of the Medical Device Amendments *see* J. Geller, *The Medical Device Amendments of 1976—Major Features and Comparisons,* 31 FOOD, DRUG, COS. L.J. 424 (1976) and Note, *Food and Drug Administration—Medical Devices Amendments to the Food, Drug, and Cosmetic Act Gives the FDA the Power to Regulate the Manufacture and Use of Medical Devices through Recommendations by Expert Panels—21 U.S.C.A. §§ 360c–360j (West Supp. 1977),* 50 TEMPLE L.Q. 1105 (1977); S. Patton, *Consumer Protection and the Medical Device Amendments: Assessing the Gains,* 9 ENVIRON. L. REV. 519 (1979).

II, "Performance Standards," includes devices for which general controls authorized by the Food, Drug, and Cosmetic Act are insufficient to assure safety and effectiveness and for which standards of performance can be established. According to the Act, a standard is intended to provide assurances of safe and effective performance, including provisions concerning construction and components of a device, testing, measurement of performance, and restrictions on sale. Condoms and diaphragms have been categorized as Class II drugs. Class III, "Premarket Approval," includes devices whose safety and effectiveness can not be assured by either general controls or performance standards and which are "purported or represented to be for use in supporting or sustaining human life or for a use which is of substantial importance in preventing impairment of human health or presents a potential unreasonable risk of illness or injury." The Act and draft regulations set forth detailed guidelines for premarket clearance.[57] IUDs made from inert materials have been classified as Class III Devices.[58] In 1977 the FDA issued regulations establishing uniform labeling for IUDs.[59] These require that each patient be given a detailed patient information brochure before having an IUD inserted.

d. Other Contraceptives. The FDA permits the use of diethylstilbestrol (DES—the so-called "morning after pill") only in cases of emergency.[60] When When the drug was initially approved for post-coital use in 1975, it was given "the most narrowly limited approval of a drug in FDA history. The approval requires that there be fully informed written consent from every person who uses the drug, that it be specially packaged for this use, and that it carry virtually every form of dire warning that could be written."[61] To date, no manufacturer has had a NDA approved by the FDA, so that, technically,

[57]For a critical commentary on the draft HEW guidelines, *see* M. Bozeman, *The Clinical Investigation of Medical Devices—A Preliminary Guide for Manufacturers,* 34 FOOD, DRUG, COS. L. J. 289 (1979).

[58]The FDA's policy of treating metalicized or medicated IUDs as "drugs" is unchanged by passage of the Medical Device Amendments. Thus, a new copper-bearing IUD could not be marketed until the FDA had approved a New Drug Application for the product, whereas a new IUD made from an inert substance would have to receive approval as a *device* before marketing. *See* FDA, MEDICAL DEVICE AND DRUG ADV. COMM. ON OB. & GYN., SECOND REPORT ON INTRAUTERINE CONTRACEPTIVE DEVICES (1978).

[59]21 C.F.R. 310.502 (1979).

[60]FDA approval, and restrictions on the use, of DES are contained in 21 C.F.R. 310.501 (1979).

[61]P. Hutt, T. Jukes, & R. Hertz, *DES: FDA and the Law,* 4 ORIG. HUMAN CANCER 1651 (1977).

DES is not available on the American market as a postcoital contraceptive.

Condoms and diaphragms are considered as Class II devices, subject to performance standards, but not premarket clearance. The FDA has regulated condoms since the 1930's, requiring that the prophylactics be subjected to a pin hole test on a 100% basis.[62] The FDA also regulates over-the-counter contraceptives such as vaginal foams and suppositories. A panel of experts recently issued a report suggesting that the FDA needed to give more emphasis to the safety and effectiveness of these contraceptives.[63]

III. INTERNATIONAL PERSPECTIVE

A. Overview

According to a survey published by the International Planned Parenthood Federation, out of 558 million women at risk of becoming pregnant, nearly 362 million were not practicing contraception.[64] However, contraceptive use had risen from 31 percent of eligible couples in 1971 to 36 percent in 1976. In the Western Pacific, Europe, and North America, more than half the couples were practicing, whereas, in much of the developing world, the level was 20 percent or below.[65]

As with voluntary sterilization, the law has not kept up with the demand for, and increased access to, contraception.[66] Many of the

[62] *See* H. Butts, *Legal Requirements for Condoms under the Federal Food, Drug, and Cosmetic Act* (paper presented at a Conference on the Condom, Battelle Human Affairs Research Center, Seattle, Washington, 1973).

[63] The committee's report is discussed in A. Hecht, *Vaginal Contraceptives: Available But . . .,* FDA CONSUMER, vol. 14, no. 1, p. 28 (1980).

[64] IPPF, SURVEY OF UNMET NEEDS IN FAMILY PLANNING, 1971–1976 (1977), Table 2.

[65] *Id.* at 9.

[66] This chapter concerns only the secular law and omits reference to religious laws on family and fertility which influence the use of contraceptives. The most important pronouncement was Pope Paul VI's encyclical *Humanae Vitae* which forbad the use of artificial contraceptives. For a comprehensive history of the Catholic viewpoint on contraception, *see* J. NOONAN, CONTRACEPTION: A HISTORY OF ITS TREATMENT BY THE CATHOLIC THEOLOGIANS AND CANONISTS (Harvard, 1965); with respect to *Humanae Vitae* specifically, *see* N. ST. JOHN-STEVAS, THE AGONIZING CHOICE: BIRTH CONTROL, RELIGION AND THE LAW (1971); for the Jewish perspective, *see* D. FELDMAN, BIRTH CONTROL IN JEWISH LAW (N.Y.U. Press, 1968); the Muslim position is discussed in ISLAM AND FAMILY PLANNING (I. Nazar, H. Karmi, & H. Zayid, eds., IPPF, 1974).

world's laws, particularly in francophone Africa and Latin America, inhibit the wider use of contraceptives, although the restrictiveness of the laws as written is often alleviated by their non-enforcement in practice.

Laws which directly affect contraceptive supply and demand deal principally with the following subjects: (1) import; (2) manufacturing; (3) distribution and sale; (4) advertising and publicity, and (5) use of the mails. The distribution of contraceptives raises the most significant legal and policy considerations, particularly whether a government will support or oppose family planning and what kinds of personnel will be permitted to distribute specific contraceptives.

B. Regional Tendencies

Laws and policies concerning contraception tend to vary widely, often in accordance with regional groupings. This is evident from the following summary published by the United Nations Fund for Population Activities in its *Survey of Contraceptive Laws: Country Profiles, Checklists, and Summaries.*[67]

1. Africa (South of the Sahara)

> The Francophone countries are predominantly pro-natalist. These countries remain under the influence of French colonial opposition to family planning and the sale of contraceptives. In particular, the old French law of 1920 seems to be technically in force in all these countries except Mali, even though it was replaced in France in 1974.[68] Cultural factors also encourage large families. The Roman Catholic religion, also part of the French heritage, discourages easy accessibility to contraceptives. Children are viewed as valuable economic assets and as their parents' "social security" for old age. Mortality rates are still high, a factor that encourages high fertility. . . .
>
> Commonwealth Africa has varying attitudes toward population growth, but in the main they have been tolerant toward contraceptive practice—no doubt influenced, at least in part, by Great Britain's long-standing liberal laws on contraceptives. For Great Britain, unlike France, has made contraceptives available for a considerable number of years, which inevitably has its impact in Anglophone

[67] UNFPA, SURVEY OF CONTRACEPTIVE LAWS: COUNTRY PROFILES, CHECKLISTS, AND SUMMARIES, 139–143 (1976).

[68] The 1920 French law prohibited the advertising of contraception and was held by a French court to prohibit the distribution of contraceptives as well. The law was modified in 1967 and again in 1974 to permit the sale of contraceptives in certain cases.—Ed.

Africa. Although family planning services are not widespread in all of these countries, import, manufacture and sale of contraceptives are legal.

2. North Africa

Tunisia led the way among the Maghreb states in legalizing the importation, advertisement and sales of all kinds of contraceptives in a 1961 law which invalidated the 1920 French-originated anti-contraceptives laws. . . .

As for Egypt, the most populous North African country, there is no law prohibiting the use, manufacture, sale or advertisement of contraceptives.

By and large, North African population is Islamic in religion, hence less susceptible to Roman Catholic influence in matters concerning contraception. Thus, Egypt, Tunisia, Morocco and Sudan all give some form of governmental support to family planning programmes. Algeria is much more restrictive in that birth control materials are only available to mothers who have had four children. Only Libya sponsors no family planning activities.

Notwithstanding the above, there are certain restrictive laws that stand in the way of easy availability of contraceptives. Presumably, family planning will continue to develop in these countries, and the passage of France's more liberal contraceptive law in 1974 may well presage the removal of the remaining French-origined anti-contraceptive laws.

3. America

Several recent policy and statutory changes in Latin America are creating an increasingly favorable atmosphere for contraceptive use. Currently, only Argentina remains actively opposed to family planning. Mexico and Brazil, long noted for their opposition to family planning, have now reversed their policy and made firm commitments to develop population programmes. Both of these countries are underscoring family planning as a basic human right, and Mexico has drafted a new sanitary code and passed a statute that integrates family planning services into public health facilities. Ecuador has made a similar pronouncement that family planning services are now available through its public health facilities. Both Chile and Mexico have taken steps to incorporate paramedical personnel into their family planning programmes, particularly for IUD insertions and pill distribution.

It may be noted that several countries have never had, or have recently dropped, prescription requirements for oral contraceptives—Chile, Honduras, Paraguay, Panama and Uruguay. El Salvador in 1974 proclaimed an official population policy. . . .

Virtually all of the Latin American countries are predominantly Iberian Roman Catholic, yet the Church in both Mexico and Brazil has not opposed Government-assisted family planning. Notwithstanding national rivalries within the Western Hemisphere and distrust of the United States—the two powerful elements which have inhibited family planning programmes in the past—they now seem to be of diminished importance considering the magnitude of the recent changes.

Viewed against the cultural, religious and political climate in which these policy shifts have taken place, the changes are all the more impressive. Thus, what has taken place merely portends what is yet to come in Latin America. There is every reason to expect that legal reform will continue to develop as population policies are increasingly legislated into reality. . . .

Both the United States and Canada have numerous laws regulating the quality of contraceptives, and prescription requirements for oral contraceptives are imposed by their respective medical associations. Nevertheless, these restrictions do not appear to present serious obstacles to accessibility to contraceptives in most instances. The availability of public and private medical services and the variety of contraceptive methods offered permit widespread utilization of contraceptives.

4. Asia and Oceania

The second most populous nation in the world, India, has had official family planning programmes for as long as 25 years. Yet only recently has India begun to encourage the use of oral pills, though still requiring prescription by medical doctors. Although Indonesia, Sri Lanka and Australia are generally in favor of family planning, they all have laws that restrict either the import of contraceptives or their advertisement. Democratic Kampuchea, the Lao People's Democratic Republic and the Socialist Republic of Viet Nam—all former French colonies—still take restrictive positions on contraceptive use, as does Burma.

Most of the countries in this geographic area are not inhibited by any religious prohibition on the use of contraceptives, although their cultural traditions coupled with illiteracy and poverty do pose problems in achieving widespread acceptance of contraceptives. However, rapid population growth in the region has provided the impetus for many of these countries to encourage family planning through contraceptive use. The Philippines, a predominantly Roman Catholic country, for example, has recently made significant progress toward making contraceptives available to their people at large. It has amended its Constitution to include a population policy, passed a Labor Code that requires certain major employers to provide free contraceptive services to their employees, repealed a former ban on the importation of contraceptives, and taken steps to utilize paramedicals in contraceptive services.

Perhaps the most successful model of a national family planning programme is provided by the People's Republic of China. Under its "birth planning" programme, extensive use of paramedicals ("barefoot doctors") is made in providing contraceptives to all its people (except for its minority peoples). A close coordination among the Ministries of Health, Labor, Finance, Commerce and Education, as well as the Cooperatives, succeeded in making contraceptives available to all who need them.

Other recent legal changes in this area that increase the availability of contraceptives include the elimination of the prescription requirement for oral contraceptives in Pakistan and in Fiji, and the legalization of pill distribution and IUD insertion by specially trained paramedicals in the Republic of Korea. Bangladesh has recently integrated family planning into its public health services, and Japan has recently approved the production and use of two types of IUDs. . . .

5. *Eastern Europe*

With the exceptions of Romania and Albania, virtually all of the countries in Eastern Europe make family planning services readily available. Easy access to medical services and a political ideology that both supplants older religious beliefs and supports mass education and individual family planning effort provide a favorable climate for use of contraceptives. Although abortion has been used to facilitate family planning in the past, there seems to be increased reliance on the use of contraceptives as an alternative to abortion. . . .

6. *Northern Europe*

Scandinavian countries have been among the leaders in making abundant supply of contraceptives available. In fact, a Swedish law of 1946 requires all pharmacies to sell contraceptives. Although there is extensive regulation of contraceptives, its purpose is not to restrict or prohibit the distribution of contraceptives, but rather to insure that medical factors are fully considered, and that quality standards are observed. General availability of subsidized medical services make the prescription requirements on oral pills easy to meet. The requirement in Finland and Sweden that IUDs be inserted by doctors is evidently not a serious deterrent to their use. The official policy of Denmark and Finland has expressed preference for contraception over abortion as a means of family planning. . . .

7. Western Europe

With the notable exceptions of Spain, Portugal and Ireland, contraceptives are generally available throughout Western Europe, though under considerable restrictions in some countries. Some of the restrictions tend to limit the widespread availability of contraceptives, while others are more concerned with regulating their quality or providing for adequate medical safeguards. Important recent changes in the laws of Belgium, Ireland, Italy and France have made contraceptives much more available in those countries. Thus, in 1973 Belgium repealed a ban on the importation, transportation, display and advertising of contraceptives. A decision by the Irish Supreme Court in late 1973 permits an individual to import contraceptives for private use. In 1971, the Italian Constitutional Court declared as unconstitutional a law prohibiting contraceptive information, which has resulted in tolerance, if not explicit approval, of contraceptive practice. France in 1974 passed a new legislation that makes contraceptives available anonymously, without charge and without regard to age. These changes represent a significant departure from the past. The Federal Republic of Germany has also proposed legislation that will make contraceptives more accessible in that country.

On the other hand, virtually all of the Western European countries require a prescription for the distribution of oral contraceptives, and a significant number require that insertion of IUDs be performed by physicians.

That the demand for contraceptives in Western Europe will increase in the future is evidenced by the recent changes in contraceptive laws described above, as well as by the decision of the Consultative Assembly of the Council of Europe in 1972 to "invite" its Member Governments to "authorize the sale of contraceptives" and to "create family planning advice bureaux in urban and rural areas."

8. The Middle East

Like North Africa, the Middle Eastern countries are predominantly Islamic in religion, whose doctrines do not proscribe the use of contraceptives in general. Some form of family planning programmes obtains in most of the more populous countries in the Middle East. Turkey, Jordan, Iran, Iraq, Lebanon and Afghanistan all provide Government assistance to family planning programmes, although current import restrictions have increased the price of contraceptives in Turkey and limited the quantity of pills imported into Iran. The Syrian Arab Republic, Saudi Arabia, Kuwait, Yemen and Democratic Yemen have no family planning programme at all, and there is little information concerning other aspects of their laws relating to family planning. . . .*

C. Import and Export, Manufacture, Advertising, and Mailing of Contraceptives[69]

1. Import and Export

Countries may choose to prohibit or restrict the import of contraceptives for a number of reasons: disapproval of contraception; protection of the local contraceptive industry or the need to conserve foreign exchange. Most countries prohibit the import of pills that do not meet local health and safety standards, although, in practice, the high cost of testing drugs means that most developing countries must rely on the findings of the United States Food and Drug Administration, or other developed country's equivalent.

Some countries forbid the importation of drugs that are not authorized for use in the country of origin. Conversely, practice in the United States prohibits the export, as part of the American foreign aid program, of drugs not authorized for use in the U.S. A concrete example of curtailing the export of a drug desired by developing countries is that of Depo-Provera, discussed on pp. 232–234, *supra.*

2. Manufacture

There appear to be few restrictions on the manufacture of contraceptives, subject to their meeting the pertinent health and safety standards. Where a strong pronatalist policy exists, as in the case of Chad, it can manifest itself in prohibition on contraception manufacturing.

3. Advertising and Publicity

A wide range of laws and policies regulate advertisement of contraceptives. Some strongly pronatalist countries (*e.g.,* Argentina,

*Reprinted with permission of the United Nations Fund for Population Activities.

[69]The following paragraphs are based, in part, on J. STEPAN & E. KELLOGG, THE WORLD'S LAWS ON CONTRACEPTIVES, *Law and Population Monograph* No. 17 (Fletcher School of Law and Diplomacy, 1974). *See also*, UNFPA, *supra* n. 67.

Ireland) prohibit advertising. Many countries permit advertising to physicians, but not to the general public, or, more commonly, advertising of prescription contraceptives to physicians only, while permitting the advertising of non-prescriptive contraceptives to the general public. Other countries permit the advertising of contraceptives, either without restriction, or upon approval of a competent administrative body. Of course, even where contraceptive advertising is permitted, publicity must not violate laws against false or misleading advertising.

4. The Use of the Mails

Many countries prohibit or severely restrict the use of the mails to transport contraceptives, whether solicited or not. Some countries forbid sending unsolicited contraceptives or contraception information, while permitting the sending of solicited contraceptives or contraceptive information.

D. Contraception Distribution

1. Family Planning Policies and Programs

There are two sources of contraceptive supply: (1) the commercial sector, consisting of pharmacies, retail stores, and other commercial outlets and (2) family planning programs, administered by either (a) private non-profit organizations such as the family planning associations affiliated with the International Planned Parenthood Federation or (b) government. Of these, the commercial sector is considered to be the major source of contraceptive supply, although family planning programs have been playing an increasingly important role.[70] In the excerpt below, Watson describes the growth and importance of family planning policies and programs.

[70]WESTINGHOUSE POPULATION CENTER, DISTRIBUTION OF CONTRACEPTIVES IN THE COMMERCIAL SECTOR OF SELECTED DEVELOPING COUNTRIES: SUMMARY REPORT (1974). For a summary and analysis of the Westinghouse Report, *see* J. Farley & S. Tokarski, *Legal Restrictions on the Distribution of Contraceptives in the Developing Nations: Some Suggestions for Determining Priorities and Estimating Impact of Change,* 6 COL. HUM. RTS. L. REV. 415 (1974–75).

a. W. Watson, "A Historical Overview," in W. Watson ed., *Family Planning in the Developing World: A Review of Programs 1-9* (Population Council, 1977)*

The Evolution of National Family Planning Policies, 1952–75

The first [family planning] policy in the developing world was adopted by India in 1952. China and Hong Kong followed in 1956. By 1959 only five countries had family planning policies . . . With the exception of Cuba, all of these were in the Asia-Pacific region, and no such policies were then in existence in Africa, Central or South America, or West Asia. As of 1975, 69 of 81 international family planning policies had been adopted within the last decade, and 36 had been adopted within the last five years, including those in Brazil, Nigeria, Mexico, and several other large countries. . . .

By the end of 1975, among the 38 developing countries with populations of 10 million or more, only Burma, North Korea, and Peru were not providing at least limited policy support for family planning, and Peru adopted a family planning policy in 1976. The proportion of the developing world's population resident in countries with policies supportive of family planning jumped from none to 22% with adoption by India in 1952 and to 51% with adoption by China in 1956; thereafter, the rise was more gradual but steady until the end of 1975, by which time 94% of the developing world's people lived in the 81 countries with governments supporting family planning. In 41 of these countries, with approximately 80% of the population of the developing world, the national policy had a demographic objective, that is, to slow population growth in order to enhance the prospects for rapid economic development, in addition to health and human rights objectives. . . .

The Evolution of Public-Sector Family Planning Services, 1952–75

. . . Services developed slowly in India after policy adoption in 1952 and in Pakistan-Bangladesh after 1960. The pace was more rapid in Hong Kong, Taiwan, South Korea, and Fiji. By 1965, significant public sector family planning services had been established in 12–14 countries (India and Pakistan-Bangladesh in South Asia; Hong Kong, Taiwan, South Korea, and presumably China in East Asia; Fiji, Singapore, and conceivably North Vietnam in Southeast Asia; Chile and possibly Cuba in Latin America; Tunisia in North Africa; and

*Reprinted with the permission of The Population Council from Walter B. Watson (ed.), "A Historical Overview," *Family Planning In The Developing World: A Review of Programs* (New York: 1977): pp. 1–9.

Mauritius in Sub-Saharan Africa) and were beginning in a few other countries. In that year, there were about 2.5 million family planning acceptors (exclusive of China, North Vietnam, and Cuba). . . . Two-thirds of them were in India. On a regional basis, the level of services as measured by acceptors amounted to a little more than 1% of the number of women aged 15–49 in South Asia, not quite 1% for East and Southeast Asia (excluding China and North Vietnam), and well under 0.1% everywhere else. . . .

By 1970 service programs had expanded tremendously in all regions of the world except Francophone Sub-Saharan Africa. The number of family planning acceptors (again excluding China, North Vietnam, and Cuba except for abortion) surpassed 9 million that year. Although the number of acceptors in India has more than doubled since 1965, the proportion of all international acceptors (excluding those in China, North Vietnam, and Cuba) contributed by India declined from 67% in 1965 to 41% in 1970 (it has since dropped to 39%) with more rapid expansion elsewhere. The number of national policies favorable to family planning rose from 19 in 1965 to 52 in 1970, and the number of countries with significant programs [defined as a program which has attracted at least 1% of the women aged 15–49] increased from 12–14 in 1965 to 33 in 1970. . . .

By the end of 1975, the number of countries with family planning policies had risen from 52 in 1970 to 81, and the number providing "real programmatic support" from 33 in 1970 to 54. The number of acceptors rose by 4.8 million in a single year to 17.4 million in 1975 (excluding China, North Vietnam, and Cuba except for abortion). This represents an increase of 37% in the year following the World Population Conference in Bucharest. Acceptors in South Asia and in East/Southeast Asia (excluding China and North Vietnam) were equivalent to 5.5% and 5.1%, respectively, of the number of women aged 15–49, suggesting substantial family planning programmatic activity in those regions. In Latin America acceptors totaled 3.0% of the number of women aged 15–49, with a major difference between the very young program in Brazil (0.8%) and the remainder of Latin America (4.4%). Although 12 countries in West Asia and North Africa had policies favorable to family planning by 1975, only four had programs of sufficient scope to serve a number of acceptors greater than 1% of women aged 15–49. Nevertheless, because of the proportion of the region's population residing in these countries, the size of the programs, and the level of activity elsewhere in the region, the number of acceptors in the region as a whole amounted to 2% of the number of women aged 15–49. By the end of 1975, 17 countries in Anglophone Sub-Saharan Africa (including Ethiopia) had policies favorable to family planning—all the countries except Malawi, Namibia, Somalia, and Sierra Leone (family planning activities have

> commenced in the last of these). But "real programmatic support" has developed in only about one-half of the countries with favorable policies, and the region as a whole does not yet approach the 1% criterion. Although six countries in Francophone Sub-Saharan Africa are judged to have policies favorable to family planning, services are at a very early stage of development and meet the 1% criterion only in Reunion. For Sub-Saharan Africa as a whole, excluding Zimbabwe (Rhodesia), where a large injectable contraceptive program exists but where statistics are uncertain, family planning acceptors numbered only about 200,000 in 1975, about 0.3% of the number of women aged 15–49. Even if subsequent data raise this crude estimate, it is evident that the availability of government family planning services is still extremely limited throughout most of the region. For the developing world as a whole (with the principal exclusions of China and North Vietnam), the 17.4 million acceptors of 1975 are equivalent to 4.0% of the 440 million women aged 15–49.

Watson added that since 1975, policies favoring family planning have been adopted in Peru, Senegal, and several smaller African countries, and previously favorable policies have been repealed in Bolivia, Laos, and Kampuchea (Cambodia). As of 1978, ninety-nine developing countries, containing 95 percent of the developing world's population, had policies that support family planning on demographic, health, or human rights grounds or all three.[71]

b. Note on Family Planning Programs in Developing Countries. In many developing countries, family planning programs began as people—often physicians—became aware of the deleterious effects of rapid population growth on quality of life and, more frequently, of the harmful effects of too many children or widespread clandestine abortion on family health and welfare. Private family planning associations were organized in the late 1950's and 1960's in response to these problems. These associations, often affiliated with the International Planned Parenthood Federation, provided clinical family planning services, information and education, and training. Gradually, as Watson observes, governments recognized that family planning was their responsibility, and national programs, generally administered by the Ministry of Health, took over much of the delivery of services. Most governments now offer family planning

[71]W. Watson, *99 LDCs Favor Family Planning/Slowing Growth, But Only 54 Show Real Programmatic Support,* 4 INT. FAM. PLAN. PERSPECTIVES AND DIGEST 129 (1978).

information and services, either through *vertical* programs, in facilities devoted exclusively to family planning, or in *horizontal* programs, where family planning is offered in conjunction with maternal-child or other health services. The private associations continue to play an important role, often providing innovative services, which governments are sometimes unable to furnish.

Some of the more innovative service delivery efforts include the development of postpartum programs, the use of village-level workers to provide contraception and primary health care, greater utilization of paramedical personnel, tapping into commercial distribution networks to market contraceptives, and the use of radio and other means of mass communication to promote family planning.[72]

Many population experts consider the birth planning program of the People's Republic of China to be the world's most innovative and successful. The program utilizes targets established for each governmental level, buttressed by a system of peer pressure that promotes late marriage and premarital celibacy and encourages married couples to have no more than an allotted number of children. Birth planning services, widely available, are offered by trained paramedical workers, including the famous "barefoot doctors."[73] Others family planning programs considered to be successful are those of Indonesia, Taiwan, Singapore, Korea, Thai-

[72]R. CUCA & C. PIERCE, EXPERIMENTS IN FAMILY PLANNING: LESSONS FROM THE DEVELOPING WORLD (Johns Hopkins, 1977) examine over 100 innovative projects. *See also* J. Ross, A. Germain, J. Forrest & J. Van Ginneken, *Findings from Family Planning Research,* REP. ON POP. FAM. PLAN., no. 12 (1972); I. SIVIN, CONTRACEPTION AND FERTILITY CHANGE IN THE INTERNATIONAL POSTPARTUM PROGRAM (Population Council, 1974); D. Altman & P. Piotrow, *Social Marketing: Does It Work,* POPULATION REPORTS, series J., no. 21 (Johns Hopkins, 1980); W. Sweeney, *Media Communications in Population/Family Planning Programs: A Review,* POPULATION REPORTS, series J, no. 16 (George Washington, 1977). Community-based distribution programs are examined in the text at pp. 252–257.

[73]A considerable literature exists on the delivery of birth planning services in China. *See, e.g.,* F. Jaffe & D. Oakley, *Observations on Birth Planning in China, 1977,* 10 FAM. PLAN. PERSPECTIVES 101 (1978); P. CHEN, POPULATION AND HEALTH POLICY IN THE PEOPLE'S REPUBLIC OF CHINA, Occasional Monograph No. 9 (Smithsonian Inst., 1976); L. CHU, PLANNED BIRTHS CAMPAIGNS IN CHINA, 1949–1976 (East-West Communications Inst., 1977); V. Sidel & R. Sidel, *The Delivery of Medical Care in China,* SCIENTIFIC AMERICAN, vol. 230, no. 4, p. 19 (1974); Y. Yu, *The Population Policy of China,* 33 POP. STUDIES 125 (1979); J. Aird, *Fertility Decline and Birth Control in the People's Republic of China,* 4 POP. & DEV. REV. 225 (1978).

land, Costa Rica, Chile, Colombia, Cuba, Mexico, Trinidad, and Barbados.[74]

Whether family planning can bring about significant declines in the birth rate or whether such declines are a function of other social and economic factors is still a much-debated question. The various perspectives on this issue are considered on pp. 380–390, *infra.*

2. Legal Provisions Concerning Contraceptive Distribution

a. J. Stepan and E. Kellogg, The World's Laws on Contraceptives 12–21, Law and Population Monograph *No. 17* (Fletcher School of Law and Diplomacy, 1974)

Provisions dealing with sale of contraceptives generally

Most modern laws do not deal with the sale or distribution of contraceptives generally (as distinguished from laws dealing specifically with condoms, the pill, or the IUD). In former times, however, many countries adopted laws prohibiting or restricting all contraceptives as a whole. . . .

Best known, and important because of its impact on the former French colonies, is the French law prohibiting contraception which lasted from July 31, 1920, until 1967. It may be noted that this law merely contained a general prohibition of abortifacients and prohibited contraceptives only when sold for the purpose of anti-conception propaganda ("dans un but de propagande anticonceptionnelle"). The expansion of the general prohibition was the result of an interpretation of this text by the French Supreme Court which held, despite the

[74]*See,* BIRTH CONTROL: AN INTERNATIONAL ASSESSMENT (M. Potts & B. Bhiwandiwala, eds., Univ. Park, 1979) [hereafter cited as M. Potts & P. Bhiwandiwala, eds.]; T. Hull, V. Hull & M. Singarimbun, *Indonesia's Family Planning Story: Success and Challenge,* POPULATION BULLETIN, vol. 32, no. 6 (Pop. Ref. Bur., 1977); B. VIEL, THE DEMOGRAPHIC EXPLOSION: THE LATIN AMERICAN EXPERIENCE (Irvington, 1976); D. Nortman, *Changing Contraceptive Patterns: A Global Perspective,* POPULATION BULLETIN, vol. 32, no. 3 (Pop. Ref. Bur., 1977); J. Stycos, *Recent Trends in Latin American Fertility,* 32 POP. STUDIES 407 (1978); G. CERNADA, TAIWAN FAMILY PLANNING READER: HOW A PROGRAM WORKS (Chinese Center for Intl. Training on Fam. Plan., 1970); S. Khoo & C. Park, *The Effect of Family Planning on Fertility in Four Asian Countries,* 4 INTL. FAM. PLAN. PERSPECTIVES AND DIGEST 67 (1978); R. Rodríguez-Barocio, J. Garcia-Nuñez, M. Urbina-Fuentes, & D. Wulf, *Fertility and Family Planning in Mexico,* INTL. FAM. PLAN. PERSPECTIVES, vol. 6, no. 1, p. 2 (1980).

language of the law, that whoever sells contraceptives acts "necessarily" with the purpose of "propagande anticonceptionnelle."

However, the general practice in most of these countries was (and is) to circumvent the prohibition. Contraceptives are sold not as contraceptives, but as articles needed on medical grounds. Condoms are sold as a means to prevent venereal disease. Pills are prescribed on "medical grounds," for cycle regulation. . . .

Another frequent way of restricting contraceptives in general is to *prohibit display* of contraceptives offered for sale. . . . It is clear that the rationale behind these provisions is that contraceptives are still considered, by some authorities, to be something indecent in and of themselves. This is clearly shown in the West German law which, as amended in 1960, still prohibits sale of contraceptives through vending machines along public roads or in public places.

An approach entirely opposite to the above provisions which are designed to limit the sales of contraceptives in general, is the *policy of ensuring an adequate supply of contraceptives,* which has appeared since World War II, starting in the Scandinavian countries. Although Sweden, in the first decades of this century, had a negative policy toward contraception, this was reversed by a Royal Order of October 18, 1946 requiring all pharmacies to sell contraceptives. . . .

Special Provisions on Condoms

. . .Two basic types of approach seem to exist. On one hand, in countries with a liberal attitude toward contraception, condoms may usually be sold in many types of stores (subject to generally applicable trade regulations), by vending machines or by mail. This is the case of the United Kingdom, Scandinavia and most of the European Socialist countries.

On the other hand, in countries with restrictive policies towards contraception, condoms may be sold in pharmacies only (as prophylactics against venereal disease). This includes Spain, the francophone African countries, Portugal, Brazil, and Venezuela. (Surprisingly, the sale of condoms is limited to pharmacies only in some countries with pro-family planning policies, such as South Korea and Ghana, despite the limited number of pharmacies in those countries). . . .

Special Provisions on the Pill

In the 1960's the oral hormonal contraceptive became the focal point of interest in family planning for two reasons: first, because it is a drug with a broad influence on bodily functions, so that its use involves medical problems which had not yet been entirely solved and, secondly, because it is the most efficient of known contraceptives and relatively easy to use.

The three types of legal restrictions which have been applied to the pill are: the general laws against contraception, the requirement that sales of pills be made in pharmacies only, and the requirement of a medical prescription. . . .

The legal requirement that *oral contraceptives be sold only in pharmacies* is found in almost all countries. . . . The primary motivation of the pharmacy monopoly is the argument that only a professional with a certain level of formal education has the knowledge required to deal with the increasingly complicated drugs of today. A second reason used very frequently as an argument in favor of this restriction, is that pills, as "ethical" drugs, are almost always sold on prescription only, and the requirement that they be dispensed in pharmacies only helps to enforce this control. In addition, there is also the tradition in most countries that medicaments be sold exclusively in pharmacies and there is clearly a certain amount of professional commercial interest in maintaining the monopoly.

Whether or not these arguments are valid, the Summary Report of the Westinghouse Population Center, which made an in-depth study of pill distribution in eight countries, concluded:

> The single greatest impediment to increase distribution of contraceptives is the lack of availability of oral pills . . . outside of pharmacies . . .

The requirement of medical prescription for sale of oral contraceptives has been enacted virtually everwhere . . . [however,] in numerous developing countries the law is disregarded and the pill is commonly available without prescription. . . .

Special Provisions on Intra-Uterine Devices

. . . Most restrictions on the use of the IUD are based not on laws regulating contraceptives, but on other kinds of law or regulation dealing with medical practice (*e.g.*, codes of medical ethics, especially in Latin America). It would appear that authorization to insert IUD's should be regarded as a practical question which depends upon the circumstances of each country rather than on the law. . . .

In nearly all European countries, and in many others, the generally accepted practice is to have the IUD inserted by a physician. In most countries there is no specific legal provision on this, and the rule is based on the laws which regulate the medical profession and give it a monopoly in the administration of medical care.

At the present time two trends away from this general rule can be discerned: one, in some developed countries, towards a stricter control, and the other, in developing countries, toward more relaxed requirements.

In some developed countries the authorization to insert IUD's is restricted to gynecologists—for example, in Finland and especially in several European socialist countries. . . .

On the other hand, in several developing countries where there is population pressure and where methods of family planning must be easily accessible to the public, the trend is in the opposite direction and to entrust trained para-medical personnel (midwives, specially trained nurses, etc.) with the insertion responsibility. This is the situation, most conspicuously, in several Asian countries (Pakistan, Thailand, Philippines, South Korea.) In the Philippines, Mexico and South Korea there are special authorities to "train para-medicals" for insertion work. On the other hand, in Brazil mid-wives have been restricted by a special provision from "applying pessaries in the uterus, whether empty or full." Another apparent limitation is the rule, in some Asian countries (*e.g.*, Indonesia) that the consent of the husband is necessary before insertion of the IUD.

b. Note on the Use of Non–physicians to Offer Contraceptive Services. There has been a worldwide trend to utilize nonphysicians to carry out family planning functions once reserved for doctors. Nurses, midwives, nurse practitioners, women's health care specialists, auxiliary nurses, and community agents have been able to offer an increasing range of family planning information and services. Evaluations in many countries have demonstrated that properly trained nurses and auxiliary nurses can perform the routine family planning tasks, including insertion of IUDs, as capably as physicians.[75] Community-based distribution (CBD) programs, in which

[75] A. Rosenfield, D. Maine & M. Gorosh, *Nonclinical Distribution of the Pill in the Developing World,* 6 INTL. FAM. PLAN. PERSPECTIVES 130 (1980); A. Rosenfield, *Family Planning: An Expanded Role for Paramedical Personnel,* 110 AM. J. OB. GYN. 1030 (1971); R. Einhorn & M. Trias, *Differences between Physicians and Nurses in Providing Family Planning Services: Findings from a Bogota Clinic,* 9 STUDIES IN FAM. PLAN. 35 (1978); H. Vaillant, G. Cummins, R. Richart & B. Barron, *Insertion of Lippes Loop by Nurse Midwives and Doctors,* 3 BRIT. MED. J. 671 (1968). Nurses, nurse-midwives, and family planning nurse practitioners have also successfully provided family planning care in the United States. D. Ostergard, E. Broen & J. Marshall, *The Family Planning Specialist as a Provider of Health Care Services,* 23 FERTILITY & STERILITY 505 (1972); M. Manisoff, *Impact of Family Planning Nurse Practitioners,* 8 J. OB. GYN. & NEONATAL NURSING 73 (1979); A. Forman & E. Cooper, *Legislation and Nurse-Midwifery Practice in the U.S.A.,* 21 J. NURSE-MIDWIFERY 1-57 (1976); R. Roemer, *The Nurse Practitioner in Family Planning Services: Law and Practice,* 6 FAM. PLAN./POP. REP 28 (1977).

trained community agents distribute contraceptives, including orals, to their neighbors, now exist in many Latin American and Asian countries. Evaluations demonstrate that CBD programs have succeeded in attracting women, particularly those living in rural areas, not otherwise served by family planning programs; continuation rates have been among the highest in the world, failure rates (*i.e.*, unwanted pregnancies) have been low, and life endangering side effects have not been reported.[76]

What are the key policy and legal issues flowing from the devolution of contraceptive service delivery to nonphysicians? There are two fundamental issues: first, what kind of personnel should be permitted to distribute contraceptives (physicians? nurses? auxiliary nurses? community agents?) and second, what kinds of contraceptives should each category of personnel be allowed to deliver (in particular, who should be allowed to deliver orals)? From these issues flow a host of subsidiary program questions that also may have legal implications: how much medical supervision should be required? what training standards should be set? what legal or administrative changes must be made to permit nonphysicians to play a greater role in fertility regulation?

The sources to determine the scope and limits of nonphysicians' family planning authority are the regulations defining the practice of medicine and other related health care professions, those relating to the prescription of drugs, and those specifically dealing with the methods of fertility regulation.[77] These might be either statutory or contained in the rules and regulations of the relevant professional society. Paxman has noted that medical practice acts, in particular, "tend to define, either explicity or implicitly, the practice of medicine in such a way as to preclude the use of non-physicians in fertility

[76]J. Foreit, M. Gorosh, D. Gillespie & G. Merritt, *Community-Based and Commercial Contraceptive Distribution: An Inventory and Appraisal,* POPULATION REPORTS, series J, no. 19 (Geo. Wash. Univ., 1978); J. Bailey & J. Correa, *Evaluation of the Profamilia Rural Family Planning Program,* 6 STUDIES IN FAM. PLAN. 148 (1975); M. Gorosh, J. Ross, W. Rodrigues, & J. Arruda, *Brazil: Community-Based Distribution in Rio Grande do Norte,* 5 INTL. FAM. PLAN. PERSPECTIVES 150 (1979); S. Isaacs, *Nonphysician Distribution of Contraception in Latin America,* 7 FAM. PLAN. PERSPECTIVES 158 (1975); I. Astawa, *Using the Local Community—Bali, Indonesia,* in M. Potts & P. Bhiwandiwala, eds., *supra* n. 74 at 55; M. Viravaidya & M. Potts, *Involving the Community—Thailand,* in M. Potts & P. Bhiwandiwala, eds., *supra* n. 74 at 71.

[77]J. Paxman, *Roles for Non-Physicians in Fertility Regulation: An International Overview of Legal Obstacles and Solutions,* 70 AM. J. PUB. HLTH. 31 (1980).

regulation. In essence, they create a closed shop."[78] According to Paxman:

> Medical practice laws, with rare exceptions, either implicity or explicitly make examination, diagnosis, prescription and the supervision of treatment the special prerogatives of doctors. Indeed, some laws specifically require that only doctors do the sorts of tasks which relate to family planning. Unauthorized involvement in these duties by non-doctors is punishable under the law.
>
> Nursing legislation and regulations require, in the main, that nurses work subject to the instructions and under the supervision of a doctor. Theoretically, they may not by themselves take the initiative in providing family planning services.
>
> Most midwifery legislation defines the practice in such a way that the provision of family planning services is not generally thought to be one of the authorized duties of a midwife.
>
> Thus, without some other form of specific authorization, professional health and auxiliary personnel may not have the *legal* authority under the laws as written to provide family planning services on their own initiative. The same is true for other types on non-doctor personnel for whom no legislation exists. . . .[79]

Notwithstanding the restrictive nature of many laws and regulations as written, in practice their restrictiveness can be eased. Physicians can delegate more authority to subordinates working under their supervision.[80] Laws or regulations can be changed to authorize specified classes of personnel to carry out family planning functions[81]

[78] *Id.* at 32.

[79] J. PAXMAN, LAW AND PLANNED PARENTHOOD: A HANDBOOK COMPILED AND EDITED FOR THE IPPF PANEL ON LAW & PLANNED PARENTHOOD 69 (IPPF, 1980); for a comprehensive review of the topic, *see,* J. PAXMAN, L. LEE & S. HOPKINS, EXPANDED ROLES FOR NON-PHYSICIANS IN FERTILITY REGULATION: LEGAL PERSPECTIVES, Law & Population Monograph No. 41 (Fletcher School of Law & Diplomacy, 1976).

[80] For examples of delegation, *see* J. PAXMAN, F. SHATTOCK & N. FENDALL, THE USE OF PARAMEDICALS FOR PRIMARY HEALTH IN THE COMMONWEALTH: A SURVEY OF MEDICAL-LEGAL ISSUES AND ALTERNATIVES 34-35 (Commonwealth Secretariat, 1979).

[81] *For example,* Ministry of Health regulations in Thailand were changed to permit midwives to dispense oral contraceptives. A. Rosenfield & C. Limcharoen, *Auxiliary Midwife Prescription of Oral Contraceptives,* 114 AM. J. OB. GYN. 942 (1972); in Chile, Ministry of Health regulations were changed to allow midwives to provide a range of family planning services, including IUD insertion and distribution of oral contraceptives. PAXMAN, LEE, & HOPKINS, *supra* n. 79 at 92.

or to eliminate the need for a physician's prescription for oral contraceptives.[82] In lieu of reform, laws restricting distribution of contraceptives can be given a liberal interpretation.[83]

Some special issues, of a legal and ethical nature, arise in connection with nonphysician distribution of oral contraceptives:

(1) *Risks versus benefits of oral contraception.* Do the benefits of the pill sufficiently outweigh the risks so as to justify nonphysician distribution? Obviously the pill does have risks—very serious ones—ranging from the severe discomfort of headaches, nausea, and weight gain to life endangering ones such as cardiovascular disease. These must be weighed against the risk of *not* using contraception, particularly the risk of maternal death in childbirth. Most medical experts who have studied the matter conclude that the risk of a mother dying in childbirth outweighs the risk of her taking the pill, particularly in less developed countries where health services are lacking.[84] Rosenfield has adapted a chart by Tietze which shows the annual number of deaths associated with control of fertility per 100,000 nonsterile women:[85]

Table 5–3 Annual Number of Deaths Associated with Control of Fertility per 100,000 Nonsterile Women by Method and Age

	Age group			
Method of contraception	*15–29 yr.*	*30–34 yr.*	*35–39 yr.*	*40–44 yr.*
None	6.4	13.9	20.8	22.6
Abortion only	1.5	1.7	1.9	1.2
Pill:				
Nonsmokers	1.4	2.2	4.5	7.1
Smokers	1.6	10.8	13.4	58.9
IUD	1.0	1.4	2.0	1.9
Traditional methods	1.5	3.6	5.0	4.2
Traditional methods plus abortion	0.2	0.3	0.3	0.2

[82]For a discussion of the legal changes easing the prescription requirement for oral contraceptives, *see* R. Cook, *Distribution of Oral Contraceptives: Legal Changes and New Concepts of Preventive Care,* 66 AM. J. PUB. HLTH. 590 (1976).

[83]Some examples of liberal interpretation of the law are given in PAXMAN, *supra* n. 79 at 72.

[84]For a review of the literature and a weighing of the risks and benefits of oral contraception, *see* A. Rosenfield, *supra* n. 8.

[85]*Id.* at 102. Adapted from C. Tietze, *New Estimates of Mortality Associated with Fertility Control,* 9 FAM. PLAN. PERSPECTIVES 74 (1977).

Based in part on the evidence presented in the table above, Rosenfield concluded:[86]

> In developing countries, the various risks of the pill and the IUD must be assessed in relation to the benefits, particularly in areas with very high maternal mortality rates. Unfortunately, adequate data on contraceptive risks in the developing world are not available, but there is some evidence that the risks of thromboembolism and other circulatory diseases are less in these developing areas, probably due to differences in diet and lifestyle. With the strikingly high maternal (and infant) mortality rates, there are those who believe the benefits of the pill heavily outweigh the possible risks. Further, it is likely that an effective family-planning effort in many developing countries will, through its preventive aspects, do more to lower the high infant and maternal mortality rates than will any other preventive or curative step one could take, in the short run. Thus, in my opinion, the decision in many developing countries to allow nonphysician health personnel and indigenous lay personnel to prescribe the pill, both in clinics and, more importantly, at the village level, is totally justifiable on medical grounds.*

(2) *The double standard.* Community-based contraceptive distribution program have been *promoted* by institutions located in developed countries, where medical practice dictates a physical examination be given before a woman can receive a medical prescription for pills, for *use* in underdeveloped countries. The justification given for this apparent double standard is the difference in health care: in the United States there is approximately one doctor per 700 people whereas in some developing countries, the ratio is 1:20,000 or even 1:100,000, with most of the doctors concentrated in the large cities. Thus, it is argued that unless contraception, and presumably other simple health services, are delivered by nonphysicians, they will not be supplied at all. Rosenfield has argued that the physician-oriented western system of health care is an inappropriate model for developing countries to follow. He writes:

> In the West we assume that only physicians can provide most medical services. Our model in the developing countries brings not higher standards and better health care delivery but restrictions on simple and effective modes of delivering many simple and effective remedies

[86] *Id.* at 103.

*Excerpted with permission from AM. J. OB/GYN, 132: 92–106, 1978 and the author; copyrighted by the C.V. Mosby Company, St. Louis, Missouri.

> for extremely serious health problems. Ethical concerns about unsupervised contraceptive usage must be viewed in this context: when the choice in developing countries is between the best care and no care at all, most people are likely to get no care at all.[87]

Notwithstanding the differences in health care between many developing and developed countries, is this enough to justify a double standard? Should the United States, under any circumstances, promote kinds of medical care abroad that are not acceptable at home?[88] Should contraceptives be taken off the list of drugs that may by given only be prescription in western countries? A British government panel recommended that the pill be taken off prescription in that country.[89] No similar movement has grown in the United States and, if anything, there seems to be an increasing awareness of the risks of oral contraception.[90]

(3) *Enforcement of the prescription requirement.* It seems generally agreed that, notwithstanding legal requirements, pills can be purchased at almost any developing country pharmacy for the asking.[91] Also, that upper and middle class women have been purchasing pills for years. Given the general accessibility of the well-to-do to oral contraception and the lack of enforcement of the laws, is it unethical *not* to distribute pills more widely? Is it a form of discrimination against the poor, sanctioned by law?

[87]A. Rosenfield, *The Ethics of Supervising Family Planning in Developing Nations,* HASTINGS CENTER REP. vol. 7, no. 1, p. 25 at 26 (1977).

[88]*See* D. Warwick, *Contraceptives in the Third World,* HASTINGS CENTER REP. vol. 5, no. 4, p. 9 (1975) and N. DEMERATH, BIRTH CONTROL AND FOREIGN POLICY: THE ALTERNATIVES TO FAMILY PLANNING (Harper & Row, 1976) for two views critical of United States government support of contraceptive distribution programs abroad.

[89]*Report of the Joint Working Group on Oral Contraceptives* (Her Majesty's Stationary Office, 1976) as reported in 9 FAM. PLAN. PERSPECTIVES 30 (1977). The Royal College of Nursing recommended that some nurses should be able to prescribe oral contraceptives, a recommendation criticized by the British Medical Association. Reported in IPPF, *Law File* (Jan. 1980).

[90]*See* E. Connell, *The Pill Revisited,* 7 FAM. PLAN. PERSPECTIVES 62 (1975).

[91]This was verified by the WESTINGHOUSE POPULATION CENTER, *supra* n. 7

CHAPTER 6

MINORS

Minors* are a population group with special problems regarding health services. Both their health problems and the legal framework surrounding them are distinctive. This is especially true in matters related to adolescent sexuality. Because of their special circumstances, minors are accorded a separate chapter. Section I explores the extent of teenage pregnancy and its consequences on health and socioeconomic factors. With this as background, Section II examines the legal aspects of fertility-related services to minors.

I. THE EXTENT AND CONSEQUENCES OF TEENAGE PREGNANCY

A. The Extent of Teenage Pregnancy

Little solid information is available on the extent of teenage pregnancy—or, in a larger context, adolescent sexuality—world-

*In these paragraphs, the words "minors," "adolescents," and "teenagers" are often used interchangeably. It should be noted, however, that "adolescent" and "teenager" are descriptive words, characterizing an age-group (whose outer limits are generally considered between 10 and 21 years of age) while "minor" is a legal term which defines the rights and obligations (or lack thereof) of a person below a specified age limit.

wide, due in part to lack of reliable data and in part to the absence of the category "adolescence" in many countries.[1] United Nations data indicate that in many countries births to women under 20 represent an increasing proportion of all births,[2] a fact partially explainable by the comparatively greater number of young people in the populations of developing countries. At the same time, a recent review disclosed "a general and unmistakable trend of decrease in the fertility rate (births per 1,000 women) of women aged 15–19 in selected developing countries having relatively good statistics. For example, the fertility rate of women aged 15–19 declined in Algeria from 122.9 (1965) to 98.4 (1969), in El Salvador from 148.5 (1960) to 134.3 (1970), and in Venezuela from 138 (1961) to 102.4 (1970)."[3] Even taking into account such declines, adolescent fertility rates in

[1]The concept of "adolescence" as a time of gradual transition from childhood to adulthood is relatively new—as, of course, is the idea that the health needs of teenagers deserve special attention. As a World Health Organization task force succinctly reported:

> In the past, many of the health needs of this age group [adolescence] were neglected. Little was known about them and little was done for them. The problems related to pregnancy and abortion, for example, were often ignored or simply included within the larger phenomenon of adult pregnancy and abortion; little attention was paid to the complex legal, social and economic implications of pregnancy and abortion.
>
> This lack of concern has been typical both of developed societies, where the problem has perhaps existed far longer, and of developing societies, where adolescents are often not even perceived as a distinct group.
>
> It is important that all countries should acknowledge the needs of adolescents and reappraise the existing situation and its significance.

[1]WHO, PREGNANCY AND ABORTION IN ADOLESCENCE 25 (Technical Report Series 583, 1975). An international conference on adolescent fertility held in 1976 tended to demonstrate both the interest in, and lack of knowledge about, the subject. *See* ADOLESCENT FERTILITY: THE PROCEEDINGS OF AN INTERNATIONAL CONFERENCE (D. Bogue, ed., Community and Family Study Center, Univ. of Chicago, 1977). To keep track of new information related to adolescent fertility, the International Planned Parenthood Federation puts out a monthly mimeographed report called *Youth Line* and the International Clearinghouse on Adolescent Fertility of the Population Institute distributes materials of interest.

[2]*See* W. Hunt II, *Adolescent Fertility—Risks and Consequences,* POPULATION REPORTS, series J, no. 10 (George Washington University, 1976).

[3]J. Chui, Policies and Programmes on Adolescent Fertility in Developing Countries: An Integrated Approach, pp. 19–20a. (unpublished, 1978).

developing countries are markedly higher than those in developed countries.[4]

Far more information is available about teenage pregnancy in the United States. It is a hot topic, the subject of TV specials, newspaper articles, and even scholarly research.[5] Surveys carried out in 1971 and 1976 by Kantner and Zelnick provide a wealth of information on adolescent sexuality and pregnancy.[6] Some of the more salient findings of research on adolescent fertility were summarized in the Alan Guttmacher Institute's booklet, *Eleven Million Teenagers:*[7]

> There are about 21 million young people in the United States between the ages of 15 and 19 years. Of these, more than half—some 11 million —are estimated to have had sexual intercourse—almost seven million young men, and four million young women. In addition, one-fifth of

[4]For example, in Bangladesh there are 203 births per thousand women between 15 and 19 years of age; in Africa and most of Latin America, there are more than 100 births per thousand women in the same age group. This compares with 58 per thousand in the United States. K. Darabi, S. Philliber & A. Rosenfield, *A Perspective on Adolescent Fertility in Developing Countries,* 10 STUDIES IN FAM. PLAN. 300 (1979).

[5]*See, e.g.,* W. Baldwin, *Adolescent Pregnancy and Childbearing—Growing Concerns for Americans,* POP. BULLETIN vol. 31, no. 2 (Pop. Ref. Bur., 1976); HEW, TEENAGE FERTILITY IN THE UNITED STATES: 1960, 1970, 1974: REGIONAL AND STATE VARIATION AND EXCESS FERTILITY (CDC, 1978); HEW, IMPROVING FAMILY PLANNING SERVICES FOR TEENAGERS (Urban and Rural Systems Assoc., 1976); FAM. PLAN. PERSPECTIVES, vol. 10, no. 4 (1978).

[6]Results of the second survey were reported as follows: M. Zelnick & J. Kantner, *Sexual and Contraceptive Experience of Young Unmarried Women in the United States, 1976 and 1971,* 9 FAM. PLAN. PERSPECTIVES 55 (1977); *First Pregnancies to Women Aged 15–19: 1976 and 1971,* 10 FAM. PLAN. PERSPECTIVES 11 (1978), and *Contraceptive Patterns and Premarital Pregnancy Among Women Aged 15–19 in 1976,* 10 FAM. PLAN. PERSPECTIVES 135 (1978). M. Zelnick, Y. Kim & J. Kantner, *Probabilities of Intercourse and Conception Among U.S. Teenage Women, 1971 and 1976,* 11 FAM. PLAN. PERSPECTIVES 177 (1979); L. Zabin, J. Kantner & M. Zelnick, *The Risk of Adolescent Pregnancy in the First Months of Intercourse,* 11 FAM. PLAN. PERSPECTIVES 215 (1979); M. Zelnick & J. Kantner, *Reasons for Nonuse of Contraception by Sexually Active Women Aged 15–19,* 11 FAM. PLAN. PERSPECTIVES 289 (1979); M. Zelnick, *Sex Education and Knowledge of Pregnancy Risk Among U.S. Teenage Women,* 11 FAM. PLAN. PERSPECTIVES 355 (1979); M. Zelnick, *Second Pregnancies to Premaritally Pregnant Teenagers, 1976 and 1971,* 12 FAM. PLAN. PERSPECTIVES 69 (1980).

[7]AGI, ELEVEN MILLION TEENAGERS 9–16 (1976). *See also* AGI, TEENAGE PREGNANCY: THE PROBLEM THAT HASN'T GONE AWAY (1981).

the eight million 13- and 14-year-old boys and girls are believed to have had intercourse. Adolescent sexual activity has been traditionally portrayed as principally affecting minorities and the poor; but recent evidence suggests that teenagers from higher income and non-minority groups are now beginning sexual intercourse at earlier ages, leading to higher rates of sexual activity and greater risk of unwanted pregnancy for teenagers generally. . . .

. . . Each year, more than one million 15–19-year-olds become pregnant, one-tenth of all women in this age group. (Two-thirds of these pregnancies are conceived out of wedlock.) In addition, some 30,000 girls younger than 15 get pregnant annually. . . .

How are the million teenage pregnancies to 15–19-year-olds resolved? In 1974:

28 percent resulted in marital births that were conceived following marriage.

10 percent resulted in marital births that were conceived prior to marriage.

21 percent resulted in out-of-wedlock births.

27 percent were terminated by induced abortion.

The remainder, 14 percent, resulted in miscarriages.

Of the additional 30,000 pregnancies experienced by girls younger than 15, 45 percent were terminated by abortion, and 36 percent resulted in out-of-wedlock births. Only six percent ended in marital births, and virtually all of these resulted from pregnancies conceived out of wedlock.

Because of the high rate of teenage pregnancy and childbearing, 608,000—or one-fifth—of all U.S. births are to women still in their teens; 247,000 are to adolescents 17 and younger, 13,000 to girls younger than 15. . . .

Like U.S. fertility generally, teenage birthrates have declined since the beginning of the 1960s. But the decline has been restricted to older adolescents. Throughout the period, the birthrates among 18- and 19-year-olds and 20–24-year-olds have shown a parallel decline. Among girls 14–17, however, fertility did not decline. Among girls younger than 14, birthrates actually rose slightly, though still barely above the one per 1,000 mark. . . .

A substantial and growing part of adolescent childbearing occurs out-of-wedlock. Between 1961 and 1974 the rate of out-of-wedlock childbearing declined by about one-quarter among women 20–24. By contrast, it increased by about one-third among 18–19-year-olds, and by three-quarters among 14–17-year olds. The nonmarital birthrate among 18–19-year-olds is now higher than that among women 20–24, reversing the trend that prevailed until the early 1970s. . . .

More than half of all out-of-wedlock births in the United States are to teenagers; one in four are to youngsters 17 and younger. Since the early 1960s, the proportion of all out-of-wedlock babies born to younger adolescents has risen by 18 percent and to older adolescents, by 40 percent. . . .

Teenage responses to national studies show that nearly two-thirds of all adolescent pregnancies and one-half of births are not intended. . .*

B. Health Consequences of Teenage Pregnancy

It is difficult to formulate a definitive statement on the health risks of adolescent pregnancy. Much of the data simply are not very good. Studies often are not comparable. More important, the classification of much vital data into the five-year grouping, 15–19, thus lumping adolescents into one category, obscures the major differences in the health risks between older teenagers and younger teenagers; 17–19-year-old females run the same comparatively low risks as those aged 20–24, while girls 16 and younger, still in the process of development, bear much higher risks.[8]

In general, pregnancy during younger adolescence increases the risks to the health of both mother and child.[9] A careful review of the domestic literature by Stepto, Keith, and Keith disclosed the most frequent complications of teenage pregnancy as:

Premature labor
Low birth weight
Increased neonatal mortality
Toxemia
Iron deficiency anemia

* Reprinted with permission of the Alan Guttmacher Institute.

[8]R. Stepto, L. Keith & D. Keith, *Obstetrical and Medical Problems of Teenage Pregnancy* in THE TEENAGE PREGNANT GIRL 87 (J. Zackler & W. Brandstadt, eds., Charles C. Thomas, 1975). [hereafter cited as R. Stepto *et al.*] This is based on data from the U.S. and other developed countries. In developing countries, where the age of menarche might be later or where physical development might take longer, a high risk of pregnancy might continue until the woman is older.

[9]The health risks of adolescent pregnancy are analyzed in some detail in D. Nortman, *Parental Age as a Factor in Pregnancy Outcome and Child Development,* REP. ON POP./FAM. PLAN., vol. 16 (1974). They are reviewed in W. Hunt II, *supra*. n. 2, which also contains an extensive bibliography.

Prolonged labor
Fetopelvic disproportion
Vaginal infections
Vaginal lacerations[10]

The risks tend to decrease with the age of the adolescent mother and increase with her parity. Although maternal age has an independent influence on the health risks, these are also influenced by other factors such as nutrition, poverty, race, etc. Writing about the risk of premature delivery, Stepto *et al.* state:

> Like toxemia, and probably related to it, prematurity rates are highest in the youngest patients. . . . The difference in the incidence of prematurity as related to maternal age is graphic. The exact cause of high rates of prematurity is unknown. Factors other than age or race alone must exert a synergistic influence on the incidence. Multiple birth, parity, improper spacing of pregnancy, social class, economic status, lack of prenatal care, and poor nutrition are some of the factors which may contribute to these high rates.[11]

In developing countries, particularly, low nutritional status, endemic diseases, and a relative lack of health care can magnify the health risks accompanying early pregnancy.[12]

C. Social and Economic Consequences of Teenage Pregnancy

Although serious physiological risks exist, particularly for very young mothers, "the psychologic impact of pregnancy in a young girl may be a great deal more detrimental than the effects or complications, however grave in nature, of biological immaturity. Pregnancy

[10]R. Stepto *et al., supra* n. 8 at 88.

[11]*Id.* at 122–124.

[12]*See* NATIONAL ACADEMY OF SCIENCES, NATIONAL RESEARCH COUNCIL COMMITTEE ON MATERIAL NUTRITION, MATERNAL NUTRITION AND THE COURSE OF PREGNANCY (1970); *see also,* S. Wishik, *The Implications of Undernutrition During Pubescence and Adolescence on Fertility,* in NUTRITIONAL IMPACTS ON WOMEN (K. Moghissi & T. Evans, eds., Harper & Row, 1977).

is frequently psychologically traumatic and, in some cases, a disaster to the person who has not fully developed."[13]

Early childbearing can affect schooling, employment, and marital status. Having a child often forces a teenage mother to drop out of school, and the younger the mother is at birth, the more likely that this will occur.[14] Since earnings are normally a function of formal education and work experience, an adolescent with a child or children would expect to find her opportunities to earn a good income greatly reduced.[15] This has been shown to be true in a study which found that teenagers with children were earning 40 percent less than a comparable group without children.[16] Additionally, women who bear their first child at a very young age tend to have more children, more unwanted children, and more out-of-wedlock births than women who postpone childbearing.[17] They are also more likely to have experienced unstable marriages or to have been married several times.[18]

In short, in the United States, teenage pregnancy, particularly for younger mothers, can be a severe personal tragedy with educational, career, and family effects that might never be overcome.[19] In considering the impact of teenage pregnancy, however, it should be remembered that, as in the case of health risks, the younger the

[13]R. Stepto *et al.*, *supra* n. 8, at 85. J. Shouse provides a comprehensive examination of the psychological problems accompanying teenage pregnancy, *Psychological and Emotional Problems of Pregnancy in Adolescence,* THE TEENAGE PREGNANT GIRL 161–168 (J. Zackler & W. Brandstadt, eds., Charles C. Thomas, 1975).

[14]J. Card and L. Wise, *Teenage Mothers and Teenage Fathers: The Impact of Early Childbearing on the Parents' Personal and Professional Lives,* 10 FAM. PLAN. PERSPECTIVES 199 (1978). In some instances it is retrogressive school policies, rather than the existence of a child, which force young mothers to leave school.

[15]T. Trussell, *Economic Consequences of Teenage Childbearing,* 8 FAM. PLAN. PERSPECTIVES 184 (1976).

[16]F. Furstenberg, *The Social Consequences of Teenage Parenthood,* 8 FAM. PLAN. PERSPECTIVES 148 (1976).

[17]T. Trussell & J. Menken, *Early Childbearing and Subsequent Fertility,* 10 FAM. PLAN. PERSPECTIVES 209 (1978).

[18]J. Card & L. Wise, *supra*. n. 14 at 202.

[19]In other countries—particularly developing countries—the consequences of early childbearing have been less well studied. In those countries which encourage youthful marriage and early childbearing and where the woman's primary role is that of a mother, many of the consequences found in the United States might not be applicable. In many countries, out-of-wedlock pregnancy is severely condemned and likely to lead to negative personal and social consequences for both the mother and the illegitimate child.

mother, the greater the consequences. It should also be remembered that illegitimacy brings with it certain adverse social consequences. A child born to a married woman will generally be cause for celebration; one born out-of-wedlock, even with today's changing morés, is far less likely to be considered a blessed event.

II. RIGHTS OF MINORS TO ABORTION, CONTRACEPTION AND STERILIZATION SERVICES

A. Minors' Consent to Medical Care Generally

1. The Common Law Rule and Exceptions to it[20]

Under the common law rule of torts, a physician could not treat a patient without first obtaining his or her informed consent. A doctor who did provide treatment in the absence of the patient's informed consent could be sued for damages under what some courts have termed a "technical assault and battery," or the doctor could be sued for malpractice. A minor, assumed not to have the judgment to know what his or her medical needs were, could not consent to treatment and, therefore, a doctor who served a minor without first obtaining parental consent might be liable for damages if the parents—or the minor upon reaching majority—chose to sue. To win, under a claim of assault and battery, a plaintiff had only to prove an unauthorized touching; it was not neccessary to prove an actual injury to the patient, or negligence or malpractice by the physician. A plaintiff could succeed even if the treatment benefitted the minor.[21]

Over the years, courts fashioned a number of exceptions that eased the restrictiveness of the common law rule of parental consent.

[20]This section is based, in part, on a paper by R. Zuckerman, *Legal Barriers to Services for Adolescents,* PROCEEDINGS OF THE BI-REGIONAL INSTITUTE OF ADOLESCENCE, REGIONS 8 AND 9 (conference sponsored by the Maternal and Child Health Service, DHEW, and the MCH Program of the School of Public Health of the University of California, Berkeley, Denver, 1978).

[21]With regard to *criminal* liability, Zuckerman, *supra* n. 20 at 20, notes:

> There are very few state statutes which expressly subject a physician to criminal liability for treating a minor without parental consent or notification or judicial authorization. Even taking the few exceptions into account, it appears that the criminal law has acted as a barrier to the adolescent's access to health care mainly when the health care sought has been abortion.

These exceptions permitted the minor to consent to treatment in emergencies and permitted emancipated and mature minors to consent to their own medical care.[22] The common law rule and exceptions have been examined in a number of articles and books.[23] Eve Paul, "The Legal Right of Minors to Sex-Related Medical Care," 6 *Columbia Human Rights Law Review* 357 (1974–1975), provides a concise summary:

> Minors have long been subject to a variety of disabilities under the law. At common law, minors were said to lack the full capacity to contract, to consent to medical treatment, to marry, to hold public office, to acquire domicile, to act as executor or administrator, to make wills, to act as agent or trustee or to appoint agents or attorneys.
>
> Minors have received further differential treatment under statutes protecting their health and morals, prescribing working conditions, and denying them the right to consent to sexual intercourse.
>
> These disabilities are sometimes said to be personal privileges conferred on minors by the law. As such they constitute limitations on the legal capacity of infants, not to defeat their rights, but to shield and protect them from their own improvidence, or from the acts of others.
>
> In cases concerning medical treatment for sex-related problems these disabilities have, however, often worked to the minor's detriment, especially because the situation has been complicated by the minor's embarrassment and disinclination to disclose the problem to a parent.

[22]The trend to permit minors to consent to their own sex-related medical care is part of a broader trend to enlarge the rights of young people generally. *See* A. SUSSMAN, THE RIGHTS OF YOUNG PEOPLE (Avon, 1977). *See also* Comment, *The Rights of Children: A Trust Model,* 46 FORDHAM L. REV. 669 (1978). Until recently, the almost universal age of majority was 21. This arbitrary dividing line between infancy and adulthood was rooted in history, supposedly having some connection with the age when a child could carry a full suit of armor. T. James, *The Age of Majority,* 4 AM. J. LEG. HIST. 22 (1960). Since the 26th amendment to the U.S. Constitution lowering the voting in federal elections from 21 to 18 years of age, nearly every state has lowered its age of majority to 18.

[23]*See, e.g.*, H. Pilpel, *Minors' Rights to Medical Care,* 36 ALBANY L. REV. 462 (1972); Note, *Parental Consent Requirements and Privacy Rights of Minors: The Contraceptive Controversy,* 88 HARVARD L. REV. 1001 (1975); Note, *The Minor's Right of Privacy: Limitations on State Action After Danforth and Carey,* 77 COLUM. L. REV. 1216 (1977); Note, *The Minor's Right to Abortion and the Requirement of Parental Consent,* 60 VA. L. REV. 305 (1974); R. Zuckerman, *supra* n. 20; Note, *Minors' Rights to Medical Care,* 14 J. FAM. LAW 581 (1975–76); R. Bennett, *Allocation of Child Medical Care Decisionmaking Authority: A Suggested Interest Analysis,* 62 VA. L. REV. 285 (1976).

The informed consent of a patient, if competent, has always been a prerequisite to surgery. If the patient was considered incompetent, then the consent of someone else who would be legally authorized to consent under the circumstances was needed.

At common law, the age of legal majority, and thus competence to consent, was fixed at 21. The law assumed that a minor was not wise or mature enough to determine what his or her medical needs were. Thus, consent was left in the hands of the minor's older and presumably wiser parent or guardian. Accordingly, a physician rendering medical care without parental consent was in danger of a possible civil suit by the parent for assault and battery, even if the contact was for the benefit of the minor. The physician was also in danger of a malpractice suit arising from a claim of performing an unauthorized operation.

Physicians were thus often reluctant to provide medical care to minors without prior parental consent, and because of the necessity of parental notification, minors were often reluctant to seek medical care, especially if the medical problem was sex-related.

However, the rule requiring parental consent has always been subject to a variety of exceptions. Courts throughout the country have held that, when confronted with an "emergency which endangers the life or health of a minor," a physician need not wait to obtain parental consent before commencing treatment. Exactly what the courts meant by an "emergency which endangers the life or health of a minor," has been subject to varying interpretations, however, and the burden of proof is usually on the physician to prove the existing emergency.

Another exception to the rule requiring parental consent which has been recognized by the courts is that of the "emancipated minor." Since emancipation is viewed as an extinguishment of parental rights and duties, most courts would probably hold, even in the absence of a statute or judicial precedent, that a completely emancipated minor can consent to his or her own medical treatment.

An "emancipated minor" is usually defined as a minor who lives apart from his or her parents and is self-supporting. Recent cases have held that a minor who contributes part of his or her own support may be emancipated even though still living at home. Various events such as marriage and military service can effect the emancipation of a minor. However, a minor may be emancipated for some purposes but not for others. Thus, a New York court recently held that while a minor was emancipated for the purpose of consenting to medical services, she was not emancipated for the purpose of altering her property rights. And several states which recognize the emancipation exception to parental consent may still require such consent under specific abortion statutes.

The most recent exception formulated by the courts has been that for the "mature minor," one who is sufficiently intelligent and mature to understand the nature and consequences of the medical treatment being sought. A physician treating a "mature minor" will not be held liable, even though parental consent has not been obtained, provided that the treatment is for the minor's benefit. The "mature minor" doctrine is a logical extension of the general rule requiring that physicians obtain "informed consent" from all patients before undertaking treatment. A "mature minor" can be defined as one who is capable of giving informed consent; this may depend in each case on the nature and seriousness of the medical treatment involved. Thus, in a recent Washington case, the exception was used to allow an eighteen-year-old minor to consent to a vasectomy because he was intelligent and mature enough to understand and appreciate the consequences of the operation. And in 1973, Judge Weinfeld of the Federal District Court for the Southern District of New York suggested a similar test in an abortion case. The surviving father of a pregnant minor sued a physician and clinic for performing an abortion on the girl without parental consent. Judge Weinfeld denied summary judgment for the plaintiff, declaring that whether the minor "was competent to exercise this right to [terminate her pregnancy] on her own behalf without her parents' consent presents an issue of fact."

Courts have elected, in the few suits that have been brought, to rely on the above exceptions. The author knows of no case holding a physician liable for damages for supplying any medical service to a minor without parental consent where the minor was older than fifteen and the treatment was for the minor's benefit and performed with the minor's consent. Nevertheless, doctors, hospitals, and health agencies have been reluctant to treat minors without parental consent, fearing exposure to suits for technical assault or malpractice. . . .*

2. State Statutory Provisions Permitting Minors to Consent to Health Care

a. R. Zuckerman, "Legal Barriers to Services for Adolescents," Proceedings Of The Bi-Regional Institute On Adolescence, Regions 8 and 9 conference sponsored by the Maternal and Child Health Service, DHEW, and the MCH Program of the School of Public Health, University of California, Berkeley (Denver 1978).

In every state and the District of Columbia, legislation has been enacted which alters, in varying degrees, the general common law requirement of parental consent to health care for minors. The scope of the statutory enactments removing the infancy disability differs markedly from state to state; and, to add to the complexity and confusion, a state often will have enacted a number of separate authorizing provisions which may overlap. Despite this considerable diversity, some generalization is possible about the kinds of statutory provisions that may exist. A cautionary word, however, is in order: because a state may have enacted only some, rather than all, of the provisions that will be described, it is always necessary to consult the statutes of a particular state before drawing any conclusions as to the precise circumstances in which, by statute, the general common law rule has been altered in that state.

One type of statutory provision frequently encountered focuses on a specific health concern about which adolescents may be especially reluctant to inform their parents—such as venereal disease, pregnancy, drug or alcohol abuse, or emotional disturbance—and authorizes some or all minors to consent to medical care relating to the specific problem or condition. For example, in every state and the District of Columbia, statutory provisions expressly authorize minors to consent to diagnosis and treatment for venereal disease. Statutory provisions expressly authorizing minors to consent to care and treatment relating to pregnancy have also been enacted in many states, but in a number of these states, consent to abortion and/or sterilization is expressly excluded. In light of recent United States Supreme Court decisions . . . the state statutes excluding consent to abortion are, however, probably unconstitutional. Where no such express statutory exclusion of abortion exists, the question has arisen whether abortion is included within the "care and treatment relating to pregnancy" provisions. To date, the courts to which this question has been addressed have concluded that consent to abortion is authorized by these statutory provisions. Also on the books in many states are statutes explicitly authorizing the provision of contraceptive services to minors without parental consent. Even in the absence of such "authorizing" provisions, a recent United States Supreme Court decision makes clear that states may not impose a parental consent requirement where a minor seeks federally subsidized family planning services under a state AFDC or Medicaid program. . . .

A second type of statutory provision which is not uncommon is that which allows certain minors to consent to virtually all kinds of medical care. Statutes in this second general group may in turn be viewed as forming a number of subcategories. A few statutes authorize the "mature minor" (defined along the same lines as the common law "mature minor" exception) to consent to medical treatment generally. Others have codified the common law emancipation doctrine, and, at times, have defined emancipation quite broadly. Still others have simply lowered the "age of majority" for purposes of medical treatment.

The third and last kind of statutory provision permitting treatment without parental consent can best be described as a codification, and in some cases a broadening, of the common law emergency exception. Occasionally these provisions depart from the common law doctrine by referring to specific medical conditions in defining "emergency." . . .

Before leaving the general subject of state legislation modifying the general common law parental consent requirement, reference should be made to one additional, albeit distinct, kind of legislative enactment—the child neglect statute. In every state, laws have been enacted which authorize court intervention for the protection of neglected children. These statutes, in turn, either implicitly or explicitly authorize the courts to order medical treatment of minors, where parental consent has been withheld, in fairly extreme cases of "medical neglect." Generally speaking, however, these statutes have been utilized in situations in which the absence of medical treatment will seriously endanger a minor, but depending upon the statutory language, courts in a number of states have ordered medical treatment in circumstances falling short of an "emergency." However, even if a neglect statute could be invoked by adolescents in some circumstances, as a practical matter, these statutes, involving as they do judicial proceedings to which a parent is a party, offer little assistance to those minors who are in need of health care relating to sexual activity, drug use and the like, but who are unwilling to inform their parents of these sensitive health problems.

3. Commentary on Minors' Consent and Physician Uncertainty

Although the emergency treatment and emancipated and mature minor doctrines provide some protection to the physician, they all have some areas of uncertainty and place the physician in the position of depending upon a court's interpretation of prior events.[24] Given this situation—and an era of defensive medicine—physicians and hospitals have sometimes been reluctant to provide medical care for minors without parental consent. As Bennett has observed, "Even in states where courts have upheld consent by a mature minor

[24]A carefully-framed statute can reduce a physician's uncertainty about when parental consent must be required and when there is potential liability for treating a minor. The relevant Maryland statute, to choose one example, states, "No physician . . . treating a minor pursuant to the minor's consent shall be liable civilly or subject to any penalty . . . solely by reason of the minor's lack of capacity to consent." MD. ANN. CODE ART. 43 § 135(b) (Supp. 1971). Pilpel notes that this kind of comprehensive medical treatment statute constitutes the best approach to reducing physician uncertainty. H. Pilpel, *supra* n. 23 at 469.

on his own behalf, the broad language of the widely-known general rule often leads doctors to insist strictly on parental consent, or to dispense with it in the belief that they are violating the law."[25]

What are the gray areas?

Emergency care. What constitutes an emergency? Courts have tended to take a narrow view of this, restricting it to imminent danger to life or health. Holder, however, suggests that a physician could prescribe contraceptives for a sexually active minor on the grounds that this condition, by itself, constitutes a medical emergency.[26]

Emancipation. Certain conditions indicating emancipation are objective: marriage, military service, parenthood. Others are less so; they vary from state to state and in accordance with the context. For example, are college students emancipated, even if their parents are paying the bills? What of boarding school students? Can a runaway child be considered emancipated—particularly one who refuses to divulge his or her parents' names?

Maturity. The "mature minor rule" is perhaps the most difficult of the three to interpret. Can a very young minor (say 11 years old) ever be mature enough to consent to treatment? Should a mature minor be able to consent to simple procedures but not complex ones? Is the degree of life-endangerment relevant? Is maturity the key factor or is it, rather, appearance of maturity? Is appearance of maturity—or maturity itself—an issue of fact for a jury to decide? One analyst, having reviewed the relevant cases, concluded that courts tended to apply the mature minor rule where the following conditions were met: the treatment was undertaken for the benefit of the minor rather than a third party; the minor was near majority (or at least in the range of 15 years or older) and was considered to have sufficient mental capacity to understand fully the nature and importance of the medical steps proposed; and the medical procedures could be characterized as something less than major or serious in nature.[27]

[25]R. Bennett, *supra* n. 23 at 306. In a similar vein *see* J. Stern, *Medical Treatment and the Teenager: The Need for Parental Consent,* 7 CLEARINGHOUSE REVIEW 1 (1973).

[26]A. HOLDER, MEDICAL MALPRACTICE LAW 28, (2d Ed., Wiley, 1978).

[27]W. Wadlington, *Minors and Health Care: The Age of Consent,* 11 OSGOODE HALL L. J. 115, 119 (1973).

With regard to a physician's liability for treating a minor without parental consent, several commentators have observed that no cases exist in which liability has been imposed on a physician or health facility on the basis of failure to secure parental consent for medical treatment where the minor was over 15.[28]

B. The Right of Minors to Consent to Abortion

In the years following the *Roe v. Wade* decision, many states enacted laws restricting abortions to those minors who had received parental consent or whose parents had been notified.[29]

In 1976, after considerable litigation in state and lower federal courts, the Supreme Court handed down two decisions concerning the rights of minors to abortion, *Planned Parenthood of Central Missouri v. Danforth* and *Bellotti v. Baird.* The 1976 *Bellotti v. Baird* (*"Bellotti I"*) decision left open a number of questions concerning a statutory requirement of parental consent for a minor's abortion. Many of the questions were answered by the Supreme Court's 1979 *Bellotti v. Baird* (*"Bellotti II"*) decision. These three cases are excerpted below.

1. Planned Parenthood of Central Missouri v. Danforth, 428 U.S. 52 (U.S. Supreme Court 1976)

Excerpts of those portions of the decision relating to minors are reprinted below. For those parts of the decision concerning other aspects of abortion, see chapter III, *supra.*

Mr. Justice Blackmun delivered the opinion of the Court . . .

Parental Consent. Section 3 (4) requires, with respect to the first 12 weeks of pregnancy, where the woman is unmarried and under the age of 18 years, the written consent of a parent or person *in loco parentis* unless, again, "the abortion is certified by a licensed physician as necessary in order to preserve the life of the mother." It is to be observed that only one parent need consent.

[28]H. Pilpel, *supra* n. 23; J. Stern, *supra* n. 25; E. Paul, *Legal Rights of Minors to Sex-Related Medical Care,* 6 COLUM. HUM. RTS. L. REV. 358 (1974–1975).

[29]*See* Note, *Implications of the Abortion Decisions: Post Roe and Doe Litigation and Legislation,* 74 COLUM. L. REV. 237, 245–247 (1974); Note, *Abortion Statutes after Danforth: An Examination,* 15 J. FAM. L. 537, 556–558; Note, *The Minor's Right of Privacy: Limitations on State Action After Danforth and Carey, supra* n. 23 at 1224–1225 (1976–77).

The appellees defend the statute in several ways. They point out that the law properly may subject minors to more stringent limitations than are permissable with respect to adults . . . Missouri law, it is said, "is replete with provisions reflecting the interest of the state in assuring the welfare of minors," citing statutes relating to a guardian *ad litem* for a court proceeding, to the care of delinquent and neglected children, to child labor, and to compulsory education . . . Certain decisions are considered by the State to be outside the scope of a minor's ability to act in his own best interest or in the interest of the public, citing statutes proscribing the sale of firearms and deadly weapons to minors without parental consent, and other statutes relating to minors' exposure to certain types of literature, the purchase by pawnbrokers or property from minors, and the sale of cigarettes and alcoholic beverages to minors. It is pointed out that the record contains testimony to the effect that children of tender years (even ages 10 and 11) have sought abortions. Thus, a State's permitting a child to obtain an abortion without the counsel of an adult "who has responsibility or concern for the child would constitute an irresponsible abdication of the State's duty to protect the welfare of minors." Parental discretion, too, has been protected from unwarranted or unreasonable interference from the State . . . Finally, it is said that § 3 (4) imposes no additional burden on the physician because even prior to the passage of the Act the physician would require parental consent before performing an abortion on a minor.

The appellants, in their turn, emphasize that no other Missouri statute specifically requires the additional consent of a minor's parent for medical or surgical treatment, and that in Missouri a minor legally may consent to medical services for pregnancy (excluding abortion), venereal disease, and drug abuse. . . . The result of § 3 (4), it is said, "is the ultimate supremacy of the parents' desires over those of the minor child, the pregnant patient." . . . It is noted that in Missouri a woman under the age of 18 who marries with parental consent does not require parental consent to abort, and yet her contemporary who has chosen not to marry must obtain parental approval. . . .

We agree with appellants and with the courts whose decisions have just been cited that the State may not impose a blanket provision such as § 3 (4), requiring the consent of a parent or person *in loco parentis* as a condition for abortion of an unmarried minor during the first 12 weeks of her pregnancy. Just as with the requirement of consent from the spouse, so here, the State does not have the constitutional authority to give a third party an absolute, and possibly arbitrary, veto over the decision of the physician and his patient to terminate the patient's pregnancy, regardless of the reason for withholding consent.

Constitutional rights do not mature and come into being magically only when one attains the state-defined age of majority. Minors, as well as adults, are protected by the Constitution and posses constitutional rights . . . The Court indeed, however, long has recognized that the state has somewhat broader authority to regulate the activities of children than of adults . . . It remains, then, to examine whether there is any significant state interest in conditioning an abortion on the consent of a parent or person *in loco parentis* that is not present in the case of an adult.

One suggested interest is the safeguarding of the family unit and of parental authority. . . . It is difficult, however, to conclude that providing a parent with absolute power to overrule a determination, made by the physician and his minor patient, to terminate the patient's pregnancy will serve to strengthen the family unit. Neither is it likely that such veto power will enhance parental authority or control where the minor and the nonconsenting parent are so fundamentally in conflict and the very existence of the pregnancy already has fractured the family structure. Any independent interest the parent may have in the termination of the minor daughter's pregnancy is no more weighty than the right of privacy of the competent minor mature enough to have become pregnant.

We emphasize that our holding that § 3 (4) is invalid does not suggest that every minor, regardless of age or maturity, may give effective consent for termination of her pregnancy. See *Bellotti v. Baird,* [*infra*]. The fault with § 3 (4) is that it imposes a special-consent provision, exercisable by a person other than the woman and her physician, as a prerequisite to a minor's termination of her pregnancy and does so without a sufficient justification for the restriction. It violates the strictures of *Roe* and *Doe.*

Mr. Justice Stewart, with whom Mr. Justice Powell joins, concurring.

With respect to the state law's requirement of parental consent, § 3 (4), I think it clear that its primary constitutional deficiency lies in its imposition of an absolute limitation on the minor's right to obtain an abortion. The Court's opinion today in *Bellotti v. Baird,* [*infra*] suggests that a materially different constitutional issue would be presented under a provision requiring parental consent or consultation in most cases but providing for prompt (i) judicial resolution of any disagreement between the parent and the minor, or (ii) judicial determination that the minor is mature enough to give an informed consent without parental concurrence or that abortion in any event is in the minor's best interest. Such a provision would not impose parental approval as an absolute condition upon the minor's right but would assure in most instances consultation between the parent and child.

There can be little doubt that the State furthers a constitutionally permissible end by encouraging an unmarried pregnant minor to seek the help and advice of her parents in making the very important decision whether or not to bear a child. That is a grave decision, and a girl of tender years, under emotional stress, may be ill-equipped to make it without mature advice and emotional support. It seems unlikely that she will obtain adequate counsel and support from the attending physician at an abortion clinic, where abortions for pregnant minors frequently take place.

Mr. Justice White, with whom The Chief Justice and Mr. Justice Rehnquist join, dissenting.

Section 3 (4) requires that an unmarried woman under 18 years of age obtain the consent of a parent or a person *in loco parentis* as a condition to an abortion. Once again the Court strikes the provision down in a sentence. It states: "Just as with the requirement of consent from the spouse, so here, the State does not have the constitutional authority to give a third party an absolute, and possibly arbitrary, veto over the decision of the physician and his patient to terminate the patient's pregnancy. . . ." The Court rejects the notions that the *State* has an interest in strengthening the family unit, or that the *parent* has an "independent interest" in the abortion decision, sufficient to justify § 3(4) and apparently concludes that the provision is therefore unconstitutional. But the purpose of the parental consent requirement is not merely to vindicate any interest of the parent or of the State. The purpose of the requirement is to vindicate the very right created in *Roe v. Wade,*—the right of the pregnant woman to decide "whether *or not* to terminate her pregnancy." (emphasis added) The abortion decision is unquestionably important and has irrevocable consequences whichever way it is made. Missouri is entitled to protect the minor unmarried woman from making the decision in a way which is not in her own best interests, and it seeks to achieve this goal by requiring parental consultation and consent. This is the traditional way by which States have sought to protect children from their own immature and improvident decisions; and there is absolutely no reason expressed by the majority why the State may not utilize that method here.

Mr. Justice Stevens, dissenting.

In my opinion, however, the parental-consent requirement is consistent with the holding in *Roe.* The State's interest in the welfare of its young citizens justifies a variety of protective measures. Because he may not forsee the consequences of his decision, a minor may not make an enforceable bargain. He may not lawfully work or travel where he pleases, or even attend exhibitions of constitutionally protected adult motion pictures. Persons below a certain age may not marry without parental consent. Indeed, such consent is essential even when the young woman is already pregnant. The State's interest in protecting a young person from harm justifies the imposition of restraints on his or her freedom even though comparable restraints on adults would be constitutionally impermissible. Therefore, the holding in *Roe v. Wade* that the abortion decision is entitled to constitutional protection merely emphasizes the importance of the decision; it does not lead to the conclusion that the state legislature has no power to enact legislation for the purpose of protecting a young pregnant woman from the consequences of an incorrect decision.

The abortion decision is, of course, more important than the decision to attend or to avoid an adult motion picture, or the decision to work long hours in a factory. It is not necessarily any more important than the decision to run away from home or the decision to marry. But even if it is the most important kind of a decision a young person may ever make, that assumption merely enhances the quality of the State's interest in maximizing the probability that the decision be made correctly and with full understanding of the consequences of either alternative.

The Court recognizes that the State may insist that the decision not be made without the benefit of medical advice. But since the most significant consequences of the decision are not medical in character, it would seem to me that the State may, with equal legitimacy, insist that the decision be made only after other appropriate counsel has been had as well. Whatever choice a pregnant young woman makes —to marry, to abort, to bear her child out of wedlock—the consequences of her decision may have a profound impact on her entire future life. A legislative determination that such a choice will be made more wisely in most cases if the advice and moral support of a parent play a part in the decisionmaking process is surely not irrational. Moreover, it is perfectly clear that the parental-consent requirement will necessarily involve a parent in the decisional process.

If there is no parental-consent requirement, many minors will submit to the abortion procedure without ever informing their parents. An assumption that the parental reaction will be hostile, disparaging, or violent no doubt persuades many children simply to bypass parental counsel which would in fact be loving, supportive, and, indeed for some, indispensable. It is unrealistic, in my judgment, to assume that every parent-child relationship is either (a) so perfect that communication and accord will take place routinely or (b) so imperfect that the absence of communication reflects the child's correct prediction that the parent will exercise his or her veto arbitrarily to further a selfish interest rather than the child's interest. A state legislature may conclude that most parents will be primarily interested in the welfare of their children, and further, that the imposition of a parental-consent requirement is an appropriate method of giving the parents an opportunity to foster that welfare by helping a pregnant distressed child to make and to implement a correct decision.

The State's interest is not dependent on an estimate of the impact the parental-consent requirement may have on the total number of abortions that may take place. I assume that parents will sometimes prevent abortions which might better be performed; other parents may advise abortions that should not be performed. Similarly, even doctors are not omniscient; specialists in performing abortions may incorrectly conclude that the immediate advantages of the procedure outweigh the disadvantages which a parent could evaluate in better perspective. In each individual case factors much more profound than a mere medical judgment may weigh heavily in the scales. The overriding consideration is that the right to make the choice be exercised as wisely as possible.

The Court assumes that parental consent is an appropriate requirement if the minor is not capable of understanding the procedure and of appreciating its consequences and those of available alternatives. This assumption is, of course, correct and consistent with the predicate which underlies all state legislation seeking to protect minors from the consequences of decisions they are not yet prepared to make. In all such situations chronological age has been the basis for imposition of a restraint on the minor's freedom of choice even though it is perfectly obvious that such a yardstick is imprecise and perhaps even unjust in particular cases. The Court seems to assume that the capacity to conceive a child and the judgment of the physician are the only constitutionally permissible yardsticks for determining whether a young woman can independently make the abortion decision. I doubt the accuracy of the Court's empirical judgment. Even if it were correct, however, as a matter of constitutional law I think a State has power to conclude otherwise and to select a chronological age as its standard.

In short, the State's interest in the welfare of its young citizens is sufficient, in my judgment, to support the parental-consent requirement.

2. Bellotti v. Baird, 428 U.S. 132 (U.S. Supreme Court 1976) [Bellotti I]

This case, decided the same day as *Danforth,* involved a challenge to § 12P of an "Act to Protect Unborn Children and Maternal Health Within Present Constitutional Limits," passed in 1974 by the Massachusetts legislature over the governor's veto. The relevant portions of Section 12P read:

> If the mother is less than eighteen years of age and has not married, the consent of both the mother and her parents is required. If one or both of the mother's parents refuse such consent, consent may be obtained by order of a judge of the superior court for good cause shown, after such hearing as he deems necessary. . . .

This section of the Act was found unconstitutional by a three judge federal district court in Massachusetts. That decision was appealed to the United States Supreme Court.

The issue decided by the Supreme Court was a procedural one: whether the federal district court should have abstained from ruling on the constitutionality of the statute until Massachusetts courts had had a chance to interpret it. In ruling that abstention was the proper course, Justice Blackmun, writing for a unanimous Court, used the following language:

> We do not accept appellees' assertion that the Supreme Judicial Court of Massachusetts inevitably will interpret the statute so as to create a "parental veto," require the superior court to act other than in the best interests of the minor, or impose undue burdens upon a minor capable of giving an informed consent.
>
> In *Planned Parenthood of Central Missouri v. Danforth,* we today struck down a statute that created a parental veto. . . . At the same time, however, we held that a requirement of written consent on the part of a pregnant adult is not unconstitutional unless it unduly burdens the right to seek an abortion. In this case, we are concerned with a statute directed toward minors, as to whom there are unquestionably greater risks of inability to give an informed consent. Without holding that a requirement of a court hearing would not unduly burden the rights of a mature adult . . . we think it clear that in the instant litigation adoption of appellants' interpretation would "at least materially change the nature of the problem" that appellants claim is presented.
>
> Whether the Supreme Judicial Court will so interpret the statute, or whether it will interpret the statute to require consideration of factors not mentioned above, impose burdens more serious than those suggested, or create some unanticipated interference with the doctor-patient relationship, we cannot now determine. Nor need we determine what factors are impermissible or at what point review of consent and good cause in the case of a minor becomes unduly burdensome. It is sufficient that the statute is susceptible to the interpretation offered by appellants, and we so find, and that such an interpretation would avoid or substantially modify the federal constitutional challenge to the statute, as it clearly would. . . .

On remand, the District Court certified nine questions to the Supreme Judicial Court of Massachusetts, the highest appellate court in Massachusetts. The Supreme Judicial Court gave the following construction of the section 12S:[30]

> 1. In deciding whether to grant consent to their daughter's abortion, parents are required by § 12S to consider exclusively what will serve her best interests.
>
> 2. The provision in § 12S that judicial consent for an abortion shall be granted, parental objections notwithstanding, "for good cause shown" means that such consent shall be granted if found to be in the minor's best interests. The judge "must disregard all parental objections, and other considerations, which are not based exclusively" on that standard.
>
> 3. Even if the judge in a § 12S proceeding finds "that the minor is capable of making, and has made, an informed and reasonable decision to have an abortion," he is entitled to withhold consent "in circumstances where he determines that the best interests of the minor will not be served by an abortion."
>
> 4. As a general rule, a minor who desires an abortion may not obtain judicial consent without first seeking both parents' consent. Exceptions to the rule exist when a parent is not available or when the need for the abortion constitutes "an emergency requiring immediate action." . . . Unless a parent is not available, he must be notified of any judicial proceedings brought under § 12S.
>
> 5. The resolution of § 12S cases and any appeals that follow can be expected to be prompt. The name of the minor and her parents may be held in confidence. If need be, the Supreme Judicial Court and the Superior courts can promulgate rules or issue orders to ensure that such proceedings are handled expeditiously.
>
> 6. Mass. Gen. Laws Ann. ch. 112, § 12F, (West. Supp. 1979) which provides, *inter alia,* that certain classes of minors may consent to most kinds of medical care without parental approval, does not apply to abortions, except as to minors who are married, widowed, or divorced . . . Nor does the State's common—law "mature minor rule" create an exception to § 12S.[31]

The case then went back to the Massachusetts federal district court, which, upon review of the state court's construction, again declared § 12S unconstitutional and enjoined its enforcement. *Baird*

[30]The numbering of the paragraph had been changed by the Massachusetts legislature from "12P" to "12S" without any change in substance.

[31]Baird v. Attorney General, 360 N.E. 2d 288 (Mass. 1977) as interpreted by the Supreme Court in Bellotti v. Baird, 443 U.S. 622, 630–631 (1979).

v. Bellotti, 428 F. Supp. 854 (1977).[32] That decision was appealed to the U.S. Supreme Court, which rendered its judgment in June 1979.

3. Bellotti v. Baird, 443 U.S. 622 (U.S. Supreme Court 1979) [Bellotti II]

Eight members of the Court voted to affirm the decision of the Massachusetts federal district court holding section 12S, as construed by the Supreme Judicial Court of Massachusetts, unconstitutional. However, no single opinion commanded a majority. Chief Justice Burger and Justices Stewart and Rehnquist joined the opinion of Justice Powell which announced the judgment of the Court. Justices Stevens, Brennan, Marshall, and Blackmun joined in a concurring opinion. Justice Rehnquist also wrote a separate concurrence, and Justice White dissented.

Parts I and II of Justice Powell's opinion have been omitted. Part I reviewed the history of the *Bellotti v. Baird* litigation. Part II examined the constitutional rights of minors and the respective roles of parents, minors, and the state.[33]

Mr. Justice Powell announced the judgment of the Court and delivered an opinion in which the Chief Justice, Mr. Justice Stewart, and Mr. Justice Rehnquist joined.

[32]The Seventh Circuit Court of Appeals struck down an Illinois statute containing language almost identical to that of the Massachusetts law. *See* Wynn v. Carey, 582 F. 2d 1375 (7th Cir. 1978).

[33]With respect to the roles of minors, their parents, and the state, courts have tended to analyze and weigh the rights and interests of the competing parties:

(1) *Minors,* as Justice Blackmun noted in *Danforth,* are protected by the Constitution and possess constitutional rights. *See, e.g.,* In re Gault, 387 U.S. 1 (1967), Tinker v. Des Moines School District, 393 U.S. 503 (1969), Goss v. Lopez, 419 U.S. 565 (1975). Although not all constitutional rights apply to minors, one of those that does is the right of privacy, a fundamental right.

(2) *Parents.* Rearing children free of state interference has long been considered a constitutional right, supported by a line of Supreme Court cases going back to 1923. Meyer v. Nebraska, 262 U.S. 390 (1923), Pierce v. Society of Sisters, 268 U.S. 510 (1925), Wisconsin v. Yoder, 406 U.S. 205 (1972). "At common law, parents' authority over their child extends to all areas of the child's life absent a strong public policy to the contrary. The potential reach of this power is virtually unlimited." Note, *The Minor's Right to Abortion and the Requirement of Parental Consent, supra* n. 23 at 319. However, courts have recognized some boundaries to parental authority, *e.g.,* in cases of child abuse or parental withholding of needed medical treatment from their children.

III

. . . In § 12S Massachusetts has attempted to reconcile the constitutional rights of a woman, in consultation with her physician, to choose to terminate her pregnancy as established by *Roe v. Wade,* 410 U.S. 113 (1973) and *Doe v. Bolton,* 410 U.S. 179 (1973), with the special interest of the State in encouraging an unmarried pregnant minor to seek the advice of her parents in making the important decision whether or not to bear a child. . . . The question before us—in light of what we have said in the prior cases—is whether § 12S, as authoritatively interpreted by the Supreme Judicial Court, provides for parental notice and consent in a manner that does not unduly burden the right to seek an abortion . . .

Appellees[34] and intervenors[35] contend that even as interpreted by the Supreme Judicial Court of Massachusetts § 12 S does unduly burden this right. They suggest, for example, that the mere requirement of parental notice constitutes such a burden . . . however, parental notice and consent are qualifications that typically may be imposed by the State on a minor's right to make important decisions. As immature minors often lack the ability to make fully informed choices that take account of both immediate and long-range consequences, a State reasonably may determine that parental consultation often is desirable and in the best interest of the minor. It may further deter-

---

(3) *The State,* as Justice Stevens observed in his dissent to the *Danforth* decision, has traditionally been considered to have interests which justify some regulation of minors: first, to protect minors from their own improvidence; second, to strengthen the family as a stable unit, and third, to maintain parental authority. The state possesses greater power to regulate the activities of children than of adults. Prince v. Massachusetts, 321 U.S. 158 (1944), Ginsberg v. New York, 390 U.S. 629 (1968).

For a comprehensive examination of the interests of the various parties in the context of abortion for minors, see Note, *The Minor's Right to Abortion and the Requirement of Parental Consent, supra* n. 23; more generally, *see* R. Bennett, *supra* n. 23; L. Teitelbaum & J. Ellis, *The Liberty Interest of Children: Due Process Rights and their Application,* 12 FAM. L. Q. 153 (1978), and A. Kleinfeld, *The Balance of Power Among Infants, Their Parents, and the State,* 4 FAM. L. Q. 320 and 410 (1970) and 5 FAM. L. Q. 64 (1971). *See also* R. MNOOKIN, CHILD, FAMILY AND STATE: PROBLEMS AND MATERIALS ON CHILDREN AND THE LAW (Little Brown, 1978).

[34]The appellees were William Baird, the Parents' Aid Society, a physician who regularly performed abortions, and "Mary Moe," a pregnant minor who, at the commencement of the suit, lived with her parents and desired to have an abortion without informing them.—Ed.

[35]The Planned Parenthood League of Massachusetts, the Crittenton Hastings House and Clinic, and Phillip Stubblefield, M.D. were the intervenors.—Ed.

mine, as a general proposition, that such consultation is particularly desirable with respect to the abortion decision—one that for some people raises profound moral and religious concerns. . . .

But we are concerned here with a constitutional right to seek an abortion. The abortion decision differs in important ways from other decisions that may be made during minority. The need to preserve the constitutional right and the unique nature of the abortion decision, especially when made by a minor, require a State to act with particular sensitivity when it legislates to foster parental involvement in this matter.

A

The pregnant minor's options are much different from those facing a minor in other situations, such as deciding whether to marry. A minor not permitted to marry before the age of majority is required simply to postpone her decision. She and her intended spouse may preserve the opportunity for later marriage should they continue to desire it. A pregnant adolescent, however, cannot preserve for long the possibility of aborting, which effectively expires in a matter of weeks from the onset of pregnancy.

Moreover, the potentially severe detriment facing a pregnant woman, see *Roe v. Wade,* is not mitigated by her minority. Indeed, considering her probable education, employment skills, financial resources, and emotional maturity, unwanted motherhood may be exceptionally burdensome for a minor. In addition, the fact of having a child brings with it adult legal responsibility, for parenthood, like attainment of the age of majority is one of the traditional criteria for the termination of the legal disabilities of minority. In sum, there are few situations in which denying a minor the right to make an important decision will have consequences so grave and indelible.

Yet, an abortion may not be the best choice for the minor. The circumstances in which this issue arises will vary widely. In a given case, alternatives to abortion such as marriage to the father of the child, arranging for its adoption, or assuming the responsibilities of motherhood with the assured support of family, may be feasible and relevant to the minor's best interests. Nonetheless, the abortion decision is one that simply cannot be postponed, or it will be made by default with far-reaching consequences.

For these reasons, as we held in *Planned Parenthood of Central Missouri v. Danforth,* . . . "the State may not impose a blanket provision . . . requiring the consent of a parent or person *in loco parentis* as a condition for abortion of an unmarried minor during the first 12 weeks of her pregnancy." Although . . . such deference to parents may be permissible with respect to other choices facing a minor, the unique nature and consequences of the abortion decision make it inappropriate "to give a third party an absolute, and possibly arbitrary, veto over the decision of the physician and his patient to terminate the patient's pregnancy, regardless of the reason for withholding consent." . . . We therefore conclude that if the State decides to require a pregnant minor to obtain one or both parents' consent to an abortion, it also must provide an alternative procedure* whereby authorization for the abortion can be obtained.

A pregnant minor is entitled in such a proceeding to show either: (1) that she is mature enough and well enough informed to make her abortion decision, in consultation with her physcian, independently of her parents' wishes; or (2) that even if she is not able to make this decision independently, the desired abortion would be in her best interests. The proceeding in which this showing is made must assure that a resolution of the issue, and any appeals that may follow, will be completed with anonymity and sufficient expedition to provide an effective opportunity for an abortion to be obtained. In sum, the procedure must ensure that the provision requiring parental consent does not in fact amount to the "absolute, and possible arbitrary, veto" that was found impermissible in *Danforth*. . . .

B

It is against these requirements that § 12S must be tested. We observe initially that as authoritatively construed by the highest court of the State, the statute satisfies some of the concerns that require special treatment of a minor's abortion decision. It provides that if parental consent is refused, authorization may be "obtained by order of a judge of the superior court for good cause shown, after such hearing as he deems necessary." A superior court judge presiding over a § 12S proceeding "must disregard all parental objections, and other considerations, which are not based exclusively on what would serve the minor's best interests."... The Supreme Judicial Court also stated: "Prompt resolution of a [§ 12S] proceeding may be expected. . . . The proceeding need not be brought in the minor's name and steps may be taken, by impoundment or otherwise, to preserve confidentiality as to the minor and her parents. . . . We believe that an early hearing and decision on appeal from a judgment of a Superior

*As § 12S provides for involvement of the state superior court in minors' abortion decisions, we discuss the alternative procedure described in the text in terms of judicial proceedings. We do not suggest, however, that a State choosing to require parental consent could not delegate the alternative procedure to a juvenile court or an administrative agency or officer. Indeed, much can be said for employing procedures and a forum less formal than those associated with a court of general jurisdiction—Footnote of the Court.

Court judge may also be achieved." . . . The court added that if these expectations were not met, either the Superior Court, in the exercise of its rulemaking power, or the Supreme Judicial Court would be willing to eliminate any undue burdens by rule or order. . . .

Despite these safeguards, which avoid much of what was objectionable in the statute successfully challenged in *Danforth,* § 12S falls short of constitutional standards in certain respects. We now consider these.

(1)

Among the questions certified to the Supreme Judicial Court was whether § 12S permits any minors—mature or immature—to obtain judicial consent to an abortion without any parental consultation whatsoever. . . . The state court answered that, in general, it does not. "[T]he consent required by [§ 12S must] be obtained for every non-emergency abortion where the mother is less than eighteen years of age and unmarried." . . . The text of § 12S itself states an exception to this rule, making consent unnecessary from any parent who has "died or has deserted his or her family." The Supreme Judicial Court construed the statute as containing an additional exception: Consent need not be obtained "where no parent (or statutory substitute) is available." . . . The court also ruled that an available parent must be given notice of any judicial proceedings brought by a minor to obtain consent for an abortion . . .

We think that, construed in this manner, § 12S would impose an undue burden upon the exercise by minors of the right to seek an abortion. As the District Court recognized, "there are parents who would obstruct, and perhaps altogether prevent, the minor's right to go to court." . . . There is no reason to believe that this would be so in the majority of cases where consent is withheld. But many parents hold strong views on the subject of abortion, and young pregnant minors, especially those living at home, are particularly vulnerable to their parents' efforts to obstruct both an abortion and their access to court. It would be unrealistic, therefore, to assume that the mere existence of a legal right to seek relief in superior court provides an effective avenue of relief for some of those who need it the most.

We conclude, therefore, that under state regulation such as that undertaken by Massachusetts, every minor must have the opportunity —if she so desires—to go directly to a court without first consulting or notifying her parents. If she satisfies the court that she is mature and well-enough informed to make intelligently the abortion decision on her own, the court must authorize her to act without parental consultation or consent. If she fails to satisfy the court that she is competent to make this decision independently, she must be permitted to show that an abortion nevertheless would be in her best interests. If the court is persuaded that it is, the court must authorize the abortion. If, however, the court is not persuaded by the minor that she is mature or that the abortion would be in her best interests, it may decline to sanction the operation.

There is, however, an important state interest in encouraging a family rather than a judicial resolution of a minor's abortion decision. Also, as we have observed above, parents naturally take an interest in the welfare of their children—an interest that is particularly strong where a normal family relationship exists and where the child is living with one or both parents. These factors properly may be taken into account by a court called upon to determine whether an abortion in fact is in a minor's best interests. If, all things considered, the court determines that an abortion is in the minor's best interests, she is entitled to court authorization without any parental involvement. On the other hand, the court may deny the abortion request of an immature minor in the absence of parental consultation if it concludes that her best interests would be served thereby, or the court may in such case defer decision until there is parental consultation in which the court may participate. But this is the full extent to which parental involvement may be required. For the reasons stated above, the constitutional right to seek an abortion may not be unduly burdened by state-imposed conditions upon initial access to court.

(2)

Section 12S requires that both parents consent to a minor's abortion. The District Court found it to be "custom" to perform other medical and surgical procedures on minors with the consent of only one parent, and it concluded that "nothing about abortions . . . requires the minor's interest to be treated differently." . . .

We are not persuaded that, as a general rule, the requirement of obtaining both parents' consent unconstitutionally burdens a minor's right to seek an abortion. The abortion decision has implications far broader than those associated with most other kinds of medical treatment. At least when the parents are together and the pregnant minor is living at home, both the father and mother have an interest—one normally supportive—in helping to determine the course that is in the best interest of a daughter. Consent and involvement by parents in important decisions by minors long have been recognized as protective of their immaturity. In the case of the abortion decision, for reasons we have stated, the focus of the parents' inquiry should be the best interests of their daughter. As every pregnant minor is entitled in the first instance to go directly to the court for a judicial determination without prior parental notice, consultation or consent, the general rule with respect to parental consent does not unduly burden the constitutional right. Moreover, where the pregnant minor goes to her parents and consent is denied, she still must have recourse to a prompt judicial determination of her maturity or best interests.

(3)

Another of the questions certified by the District Court to the Supreme Judicial Court was the following: "If the superior court finds that the minor is capable [of making], and has, in fact, made and adhered to, an informed and reasonable decision to have an abortion, may the court refuse its consent on a finding that a parent's, or its own, contrary decision is a better one?" . . . As stated above, if the minor satisfies a court that she has attained sufficient maturity to make a fully informed decision, she then is entitled to make her abortion decision independently. We therefore agree with the District Court that § 12S cannot constitutionally permit judicial disregard of the abortion decision of a minor who has been determined to be mature and fully competent to assess the implications of the choice she has made.

IV

Although it satisfies constitutional standards in large part, § 12S falls short of them in two respects: First, it permits judicial authorization for an abortion to be withheld from a minor who is found by the superior court to be mature and fully competent to make this decision independently. Second, it requires parental consultation or notification in every instance, without affording the pregnant minor an opportunity to receive an independent judicial determination that she is mature enough to consent or that an abortion would be in her best interests. Accordingly, we affirm the judgment of the District Court insofar as it invalidates this statute and enjoins its enforcement.

[A separate concurring opinion of Justice Rehnquist is omitted.]

Mr. Justice Stevens, with whom Mr. Justice Brennan, Mr. Justice Marshall, and Mr. Justice Blackmun join, concurring in the judgment.

. . . In *Planned Parenthood of Central Missouri v. Danforth,* this Court invalidated statutory provisions requiring the consent of the husband of a married woman and of one parent of a pregnant minor to an abortion . . . As to the parental consent, the Court held that "Just as with the requirement of consent from the spouse, so here, the State does not have the constitutional authority to give a third party an absolute, and possibly arbitrary, veto over the decision of the physician and his patient to terminate the patient's pregnancy, regardless of the reason for withholding the consent."... These holdings, I think, equally apply to the Massachusetts statute. The differences between the two statutes are few. Unlike the Missouri statute, Massachusetts requires the consent of both of the woman's parents. It does, of course, provide an alternative in the form of a suit initiated by the woman in superior court. But in that proceeding, the judge is afforded an absolute veto over the minor's decisions, based on his judgment of her best interests. In Massachusetts, then, as in Missouri, the State has imposed an "absolute limitation on the minor's right to obtain an abortion," . . . applicable to every pregnant minor in the State who has not married.

The provision of an absolute veto to a judge—or, potentially, to an appointed administrator—is to me particularly troubling. The constitutional right to make the abortion decision affords protection to both of the privacy interests recognized in this Court's cases: "One is the individual interest in avoiding disclosure of personal matters, and another is the interest in independence in making certain kinds of important decisions." *Whalen v. Roe,* 429 U.S. 589, 599–600. It is inherent in the right to make the abortion decision that the right may be exercised without public scrutiny and in defiance of the contrary opinion of the sovereign or other third parties. In Massachusetts, however, every minor who cannot secure the consent of both her parents—which under *Danforth* cannot be an absolute prerequisite to an abortion—is required to secure the consent of the sovereign. As a practical matter, I would suppose that the need to commence judicial proceedings in order to obtain a legal abortion would impose a burden at least as great as, and probably greater than, that imposed on the minor child by the need to obtain the consent of a parent. Moreover, once this burden is met, the only standard provided for the judge's decision is the best interest of the minor. That standard provides little real guidance to the judge, and his decision must necessarily reflect personal and societal values and morés whose enforcement upon the minor—particularly when contrary to her own informed and reasonable decision—is fundamentally at odds with privacy interests underlying the constitutional protection afforded to her decision.

In short, it seems to me that this case is governed by *Danforth;* to the extent this statute differs from that in *Danforth,* it is potentially even more restrictive of the constitutional right to decide whether or not to terminate a pregnancy. Because the statute has been once authoritatively construed by the Massachusetts Supreme Judicial Court, and because it is clear that the statute as written and construed is not constitutional, I agree with Mr. Justice Powell that the District Court's judgment should be affirmed. Because his opinion goes further, however, and addresses the constitutionality of an abortion statute that Massachusetts has not enacted, I decline to join his opinion.

Mr. Justice White, dissenting.

I was in dissent in *Planned Parenthood of Central Missouri v. Danforth,* on the issue of the validity of requiring the consent of a parent when an unmarried woman under 18 years of age seeks an abortion. I continue to have the views I expressed there and also agree with much of what Mr. Justice Stevens said in dissent in that case. I would not, therefore, strike down this Massachusetts law. . . . Until now, I would have thought inconceivable a holding that the United States Constitution forbids even notice to parents when their minor child who seeks surgery objects to such notice and is able to convince a judge that the parents should be denied participation in the decision. . . .

4. Issues and Commentary

Three differing fact situations of parental intervention in a minor's abortion decision have been posited: (a) a simple requirement of parental *consent;* (b) a requirement of a parental consent with an appeal mechanism in case of parental refusal; and (c) a requirement of parental *consultation* or *notification.* The Court's decision in *Danforth* disposed of the first alternative and in *Bellotti II* established some rules for the second. Thus, the key remaining issue is that of parental notification or consultation.

a. Parental Notification—Mature Minors. How much guidance does *Bellotti II* provide on the constitutionality of a statute requiring a minor to *consult with* or *seek the guidance of* her parents before obtaining an abortion?[36] The language of the Massachusetts statute required parental consent, not consultation. From the language of Justice Powell's opinion, it would appear that a statute requiring even parental notification by a mature minor would be unconstitutional. Recall his statement that:

If she [the minor seeking an abortion] satisfied the court that she is mature and well-enough informed to make intelligently the abortion

[36]Justice Stevens' concurrence observes in a footnote not excerpted that neither *Danforth* nor *Bellotti II* determines the constitutionality of a statute which only requires notice to the parents without affording them or any other third party an absolute veto.

decision on her own, the court must authorize her to act *without parental consultation* or consent. (emphasis added)

Of course, in Massachusetts, a judicial mechanism was provided to make a decision on a minor's maturity.[37] What happens in a situation where there is no provision for access to the courts or other administrative body? For example, where a statute simply states that parental consultation is required before a physician performs an abortion on a minor? Would a physician's judgment on maturity be conclusive? The practical consequences for physicians were discussed, in the context of *Danforth* (before *Bellotti II* was decided), in the Columbia Law Review:

> However, if *Danforth* emancipates only the "mature" child, leaving states free to impose parental consent requirements on unemancipated minors, the common law would remain in partial effect. Physicians performing abortions on minors not protected by *Danforth* would still have to obtain prior parental approval or risk subsequent tort actions by the minor's parents. Thus, the net effect of *Danforth* would be to require states to incorporate the common law's "mature minor" exception . . . into any legislation restricting juvenile access to abortions. It seems likely, however, that in such a situation physicians would refrain from performing abortions on *any* minor, pending a clear determination that the child was, as a matter of law, authorized to make the abortion decision. . . .[38]

b. Parental Notification—Immature Minors. Justice Powell's opinion also appears to establish guidelines for parental consultation where a minor is found to be too young to make the abortion decision on her own:

> If, all things considered, the court determines that an abortion is in the minor's best interests, she is entitled to court authorization *without any parental involvement.* On the other hand, the court may deny the abortion request of an immature minor in the absence of parental consultation if it concludes that her best interests would be served thereby, or the court in such a case defer decision until there is parental consultation in which the court may participate. But *this is the full extent to which parental involvement may be required* (emphases added).

[37]The Court does not address the question of whether minors will, in fact, know that a judicial remedy is available to them.

[38]Note, *The Minor's Right of Privacy: Limitations on State Action After Danforth and Carey, supra* no. 23 at 1228 n. 66.

Determining what is in a minor's best interest is complex and difficult, not only in the abortion context, but in all situations concerning minors. Justice Powell observed that "parents naturally take an interest in the welfare of their children," a consideration that may be taken into account by a court asked to determine whether an abortion is in an immature minor's best interest.

c. Summary. To summarize: under *Danforth,* a state cannot give a parent the right to consent to a minor's abortion decision. Under *Bellotti II,* in states passing statutes similar to the Massachusetts legislation, a minor has the right to go directly to court or other designated administrative body. If it is determined that she is either (a) a mature minor or (b) an immature minor and an abortion would be in her best interest, she has the right to have an abortion without parental involvement. This applies to abortion at any stage of the pregnancy.[39] In 1981 the Supreme Court, in *H.L. v. Matheson,* 49 *U.S. Law Week* 4255, upheld a parental *notification* requirement where the minor was living with and dependent upon her parents, was not emancipated, and had made no claim regarding her maturity or relations with her parents. Two concurring justices emphasized that parental notification could not constitutionally be required of mature minors or immature minors whose best interests would not be served by notifying the parents. Three dissenting justices felt that the notification statute should have been declared unconstitutional.

d. Parental Notification and Physician Confidentiality. Does a requirement that physicians must notify parents of minors before per-

[39]Paul and Pilpel summarize the implications of *Danforth* and *Bellotti* II on the law of medical malpractice in the following terms:

> The Supreme Court in effect approved in *Danforth* the rule that minors sufficiently mature and intelligent to understand the nature of a medical problem and the risks and benefits of the treatment may give effective consent for abortion. More explicitly, the Court held in *Bellotti II* that states "cannot constitutionally permit disregard of the abortion decision of a minor who has been determined to be mature and fully competent to assess the implications of the choice she has made." This affirmation of the mature minor rule indicates that damages cannot be assessed against a physician or other health care provider for performing an abortion on a mature minor without parental consent, since such an award would violate the minor's constitutionally established right to privacy in the same way as would a state law requiring parental consent.

E. Paul & H. Pilpel, *Teenagers and Pregnancy: The Law in 1980,* 11 FAM. PLAN. PERSPECTIVES 297 at 299 (1979).

forming an abortion force them to breach a confidential relationship with their adolescent patient? Zuckerman points out that state laws vary widely—many are silent about parental notification, a few require it, while others state it is not required, but leave open whether it is permitted. Even where disclosure is permitted by statute, the laws do not always provide criteria to guide the health professional's exercise of discretion.[40] Compare Holder who concludes: "If the physician does not feel the need to obtain consent of the parents to treat the child, he is by that decision assuring the child that the normal physician-patient relationship that would obtain if he were an adult has begun to apply."[41]

e. A Minor's Right to Refuse Consent. If a minor has the right to consent to an abortion, does she also have the right to refuse consent? Should parents be able to compel their very young daughter to undergo an abortion? To use an IUD? Very few cases have been litigated on this point.[42] It seems likely that a physician who performed an abortion on an objecting minor, at her parents' request, would run the risk of being sued for assault and battery when the youngster reached the age of majority. The issue presented herein is in some ways analogous to the issue of sterilization of minors based on parental consent, which is prohibited under current HEW regulations.

C. A Minor's Right to Obtain Contraceptives

1. Carey v. Population Services International 431 U.S. 678 (U.S. Supreme Court (1977)

The case involved a challenge to § 6811(8) of the New York Education law, which made it a crime for (a) any person to sell or distribute contraceptives to a minor under the age of 16, (b) anyone other than a licensed pharmacist to distribute contraceptives to persons over 16, and (c) anyone, including licensed pharmacists, to advertise or display contraceptives. The Supreme Court struck down all three provisions as unconstitutional. Those portions of the decision dealing with advertising of contraceptives and distribution by

[40] R. Zuckerman, *supra* n. 20 at 17–18.

[41] A. HOLDER, LEGAL ISSUES IN PEDIATRICS AND ADOLESCENT MEDICINE (Wiley, 1977).

[42] *See, e.g.,* In re Smith, 295 A. 2d 238 (Md. 1972).

pharmacists only are discussed in Chapter 5. That portion of the opinion dealing with minors (Section IV), as well as the relevant concurrances and dissents, are excerpted below.

Justice Brennan announced the judgment relating to minor's access to contraception; he was joined in this part of the decision by Justices Stewart, Marshall, and Blackmun.

IV

The District Court also held unconstitutional, as applied to nonprescription contraceptives, the provision of § 6811(8) prohibiting the distribution of contraceptives to those under 16 years of age. Appellants contend that this provision of the statute is constitutionally permissible as a regulation of the morality of minors, in furtherance of the State's policy against promiscuous sexual intercourse among the young.

The question of the extent of state power to regulate conduct of minors not constitutionally regulable when committed by adults is a vexing one, perhaps not susceptible to precise answer. We have been reluctant to attempt to define "the totality of the relationship of the juvenile and the state." ... Certain principles, however, have been recognized. "Minors, as well as adults, are protected by the Constitution and possess constitutional rights." ... "Whatever may be their precise impact neither the Fourteenth Amendment nor the Bill of Rights is for adults alone."... On the other hand, we have held in a variety of contexts that "the power of the state to control the conduct of children reaches beyond the scope of its authority over adults." *Planned Parenthood of Central Missouri v. Danforth.*

Of particular significance to the decision of this case, the right to privacy in connection with decisions affecting procreation extends to minors as well as to adults.... State restrictions inhibiting privacy rights of minors are valid only if they serve "any significant state interest ... that is not present in the case of an adult." ...

Since the State may not impose a blanket prohibition, or even a blanket requirement of parental consent, on the choice of a minor to terminate her pregnancy, the constitutionality of a blanket prohibition of the distribution of contraceptives to minors is *a fortiori* foreclosed. The State's interests in protection of the mental and physical health of the pregnant minor, and in protection of potential life are clearly more implicated by the abortion decision than by the decision to use a nonhazardous contraceptive.

Appellants argue, however, that significant state interests are served by restricting minors' access to contraceptives, because free availability to minors of contraceptives would lead to increased sexual activity among the young, in violation of the policy of New York to discourage such behavior.* The argument is that minors' sexual activity may be deterred by increasing the hazards attendant on it. The same argument, however, would support a ban on abortions for minors, or indeed support a prohibition on abortions, or access to contraceptives, for the unmarried, whose sexual activity is also against the public policy policy of many States. Yet, in each of these areas, the Court has rejected the argument, noting in *Roe v. Wade,* that "no court or commentator has taken the argument seriously." . . . The reason for this unanimous rejection was stated in *Eisenstadt v. Baird.* "It would be plainly unreasonable to assume that [the state] has prescribed pregnancy and the birth of an unwanted child [or the physical and psychological dangers of an abortion] as punishment for fornication." . . . We remain reluctant to attribute any such "scheme of values" to the State.

Moreover, there is substantial reason for doubt whether limiting access to contraceptives will in fact substantially discourage early sexual behavior. Appellants themselves conceded in the District Court that "there is no evidence that teenage extramarital sexual activity increases in proportion to the availability of contraceptives, . . ." and accordingly offered none, in the District Court or here. Appellees, on the other hand, cite a considerable body of evidence and opinion indicating that there is no such deterrent effect. Although we take judicial notice, as did the District Court, that with or without access to contraceptives, the incidence of sexual activity among minors is high, and the consequences of such activity are frequently devastating, the studies cited by appellees play no part in our decision. It is enough that we again confirm the principle that when a State, as here, burdens the exercise of a fundamental right, its attempt to justify that burden as a rational means for the accomplishment of some significant State policy requires more than a bare assertion, based on a conceded complete absence of supporting evidence, that the burden is connected to such a policy . . .

*Appellees argue that the State's policy to discourage sexual activity of minors is itself unconstitutional, for the reason that the right to privacy comprehends a right of minors as well as adults to engage in private consensual sexual behavior. We observe that the Court has not definitively answered the difficult question whether and to what extent the Constitution prohibits state statutes regulating such behavior among adults. See generally Note, On Privacy: Constitutional Protection for Personal Liberty, 48 N.Y.U.L. Rev. 670, 719–738 (1973). But whatever the answer to that question, *Ginsberg v. New York,* 390 U.S. 629 (1968), indicates that in the area of sexual mores, as in other areas, the scope of permissible state regulation is broader as to minors than as to adults. In any event, it is unnecessary to pass upon this contention of appellees, and our decision proceeds on the assumption that the Constitution does not bar state regulation of the sexual behavior of minors.—Footnote of the Court.

The Chief Justice dissents.

Mr. Justice White, concurring in the result.

I concur in the result in Part IV primarily because the State has not demonstrated that the prohibition against distribution of contraceptives to minors measurably contributes to the deterrent purposes which the State advances as justification for the restriction. Again, however, the legality of state laws forbidding premarital intercourse is not at issue here. . . .

Mr. Justice Powell, concurring in the judgment.

. . . Although I concur in the judgment of the Court, I am not persuaded that the Constitution requires the severe constraints that the Court's opinion places upon legislative efforts to regulate the distribution of contraceptives, particularly to the young. . . .

There is also no justification for subjecting restrictions on the sexual activity of the young to heightened judicial review. Under our prior cases, the States have broad latitude to legislate with respect to adolescents. The principle is well settled that "a State may permissibly determine that, at least in some precisely delineated areas, a child . . . is not possessed of that full capacity for individual choice" which is essential to the exercise of various constitutionally protected interests. . . .

Until today, I would not have thought it was even arguably necessary to review state regulation of this sort under a standard that for all practical purposes approaches the "compelling state interest" standard. . . . The relevant question in any case where state laws impinge on the freedom of action of young people in sexual matters is whether the restriction rationally serves valid state interests . . .

With these considerations in mind, I turn to the specific provisions of the New York statute limiting the distribution of contraceptives.

New York has made it a crime for anyone other than a physician to sell or distribute contraceptives to minors under the age of 16 years. . . . This element of New York's program of regulation for the protection of its minor citizens is said to evidence the State's judgment that the health and well-being of minors would be better assured if they are not encouraged to engage in sexual intercourse without guidance. Although I have no doubt that properly framed legislation . . . would meet constitutional standards, the New York provision is defective in two respects. First it infringes the privacy interests of married females between the ages of 14 and 16 . . . in that it prohibits the distribution of contraceptives to such females except by a physician. . . .

Second, this provision prohibits parents from distributing contraceptives to their children, a restriction that unjustifiably interferes with parental interests in rearing their children. . . .

But in my view there is considerably more room for state regulation in this area than would be permissible under the plurality's opinion. It seems clear to me, for example, that the State would further a constitutionally permissible end if it encouraged adolescents to seek the advice and guidance of their parents before deciding whether to engage in sexual intercourse. . . .

Requiring minors to seek parental guidance would be consistent with our prior cases. . . . A requirement of prior parental consultation is merely one illustration of permissible regulation in this area. As long as parental distribution is permitted, a State should have substantial latitude in regulating the distribution of contraceptives to minors.

Mr. Justice Stevens, concurring in the judgment.

There are two reasons why I do not join Part IV. First, the holding in *Planned Parenthood of Central Missouri v. Danforth* that a minor's decision to abort her pregnancy may not be conditioned on parental consent, is not dispositive here. The options available to the already pregnant minor are fundamentally different from those available to non-pregnant minors. The former must bear a child unless she aborts; but persons in the latter category can and generally will avoid childbearing by abstention. Consequently, even if I had joined that part of *Planned Parenthood,* I could not agree that the Constitution provides the same measure of protection to the minor's right to use contraceptives as to the pregnant female's right to abort.

Second, I would not leave open the question whether there is a significant state interest in discouraging sexual activity among unmarried persons under 16 years of age. Indeed, I would describe as "frivolous" appellee's argument that a minor has the constitutional right to put contraceptives to their intended use, notwithstanding the combined objection of both parents and the State.

For the reasons explained by Mr. Justice Powell, I agree that the statute may not be applied to married females between the ages of 14 and 16, or to distribution by parents. I am not persuaded, however, that these glaring defects alone justify an injunction against other applications of the statute. Only one of the three plaintiffs in this case is a parent who wishes to give contraceptives to his children. The others are an Episcopal minister who sponsors a program against venereal disease, and a mail-order firm, which presumably has no way to determine the age of its customers. I am satisfied for the reasons that follow, that the statute is also invalid as applied to them. . . .

Common sense indicates that many young people will engage in sexual activity regardless of what the New York Legislature does; and further, that the incidence of venereal disease and premarital pregnancy is affected by the availability or unavailability of contraceptives. Although young persons theoretically may avoid those harms by practicing total abstention, inevitably many will not. The statutory prohibition denies them and their parents a choice which, if available, would reduce their exposure to disease or unwanted pregnancy.

The State's asserted justification is a desire to inhibit sexual conduct by minors under 16. Appellants do not seriously contend that if contraceptives are available, significant numbers of minors who now abstain from sex will cease abstaining because they will no longer fear pregnancy or disease. Rather appellants' central argument is that the statute has the important *symbolic* effect of communicating disapproval of sexual activity by minors. In essence, therefore, the statute is defended as a form of propaganda, rather than a regulation of behavior.

Although the State may properly perform a teaching function, it seems to me that an attempt to persuade by inflicting harm on the listener is an unacceptable means of conveying a message that is otherwise legitimate. The propaganda techinque used in this case significantly increases the risk of unwanted pregnancy and venereal disease. It is as though a State decided to dramatize its disapproval of motorcylces by forbidding the use of safety helmets. One need not posit a constitutional right to ride a motorcycle to characterize such a restriction as irrational and perverse.

Even as a regulation of behavior, such a statute would be defective. Assuming that the State could impose a uniform sanction upon young persons who risk self-inflicted harm by operating motorcycles, or by engaging in sexual activity, surely that sanction could not take the form of deliberately injuring the cyclist or infecting the promiscuous child. If such punishment may not be administered deliberately, after trial and a finding of guilt, it manifestly cannot be imposed by a legislature, indiscriminately and at random. This kind of government-mandated harm, is, in my judgment, appropriately characterized as a deprivation of liberty without due process of law . . .

Mr. Justice Rehnquist, dissenting.

Those who valiantly but vainly defended the heights of Bunker Hill in 1775 made it possible that men such as James Madison might later sit in the first Congress and draft the Bill of Rights to the Constitution. The post-Civil War Congresses which drafted the Civil War Amendments to the Constitution could not have accomplished their task without the blood of brave men on both sides which was shed at Shiloh, Gettysburg, and Cold Harbor. If those responsible for these Amendments, by feats of valor or efforts of draftsmanship, could have lived to know that their efforts had enshrined in the Constitution the right of commercial vendors of contraceptives to peddle them to unmarried minors through such means as window displays and vending machines located in the men's room of truck stops, notwithstanding the considered judgment of the New York Legislature to the contrary, it is not difficult to imagine their reaction.

I do not believe that the cases discussed in the Court's opinion require any such result, but to debate the Court's treatment of the question on a case-by-case basis would concede more validity to the result reached by the Court than I am willing to do. There comes a point when endless and ill-considered extension of principles originally formulated in quite different cases produces such an indefensible result that no logic chopping can possibly make the fallacy of the result more obvious . . .

. . . The majority of New York's citizens are in effect told that however deeply they may be concerned about the problem of promiscuous sex and intercourse among unmarried teenagers, they may not adopt this means of dealing with it. The Court holds that New York may not use its police power to legislate in the interests of its concept of the public morality as it pertains to minors. The Court's denial of a power so fundamental to self-government must, in the long run, prove to be but a temporary departure from a wise and heretofore settled course of adjudication to the contrary. I would reverse the judgment of the District Court.

2. Commentary and Issues

a. The Significant State Interest Test. Justice Brennan, writing for four members[43] of the Court in *P.S.I.,* adopted the language used in *Danforth* to posit that a state must have *significant* state interest to justify an infringement on the privacy rights of a minor. The plurality suggests that this standard is less rigorous than the *compelling* state interest test used where fundamental rights of adults are involved.[44] The plurality then found that since the state's interest in

[43]Three Justices (Powell, Stevens, and White) concurred in the result, but not the reasoning, of the plurality. Chief Justice Burger and Justice Rehnquist dissented.

[44]However, Justice Powell noted that the *significant interest* test for all practical purposes approaches the *compelling state interest* standard. A note in the Columbia Law Review challenged the reasoning behind the significant state interest standard:

protecting the health of the mother or the life of the unborn fetus did not justify state intervention in the first trimester of pregnancy, *a fortiori* it was not sufficiently significant to justify a ban on contraceptives. The scope of significant state interest will be litigated in the future. Also to be litigated is the question of what are rational means to fulfill even a significant end. For example, even if a state has a significant interest in curbing adolescent sex, it must demonstrate that a requirement of parental guidance or notification will, in fact, deter teenage sexual activity. The plurality in *P.S.I.* found no evidence to support the "bare assertion" that limiting access to contraceptives would reduce teenage sexual activity.

b. Parental Consent and Consultation for Contraceptives. Although *Carey v. P.S.I.* does not specifically consider a parental consent requirement, the decision is certainly relevant should the issue arise. Could a state require parental consent for a minor to use contraception? Following the logic of *Danforth*, a parent would not be likely to have the power to do this since the state is prohibited from doing it. In this regard, it should be noted the Supreme Court affirmed a federal district court decision that the provisions of AFDC and Medicaid statutes mandating the provision of family planning services to minors desiring them precluded a parental consent requirement in those programs. *T_H_ v. Jones,* 425 U.S. 986 (1976), *aff'g. mem.* 425 F. Supp. 873 (D. Utah, 1975). The decision was based on statutory, not constitutional, grounds.

What about the constitutionality of parental notification or consultation requirement? The issues are similar to those examined in relation to parental notification for abortion, pp. 288–291, *supra*. Are there differences between parental notification of contraceptive use and notification of abortion? Would the state interest in requiring

---

. . . By positing a lower standard for action affecting minors, the Court essentially established a two-tiered system of constitutional protection; a minor, even though technically possessing the same constitutional right against government interference, is potentially subject to greater infringements.

A more logical approach would be to maintain a uniform compelling interest requirement for state action affecting fundamental rights while recognizing that, in the case of minors, the state may possess additional compelling interests not applicable to adults. Such as approach avoids relegating the constitutional rights of minors to a second class status but still allows for expression of special state concerns with respect to minors.

Note, *The Minor's Right of Privacy: Limitations on State Action after Danforth and Carey,* supra n. 23 at 1232, n. 88.

parental notification for contraception be greater or less than for abortion?[45]

c. Prescriptive and Non-Prescriptive Contraceptives. Although the New York law in *P.S.I.* prohibited the distribution of all contraceptives to minors, the plurality went out of its way to limit its holding to *non-prescriptive* or *non-hazardous* contraceptives. It should be noted that, in *P.S.I.*, the state of New York conceded that physicians were free to provide prescriptive contraceptives to minors of any age. Thus, the question of consent for prescriptive contraceptives was not before the Court. Does the language or reasoning of *P.S.I.* lead to the conclusion that a requirement of parental consent or notification prior to the distribution of oral contraceptives would also be unconstitutional? For a viewpoint arguing that the state has no significant interest in imposing a parental consent requirement for prescriptive contraceptives that it would not have with respect to nonprescriptive contraceptives, see Comment, "Carey v. Population Services International: Closing the Curtain on Comstockery," 44 *Brooklyn L. Rev.* 565, 590–59 (1978). For an opposing view, see *Doe v. Irwin,* which, emphasizing the risks of oral contraceptives, noted that a minor on the pill without the knowledge of her parents and physician might not be properly treated in case of a serious complication, even though her parents remain responsible for the expenses of any treatment she may require.[46]

d. A Parental Right of Notification? The recent case of *Doe v. Irwin, supra*, raised the issue of parental notification from the per-

[45]For an argument that the state has less of an interest in requiring parental notification of a contraceptive than an abortion decision, see Comment, *Constitutional Law: Minors' Access to Contraceptives Freed from Future Restraints?* 29 UNIV. OF FLA. L. REV. 1019, 1027-1029 (1977) and Note, *The Minor's Right of Privacy: Limitations on State Action After Danforth and Carey,* supra n. 23 at 1242-1243 (1977). The degree to which a requirement of parental notification would discourage minors from getting contraception or abortions is not known. A recent study of Planned Parenthood birth control clinics disclosed that 55 percent of the minors told their parents they attended the clinic and that 45 percent had not told their parents and would stop coming to the clinic if their parents had to be notified. A. Torres, *Does Your Mother Know . . . ?* 10 FAM. PLAN. PERSPECTIVES 280 (1978).

[46]428 F. Supp. 1198 (W. D. Mich. 1977), *vacated and remanded*, 559 F. 2d 1219 (6th Cir. F. 2d 1977), *aff'd on remand,* 441 F. Supp. 1247 (W. D. Mich, 1977), *rev'd* 615 F. 2d 1162 (6th Cir. 1980).

spective of a parent's, not a minor's, right. The case arose in the unusual posture of parents challenging the distribution of oral contraceptives to minors, without parental consent, by a state-funded family planning clinic. A federal district court found that parents had a constitutionally-guaranteed right to raise their children free of state interference and that the clinic's policy not to inform parents infringed this right.[47] On appeal, the Court of Appeals for the Sixth Circuit remanded the case to the federal district court[48] which affirmed its earlier opinion.[49] On appeal again to the Sixth Circuit Court of Appeals, the decision was reversed, the court stating:

> The State of Michigan . . . has imposed no compulsory requirements or prohibitions which affect rights of the plaintiffs [the parents]. It has merely established a voluntary birth control clinic. There is no requirement that the children of the plaintiffs avail themselves of the services offered by the Center and no prohibition against the plaintiffs' participating in decisions of their minor children on issues of sexual activity and birth control. The plaintiffs remain free to exercise their traditional care, custody and control over their unemancipated children. . . . We can find no deprivation of the liberty interest of parents in the practice of not notifying them of their children's voluntary decisions to participate in the activities of the Center.[50]

D. A Minor's Right to Voluntary Sterilization

The legal right of minors to sterilization rarely is litigated since few adolescents request sterilization.[51] Generally the issue of sterilization of minors arises in the context of a parent requesting that a child, often retarded, be sterilized. Although the logical extension of *Griswold, Roe, Danforth,* and *Carey* would be to place voluntary sterilization within the scope of the privacy right for minors, the permanence of the operation, coupled with the potential for abuse, give the state some additional interests not present in the abortion and contraception situations.[52] Whether these interests reach the level of *compelling* or *significant* has not been determined. Under

[47]428 F. Supp. 1198 (W.D. Mich. 1977).

[48]559 F. 2d 1219 (6th Cir. 1977).

[49]441 F. Supp. 1247 (W.D. Mich. 1977).

[50]615 F. 2d 1162, 1168 (6th Cir. 1980)

[51]E. Paul, H. Pilpel & N. Wechsler, *Pregnancy, Teenagers, and the Law,* 8 FAM. PLAN. PERSPECTIVES 16, 20 (1976).

[52]These are examined in Chapter 4, *supra* pp. 148–158.

current federal guidelines, U.S. government funds cannot be used to pay for the sterilization of a person under 21 years of age.[53] Where federal funding is not involved, the right of minors to consent to sterilization varies according to state. Nine states have minimum age requirements for sterilization, four states and the District of Columbia specifically exclude sterilization from those medical procedures to which a minor can consent, and one state permits only married, widowed, or divorced minors to consent to sterilization.[54]

E. Rights of Minors to Fertility-Related Services Internationally

Internationally, rights of minors to fertility-related services vary greatly.[55] Each country differs in its laws, regulations, and orders concerning age of majority, sex education, contraception, abortion, age of marriage, etc. These are reviewed in J. Paxman and R. Zuckerman, "Adolescent Sexual and Reproductive Health Care: A Survey of Legal and Policy Alternatives" in WHO, *Legislation On Adolescent Health Care* (in press); L. Lee and J. Paxman, "Pregnancy and Abortion in Adolescence: A Comparative Legal Survey and Proposals for Reform," 6 *Colum. Hum. Rts. L. Rev.* 307 (1974–75), and J. Paxman, *"Law, Policy and Adolescent Sexuality,"* 5 *J. Biosocial Science Supp.* 187 (1978).

F. Sex Education and Population Education

A related topic, which has legal and policy overtones, is the teaching of sex education or population education in the school system. Although some states have prohibited or mandated the teaching of sex or population subjects, it is a matter usually left to local school districts.[56] The teaching of sex education in the schools

[53]42 C.F.R. §50.203 (1979).

[54]E. Paul & H. Pilpel, *supra*, n. 39 at 302.

[55]Paxman and Zuckerman concluded their comprehensive study by noting that "the diversity in laws affecting adolescent sexual behavior is so great that it is difficult to make generalized statements which could be useful in solving the [pertinent] legal issues." J. Paxman & R. Zuckerman, *Adolescent Sexual and Reproductive Health Care: A Survey of Legal and Policy Alternatives* in WHO, LEGISLATION ON ADOLESCENT HEALTH CARE (in press).

[56]For a general review of sex education programs in the United States, *see* HEW, AN ANALYSIS OF U.S. SEX EDUCATION PROGRAMS AND EVALUATION METHODS (CDC, 1979) and A. Kenney & S. Alexander *Sex/Family Life Education in the Schools: An Analysis of State Policies,* 9 FAM. PLAN./POP. REP. 44 (1980).

has been challenged on a number of constitutional grounds: violation of the First Amendment provisions relating to the establishment, or free exercise of, religion, violation of the right of privacy, or violation of substantive due process.[57] These challenges have almost always failed and where "provision has been made that students whose parents object can be excused, the giving of a sex education course has been uniformly upheld in the few cases in which the matter has been adjudicated."[58] Similarly, with few exceptions, the right of students to publish articles on birth control, abortion, and venereal disease in their school newspaper has been upheld as protected by the First Amendment.[59] Most controversy has concerned introduction of *sex education. Population education* appears to be comparatively more acceptable. In 1978 Congress passed the Population Education Act which authorizes a program of grants and contracts to public and private agencies to develop population education programs in elementary and secondary schools, to train teachers in population education, to develop instructional materials, and to conduct other activities related to the incorporation of population education into the school curriculum.[60] However, the program did not receive Congressional funding in 1980.

Internationally, laws on sex and population education vary considerably. Kellogg, Kline, and Stepan have reviewed the world's laws on these topics, as follows:[61]

[57]For analyses of relevant litigation, *see* M. Solberg, *Sex Education Courses: What Have Courts Permitted and Prohibited,* 9 SCHOOL L. BULL. 1 (1978); Note, *Sex Education: The Constitutional Limits of State Compulsion,* 43 SO. CALIF. L. REV. 548 (1970).

[58]Annot., *Validity of Sex Education Programs in Public Schools,* 82 A.L.R. 3d 579, 582 (1978).

[59]*See, e.g.,* Bayer v. Kinzler, 383 F. Supp. 1164 (E.D.N.Y. 1974), *aff'd mem.,* 515 F. 2d 504 (2d Cir. 1975); *compare* Trachtman v. Anker, 563 F. 2d 512 (2d Cir. 1977), *cert. denied* 435 U.S. 925 (1977). For a review of this topic generally and a criticism of the Trachtman decision, *see* Comment, *Constitutional Law—First Amendment—School Authorities May Prohibit High School Student's Distribution of Sex Questionnaire to Prevent Possible Psychological Harm to Other Students,* 31 VAND. L. REV. 173 (1978).

[60]Population Education Act, Pub. L. No. 95–561, 20 U.S.C. §§ 3061–2 (1978). For an analysis of population education generally, *see* C. Huether & S. Gustavus, *Population Education in the United States,* POP. REF. BUR. REP., vol. 3., no. 2 (1977).

[61]E. KELLOGG, D. KLINE, & J. STEPAN, THE WORLD'S LAWS AND PRACTICES ON POPULATION AND SEXUALITY EDUCATION 23–32 Law and Population Monograph No. 25 (Fletcher School of Law & Diplomacy, 1975).

Western and Northern Europe
As might be expected, the Northern and Western European countries are, with a few exceptions, the leaders in the field of sexuality education. Their motivation has been human rights and welfare. Since population pressures are no longer a problem in most of these countries, and since there has not been any need to inculcate the small family ideal, there has not been much attention given to population education, except insofar as certain countries have sought to deal with problems of low fertility and internal migration.

With the exception of Ireland, most of the countries in this area favor sexuality education, and are taking steps to provide it. However, the governments are all aware of the danger of negative popular reactions and are proceeding with caution.

Some governments make sexuality education compulsory (e.g., Sweden and West Germany). Some make it theoretically compulsory but permit parents to withdraw their children from specific courses (France). Others leave the matter to the local authorities (Belgium and the United Kingdom). Contraception information is, or may be, covered in each of these countries. . . .

Eastern Europe
The socialist countries of Eastern Europe have for many years provided a much more liberal resort to abortion than the other European countries. However, since 1971 they have indicated a desire to limit excessive abortions and have been stressing contraception as a preferred alternative. This has meant greater emphasis on sexuality education. . . .

In the USSR, education is a matter controlled by the constituent Union republics, and fertility related education seems not to cover more than the topics of menstruation, hygiene and venereal diseases. . . . In Czechoslovakia, where sexuality education was introduced several years ago, and in East Germany, the curricula include family planning and contraception. . . .

Conservative European Countries
In this category are Eire, Italy, and Spain, all of which are very strongly influenced by the Roman Catholic Church, and all but Eire have been subjected to the pro-natalist influences of dictatorship governments. In all these countries, population and sexuality education were either forbidden, or if theoretically tolerated, rare. . . .

East and South Asia
In this area there is a significant anomaly in that, on one hand, there is maximum population pressure, almost all the Governments have policies favoring the control of population growth, and there appears

to be comparatively little popular objection to the idea of contraception. On the other hand, the taboo against in-school sexuality education—i.e., the discussion of sex-related matters with the young—is so strong that, except for the Philippines, Japan, and Taiwan, no Government apparently dares to consider sexuality education on a large scale (and Taiwan is proceeding with great caution). . . .

Peoples' Republic of China

China has a specially severe problem of population pressure, and has attempted a specially drastic solution, of which population and sexuality education form an essential part. . . . Education in and out of school is believed to be complete and thorough on sex matters, and this is backed up by home visits from "barefoot doctors" and other community workers. The educational process indoctrinates children with the idea that the government will provide illness and old age protection . . .

Moslem West Asia and North Africa

Moslem countries of South and South East Asia [face considerable difficulties] with regard to sexuality education. The same difficulties also apply to the Arab and other Moslem countries of West Asia and North Africa, but in at least two of them an effort seems to be underway to face the problem. Egypt has apparently been successful in getting sexuality education into the schools and Tunisia is getting into the field on an experimental pilot basis. Both have population education materials dispersed through their regular courses on economics, geography, etc. . . .

On the other hand, in Lebanon, where the question of population predominance (as between Christians and Moslems) is a difficult political issue, there is no indication that the Government will deal with the question. In Syria, Libya and Morocco, the subject is apparently not raised, and in Turkey, despite the government's policy of favoring family planning, there appears to be little effort in either population or sexuality education below the university level, outside of some nonschool publicity in support of family planning services.

Africa South of the Sahara

In Africa south of the Sahara the subjects of population and sexuality education in school have only recently received any attention. In former times, sexuality education was dealt with by tribal authorities on a customary basis, and the idea of population education did not exist. There has until recently been little consciousness of population pressures and a need for population education has not been felt except in one or two countries. The two types of education are now beginning to be recognized as desirable, at least in some countries. . . .

Latin America and Caribbean Countries
In this area the full gamut of attitudes and programs is represented, varying from the extreme negative position of Argentina to the full and active in-school programs of some of the island countries of the Caribbean. Argentina, by a recent decree, has forbidden all dissemination of birth control information. (Whether this ban covers the teaching of human reproduction is not yet known.) On the other hand, some of the Caribbean countries, such as Barbados and the Netherlands Antilles, whose island confines may make the people more aware of crowding, have vigorous programs expressly aimed at population stabilization—both in and out of school. Nearly every other possible arrangement between these extremes may be found in one or more of the countries of the region. . . .

First, most of the countries of the region are moving into the field, with more interest in sexuality education than in population information. The International Council on Education, Science and Culture of the Organization of American States in its Resolution 69 adopted at Santo Domingo in 1973 called for sexuality education in all the American states. The Governments are, however, moving with extreme caution and mostly on an experimental basis. Reluctance to implement policy decisions is obvious, and fear of popular reaction is prevalent. In this regard, the Latin American education authorities resemble their Asian and some European "opposite numbers."

Second, it would appear that the Catholic Church, which predominates in all of the countries except some of the Caribbean Islands, has become more "flexible," and has not taken a fixed position. Whether or not there is any significance in the fact that Barbados and the Netherlands Antilles, which are not predominantly Catholic, have gone the farthest is not clear. The fact that these are small island countries where pressures are most obviously visible may be the reason behind their action in this field.

Australia, Canada and the United States
The situation in these countries in some ways resembles that in Northern and Western Europe. All three countries have federal constitutions and a British-oriented legal and cultural tradition.

Although it is clear that sexuality education is gaining in acceptance, and that in-school courses will eventually be generally available, the same caution and hesitation is visible here which we have seen in European countries. The Governments appoint study commissions for official inquiries which take time to prepare their reports. There is quite obvious concern as to popular reaction and the courses are usually voluntary (except in the case of some laws requiring instructions on venereal disease) and parents may be authorized to withdraw their children. . . .

Kellogg and Stepan, in a later publication, discuss the four principal legal issuss raised by the teaching of sex education:

> The question of obscenity;
> The questions raised by the presence, or prohibition, of an established religion;
> The question of "freedom of religion"—does it give parents the right to object to sex education on the basis of their religious conviction?
> The possible conflicts between the rights of parents and the rights and interests of their children.[62]

[62]E. Kellogg & J. Stepan, *Legal Aspects of Sex Education,* 26 AM. J. COMP. L. 573 (1978).

CHAPTER 7

INCENTIVES AND DISINCENTIVES: SOCIO-ECONOMIC LAWS AND POLICIES

I. INTRODUCTORY NOTE

This chapter examines the use of social or economic laws and policies to influence reproductive behavior. It also explores policies and laws which, although not primarily intended to affect fertility, are thought to have an ancillary effect on it.

The use of economic incentives to lower fertility has been associated chiefly with Asian population programs. For example, Singapore has tried to lower its population growth rate through the use of *disincentives* (discouragements, or *negative incentives*), in this case, the withdrawal of benefits or privileges to people having more children than the prescribed limit.[1] India has relied on positive economic incentives, such as cash payments to men undergoing sterilization, to induce people to have fewer children. Since Singapore and India have had the greatest experience in the use of incentives to reduce fertility, the measures used in these countries are explored in some depth.

[1]The distinction between positive and negative incentives, although useful for analytical purposes, is somewhat artificial and blurred in reality. For example, a law which permits a $100 tax exemption for the first three children and no exemption for the fourth child or additional children could be seen as a positive inducement (giving people $100 for each of the first three children) or a negative incentive, punishing them for the fourth child and later children.

On the other hand, France, Belgium, the Soviet Union and many Eastern European countries have used economic stimuli as an avowed measure to *increase* fertility. The most important of these stimuli are family allowances, a periodic government payment to families with children. In evaluating incentives, it is often difficult to disentangle the pronatalist motivation from that of social welfare. Many European countries provide family allowances not to encourage fertility but rather to alleviate the financial hardship of supporting a large family. And, in some countries, the motivation is a mixture of social welfare and pronatalism. As European countries display greater concern about negative rates of population growth and their implications for their economies, economic incentives to increase fertility may take on more importance.

In addition to economic incentives or disincentives, other laws and policies can have a significant indirect influence on fertility. Although there is considerable debate over the extent to which social and economic legislation affects reproductive behavior, in the long run changes in education, the status of women (particularly education and employment), health care (particularly as it reduces infant mortality), ease of marriage and divorce, urbanization and housing, and personal income are thought to influence choice of family size and, on a national scale, rates of population growth.[2] A comprehensive analysis of the legal aspects of the so-called determinants of fertility, which on a macro level might be termed aspects of population policy, is beyond the scope of this chapter. However, the legal aspects of some of the major fertility-related socioeconomic policies are examined.

II. DISINCENTIVES TO REDUCE POPULATION GROWTH

A. Use of Disincentives in Singapore

After achieving independence from Great Britain in 1965, Singapore implemented a number of policies designed to reduce its rate of population growth from 2.3 percent a year to zero. It created a

[2]For reviews of the research literature concerning the determinants of fertility, *see* N. Birdsall, *Analytical Approaches to the Relationship of Population Growth and Development,* 3 POP. & DEV. REV. 63 (1977); R. Cassen, *Population and Development: A Survey,* 4 WORLD DEVELOPMENT 785 (1976); POPULATION AND DEVELOPMENT: THE SEARCH FOR SELECTIVE INTERVENTIONS (R. Ridker, ed., Johns Hopkins, 1976); L. CORSA & D. OAKLEY, POPULATION PLANNING (Michigan, 1979).

national Family Planning and Population Board, expanded contraceptive distribution, embarked on a widespread educational campaign promoting the two-child family, made sterilization accessible to people over 21 and to married people under 21, and liberalized its abortion law to make the procedure available on demand through the twenty-fourth week of pregnancy. It also established a number of disincentive policies, which are summarized below:

K. Wee, "Legal Aspects of Population Policies," in *Public Policy and Population Change in Singapore* 34–37 (P. Chen & J. Fawcett, eds., Population Council, 1979)*

Sterilization. In addition to the liberal provisions on contraception, abortion, and sterilization, the government has implemented a number of measures designed to discourage large families. The following measures relating to undergoing sterilization are directly aimed at the practice of family planning:

1. Delivery fees will be waived for B and C class patients if either the husband or wife is sterilized within six months of delivery.
2. Civil servants who undergo sterilization are given seven days' unrecorded full-pay leave.
3. Ward charges (*i.e.,* charges for bed and board) for C class patients will be refunded if either husband or wife is sterilized and if certain other conditions are satisfied.
4. Female government servants who are sterilized six months after delivery or abortion will receive medical leave on generous terms.

In addition, a number of measures are designed to exert financial and other pressure on couples to limit their family size.

Limitations on Maternity Benefits. The Employment Act originally provided for paid maternity leave up to the third pregnancy. Every married female worker was entitled to absent herself from work for four weeks before and after confinement and to receive the whole or a part of her salary during this period. The Employment (Amendment) Act of 1972, however, as an inducement to accepting the two-child norm, provided that maternity leave would not be given for delivery of the third and each subsequent child.

Delivery Fees. Delivery fees in government hospitals, first levied in 1964, have been gradually increased on a sliding-scale basis, depending on the birth order of the child. After the latest amendments (in 1975) the fees now stand as follows (with comparative 1973 figures):

*Reprinted with the permission of the Population Council from Peter S. J. Chen and James T. Farcett, eds., *Public Policy and Population Change in Singapore,* 1979: "Legal Aspects of Population Policies" by Kenneth K. S. Wee, pp. 34–37.

	A Class		*B Class*		*C Class*	
Birth order	*1973*	*1975*	*1973*	*1975*	*1973*	*1975*
First child	S$250	S$300	S$100	S$120	S$ 50	S$ 60
Second child	300	360	150	180	75	90
Third child	350	420	200	240	100	120
Fourth child	400	480	250	300	200	240
Fifth and each subsequent child	400	480	300	360	250	300

NOTE: S$2.50 = U.S.$1.00.

About 80 percent of the babies born in Singapore in recent years have been delivered in government hospitals.

Tax Deductions. Before 1 August 1973 the Income Tax Act permitted a taxpayer the following deductions from his taxable income: S$750 for the first child, S$500 each for the second and third child, and S$300 each for the fourth and fifth child. For a child born on or after that date, however, a taxpayer may deduct S$750 if it is his first or second child and S$500 if it is his third child. A deduction is no longer allowed, therefore, for a fourth or subsequent child. To qualify for a deduction the child must also be unmarried and must either be under age 16 or meet certain other conditions such as attending school full time or suffering from mental or physical infirmity.

As an incentive to some married women to enter the work force, the Income Tax Act permits a married woman with earned income who is university educated or is in certain professions to claim deductions for her children (provided her husband does not do so) as follows: S$2,000 or 5 percent of her earned income, whichever is less, for each of the first two children; S$2,000 or 3 percent of her earned income, whichever is less, for her third child. . . .

Allocation of Housing. The Housing and Development Board (HDB), the main government body responsible for Singapore's Public Housing Programme, provides low-cost housing for Singapore citizens. At present over 50 percent of Singaporeans live in flats built by the HDB, and 44 percent of this group own their flats. No formal legislation governs the allocation of HDB housing; the board accordingly sets its own policy (subject, of course, to Cabinet approval). Formerly, flats were allocated to families, whether on purchase or rental, on a "points" system that gave priority to couples with larger families. This policy was revised in 1972, however, so that small families are not hindered in their eligibility for HDB flats. In addition, families with fewer than four children are eligible to sublet rooms in their HDB flats under certain conditions. (Unauthorized subletting may result in eviction, regardless of whether the flat is rented or purchased.) Moreover, under the present HDB allocation policy an unmarried person is not eligible to rent or purchase a flat, except under exceptional circumstances.

There is some evidence that the government would have liked to go further in using housing policy as a disincentive to having large families. In October 1972 the Minister of Health announced that priority would go to smaller families. In July 1973, however, the Minister of Law and National Development said that the government had found it difficult to work out a fair method of allocation according to family size. Furthermore, rather than penalize large families, it would be better to give inducements to those with smaller families.

Primary-School Registration. Singapore's population is very young —about 40 percent is under age 20—and schooling, though not compulsory, is almost universal. Primary education (the first six years) is heavily subsidized, as are the following four years of secondary education.

Since 1 August 1973, the Ministry of Education has given lower priority in the choice of primary schools to children of the fourth birth order and above, while simultaneously raising the priority of children whose father or mother has been sterilized. Present policy gives higher priority to children whose mother or father has been sterilized after the first or second child if the parent was sterilized before reaching age 40 (except for second and third children with a sibling already enrolled in the school, who are admitted ahead of all others). Some priority is given to the third or subsequent child of a parent who has been sterilized before age 40.

The significance of this policy is that great inconvenience may be caused to parents whose children might have to attend schools in different areas of the city. Furthermore, those with higher priority may be able to choose better schools. . .

B. Disincentives in Other Countries

Although Singapore provides the most striking use of economic disincentives to lower fertility, other Asian countries have also experimented with disincentives. For example, in Seoul, Korea, housing priority is given to parents, at least one of whom has been sterilized. The government of Indonesia has reduced from ten to seven the number of dependents that can be claimed as tax deductions.[3] Thai-

[3]B. Vumbaco, *Recent Law and Policy Changes in Fertility Control,* POPULATION REPORTS, series E, no. 4 (George Washington Univ., 1976).

land recently limited its payment of family allowances to three children per family.[4] The Philippines put into effect a wideranging antinatalist population plan which included restricting tax relief to four dependents and permitting maternity leave only for a woman's first four deliveries.[5] And the Indian state governments, during the period when Indira Gandhi was Prime Minister, had invoked a variety of strong disincentives, ranging from:

> . . . the seemingly mild (West Bengal's refusal to cover government servants' leave travel costs for more than two children) to the distressingly cruel (Bihar's denial of public food rations to families with three children). Some were directed toward the general public (Orissa's granting of government loans only to sterilized persons or people with small families); others affected only government servants (Rajasthan's rule that no one having more than three children would be eligible for a government job unless sterilized). Many affected individuals directly; others were on a community basis (Madhya Pradesh's granting of irrigation water at subsidized rates to all persons from villages producing specified numbers of sterilization patients).[6]

The Chinese government, in an effort to achieve zero population growth by the year 2000, is reported to be considering enactment of disincentives based on the Singapore model. According to Deputy Prime Minister, Chen Muhua:

> In order to encourage the one-child family, a series of social and economic measures are being formulated. One of the methods is to give material rewards—for example, by issuing child care funds, work point awards, extra retirement funds, and so forth. Another method of encouragement is to give institutional guarantees—for example, appropriate consideration to the one-child family in urban and rural employment and in the distribution of urban housing, rural private plots, and rural lots for housing. Those who insist on having many children after patient persuasion and education will be taxed.[7]

[4] *Far Eastern Economic Review,* Jan. 19, 1979, as cited in IPPF, *Law File* (Feb. 1979).

[5] *Philippine Laws, Regulations Back Policy to Contain Population Growth,* POP. DYNAMICS Q. vol. 2, no. 2, p. 3 (1974).

[6] D. Gwatkin, *Political Will and Family Planning: The Implications of India's Emergency Experience,* 5 POP. & DEV. REV. 29, 38 (1979).

[7] C. Muhua, *For the Realization of the Four Modernizations, There Must Be Planned Control of the Population,* as it appeared in translation in 5 POP. & DEV. REV. 723, 727 (1979).

In 1970, the United States Supreme Court, in *Dandridge v. Williams,* let stand a Maryland regulation that imposed a $250 monthly ceiling on welfare payments, irrespective of family size or need. Although the regulation was enacted for fiscal, not demographic, reasons, it was argued that the welfare ceiling penalized children of large families, thus serving as an antinatalist disincentive. The Court upheld the regulation as a rational exercise of the state's police power and avoided discussion of issues related to population policy.[8]

C. Commentary and Issues

1. Effectiveness of Disincentives

Several evaluations have assessed the effectiveness of Singapore's disincentives policies. Salaff and Wong, examining the enforcement of the measures, found that severe limitations existed in applying all of the disincentives.[9]

For example, there is no administrative mechanism whereby the government can actually withdraw housing from families with too many children. Hospitals, which make only a one-in-ten spot check of parity, are not likely to take a woman to court for refusing to pay the accouchment fee. Despite these difficulties, the authors concluded that the measures were "not ineffective" from the government's perspective:

> They work by creating an image of comprehensiveness and stringency, and enable the government to bring people into line with its official policies without actually devoting substantial resources to their enforcement.[10]

A later survey by the same evaluators found that although Singapore's disincentives influenced behavior of people who tended to plan their activities, "most nonplanners are totally unaffected by the disincentives."[11] A survey by Tan, Lee, and Ratnam of approxi-

[8]397 U.S. 471 (1970). For a comprehensive discussion of *Dandridge* and its implications, *see* Note, *Legal Analysis and Population Control: The Problem of Coercion,* 84 HARV. L. REV. 1856 (1971).

[9]J. Salaff & A. Wong, *Are Disincentives Coercive? The View from Singapore,* 4 INTL. FAM. PLAN. PERSPECTIVES & DIGEST 50 (1978).

[10]*Id.* at 52.

[11]A. Wong & J. Salaff, *Planning Births for a Better Life: Working-Class Response to Population Disincentives,* in PUBLIC POLICY AND POPULATION CHANGE IN SINGAPORE, 109, 125 (P. Chen & J. Fawcett, eds., Pop. Council, 1979). [hereafter cited as P. Chen & J. Fawcett, eds.]

mately 1,000 women hospitalized for abortion and 1,000 women hospitalized for childbirth found that the disincentives were known to a substantial proportion of the pregnant women, although known better to the well educated than the less educated. Four of the five disincentive measures appear to have succeeded in affecting the decisions of the target group to some degree; only the taxation policy had a negligible effect. The most widely known measures were the maternity fee and the school admission policy, both of which were cited by the women as most influencing their decisions on present and future pregnancies.[12] These findings were, in general, corroborated by Hassan, who concluded:

> . . . the policy on graduated delivery fees appears to be the most widely effective, followed by the policy on waiving delivery fees if sterilization follows delivery and the policy on lower priority for choice of primary school for the fourth and each subsequent child.[13]

To implement a successful disincentive program, it has been said that a country must make contraception, voluntary sterilization, and abortion readily available. Singapore's sterilization and abortion laws are among the most liberal in the world, and contraception is readily available.

The apparent success of Singapore's disincentives policies raises some questions about that country as a model to be followed by other nations. To what extent is the Singapore experience replicable in other countries and to what extent is its apparent success dependent on Singapore's unique characteristics? How important is it that Singapore is a small island state? That it is a country with strong one-man rule? That the government controls almost 100 percent of the nation's housing, education, and health services? That it is a country with a relatively homogenous ethnic Chinese population? That most of the population endorse the disincentives as a proper means to influence fertility behavior and do not feel themselves unduly restricted by them?

2. Ethical Considerations

The use of disincentives to influence fertility behavior raises important ethical questions. To what extent are the Singapore laws

[12]S. Tan, J. Lee & S. Ratnam, *Effects of Social Disincentive Policies on Fertility Behavior in Singapore,* 68 AM. J. PUB. HLTH. 119 (1978).

[13]R. Hassan, *Perception of Population Policies,* in P. Chen & J. Fawcett, eds., *supra* n. 11 at 144.

coercive and to what extent can they be justified as a use of the government's police power to safeguard the health and welfare of Singapore's citizens? Are some of the laws more coercive than others? Is it easier to justify laws that restrict housing and therefore penalize parents than those which restrict choice of schools and thereby punish children? If you feel that Singapore's laws are coercive, how do you respond to those who argue that most family-related laws tend to be pronatalist and that disincentives merely provide a balance?

By what ethical standards are disincentives to be measured?[14] Consider Daniel Callahan's guidelines:[15]

> Freedom of choice must be protected; the first order of business is the establishment of effective voluntary family planning programs.
>
> If voluntary programs are not successful, governments have the right to go beyond family planning.
>
> In choosing among programs which go beyond family planning, governments must first try those which, comparatively, respect freedom of choice. This means, for example, that positive incentives should be attempted before negative ones.
>
> If circumstances force a government to choose programs that are quasi or wholly coercive, they can justify such programs if, and only if:
>
> (1) in the light of primacy of free choice, a government has discharged the burden of proof necessary to justify a limitation of free choice. This burden may be discharged by demonstrating that continued unrestricted liberty poses a direct threat to distributive justice or security-survival, and
>
> (2) in light of the right of citizens to take part in the government of their country, the proposed limitations on freedom promise, in the long run, to increase the options of free choice, decisions to limit freedom are collective decisions, the limitations on freedom are legally regulated and the burden falls upon all equally, and the chosen means of limitation respect human dignity, which will here be defined as respecting those rights specified in the United Nations' "Universal Declaration of Human Rights."

[14]Berelson and Lieberson propose an ethical framework for assessing fertility-regulation policies and, within that, incentives and disincentives. B. Berelson & J. Lieberson, *Government Efforts to Influence Fertility: The Ethical Issues,* 5 POP. & DEV. REV. 581 (1979). [hereafter cited as B. Berelson & J. Lieberson] Callahan, *infra* n. 15, and Veatch, *infra* n. 24, also provide guidelines for evaluating the ethics of fertility regulation programs.

[15]D. Callahan, *Ethics and Population Limitation,* 175 SCIENCE 487 (1972).

III. INCENTIVES TO REDUCE POPULATION GROWTH

A. India: M. Franda, "Mass Vasectomy Camps and Incentives in Indian Family Planning," *Fieldstaff Reports,* South Asia Series, vol. 16, no. 7 (American Universities, 1972)

. . . The idea of providing incentives to men willing to submit to a vasectomy was first widely discussed in India in the late 1950s, at a time when nominal monetary reimbursements were being given to compensate for time lost from gainful employment or for personal inconvenience. Finding that the number of men willing to submit to a vasectomy increased almost proportionately with the size of their "reimbursement," a number of family planners began to propose schemes that would convert compensation fees into outright cash incentives. As one might expect, it did not take long after that for experimental programs to arise, testing the efficacy of larger and larger amounts of cash as opposed to other material incentives, while exploring the possibilities for greater inducements to doctors and nurses, as well as to various kinds of promoters (or what are now known as "motivators," *i.e.,* a go-between who can help "motivate" men to accept a vasectomy operation, the men on whom the operations are performed being known as "acceptors"). When all of these efforts began to meet with some success the next logical step seemed to be a large-scale vasectomy camp, at which thousands of vasectomy operations could be performed in a fairly efficient manner over a short space of time.

Vasectomy camps—which might not go over too well in many other cultures—seem somewhat at home in the Indian environment. The camps are organized much like the usual rural *tamashas* (festivals), with cultural exhibits and programs inspired by nationalist and regionalist causes, performances by leading artists, movie stars, poets, and writers, and speeches by eminent personalities and political figures, all provided for the benefit of those visiting the camps. Frequently, the campaign for participation in the vasectomy camps (or "family planning festivals," as they are popularly known) will be led by village *panchayats* (councils of elders or elected officials), so that almost entire villages will be prompted to come to a festival, often in *Jathas* (marching demonstrations), accompanied by floats and decorated vehicles, colorfully adorned bullocks, folk dancers, blaring loudspeakers playing Hindi film songs, and by men shouting slogans in support of family planning. . . . While vasectomy camps have been organized in India since 1967, the first camp to offer incentives approaching the 100 rupee figure was a mass sterilization camp organized in Ernakulam district in Kerala (November-December

1970). . . . During the first mass vasectomy camp, a total of 15,005 men underwent sterilization operations in the space of a month, with high rates of incentives (almost a hundred rupees) being provided largely from contributions by businesses, industries, local bodies, service organizations, and the general public in Ernakulam district. . . . Mr. Krishnakumar (the District Collector) established an original target of 20,000 sterilizations for his second mass vasectomy camp at Ernakulam in July 1971. However, when he found himself more than a third of the way toward his target after only five days of the operation of the camp, Mr. Krishnakumar immediately upped his target to 50,000 sterilizations for the month, and then proceeded to go way beyond his new target. By the time the camp ended, a total of 66,357 men had presented themselves for sterilization, and a total of 63,418 vasectomies had been performed (those who were refused vasectomies included men whose wives were older than 45; those with general constitutional diseases or local infections that prevented surgery; unmarried men or men with only one or no children; and a few men who had been sterilized before but were still hoping to cash in again on the incentives).

On the basis of the success of the vasectomy camps in Ernakulam, a number of other Indian states are now contemplating similar ventures, and two mass vasectomy drives (in Gujarat and Uttar Pradesh) have already been completed. The most successful of these latter campaigns was the one in Gujarat (November 15, 1971 through January 15, 1972), which was organized in a slightly different fashion than the Ernakulam camps. Instead of one large central camp (such as the Town Hall in Ernakulam), to which all festival participants would travel, the Gujarat government established more than 100 smaller stationary camps, scattered throughout the 19 districts of Gujarat state, and several mobile "minicamps" that moved about in the more remote areas. According to the Gujarat state Family Planning Ministry, a conscious decision was made to "decentralize" the camps . . .

Operating out of these smaller camps scattered throughout the state, the Gujarat authorities were able to provide a total of 223,060 vasectomies in two months, exceeding their original target of 150,000 vasectomies despite the fact that India was at war with Pakistan during two of the weeks that the camp was in operation . . . In contrast to Ernakulam, for example, the Gujarat government gave larger *cash* incentives (Rs. 60-80 per person) to acceptors, but smaller grants in terms of services and goods. At the same time, Gujarat also gave larger incentives to most motivators, either in cash or in prizes awarded for a given number of acceptors that were brought to the camps (for example, in Panchmahals district of Gujarat, a motivator received an umbrella as a prize for five cases; an alarm clock for 15 cases; a transistor radio for 25 cases; and a bicycle as a prize for 40 cases—all in addition, of course, to his regular 10 to 20 rupee motivator incentive fees).

As was the case in Gujarat, the vasectomy campaign in Gorakhpur division of Uttar Pradesh in February 1972 was organized around a number of camps, scattered throughout the four districts of Gorakhpur division (Gorakhpur, Basti, Deoria, and Azamgarh). But in contrast to both Gujarat and Ernakulam, the camps in Gorakhpur encountered a number of public relations problems that could conceivably discourage other regions from trying the mass vasectomy approach. Many of these, of course, stemmed from the 11 tetanus deaths in late February, but even before the tetanus deaths there were reports from Gorakhpur that the leaders of the sterilization drive had been acting very hastily and aggressively "out of fear [that they] might not be able to equal the feat of the Ernakulam one-month camp held last year."

The highly ambitious goals of the Gorakhpur leadership were evident from their target of 76,000 vasectomies for the month, considerably more than the 63,000 that had been performed at Ernakulam in July 1971. To help achieve this target, the Gorakhpur leadership provided incentives up to Rs. 140 per acceptor, with unspent state flood relief money reportedly being used to cover the cost of the program. In contrast to both Ernakulam and Gujarat, there were a number of reports from Gorakhpur (again, even before the 11 tetanus deaths) that "violence was being used [by motivators];" that motivators were being allowed to operate "without having the answers to all of the doubting questions they were likely to face;" that "sometimes the post-operation performance [of the Gorakhpur camp] did not match the pre-operation assurance;" and that "to stifle protest, officials [were using] a heavy-handed approach."

B. Other Incentive Plans: B. Herz, "Socio-economic Policies to Encourage Smaller Families," in Inter-Governmental Coordinating Committee, Southeast Asia Regional Cooperation in Population and Family Planning. *Reducing Fertility through Beyond Family Planning Measures* 20–27 (1976).

Although the incentives paid to vasectomy acceptors in India have generated the most publicity and controversy, other Asian countries have experimented with economic incentives to induce families to have fewer children. These were reviewed by Herz in an article from which some parts are excerpted below:

1. *Taiwan Educational Bonds*[16]

The program offers to couples with 0-2 children an annual deposit in a savings account for each year that they have no more than two children. If a third child is born, the value of the account is reduced by 50%. If a fourth child is born, the account is cancelled and funds revert to the bank. The account earns interest. After 10–14 years the account can be cashed for an amount ranging from about $268 to about $385 depending on the term, enough to cover a significant portion of the costs of higher education. The savings account records are retained primarily by the participating women to ease administration. Thus far the program's administrative burden appears manageable, and no major attempts to defraud have been reported.

At the end of the first year of enrollment in 1972, over two-thirds of eligible couples had joined, with almost all continuing past a year. Many of those who failed to enroll indicated they were unaware of the program or wanted more children; relatively few said the program was in itself unappealing. Generally the program appears to be averting a substantial number of births, though an updated evaluation would give a clearer picture.

2. *India Tea Estate Program*[17]

For each female worker capable of having children the estates set up a joint savings account in the name of the company and the woman. The estate pays into the account about five rupees for every month that the woman does not appear pregnant. The account cannot be drawn upon until the woman completes her childbearing years, but it accumulates interest in the interim. If the woman has more than three children, she forfeits a substantial part of her accumulated account. If she has a fifth child, she forfeits the whole account. (The funds revert to the estates to help defray the costs of caring for the additional children.) The accounts draw interest at about 5%. For a woman who participates for 30 years and has only two children, the savings account is reportedly worth over Rs. 2000 (about $270), nearly a year's earnings, at retirement.

[16]For a more detailed description *see* O. Finnigan III & T. Sun, *Planning, Starting and Operating an Educational Incentives Project,* 3 STUDIES IN FAM. PLAN. 1 (1972) and C. Wang & S. Chen, *Evaluation of the First Year of the Educational Savings Program in Taiwan,* 4 STUDIES IN FAM. PLAN. 157 (1973) —Ed.

[17]For a more detailed description *see* V. Chacko, *Comprehensive Approach to a Population Programme in the Plantations of Southern India,* IGCC, REDUCING FERTILITY THROUGH BEYOND FAMILY PLANNING MEASURES, 46–65 (1976) and R. Ridker, *Savings Accounts for Family Planning: An Illustration from the Tea Estates of India,* 2 STUDIES IN FAM. PLAN. 150 (1971) —Ed.

The discounted cost to the tea estates of a birth is approximately Rs. 1500 ($200). The discounted cost of paying Rs. 5 per month for 13 years is far less. In other words, if the company paid Rs. 5 per month to a woman for 13 years, and, as a result, she had only one less child than she otherwise would have had, the company would more than break even.

However, when the normal pattern of childbirth and child spacing among tea plantation employees was reviewed, it was found to be more likely that two, three, or even four births would be prevented. Since each birth prevented saves the company Rs. 1500, the plan pays for itself several times over. Since administrative procedures have been streamlined, the administrative burden is manageable.

Initial results of the tea estate program are so favourable as to suggest a major breakthrough in designing programs to lower fertility. Over 90% of eligible women on the three estates with the incentive program have elected to join; it appears that in the four years of the program's operation, birth rates on those three estates have declined by over a third, from the mid-thirties to around twenty per thousand population. Birth rate declines on estates where no incentives were offered have been far less impressive.

3. *Malaysia Proposal*[18]

The scheme would offer each married woman above a certain age an incentive to visit a health clinic with her children for a periodic health check-up, during which the children could receive immunizations and general MCH care would be provided to minimize future health problems. The incentive would be provided, however, only if the woman were found not to be pregnant. Apart from a small immediate payment, perhaps the bulk of this incentive would be deferred, payable to the woman and her husband upon retirement. The size of the retirement or pension fund would vary inversely with the number of surviving children they have, being largest for zero or one child, smaller for three, and becoming zero for four or more children. Administratively, the program posed no substantial problem because record keeping in Malaysia, particularly at health centers, is generally very good.

4. *Pakistan Life Insurance Proposal*

In Pakistan, the State Life Insurance Company has been considering a pilot program to insure the life of the son of couples who practise family planning. The pilot program would be limited to couples under

[18]For a more detailed description *see* R. Ridker and R. Muscat, *Incentives for Family Welfare and Fertility Reduction: An Illustration for Malaysia,* 4 STUDIES IN FAM. PLAN. 1 (1973) —Ed.

thirty who have no more than three children, including at least one son over two years old; having a fourth child might require forfeiting the policy. Such a program would hopefully discourage parents from having "extra" children to insure that some son survives.

C. Commentary and Issues

1. Ethical Considerations

Incentives raise many of the same ethical questions as disincentives, albeit in a milder form since the apparent punitive aspects appear to be reduced.[19] Some of the key issues are the following.

> The Indian vasectomy camps have been criticized as being coercive in practice. Is payment of money to a contraceptive user conceptually coercive? Does the answer depend on the amount of money offered as an incentive relative to the financial status of the recipient? In a 1968 study of 297 vasectomized men, 43 percent stated that money was the "sole motivating factor" in their decision to have the operation.[20] What does this indicate about the quality of acceptance? Although incentive payments have reached relatively high amounts, it should be remembered that the original justification for payments was as reimubursement for transportation and time lost from work.

> Is payment of a motivator—particularly payment based on the number of referrals—inherently coercive? In practice, there is no question that payment to motivators has led to abuse. Repetto, studying the program in Madras, estimated

[19]Berelson and Lieberson, *supra* n. 14 at 591, regard positive incentives as ethically permissible as long as the recipient has an effective choice of accepting or rejecting the offer. They write:

> In our view, positive incentives serve to enlarge options, not diminish them, and hence can serve both freedom and (interclass) justice.

Negative incentives, they note, have special problems, the most important being the effect on children born in disregard of the incentives.

[20]K. Srinivasan & M. Kachirayan, *Vasectomy Follow-up Study: Findings and Implications,* 3 BULL. GHANDIGRAM INST. RUR. HLTH. & FAM. PLAN. 12 (1968), as cited in E. Rogers, *Incentives in the Diffusion of Family Planning Innovations,* 2 STUDIES IN FAM. PLAN. 241 (1971).

that abuse occurred in half of the vasectomy cases.[21] Is an incentive payment for referral, or for performing a service, conceptually different from the profit that a pharmacy makes on the sale of pills? From the incentive of a small profit on a sale of pills earned by a village distributor in a nonclinical contraceptive distribution program?

c. Critics have objected that incentive programs are regressive by persuading (bribing) the poorest people. On the other hand, supporters have lauded this same feature, pointing out that incentives are among the few known ways of convincing poor people to change their fertility behavior. Is the fact that incentive programs reach the poorest, least advantaged, populace a positive or negative feature?

d. In considering incentives, how important is it to distinguish among types of recipient? That is, does it make a difference whether the recipient is the acceptor? The doctor who performs the service (*e.g.,* a physician performing vasectomies at a piece-work rate)? A village leader who refers clients to a physician? The community as a whole?[22]

What standards should be used to measure the morality of incentive programs? Compare the statement by Wishik,

> The morality of incentives is subject to individual interpretation. . . . I think it is legitimate to consider incentives but only after social consensus has been achieved and family planning services, including abortion and sterilization, are fully available and readily accessible to all persons who want them.[23]

with the guidelines proposed by Veatch for the ethical acceptability of an incentives program:

[21]R. Repetto, *India: A Case Study of the Madras Vasectomy Program,* 31 STUDIES IN FAM. PLAN. 8 (1968). He cites opposition on ethical grounds to "creating a class of touts in the family planning programme."

[22]The Indian population policy of 1976 gave considerable emphasis to payment of incentives at all levels, ranging from acceptors of sterilization to local councils. *See infra* pp. 405–406.

[23]S. Wishik, *The Use of Incentives for Fertility Reduction,* 68 AM. J. PUB. HLTH. 113, 114 (1978).

It should preserve freedom by avoiding incentives that are, in effect, coercive.

It should avoid harming children.

It should minimize the monetizing of childbearing decisions.

It should avoid promoting population-related decisions primarily for purposes of immediate financial gain.

It should avoid deception both in its announced intent and in its administrative procedures.

It should distribute the burden of change in population-related behavior equally rather than limiting it to one class or group.

It should avoid flat-rate incentives until such incentives can be shown to be nondiscriminatory.

It should apply to all childbearing decisions equally rather than being limited to decisions after the Nth child.[24]

2. Program Considerations

As indicated by the above excerpts, a variety of incentive schemes have been attempted and proposed. Most proposals were made in the early 1970s;[25] the literature on incentives in the late 1970s is relatively barren and evaluations of proposals that were implemented are almost nonexistent. Some of the key issues have been:

a. Immediate versus delayed incentives. In the Indian tea estate proposal, incentives serve as a form of old-age social security. Kangas questions whether people can delay gratification for so long or have sufficient faith in the long-term dependability of institutions.[26] The idea behind delayed incentives also raises a question whether any system of

[24]R. Veatch, *Governmental Population Incentives: Ethical Issues at Stake,* 8 STUDIES IN FAM. PLAN. 100 (1977).

[25]For comprehensive reviews of projects and proposals, *see* E. POHLMAN, INCENTIVES AND COMPENSATIONS IN BIRTH PLANNING (North Carolina, 1971) and WORLD BANK, POPULATION POLICIES AND ECONOMIC DEVELOPMENT (Johns Hopkins, 1974); *see also* V. Chacko, *Some Considerations of Incentives and Disincentives in the Promotion of Family Planning: India's Experience,* in UNFPA, THE SYMPOSIUM ON LAW AND POPULATION (1975) and UNFPA, *The Role of Incentives in Family Planning Programmes* (1980).

[26]L. Kangas, *Integrated Incentives for Fertility Control,* 169 SCIENCE 1278 (1970).

incentives can work without an adequate system of providing care for aged parents.[27]

b. Should incentives be made available to an individual or to the community?

c. With respect to individuals, who should receive incentives: the acceptor, the motivator, or the provider?

d. Should incentives be paid at a flat rate or at graduated rates?

3. Effectiveness

The richness of the literature proposing various incentive schemes contrasts markedly with the paucity of materials evaluating them. A recent evaluation of the Indian tea estate idea, *supra* p. 319, revealed that only slight changes in fertility could be attributed to the incentives, in part because the project was not implemented as originally planned, in part because of administrative difficulties.[28] Berelson rated the Indian sterilization camps as a moderately effective means of fertility regulation, giving them a 5.5 ranking out of a possible score of 10.[29]

Use of incentives assumes people respond to economic inducements in making childbearing decisions, be they in the form of an immediate cash payment or, on a more sophisticated level, education for their children or care during old age. This raises the question whether parenthood is, in fact, a conscious decision that can be affected by economic inducements.[30] It raises a further question

[27] J. Spengler in *Population Problem: In Search of a Solution,* 166 SCIENCE 1234 (1969) proposed an interesting variation of old-age security as an incentive. Positing that a major reason for excessive reproduction in developing countries is the need for support in old age, he proposed the gradual introduction of a social security system for people over, say, 65. Entrance into the system would be limited only to those with X number of children where X is approximately equal to the replacement rate.

[28] R. Ridker, *The No-Birth Bonus Scheme: The Use of Savings Accounts for Family Planning in South India,* 6 POP. & DEV. REV. 31 (1980).

[29] B. Berelson, *Paths to Fertility Reduction: The "Policy Cube,"* 9 FAM. PLAN. PERSPECTIVES 214 (1977). *See also* S. Krishnakumar, *Kerala's Pioneering Experiment in Massive Vasectomy,* 3 STUDIES IN FAM. PLAN. 177 (1972) and V. Thakor & V. Patel, *The Gujarat State Massive Vasectomy Campaign,* 3 STUDIES IN FAM. PLAN. 186 (1972).

[30] Some economists have argued that as the cost of raising children rises, people will tend to have fewer children. According to this economic analysis, children are viewed as "goods," competing with other goods, and the number of children a couple will have is a function of the "opportunity cost" of children. *See* R. Easterlin, *Relative Economic Status and the American Fertility Swing,* in FAMILY ECO-

concerning the size of an incentive, a question that reappears in considering pronatalist incentives, pp. 332–335, *infra.* Consider in this regard Wishik's proposition:

> In general, it becomes clear that the size of an incentive must be appreciable to have significant effect. Granting appreciable incentive to a large portion of the population is, in effect, a redistribution of wealth. The leaders of very few non-socialist poor countries have serious interest in such redistribution. Hence, incentives in most countries remain inconsequential token payments with little if any effectiveness.[31]

IV. INCENTIVES TO INCREASE POPULATION GROWTH

A. INTRODUCTORY NOTE

Most countries have enacted legislation to protect and strengthen the family. In fact, the United States is the only developed country without a general family allowance plan.[32] In many cases, the motivation behind the legislation is social welfare, *i.e.,* to ease the financial burden of children on parents and to assure that children are given adequate care. In some countries, this legislation forms part of the state social security system. Sometimes mingled with the humanitarian motivation is another, that of persuading people to have larger families. The primary incentive used to promote population growth is the "family allowance," a periodic payment to families that can vary with the number of children they have. Other monetary incentives include a direct cash payment upon the birth of a child or an income tax credit for dependent children. Incentives can also be nonmonetary, such as housing priority for large families or awards to mothers of many children. Making motherhood more attractive

---

NOMIC BEHAVIOR PROBLEMS AND PROSPECTS (E. Sheldon, ed., Lippincott, 1973); *New Economic Approaches to Fertility,* 81 J. POL. ECON. S1-S299 (T. Schultz, ed., 1973); H. Leibenstein, *An Interpretation of the Economic Theory of Fertility: Promising Path or Blind Alley?*, 12 J. ECON. LIT. 457 (1974). A somewhat broader approach has been taken by the trans-national "value of children" project; for a review of the project in six countries, *see* A. Simmons, *The VOC Approach to Population Policies: New Hope or False Promise?* 1 PROCEEDINGS INTL. POP. CONF. OF THE IUSSP, MEXICO (1977).

[31] S. Wishik, *supra* n. 23 at 114.

[32] H.E.W., SOCIAL SECURITY PROGRAMS THROUGHOUT THE WORLD, 1977 (HEW Publication No. SSA 78-11805, 1977).

by providing extended maternity leave or providing day care for young children are other kinds of nonmonetary incentives.

Family allowances and other incentives to promote population growth were initially attempted on a major scale by France, Germany, and Italy between World Wars I and II.[33] Today, they are associated primarily with Belgium, France, the USSR, and the socialist countries of Eastern Europe.[34]

In examining family allowances and other incentives, it must be cautioned that these are part of each country's complex systems of laws regulating the family, housing, employment, etc., that few countries have wholly consistent population policies, and that population objectives are often hard to disentangle from other social or economic objectives.

B. Overview of Pronatalist Incentives: United Nations, Measures, Policies and Programmes Affecting Fertility, With Particular Reference To National Family Planning Programmes 17–33. (1972).

Family Allowances

Family allowances can be broadly defined as "systematic payments made to families with dependent children, either by employers or by the Government for the primary purpose of promoting the welfare of such children." Of all measures considered here, with the possible exception of income tax exemptions for children, family allowances are the most widespread.

As of early 1967, 64 countries had introduced family allowance

[33]J. Vadakin provides an enlightening history of family allowances in FAMILY ALLOWANCES: AN ANALYSIS OF THEIR DEVELOPMENT AND IMPLICATIONS (Miami, 1958).

[34]For more detailed analyses of specific country legislation, *see* POPULATION POLICY IN DEVELOPED COUNTRIES (B. Berelson, ed., McGraw Hill, 1974) [hereafter cited as B. Berelson, ed.]; LAW AND FERTILITY IN EUROPE (M. Kirk, M. Livi Bacci & E. Szabady, eds., Ordina, 1975) [hereafter cited as Kirk *et al,* eds.]; M. Livi Bacci, *Population Policies in Western Europe,* 28 POP. STUDIES. 191 (1974); M. Macura, *Population Policies in Socialist Countries of Europe,* 28 POP. STUDIES. 369 (1974); D. GLASS, POPULATION POLICIES AND MOVEMENTS IN EUROPE (Clarendon, 1940, reprinted by Cass, 1967); COUNCIL OF EUROPE, FAMILY POLICY: LAWS AND REGULATIONS DESIGNED TO COMPENSATE FOR FAMILY COMMITMENTS (1967); D. Heer & J. Bryden, *Family Allowances and Fertility in the Soviet Union,* 18 SOVIET STUDIES 153 (1966); the country studies published as monographs by the Law and Population Program, Fletcher School of Law and Diplomacy, Tufts University.

programmes. Included were all 27 European countries, 21 African countries (mostly former French colonies), 7 countries of North and South America, and 9 in Asia and Oceania. France and Belgium were the first to introduce family allowances on a nation-wide scale in the early 1930s. Since that time, many Governments have assumed greater responsibility for the economic and social well-being of their people, and the use of family allowance programmes has become widespread since the Second World War. . . .

Family allowance schemes may be classified in two major categories: those covering, in principle, all families ordinarily resident in the country; and those under which entitlement to the benefit depends upon the existence of employment relationship. Under the schemes belonging to the first category, it is usual for the entire cost to be borne by the Government, whereas, in the case of the second category, costs are met at least in a substantial part from contributions paid by employers. In a number of developed countries, the Government finances the entire cost of the programme through special or general tax revenue and, in most cases, all resident families are eligible for payment.

In general, eligibility is determined mainly by the age and birth order of children. The maximum age ranges from 12 to 18 years among less developed countries and from 14 to 21 years in developed nations. However, the maximum in most countries centers around the ages of 14 to 18, though it is often higher in the case of students, apprentices, invalids, and sometimes of unmarried girls who remain at home. A major exception is the Soviet Union, which pays the allowances only for children between the ages of 1 and 5 years.

Most countries pay allowances to all families with eligible children from the first child on. However, some begin payments only with the second child; some are known to commence with the third child; and at least two with the fourth child. Several countries have established limits on the number of children that the Government will support in one family. In addition, some countries pay allowances to other dependent members of the family as well, most notably the non-working wife.

A fixed allowance per child is the most common arrangement, although it by no means prevails uniformly. In many countries, payments per child increase with the number of children in the family, and in some payments are increased with the age of the child, presumably because it is more costly to provide for an older child. Five countries have special additional allowances for large families. In addition, several countries pay supplementary allowances to children who attend school to cover some of the extra expenses involved. On the other hand, a few diminish the size of payments as the number of children in the family increases, and some have a system whereby allowances decrease as other income increases to some maximum. . . .

Systems of Taxation on Income

In most countries some system exists whereby persons subject to income taxation are granted a reduction in the size of their tax payments if they have family responsibilities. Such a system recognizes that family responsibilites necessitate additional expenditure and is therefore similar in purpose to a family allowance programme. The size of tax savings from taxable income increases with the size of the deductions allowed for each dependent. In some cases, the tax rate itself may vary with family size. Figures available for several European countries indicate that a family with two minor children earning a typical income pays significantly less in taxes than a bachelor with the same income. . . .

In some tax systems, married couples, even without children, may benefit from special tax treatment. Exceptionally, as in Romania, the imposition of taxes for bachelorhood and childlessness may be a means of achieving higher national birth rates. But where a policy favouring lower fertility is in effect, tax discrimination against unmarried persons may be eliminated, as in India (1965), so as not to give special favour to the state of marriage in itself. . . .

Aid to Maternity and Rewards to Motherhood

Many Governments aid expectant mothers, and some reward motherhood with special grants and services. Pre-natal grants and birth grants are paid to aid a woman with the extra expenses incurred upon the arrival of a new child. Maternity insurance and maternity benefits for employed women are provided to cover the loss of income of mothers who can no longer work and also to enable mothers to procure necessary medical and child-care services. . . .

France and fourteen African countries formerly administered by France provide pre-natal allowances to expectant mothers for the nine months preceding birth. More than twenty-five developed and developing countries award a lump-sum birth grant as part of their family allowance programmes, the conditions ranging from a limitation to the first three births only, to variations in the size of payments with parity. The grants are frequently provided as a part of a maternity insurance programme. As of early 1967, 82 countries had such schemes, and 24 were less developed countries, which had no family allowance programmes. Maternity insurance is generally financed by employers' or by joint employees' and employers' contributions. Thus, eligibility is linked to employment status, entitlement is restricted to female employees and, in some countries, to wives of employees. In all countries where it is provided, maternity insurance is calculated at some percentage of earnings and in all but a few less developed countries it also includes complete or partial coverage for hospitalization and maternity care. . . .

Other Measures Related to the Family

Although less widespread then those considered above, there are other measures aiding families in certain countries which may influence fertility. They include (a) grants and loans to newly married couples; (b) the subsidization of many services used largely by families; (c) special privileges granted to family members in employment and military services. Measures involving the treatment of illegitimate children may also be of importance. . . .

Government provision of benefits in kind in the areas of housing, transportation, education, child care, vacations and the like, are intended to reduce the impact of family size upon a family's standard of living. Such benefits are found almost exclusively among developed countries.

A system of child care or creches for children whose mothers are working is a means utilized by several countries to aid the mother and the family. Creches—usually for pre-school children—are used most widely in the USSR and most Eastern European countries and are intended primarily to guarantee women the right to work as well as privileges that flow from work. In a great many of the less developed countries, all business enterprises employing more than a specified number of women are required to provide infant and child-care facilities. Argentina and Italy, among the more developed nations, have similar regulations.

Other measures widely used to alleviate the financial burden of parenthood include a reduction in the price of public transportation for children below a certain age; school meals and free health care for school children in addition to free schooling; and special aid to large families for school attendance. In addition, there are maternal and child health care centres in many countries; and free or partially subsidized holidays for mothers and children. . . .

C. Commentary and Issues

1. Population and Social Welfare Policies

Summarizing extensive reviews of the population policies of 24 developed countries, Berelson wrote:

> . . . Each country reviews its own situation in the light of its own history and tradition, its own values and operating procedures, and determines its position accordingly. Thus the whole issue of population, already complicated in its very nature, becomes involved in a range of economic and social concerns of national importance and becomes progressively defined and decided in that light. . . .
>
> But population is not an issue of really high priority in these countries except perhaps in a few cases seeking to increase fertility. "Population policy" is much more likely to surface as one factor in social policy, as illustrated particularly by the Soviet Union, rather than "in its own right"—as incidental to social welfare rather than directly demographic in cause and consequence.[35]

As has been noted above, many countries provide family allowances for both social welfare and fertility reasons. Can the two be separated? One way might be to examine whether the benefits are progressive or not. If equal benefits are paid for each child, then the prime motivation is more likely to be family welfare than it is if benefits are graduated, *i.e.,* higher for, say, the fourth and later child. Paillat has prepared an index for a number of European countries reprinted as Table 7–1.[36] Commenting on this index, Paillat noted that:

> Many countries have progressive scales, but in very different forms. There may be a fixed rate starting with the second child (Greece), the third (Great Britain, Belgium, France), the fifth (Federal Republic of Germany) or even the eighth (Netherlands). The situations of first, and sometimes of second, children cover a very wide range. In relation to the figure 100 (3 children), the index for the first child lies between 0 (Great Britain and the Federal Republic of Germany) and 50 (agricultural wage-earners in Switzerland), but it is generally lower than 33 (the figure on the non-progressive scale).
>
> In France, it is sharply reduced (from 26 to 11) at the second birthday if no younger child is born by then. Bulgaria is least generous to the second child, excepting, of course, for Poland where no allowances are paid until the fourth child. The differences in allowances for the fifth child are marked, even excluding Bulgaria: 150 (Serbia), 205 (Great Britain), 253 (Federal Republic of Germany).
>
> One relatively recent development is worth noting. Whereas originally allowances virtually stopped after the age of compulsory education and even now are no longer paid to all children after the age of

[35] B. Berelson, *Summary,* in B. Berelson, ed., *supra* n. 34 at 771 and 774.

[36] P. Paillat, *Economic and Social Assistance to Families,* in M. Kirk *et al.,* eds., *supra* n. 34 at 69.

Table 7–1 Graduation of Allowances for Children Under 16 Years of Age in Relation to the Allowance for 3 Children (= 100)

	No. of children				
Country	*1*	*2*	*3*	*4*	*5*
Federal Republic of Germany	–	29	100	171	253
France*	–	37	100	163	225
Great Britain	–	47	100	153	205
Belgium	20	53	100	147	194
Netherlands	31	65	100	148	192
France*	26	54	100	146	192
France*	11	49	100	146	192
Rumania** (3)	29	62	100	150	190
(2)	30	63	100	148	186
(1)	31	63	100	145	183
Finland	28	61	100	139	179
Slovenia** (2)	27	63	100	137	173
Czechoslovakia	10	49	100	145	173
Austria	25	56	100	134	170
Croatia, Denmark, Hungary, Italy, Sweden, Switzerland (industry and commerce)	33	67	100	133	167
Switzerland (agricultural workers)	50	66	100	132	165
Slovenia** (1)	35	68	100	133	165
Serbia** (2)	30	67	100	133	150
Serbia** (2)	27	67	100	133	150
Greece	21	35	100	113	127
Bulgaria	8	32	100	108	116

*France is listed three times. The first shows allowances for households with more than one wage-earner and with children under ten years old; the second shows allowances for households with one wage-earner and one child under two years old, and the third shows allowances for households with one wage-earner but no children under two years old.—. Ed.
**(1), (2), and (3) refer to family's income bracket.

15 or 16, more and more countries are extending them to families whose children continue their studies (provided proof is given of this) while remaining dependent on them; some countries even continue to pay allowances up to 27 years (Federal Republic of Germany) or 26 (Italy, Czechoslovakia, Yugoslavia) in the case of university students. . . .

Increases linked to the age of the children (Belgium, France) reflect a desire to ensure that the aid granted is more in keeping with changes in the household budget as the children grow up, although the conditions may sometimes be questionable.[37]

[37] *Id.* at 68.

Some family allowances are paid only to poor families, while others are provided whatever the family's income. Reviewing family allowances in France, Doublet and de Villedary noted that increasing attention is being given to family resources in determining the right to family allowances.[38] This would appear to be based primarily on family welfare considerations and only secondarily on demographic grounds. More recently, the French government adopted an avowedly pronatalist policy and adopted six measures to promote large families; these include increased family allowances, longer maternity leaves, and payment of a maternity grant upon the birth of a third or subsequent child.[39]

2. Do Pronatalist Incentives Work?

There have been very few studies evaluating whether pronatalist incentives actually do increase fertility. Those studies that have been done tend to indicate that incentives have not been successful in raising fertility—at least not very successful. It is not known, however, whether pronatalist incentives are conceptually unsound or whether they simply have not been large enough.

Generally, fertility has not increased in those countries that have used family allowances and other economic inducements to increase it. Glass observed in 1940, "Examination of the gross reproduction rates for France as a whole and for the individual Départements does not bring much evidence to support any contention that French population policy has succeeded in raising fertility. . . . On the contrary, fertility has fallen more rapidly in the last few years in spite of more widespread and, in terms of money, more significant allowances. . . ."[40] This conclusion was echoed by Heer and Bryden's analysis of family allowances in the Soviet Union, "It is not possible to offer conclusive proof concerning the effects of any family allowance. . . . However, we think we have produced sufficient evidence to show that at the present time the Soviet programme of family allowances has little overall positive effect on fertility."[41] McIntyre, having reviewed pronatalist programs in four Eastern

[38] J. DOUBLET & H. de VILLEDARY, LAW AND POPULATION GROWTH IN FRANCE, 49–60, Law and Population Monograph No. 12 (Fletcher School of Law & Diplomacy, 1973).

[39] *Le Monde,* November 24, 1979, as reported in IPPF, *Law File* (December, 1979).

[40] D. GLASS, *supra* n. 34 at 202. Some French demographers have expressed a view contrary to that of Glass. *See, e.g.,* the statements of Henry and Rain, quoted in Vadakin, *supra* n. 33 at 113.

[41] D. Heer & J. Bryden, *supra* n. 34 at 161.

European countries, refused to give a judgment, stating only, "It is . . . too early to offer an empirical conclusion, despite the existence of some positive natality signs. . . ."[42] Frejka, commenting on fertility policies in Czechoslovakia, which has enacted a comprehensive and wideranging series of pronatalist incentives, found evidence that the policies *were* effective. He wrote:

> Although the foregoing analysis does not permit us to draw decisive conclusions about the causal role of pronatalist policy measures in the increase in fertility in the 1970's, it does provide reasonably solid ground for the inference that the fertility trends were in part brought about by those measures.[43]

Two studies using techniques of multivariate regression analysis failed to find a correlation between family allowances and increased fertility. Utilizing data for 67 countries, Hohm concluded that family allowances did *not* increase fertility. He found no correlation between the size of the benefit and fertility and even uncovered an inverse relationship between the extent of coverage and fertility, *i.e.*, as more children were covered by family allowances, fertility declined. Hohm attempted to explain this surprising finding by speculating that the causal relationship might be inverse, that is, decreasing fertility leads governments to increase coverage of family allowances.[44] Lloyd, analyzing data from a number of developed countries concluded that "no pronatalist effect of family allowances was observed. . . . Further empirical investigation into the determinants of the size of family allowances revealed that relatively low birth rates were more likely to be the cause of than the result of generous child subsidies". . . .[45]

These results—that family allowances do not influence couples to have large families—challenge the conventional economic wisdom

[42]R. McIntyre, *Pronatalist Programmes in Eastern Europe,* 7 SOVIET STUDIES, 366, 378 (1975).

[43]T. Frejka, *Fertility Trends and Policies: Czechoslovakia in the 1970's,* 6 POP. & DEV. REV. 65, 89 (1980).

[44]C. Hohm, *An International Analysis of the Effects of Family Allowance Programs on Fertility Levels,* 6 INTL. J. SOC. FAM. 45 (1976). Hohm concluded that "if a country desires to implement or expand family allowance programs in order to raise the living standard of its children, the data in this study suggest that [this] can be done without fear of raising the fertility level." *Id.* at 55.

[45]C. Lloyd, *An Economic Analysis of the Impact of Government on Fertility,* 22 PUB. POLICY 489 at 497–498 (1974).

that, as the cost of children decreases, people tend to have more.[46] It raises questions about why pronatalist incentives have not been more successful. Is parenthood such a personal matter that people fail to respond to economic stimuli? Has a mental "set" toward small families, which even child subsidies cannot break, somehow been established? Have incentives thus far been so trivial that people have not responded to them?

3. The Size of Pronatalist Incentives

Data on the size of family allowances, particularly in relation to earning power, are not easy to obtain. Most information is rather old. Cross national comparisons are difficult to make, and, insofar as they can be made, must be frequently revised to account for inflation. Notwithstanding the methodological difficulties, a general, though somewhat tentative, consensus has been reached that pronatalist incentives have not been of sufficient size to influence reproductive decisions.[47]

Utilizing the family allowance payments as a percentage of national income (a surrogate for family allowance as a percentage of family income), Heer and Bryden provided the following table, based on 1961 data:[48]

Table 7–2 Family Allowance Payments as a Percentage of National Income

Country	*Family allowance as percentage of national income*
Belgium	3.12%
Canada	1.83%
France	4.76%
West Germany	0.39%
Italy	2.57%
Netherlands	1.54%
Sweden	1.30%
United Kingdom	0.64%
USSR	0.32%
United States (AFDC benefits)	0.29%

[46]Lloyd grapples with this conceptual problem. *Id.* at 490 *et seq. See* the references *supra* n. 30 for analysis of the economic value of children.

[47]B. Berelson, *Summary,* in B. Berelson, ed., *supra* n. 34 at 780–781 provides a table of the dollar value of family assistance programs in 24 developed countries.

[48]D. Heer & J. Bryden, *supra* n. 34 at 160.

They concluded, at least regarding the Soviet Union, that the family allowance benefits have been too trivial to influence fertility. Based on his analysis of family allowances in Europe, Paillat concurred in this judgment and observed further that "very few allowances are based on the movement of prices.... In the circumstances one cannot see how they can still serve as an inducement, since even from the point of view of social justice they leave much to be desired."[49] Similar conclusions were reached by Plank with regard to family allowances in Chile.[50]

If the small size of family allowances does account for their lack of success, what would it take to reverse this? Can threshold levels be established beyond which incentives would become effective? What would be the social implications of such massive income transfer? Might inducements affect primarily the poorer segments of society and would governments be willing to spend large amounts of money so the poor would have more children? If fertility in the developed world continues to fall below replacement level, would these countries institute massive payments to promote childbirth?[51] Several European countries, already concerned about falling birth rates, have increased pronatalist incentives to induce couples to have larger families.[52]

4. Welfare and Fertility in the United States

The closest analogue in the United States to the European system of family allowances is welfare payments made under the Aid to Families with Dependent Children (AFDC).[53] Payment of welfare benefits to mothers with dependent children has provoked criticism that AFDC acts to encourage childbearing and has led to

[49] P. Paillat, *supra* n. 36 at 70.

[50] S. Plank, *Family Allowance and Family Planning in Chile,* 68 AM. J. PUB. HLTH. 989 (1978).

[51] This possibility is suggested by C. Westoff, *Marriage and Fertility in the Developed Countries,* 239 SCIENTIFIC AMERICAN 51 (1978).

[52] In an attempt to raise birth rates, the West German government increased family allowances and maternity leave, *The Economist,* Feb. 3, 1979, as reported in IPPF, *Law File* (Feb. 1979), the East German government expanded its day care system and increased the amount of baby bonuses, *The Guardian,* Aug. 7, 1979, as reported in IPPF, *Law File* (Sept. 1979), and France has enacted six measures, including larger family allowances, *Le Monde, supra* n. 39.

[53] 42 U.S.C. §§ 601 *et seq.* (1976).

suggestions that "welfare mothers" be given incentives to limit childbearing.[54]

The charge that welfare encourages childbearing has come under increasing criticism by social demographers. For example, a study by Presser and Salsberg concluded:

> We found that women in households receiving public assistance want fewer children than those in non-recipient households. Moreover, there is no significant difference between recipients and non-recipients on other indices of fertility-related attitudes and behavior.[55]

These findings corroborate the results of the European studies discussed *supra* pp. 332–333. Cain has observed that AFDC should be expected to have little pronatal effect since the two conditions for being on welfare, abject poverty and an absent father, do not, in economic terms, lend themselves to motivating mothers to have large families.[56] Additionally, welfare payments might be too small to encourage additional offspring. However, Winegarden has presented data which indicate that neither larger AFDC payments nor additional payments per child increased fertility among welfare recipients.[57]

V. OTHER SOCIOECONOMIC POLICIES AND LAWS INFLUENCING FERTILITY

A. Introductory Note

A panoply of laws and policies enacted for social welfare or humanitarian reasons can, either directly or indirectly, affect fer-

[54]*See, e.g.,* N. Dembitz, *Should Public Policy Give Incentives to Welfare Mothers to Limit the Number of Their Children?,* 4 FAM. L.Q. 130 (1970), and the reply by H. Pilpel, *A Dissenting Viewpoint: Should Public Policy Give Incentives to Welfare Mothers to Limit the Number of Their Children?,* 4 FAM. L.Q. 146 (1970).

[55]H. Presser & L. Salsberg, *Public Assistance and Early Family Formation: Is There a Pronatalist Effect?,* 23 SOCIAL PROBLEMS 226 (1975). *See also* the similar conclusions reached by the U.S. COMM. ON POP. GROWTH & THE AMER. FUTURE, POPULATION AND THE AMERICAN FUTURE 158 (Signet, 1972); P. Placek & G. Hendershot, *Public Welfare and Family Planning: An Empirical Study of the "Brood Sow" Myth,* 21 SOCIAL PROBLEMS 658 (1974); K. Moore & S. Caldwell, *The Effect of Government Policies on Out-of-Wedlock Sex and Pregnancy,* 9 FAM. PLAN. PERSPECTIVES 164 (1977).

[56]G. Cain, *The Effect of Income Maintenance Laws on Fertility in the United States,* in U.S. COMM. ON POP. GROWTH & THE AMER. FUTURE: RESEARCH REPORTS 323 (vol. 6, R. Parke & C. Westoff, eds., 1972).

[57]C. Winegarden, *The Fertility of AFDC Women: An Econometric Analysis,* 26 J. ECON. & BUS. 159 (1974).

tility. The remainder of this chapter explores some of the most important of these laws and policies.

B. Laws Regulating Marriage and Divorce

1. United Nations. Measures, Policies and Programmes Affecting Fertility, with Particular Reference to National Family Planning Programmes 49–54 (1972)

Age at marriage

Throughout the world, the legal minimum age for marriage ranges from 12 to 18 for females and from 14 to 21 for males. In general, higher legal minimum ages for marriage are found in the developed countries and lower legal minimum ages in less developed countries. However, some interesting exceptions to this rule can be found. In Ireland, the minimum is 12 for females and 14 for males, and in some states of the United States, 16 is the minimum for males and 14 for females. By contrast, in Ethiopia and Peru, both considered to be less developed countries, legal minimum age for females is 18 and for males 18 in Ethiopia and 21 in Peru. In Canada, the minimum age is 12 for females and 14 for males. In the Ivory Coast the minimum age is 20 for females and 21 for males.

In the last 20 years, several countries have raised the minimum age at marriage in the interests of child welfare and/or a reduction in the rate of population growth. In 1950, China (mainland) raised the minimum age at marriage of females to 18 and of males to 20, and in recent years, the age for both sexes is reported to have been further advanced. In 1949 the Child Marriage Restraint (Amendment) Act in India raised the minimum age of marriage of females from 14 to 15 years. The minimum age for males remained 18, the age which had been established by the Sarda Act of British India in 1929. However, because according to Hindu law, children of any age may be validly married, this law has been difficult to implement effectively. Also in 1961 Pakistan raised the minimum age for females from 14 to 16. In the USSR a new marriage and family law was ratified in June 1968 which introduced a minimum age of 18 for both males and females, giving individual republics the right to lower it, but by no more than two years. . . .

It is generally known that the average completed family size is likely to be larger in a society with a very high proportion of young marriages than in one where a high proportion of the population marries at a later age. . . .

While age at marriage tends to be generally related to fertility, it does not follow that a rise in the legal minimum age of marriage will necessarily lead to a decline in fertility. In cases such as India, where even the existing minimum age is not enforced, legislation providing for an additional increase could hardly be expected to have practical consequences for fertility. This is not to deny the fact that, hypothetically, such a change could contribute to a decline in fertility if the higher minimum age at marriage could be enforced. Also, in those instances where large proportions of the population marry later than the minimum established by law, increasing the age at marriage would not be expected to affect fertility.

Polygamy

Most countries do not permit plural marriages. However, Islamic law permits a man to be married to a maximum of four wives at any one time. The laws of Moslem countries seek to conform with the Koran's instruction that four wives are permissible if they are treated equally, but they may have different interpretations. The Tunisian Government abolished polygamy under the Code of Personal Status of 1956 (article 18), taking the stand that a man could only have one wife under Islamic law, because it is humanly impossible to treat several equally, and polygamy has been illegal in Turkey since 1926. In other Moslem countries, it is still legal. . . .

Several studies comparing the fertility of monogamous and polygamous marriages have found that polygamy reduces fertility. . . . However, despite its acknowledged effect on fertility, polygamy is probably not sufficiently widespread in any country to exert an appreciable effect on the overall birth-rate. In a society where an important number of women would not have the opportunity to marry under a monogamous system, polygamy will increase the number of married women. Therefore, the effect of reduced fertility per married woman on the birth rate in a polygamous society might be counteracted to some extent by the effect of an increased number of married women.

Divorce

The right to divorce is not universally granted and the permissible grounds for divorce vary among those countries where it is legal. In some predominantly Catholic countries, under no condition is divorce permitted and only the physical separation of the spouses without the dissolution of the marriage bond may be authorized. In one or two, only non-Catholics may divorce.

In most other countries, divorce is legal, although the ease with which it can be obtained varies from place to place. In those European countries where divorce is possible, it is generally permitted by judicial decision only on the grounds of adultery, desertion, cruelty or imprisonment. There are some exceptions, however, as in Czechoslovakia, where divorce may be deemed contrary to the interests of minor children in the marriage, though normally deep and permanent dissension between the couple provides adequate grounds.

Grounds for divorce in the United States vary from one state to another, but the trend in recent years has been toward liberalization of the statutes. Costa Rica and Panama are examples of two South American countries where divorce is permitted on various grounds: adultery of the wife and mutual consent are among eleven acceptable reasons in Panama.

Laws change rapidly, especially in the midst of such revolutionary social changes as are taking place in the emerging countries. Thus, inventories of legal questions are frequently out of date before they are published. . . .

2. Note on Age of Marriage and Fertility Change

Theoretically, legislation increasing the age of marriage reduces rates of population growth by decreasing the number of childbearing years (at least where nonmarital fertility, is low) and by lengthening the interval between generations.[58] Practically, however, it has been questioned whether legal change has this effect since enforcement is often difficult, childbearing may be a culturally related decision not governed by the law, and many couples, particularly in rural areas, are physically beyond the reach of social legislation.[59] Nonetheless, where laws are enforceable, raising the age of marriage is thought to have had a considerable impact on fertility.[60] According to one report, of 26 developing countries with populations of over one million in which fertility has declined during the past two decades, rising age at marriage has contributed substantially to total fertility declines in eight.[61]

[58]A. Henry & P. Piotrow, *Age at Marriage and Fertility,* POPULATION REPORTS, series M, no. 4 (Johns Hopkins, 1979).

[59]This conclusion was reached by the Report of the Special Rapporteur, Commission on the Status of Women, United Nations Economic and Social Council, *Study on the Interrelationship of the Status of Women and Family Planning* (1973), reprinted in UNESCO, READINGS ON POPULATION FOR LAW STUDENTS 59 *et seq.* (1977).

[60]*See* M. BADRUD DUZA & C. BALDWIN, NUPTIALITY AND POPULATION POLICY 1–4 (Pop. Council, 1977).

[61]A. Henry & P. Piotrow, *supra* n. 58.

C. Public Health Measures

Improved health and nutrition, particularly insofar as they improve the life chances of children, tend to be correlated with lower fertility, at least in the long run.[62] According to a recent report of the U.S. National Academy of Sciences, basic health services do not reach, or are inaccessible to, perhaps as many as 80–85 percent of the population in need in developing countries.[63] A major reason "is an inadequate health care system or infrastructure, which includes the personnel who work within it, physical facilities, the arrangement and logistical support systems, and the health care methodology and technology that flow through it."[64] How to improve health care delivery is a complex question that generates considerable controversy. Some of the key issues include: Should greater use be made of nonphysicians or community leaders in delivering health services (a question stimulated by the "barefoot doctors" of China and community-based family planning programs)? Is the western health delivery model an appropriate one for the developing world? Will improvements in the health care delivery system, apart from other societal changes, have a significant effect in reducing fertility? What should be the priorities in determining health interventions?[65]

D. Housing

Housing may represent a policy variable that can affect fertility. Recall that Singapore's disincentive measures withdrew the priority

[62] *See* T. Schultz, *Interrelationships Between Mortality and Fertility,* in POPULATION AND DEVELOPMENT: THE SEARCH FOR SELECTIVE INTERVENTIONS 239 (R. Ridker, ed., Johns Hopkins, 1976); W. Butz & J-P Habicht, *The Effects of Nutrition and Health on Fertility: Hypotheses, Evidence, and Interventions, id.* at 210; THE EFFECTS OF INFANT AND CHILD MORTALITY ON FERTILITY (S. Preston, ed., Academic, 1978).

[63] REPORT OF A STUDY ON U.S. INITIATIVES FOR THE U.N. CONFERENCE ON SCIENCE AND TECHNOLOGY FOR DEVELOPMENT (NATL. ACAD. SCIENCES, 1978).

[64] *Id.* at 96.

[65] For examination of public health issues, *see* J. BRYANT, HEALTH AND THE DEVELOPING WORLD (Cornell, 1969); A. Rosenfield, *Modern Medicine and the Delivery of Health Services: Lessons from the Developing World,* 2 MAN & MED. 279 (1977); V. Navarro, *The Underdevelopment of Health or the Health of Underdevelopment: An Analysis of the Distribution of Human Health Resources in Latin America,* 4 INTL. J. HLTH. SERV. (1974); M ROEMER, COMPARATIVE NATIONAL POLICIES ON HEALTH CARE (Dekker, 1977); R. KOHN & K. WHITE, HEALTH CARE: AN INTERNATIONAL STUDY (Oxford, 1976).

in allocation of government housing for large families and that some European countries provide housing loans or priorities to families with many children. Lack of housing, insofar as it makes having a large family less desirable, has conflicted with the pronatalist tendencies of Eastern European countries.[66]

E. STATUS OF WOMEN

The importance of improving the status of women, both as a goal in itself and as it tends to reduce fertility, has received considerable attention.[67] The 1975 International Women's Year Conference in Mexico and its domestic follow-up in Houston, Texas, are but two examples.[68] International agencies are now tending to look more favorably upon so-called "women's projects" and to include funds to improve the lives of women in projects whose goals are not specifically aimed at women.[69] As Zeidenstein has observed, "In every development situation there are, indeed, identifiable contributions, potentials, and needs of women that can be adequately understood, addressed, and integrated into development undertakings."[70]

The two most important aspects of the relationship between

[66]Scarcity of housing and pronatalist population policy has been explored by P. MAGGS, LAW AND POPULATION GROWTH IN EASTERN EUROPE 18–19, Law and Population Monograph No. 3 (Fletcher School of Law & Diplomacy, 1972).

[67]*See, e.g., Law and the Status of Women: An International Symposium,* 8 COLUM. HUM. RTS. L. REV, 1–371 (1977); E. BOSERUP, WOMAN'S ROLE IN ECONOMIC DEVELOPMENT (St. Martin's 1970); A. Germain, *Status and Roles of Women as Factors in Fertility Behavior: A Policy Analysis,* 6 STUDIES IN FAM. PLAN. 192 (1975); J. Bruce, *Women's Organizations: A Resource for Family Planning and Development,* 8 FAM. PLAN. PERSPECTIVES 291 (1976); K. NEWLAND, WOMEN AND POPULATION GROWTH: CHOICE BEYOND CHILDBEARING 15–22 (Worldwatch Inst., 1977).

[68]For a cogent report on the International Women's Year conference, *see* A. Germain, *Women at Mexico: Beyond Family Planning Acceptors,* 7 FAM. PLAN. PERSPECTIVES 235 (1975). Germain noted that third world women at Mexico were concerned with basics such as eradication of illiteracy, more productive labor for all, development problems, and assistance from wealthier countries. Western women would have liked more attention given to redefining protective legislation, elimination of unequal work conditions, and equal access to paid (especially professional) employment.

[69]For a review of some current projects which attempt to improve the lives of rural women *see Learning about Rural Women* (S. Zeidenstein, ed.), 10 STUDIES IN FAM. PLAN. 309–422 (1979).

[70]G. Zeidenstein, *Including Women in Development Efforts* (presidential address, Population Council, 1978).

women's status and fertility are considered to be education and employment. In the excerpts that follow, Birdsall reviews the relationship between these two variables and fertility and Piepmeier discusses some specific ways in which law can help improve the educational and employment opportunities of women.

1. N. Birdsall, "Analytical Approaches to the Relationship of Population Growth and Development," 3 *Population and Development Review* 63, at 86–87 (1977).

Female Education and Labor Force Participation

Female education bears one of the strongest and most consistent negative relationships to fertility for a variety of reasons: through its effect on raising age of marriage; because it may improve the likelihood that a woman has knowledge of and can use modern contraceptives; and because it has some intangible effect on the woman's ability to plan, her interest in nonfamilial activities, and so on. No need to invoke fertility reduction to justify improving educational opportunities for women: better educated women will be more productive workers, better parents, and better-informed citizens; however, where male/female student ratios indicate that women suffer some schooling disadvantage, fertility effects provide additional justification for rectifying the imbalance. . . .

But female labor-force participation appears to have an independent effect on fertility only for those women who work in high-prestige, modern-sector jobs. High rates of female labor-force participation, like virtually all other variables, are neither a necessary condition for fertility decline (consider Korea, Turkey) nor a sufficient condition for it (consider countries of West Africa). On the other hand, increasing opportunities for women to work in the modern labor force can accelerate a fertility decline; where women may desire more children than their husbands (as is possible in the middle East and Pakistan, where custom deprives most women of opportunities in other endeavors), offering women some other avenue of activity than child rearing may reduce family size. Good earnings opportunities, like higher education, can increase the age of marriage for women. . . .

From the point of view of policy, an important conclusion emerging from these analyses is the highly tentative nature of the effect of "status of women" on fertility. But "status of women" does not define an area where public intervention is possible; education and jobs for women do. Improving women's opportunities for education and for modern jobs, like reducing infant mortality, has its own justification;

piggybacking its fertility-reducing benefit onto programs and projects geared to improving women's lives increases the measured benefits of such projects relative to their given costs.

2. K. Piepmeier, "Changing Status of Women Through Law," *Law and Planned Parenthood* (J. Paxman, ed., IPPF, 1980) 91–106.

Education

One of the keys to equal status and opportunities is education and training. . . . Appropriate measures, including legislation, are necessary to guarantee that women, whether married or unmarried, have equal rights with men in access to education. Formal schooling should be made compulsory as a means of guaranteeing girls, who are often kept out of school to help at home, the same educational opportunities as boys. In addition, women must be guaranteed equal access to education of all types and at all levels, to the same examinations, the same curricula and to teaching staff, premises and equipment of the same standard. . . . Possible strategies for eliminating educational discrimination against women include:

Compulsory schooling for boys and girls.

Appropriate measures including legislation to ensure girls' and boys' access to the same institutions, curricula, examinations, standard of teaching and equipment, as well as scholarships and grants.

Abolition of child labor in order to discourage parents from sending children to work instead of school.

Waiver of school fees for girls or tax incentives for educating girls beyond a certain age.

Provision of out-of-school education, including functional literacy training, which is designed to fit the life-style of the women taught.

Prohibition against permanent dismissal of pregnant girls from school. . . .

Employment

Genuine economic equality is perhaps the most significant factor in bringing about social equality. It is also important because if denied full participation in economic production, women cannot contribute on an equal basis with men to the development of their societies. . . .

A host of factors have militated against the full participation of women in productive work. These include among others: existing power structures in which women have not been well represented;

maternal and domestic responsibilities; lack of education and training; high unemployment in general. While the law cannot erase totally such impediments, it can make some contribution toward improving a woman's chances for active participation in economic life and toward equal remuneration for her work. Law can be used to establish the principle of equal rights of men and women in employment by providing sanctions against discrimination based on sex as well as through regulations intended to encourage and facilitate women's involvement in productive work. . . .

Possible approaches to the establishment of equality of opportunity, treatment and pay for women workers include:

Adoption of equal pay and equal employment opportunity acts.

Establishment of equal-pay or equal-opportunities commissions to implement such legislation.

Development of regulations prohibiting government or institutions which receive government funds from discriminating against women in employment matters.

Establishment of affirmative action programmes to eliminate discrimination and promote equality of opportunity.

Review of protective legislation for women workers (outside of maternity protection) to determine whether it forecloses or inhibits equal opportunities and pay for women.

Adoption of legislation providing maternity protection for women.

Provision of parenthood benefits and leave from employment for parents of small children.

Development of legislation or other policies to promote child-care facilities for children of working parents.

Approval of tax deductions for private child care arrangements.

Definition of women's unpaid domestic work as a job with an economic value which can be taken into account in calculating social security and welfare benefits.

Legislation guaranteeing women and men equal access to credit and loans.

Development of policies or other measures to provide rural women with equal access to marketing facilities, technology, membership in cooperatives and equal treatment in land and agrarian reforms.

3. Note on Women's Employment

The traditional reason given for the generally inverse relationship between women's employment and fertility was the incompatibility of the roles of motherhood and worker. Although this has been demonstrated to be true in many instances, studies have highlighted the importance of the *kind* of employment on fertility.[71] Enforcement of equal opportunity and equal pay laws, where they exist, has often been weak, thus permitting major differences between the *de jure* and *de facto* situations.[72] And where laws are implemented, they may not have the effect originally intended. For example, Livi Bacci, after reviewing Western European legislation, observed that the greater protection afforded the working mother and employed women in general has tended to make the cost of a unit of female labor higher than a comparable unit of male labor, thus reducing female employment or, where labor supply is abundant, driving women out of the job market.[73]

In the United States, sex discrimination cases are litigated with increasing frequency. The primary vehicles for obtaining equal access to employment opportunities for women have been the equal protection clause of the Fourteenth Amendment and Title VII of the Civil Rights Act.[74] Title VII of the Civil Rights Act makes it unlaw-

[71]The relationship between female employment and fertility is explored in R. Dixon, *Women's Rights and Fertility,* REP. ON POP./FAM. PLAN., No. 17 (1975) and S. Preston, *Female Employment Policy and Fertility* in U.S. COMM. ON POP. GROWTH & THE AMER. FUTURE: RESEARCH REPORTS 379 (vol. 6, R. Parke & C. Westoff, eds., 1972).

[72]K. Piepmeier, *Changing the Status of Women Through Law,* in LAW AND PLANNED PARENTHOOD 91, 106 (J. Paxman, ed., IPPF, 1980), after reviewing the world's laws on the status of women concluded, "While a great many legislative reforms have attempted to achieve equality between men and women, the *de facto* situation of women is still unsatisfactory."

[73]M. Livi Bacci, *supra* n. 34 at 199.

[74]Courts have read the equal protection guarantees of the Fourteenth Amendment as applying to the federal government through the due process clause of the Fifth Amendment. Some of the key cases reaching the U.S. Supreme Court in which laws or policies were challenged on the grounds that they violated the equal protection clause are: Reed v. Reed, 404 U.S. 71 (1971) (statute giving men preference over women as administrators of decedents' estates held unconstitutional); Frontiero v. Richardson, 411 U.S. 677 (1973) (statute which required women, but not men, in the armed forces to prove dependency of spouse before spouse would be eligible for benefits held unconstitituonal. The four-justice plurality opinion found classification on the basis of gender to be constitutionally "suspect" and meriting "strict scrutiny"

ful, *inter alia,* for any employer "to fail or refuse to hire or to discharge any individual or otherwise to discriminate against any individual with respect to his compensation, terms, conditions or privileges of employment because of such individual's race, color, religion, sex or national origin."[75]

The proposed Equal Rights Amendment to the U.S. Constitution states in part: "Equality of rights under the law shall not be denied or abridged by the United States or by any State on account of sex." It had been ratified by 35 states as of 1981.[76]

Lack of child care, too, may be an obstacle to greater female participation in the labor force. It is probably a more important

---

of the law in question); Taylor v. Louisiana, 419 U.S. 522 (1975) (exclusion of women from juries found unconstitutional); Stanton v. Stanton, 421 U.S. 7 (1975) (statute specifying a higher age of majority for males than females held unconstitutional); Craig v. Boren, 429 U.S. 190 (1976) (statute prohibiting the sale of 3.2% beer to males under 21 and females under 28 held unconstitutional-the Court announced an intermediate standard of review in sex discrimination cases); Weinberger v. Wiesenfeld, 420 U.S. 636 (1975) (statute denying survivors' insurance to surviving widowers with children while authorizing similar mothers' benefits to widows held unconstitutional); Califano v. Goldfarb, 430 U.S. 199 (1977) (statute stating that survivors benefits based on husband's earnings payable automatically to wife, but benefits based on wife's earnings payable to husband only on proof of dependency held unconstitutional); Geduldig v. Aiello, 417 U.S. 484 (1974) (exclusion of pregnancy from employee disability plan held not a violation of equal protection).

[75]42 U.S.C. § 2000 e. § 703(a)(1). Some of the Key Title VII cases reaching the U.S. Supreme Court have been: General Electric Co. v. Gilbert, 429 U.S. 125 (1976) (exclusion of pregnancy from employee disability plan does not violate Title VII); City of Los Angeles, Department of Water and Power v. Manhart, 435 U.S. 702 (1978) (requirement that female employees make larger contribution to pension fund than male employees violates Title VII); Nashville Gas Co. v. Satty, 434 U.S. 136 (1977) (loss of seniority resulting from maternity leave, but not other disabilities, held to violate Title VII); Dothard v. Rawlinson, 433 U.S. 321 (1977) (gender-based requirement for prison guards upheld as a "bona fide occupational qualification"). *See also* Corning Glass Works v. Brennan, 417 U.S. 188 (1974) (higher pay for night inspectors (male) than day time inspectors (female) violated the Equal Pay Act of 1963). For a comprehensive review of this topic, *see* K. DAVIDSON, R. GINSBURG & H. KAY, TEXT, CASES AND MATERIALS ON SEX-BASED DISCRIMINATION (West, 1974) and R. GINSBURG & H. KAY, 1978 SUPPLEMENT TO DAVIDSON, GINSBURG & KAY'S CASES AND MATERIALS ON SEX-BASED DISCRIMINATION (West, 1978).

[76]For comprehensive discussions of the ERA, *see* B. Brown, T. Emerson, G. Falk & A. Freedman, *The Equal Rights Amendment: A Constitutional Basis for Equal Rights for Women,* 80 YALE L. J. 871 (1971) and B. BROWN, A. FREEDMAN, H. KATZ & A. PRICE, WOMEN'S RIGHTS AND THE LAW: THE IMPACT OF THE ERA ON STATE LAWS (Praeger, 1977).

consideration in developed countries, with a pattern of nuclear families, than in developing countries, with a tradition of extended families. In the United States legislation establishing a national day care program was vetoed by President Nixon in 1972. There now exist provisions for day care under various federal and state laws.[77]

[77]For analyses and discussion of child care, *see* S. LEVITAN & K. ALDERMAN, CHILD CARE & ABC's TOO (Johns Hopkins, 1975); G. STEINER, THE CHILDREN'S CAUSE (Brookings, 1976); S. Woolsey, *Pied Piper Politics and the Child-Care Debate,* 106 DAEDALUS 127 (1977); NATL. RESEARCH COUNCIL, ADVISORY COMM. ON CHILD DEVEL., TOWARD A NATIONAL POLICY FOR CHILDREN AND FAMILIES (1976); B. Bruce-Biggs, *"Child Care": The Fiscal Time Bomb,* 49 PUB. INTEREST 87 (1977).

CHAPTER 8

POPULATION POLICY FROM INTERNATIONAL PERSPECTIVE

I. INTRODUCTION

Policy and law flow into each other and at times are indistinguishable. In a broad sense, a book about legal aspects of population is also a book about population policies. There is, however, a body of materials on "population policy" that contains elements of population law but that also stands apart from it. The primary source of materials on population policy is the United Nations, and the starting point in understanding the major issues is the World Population Conference of 1974.

This chapter examines population policy from an international perspective, particularly from that of the United Nations. It explores definitions of population policy, discusses fertility regulation as a human right, and, in the context of the World Population Plan of Action, examines the most important unresolved population policy issue, the relationship between population and development. This is followed in Chapter 9 by an examination of how national governments have actually handled population policy issues. Specifically, through a comparative analysis of several explicit population policies, it provides some guidelines for the content of explicit policies and the manner of their enunciation and implementation.

II. THE DEFINITION OF POPULATION POLICY

There are almost as many definitions of population policy as there are commentators on the topic. Compare, for example, the following:

> An operational definition that seemed acceptable was that a population policy exists when the public sector takes a stance vis-a-vis mortality, fertility or spatial distribution.[1]
> Population policies may be defined as legislative measures, administrative programs, and other governmental action intended to alter or modify existing population trends in the interest of national survival and welfare.[2]
> Population policy comprises measures aimed at closing the gap between the sum of actual births in a society and the number that would be socially optimal (under some specified means of determining social objectives).[3]
> I would define policy as a statement of important goals, accompanied by a specific set of means to achieve them.[4]
> . . . both direct and indirect measures, formulated by the whole range of social institutions including government, which, whether intended or not, may influence the size, distribution, or composition of human population.[5]
> . . . a deliberate effort by a national government to influence the demographic variables: fertility, mortality, and migration.[6]
> . . . deliberate attempts by a government to affect the size, structure, or geographic distribution of the population. . . .[7]
> . . . population policy [means] a set of coordinated laws aimed at reaching some demographic goals. . . .[8]

[1]NATL. ACAD. SCIENCES, IN SEARCH OF POPULATION POLICY: VIEWS FROM THE DEVELOPING WORLD 45 (1974).

[2]H. Eldridge, *Population: Population Policy* in INTL. ENCYC. SOC. SCIENCES 381 (Vol. 12, Macmillan & Free Press, 1968).

[3]G. McNicoll, *Community-Level Population Policy: An Exploration,* 1 POP. & DEV. REV. 1, 2 (1975).

[4]J. Stycos, *Population Policy and Development,* 3 POP. & DEV. REV. 103, 106 (1977).

[5]E. DRIVER, WORLD POPULATION POLICY: AN ANNOTATED BIBLIOGRAPHY xvii (Lexington, 1972).

[6]K. ORGANSKI & A. ORGANSKI, POPULATION AND WORLD POWER 182 (Knopf, 1961).

[7]POPULATION POLICIES AND ECONOMIC DEVELOPMENT: A WORLD BANK STAFF REPORT 57 (John Hopkins, 1974). [Hereafter cited as POPULATION POLICIES.]

[8]J. Bourgeois-Pichat, *France,* in POPULATION POLICY IN DEVELOPED COUNTRIES 546 (B. Berelson, ed., McGraw-Hill, 1974).

A review of these definitions reveals major disagreements about the nature of population policy.[9] One issue is whether a population policy must be in the form of an explicit statement or declaration by the government or whether it can be inferred from a series of governmental actions. With regard to explicit policies, who should be considered authorized to make an explicit policy? For example, should a statement by a country's Health Minister about demographic goals be considered a population policy? Should the statement of the Brazilian representatives to the World Population Conference that Brazil had no national policy to reduce population growth but that every couple had the right to the number and spacing of children it desired and that government should provide information and services to the needy, be considered as the population policy of Brazil?

With regard to implicit policies, what actions should be considered in determining whether a country has a population policy or what it is? Must they be actions with an intention to change population variables? Does one look to a "set of administrative programs and other governmental action," "direct and indirect measures formulated by the whole range of social institutions," or "a coordinated set of laws," as proposed by the various commentators quoted above? To what extent is analysis of government budget allocation the key to determining a country's policy? Is fertility the only important element in a population policy, or does a population policy also have to affect mortality and migration?[10] With regard to fertility, it must be recognized that a continuum of activities can influence it. The World Bank has listed the following on the spectrum of governmental policies which can influence fertility:[11]

[9] Issues in population policy formation are discussed in L. CORSA & D. OAKLEY, POPULATION PLANNING (Michigan, 1979), 155–194, and INTL. REV. GROUP SOC. SCIENCE RESEARCH ON POP. & DEV., SOCIAL SCIENCE RESEARCH FOR POPULATION POLICY: DIRECTIONS FOR THE 1980s (Colegio de Mexico, 1979) [hereafter cited as IRG].

[10] B. Berelson, *Paths to Fertility Reduction: The "Policy Cube,"* 9 FAM. PLAN. PERSPECTIVES 214 (1977) has observed:

> If a country seeks to reduce the rate of population growth, there are in principle three ways to do so: encourage emigration, raise mortality or lower fertility. The first has occasionally been utilized in a few small island societies but clearly is not feasible for most developing countries in today's world. . . . The second is virtually unthinkable as a matter of public policy. . . . That leaves fertility as the means of choice.

[11] POPULATION POLICIES, *supra* n. 7 at 59.

Pronatalist

- Use of contraceptives prohibited
- Contraceptive sales allowed, advertising illegal
- Pronatalist Incentives
- Contraceptive sales illegal
    - Income tax deductions for children
    - Maternity benefits
    - Child allowances
    - Public housing preferences for large families
    - Scholarships

Laissez Faire

Antinatalist

- Official support of voluntary family planning programs
    - Cash subsidies to private organizations
    - Facilities provided free or at subsidized rents
- Official family planning program
    - Use of public health services to supply family planning services
    - Health advantages advertised
- Official family planning program including motivation campaign
- Demographic target
    - Use of mass communications, group meetings, home visits, postpartum program
- Population education
- Official family planning program with economic incentives
    - Payments for acceptance (immediate or deferred)
    - No-birth/no-pregnancy bonus schemes
    - Dowry for late marriages
    - Scholarships for children of small families
- Curtailment of rights and privileges with excess children
    - Social security benefits conditional on small families
    - Discrimination in favor of small families for public housing
    - Curtailment of maternity leave for higher parity pregnancies
- Restraints on marriage
    - High minimum legal age
    - Social sanctions, *e.g.,* housing restrictions, scholarships

Restrictions on number of children
- Marketable licenses to have children
- Social sanctions
- Taxes on children

Involuntary fertility control
- Temporary sterilizing agent
- Compulsory sterilizing agent*

Finally, it should be noted that although analysis of legislative, administrative, programmatic, and budgetary actions can give a sophisticated and comprehensive understanding of a country's population policy direction, many donor agencies mean nothing more of population policy than a statement by a high-level official setting demographic goals (particularly reduction of birth rates to a certain level by a certain year).

III. FERTILITY CONTROL AS A HUMAN RIGHT

The United Nations has taken on the role as a speaker for human rights, including the right of couples to determine the number and spacing of their children.[12] Although this right was omitted from the 1948 United Nations Declaration on Human Rights, it was included, twenty years later in the Final Act of the International Conference on Human Rights held in Teheran and has since been affirmed in other United Nations' instruments. The salient sections of these documents are quoted below.

A. Final Act of the International Conference on Human Rights, Teheran, 1968[13]

> . . . *Believing* that it is timely to draw attention to the connexion between population growth and human rights [the conference]:

*Reprinted with permission of the Johns Hopkins University Press from POPULATION POLICIES AND ECONOMIC DEVELOPMENT: A WORLD BANK REPORT.

[12]For a historical review, *see* R. SYMONDS & M. CARDER, THE UNITED NATIONS AND THE POPULATION QUESTION: 1945–1970 (McGraw-Hill, 1973).

[13]Resolution XVIII adopted at the U.N. Conf. on Hum. Rts. at Teheran, reprinted in UNFPA, THE UNITED NATIONS AND POPULATION: MAJOR RESOLUTIONS AND INSTRUMENTS 50 (1974). [Hereafter referred to as THE U.N. AND POPULATION]

1. *Observes* that the present rapid rate of population growth in some areas of the world hampers the struggle against hunger and poverty, and in particular reduces the possibilities of rapidly achieving adequate standards of living, including food, clothing, housing, medical care, social security, education and social services, thereby impairing the full realization of human rights;

2. *Recognizes* that moderation of the present rate of population growth in such areas would enhance the conditions for offering greater opportunities for the enjoyment of human rights and the improvement of living conditions for each person;

3. *Considers* that couples have a basic human right to decide freely and responsibly on the number and spacing of their children and a right to adequate education and information in this respect;

4. *Urges* Member States and United Nations bodies and specialized agencies concerned to give close attention to the implications for the exercise of human rights of the present rapid rate of increase in world population.

B. Declaration on Social Progress and Development[14]

Objectives . . . Article 11 . . .

. . . The protection of the rights of the mother and child; concern for the upbringing and health of children; the provision of measures to safeguard the health and welfare of women and particularly of working mothers during pregnancy and the infancy of their children, as well as of mothers whose earnings are the sole source of livelihood for the family; the granting to women of pregnancy and maternity leave and allowances without loss of employment and wages.

Means and Methods . . . Article 22

(a) The development and coordination of policies and measures designed to strengthen the essential functions of the family as a basic unit of society;

(b) The formulation and establishment, as needed, of programmes in the field of population, within the framework of national demographic policies and as part of the welfare medical services, including education, training of personnel and the provision to families of the knowledge and means necessary to enable them to exercise their right to determine freely and responsibly the number and spacing of their children;

(c) The establishment of appropriate child-care facilities in the interest of children and working parents.

[14]Gen. Ass. Res. 2542 (XXIV), reprinted in THE U.N. AND POPULATION *supra* n. 13 at 54-56.

C. World Population Plan of Action, Bucharest, 1974[15]

Article 14 (f): All couples and individuals have the basic right to decide freely and responsibly the number and spacing of their children and to have the information, education and means to do so; the responsibility of couples and individuals in the exercise of this right takes into account the needs of their living and future children, and their responsibilities towards the community.

D. Resolution of World Food Conference, Rome, 1974[16]

Resolution IX

The World Food Conference . . . Now calls on all Governments and on people everywhere . . . to support . . . rational population policies ensuring to couples the right to determine the number and spacing of births, freely and responsibly, in accordance with national needs within the context of an over-all development strategy.

E. Declaration of International Women's Year Conference, Mexico, 1975[17]

Article 11: It should be one of the principal aims of social education to teach respect for physical integrity and its rightful place in human life. The human body, whether that of woman or man, is inviolable and respect for it is a fundamental element of human dignity and freedom.

Article 12: Every couple and every individual has the right to decide freely and responsibly whether or not to have children as well as to determine their number and spacing, and to have information, education and means to do so.

Although the United Nations has taken the lead in asserting the right of couples to space and limit the number of children, it is not the only advocate of this view. On "Human Rights Day," December 10, 1966, twelve heads of state signed a *Declaration on Population by World Leaders* in which they said:

[15] UNITED NATIONS, REPORT OF THE WORLD POPULATION CONFERENCE (U.N. Doc. E/CONF. 60/19, 1974).

[16] UNITED NATIONS, REPORT OF THE WORLD FOOD CONFERENCE (U.N. Doc. E/CONF. 65/20, 1974).

[17] UNITED NATIONS, REPORT OF THE WORLD CONFERENCE ON THE INTERNATIONAL WOMEN'S YEAR (U.N. Doc. E/CONF. 66/34, 1975).

> We believe that the majority of parents desire to have the knowledge and the means to plan their families; that the opportunity to decide the number and spacing of children is a basic human right.[18]

Heads of 18 other states concurred in this statement by signing it in the following year.

More recently, the International Conference of Parliamentarians on Population and Development called on governments to:

> ensure that all couples and individuals can exercise their basic right to decide freely and responsibly the number and spacing of their children and have the information, education and means to do so.[19]

The repeated assertions of the right of couples to control their fertility raises a number of fundamental questions about human rights in general and specifically the right of fertility regulation:

To what extent are sovereign states bound by United Nations' declarations on human rights? Are United Nations' declarations more than moral pronouncements? If so, how much more?[20]

If fertility control exists as a human right, what is the mechanism for enforcement? If none exists, can it be said to be a right? A logical enforcement body is the International Court of Justice. This, however, is a court of limited jurisdiction whose decisions are binding only if agreed to by both parties to a dispute. Some countries, such as the United States, do not allow the International Court of Justice jurisdiction over internal matters, as defined by the country itself.

Is the right of a couple to determine the number and spacing of their children truly a human right? Frankel has written that to be considered a human right, a concept must meet two tests: it must be a genuinely felt choice, and it must be deliverable. If it does not meet these tests, it should be considered a "human need" or a "human aspiration."[21] If fertility control is a human right, how does it com-

[18]Quoted in L. Lee, *Law, Human Rights and Population: A Strategy for Action,* 12 VA. J. INTL. L. 309, 316 (1972).

[19]UNFPA, COLOMBO DECLARATION ON POPULATION AND DEVELOPMENT, ISSUED BY THE INTERNATIONAL CONFERENCE OF PARLIAMENTARIANS ON POPULATION AND DEVELOPMENT (1979).

[20]Compare the views of L. Lee, *supra* n. 18 and J. BRIERLY, THE LAW OF NATIONS: AN INTRODUCTION TO THE INTERNATIONAL LAW OF PEACE, 292–299 (6th Ed. H. Waldock, ed., Oxford, 1963).

[21]C. Frankel, *Human Rights and Imperialism,* in HUMAN RIGHTS: A SYMPOSIUM 22 (Proceedings of the General Education Seminar, vol. 6, no. 1, Colum. Univ. 1977).

pare with, say, the right not to be tortured or the right to fair criminal procedures? On a more general level, should economic and social rights be given the same importance as political and civil rights?[22]

A right to control one's fertility presumably encompasses the right to have many as well as few children. To what extent are coercion, incentives, or even propaganda to persuade people to have fewer children compatible with this aspect of the right to control one's own fertility?

Does the right of couples to determine the number and spacing of their children imply a state duty to provide the means of exercising the right? If so, what does this mean in terms of a governmental obligation to provide information and services? Contraceptives? All kinds of contraceptives? Sterilization or abortion services? Subsidized services for the indigent? The experience in the United States with federal funding of abortion, *supra* p. 88–110 is relevant.

IV. MAJOR ISSUES IN POPULATION POLICY: THE 1974 WORLD POPULATION CONFERENCE

A. Antecedents: The Davis-Berelson Debate

Should population policy concern itself only, or primarily, with fertility? Is population policy really the same as family planning policy? In terms of practical programmatic aspects, what more than family planning can be done? These and other related issues were argued during the late 1960's in a classic debate in *Science* magazine between Kingsley Davis, Professor of Sociology at the University of California, and Bernard Berelson, President of The Population Council.

Davis, in an article entitled *Population Policy: Will Current Programs Succeed?,*[23] criticized family planners for failing to establish specific population growth targets, such as zero population growth, and for assuming that family planning programs, which rely on free choice, will lower fertility since most people want more than two or three children. He emphasized the conflict between population control, where a societal good of zero population growth is paramount, and family planning, which relies on individual choice, and suggested that societal change which discouraged childbearing

[22]For discussion of this point, *see* L. Henkin, *Rights: American and Human,* 79 COLUM. L. REV. 405 (1979).

[23]158 SCIENCE 730 (1967).

would be necessary before population growth could be halted. He concluded:

> The things that make family planning acceptable are the very things that make it ineffective for population control. By stressing the right of parents to have the number of children they want, it evades the basic question of population policy, which is how to give societies the number of children they need. By offering only the means for *couples* to control fertility, it neglects the means for societies to do so.

Responding to Davis and other critics of family planning, Berelson measured 29 ideas to reduce family size that went "beyond family planning" against six criteria: (1) scientific/medical/technological readiness, (2) political viability, (3) administrative feasibility, (4) economic capability, (5) moral/ethical/philosophical acceptability, and (6) presumed effectiveness. He concluded, *inter alia:*

> Family planning programs do not compare unfavorably with specific other proposals—especially when one considers that any *actual* operating program is disadvantaged when compared with any competitive *ideal* policy. Indeed, on this showing, if family planning programs did not exist, they would have to be invented: it would appear that they would be among the first proposals to be made and the first programs to be tried, given their generally acceptable characteristics.[24]

Over the years Berelson has refined his viewpoint on population policy. In *Paths to Fertility Reduction: The Policy Cube,*[25] he divided "policy paths" to fertility reduction into two categories: those which affect supply and those which affect demand. Those which affect supply are (1) improved access to modern means of fertility and providing a better service and (2) an improved product, *i.e.,* new means of fertility control. On the demand side are (1) the promotion of basic socioeconomic determinants of fertility such as increased income, improving the status of women, reducing infant-child mortality, (2) more and better information and education, (3) manipulation of incentives and disincentives, (4) politically-guided community pressure to develop an antinatalist community consensus,

[24]B. Berelson, *Beyond Family Planning,* 163 SCIENCE 533 (1969).

[25]9 FAM. PLAN. PERSPECTIVES 214 (1977). *See also* B. Berelson & R. Haveman, *On the Efficient Allocation of Resources for Fertility Reduction,* 5 INTL. FAM. PLAN. PERSPECTIVES 133 (1979).

and (5) legal sanctions. Specific proposals are then measured against their acceptability, feasibility, and effectiveness. Once again family planning programs rate pretty high.[26]

B. Background to the World Population Conference

The World Population Conference was held in Bucharest, Romania, in August, 1974, under the sponsorship of the United Nations. Two earlier world population conferences held under U.N. auspices (Rome, 1954, and Belgrade, 1965) brought together population specialists to discuss relatively technical questions. In contrast, the Bucharest conference was highly political in nature and brought to the fore major policy issues of the day. In some ways, the struggle to draft a Plan of Action acceptable to the 136 delegates pitted the aspirations of the developing world against the complacency of the developed. In another sense, it was a battle between the *family planners* and the *developmentalists.* Whatever one's perspective on the fundamental issues, the World Population Plan of Action (WPPA) that emerged from the conference is a document of considerable importance and has become the reference point for population policy analysis in the 1970's and 1980's. Key sections of the WPPA are printed on pp. 366–379, *infra.* They are preceded by excerpts from Finkle and Crane's article reviewing the political jockeying that went on during the conference and are followed by an examination of major issues raised by the WPPA.

1. J. Finkle and B. Crane, "The Politics of Bucharest: Population, Development, and the New International Economic Order," 1 *Population and Development Review* 87 (1975).*

The World Population Conference in Bucharest in August 1974 was the first global conference of official government representatives to

[26]Another way at looking at what Berelson terms supply and demand factors is the paradigm of J. Bongaarts, *A Framework for Analyzing the Proximate Determinants of Fertility,* 4 POP. & DEV. REV. 105 (1978) which, building on the model of K. Davis & J. Blake, *Social Structure and Fertility: An Analytical Framework,* 4 ECON. DEV. & CULT. CHANGE 211 (1956), divides determinants of fertility into "direct determinants" (intermediate variables such as proportion married, contraception, induced abortion, lactational infecundability) and "indirect determinants" (socioeconomic, cultural, and environmental variables).

*Reprinted with the permission of The Population Council from J. Finkle and B. Crane, "The Politics of Bucharest: Population, Development, and the New International Economic Order," *Population and Development Review* 1, no. 1 (September 1975): pp. 87–114.

confront the highly sensitive question of population and its relationship to development as well as to consider population policies and action programs. Despite the many achievements now claimed for the Conference, one thing that it failed to do was to follow the scenario constructed by its principal organizers. The inspiration for the Conference came mainly from the United States and, to a lesser extent, from a small group of Western European and Asian nations actively concerned with global population trends. For roughly a decade, these nations had sought to make the international community aware of the burden that rapid population growth imposed on development and had promoted efforts to limit fertility in the developing nations. They intended the Bucharest Conference to consolidate the policy gains that had already been made in almost every agency of the United Nations system as well as in developing countries. More than that, they hoped that Bucharest would stimulate governments and international agencies to move ahead with greater energy and determination than in the past in dealing with population problems.

Most of the hopes and expectations of those who had taken the lead in convening the Conference were embodied in the Draft World Population Plan of Action, which had been prepared by the UN Secretariat based on consultations with member governments, population experts, and other UN agencies. The nations represented at Bucharest did adopt a Plan of Action by consensus on the final day of the Conference, but it differed in important respects from the Draft Plan and was approved only after intense conflict and difficult negotiations. More than 300 amendments to the Draft Plan were introduced and debated. Midway through the Conference many delegates and even members of the Secretariat openly acknowledged the real possibility that it would adjourn without a Plan being approved. . . .

The final version of the World Population Plan of Action was a product of strained compromise that neither synthesized nor fully reflected the different positions that initially divided the delegates. It had undergone extensive changes in spirit and substance, especially in the provisions relating to fertility and population growth. Whereas the Draft Plan submitted to the Conference had as its purpose "to affect population variables," the final version stated its purpose as "to help coordinate population trends and the trends of economic and social development," noting that "the basis for an effective solution of population problems is, above all, socioeconomic transformation." The Draft Plan stressed the need to limit population growth through implementing population and social welfare policies with direct effects on fertility. The final Plan, by contrast, conveyed a strong sense of urgency about the need to accelerate socioeconomic development in general and to bring about a new and more equitable international economic order. Language inserted in the Background section of the Plan indicates the attitude of a majority of delegates at Bucharest that "population problems" are really symptoms of imbalances in the development process, which are, in turn, a consequence of the international economic system. . . .

The Dual Ancestry of Bucharest

The long and complex ancestry of the Bucharest Conference helps to explain the conflicts and divisions that developed there. . . .

The Population Ancestry. The population issue had been discussed in both national and international forums prior to the 1960s, but it was not until then that governments and the UN system itself began to address the question seriously and to adopt policies aimed at controlling fertility. In the decade from 1962 to 1972, a series of resolutions on population were adopted in the governing bodies of UN agencies. The resolutions were usually initiated and supported by Western and Asian countries, including Sweden, the United States, and India, who felt that rapid population growth was a serious impediment to development and that population and family planning programs were urgently needed. This view met with considerable opposition and resistance from Catholic, Socialist, and African nations. During the 1960s, however, governments of many of these nations became increasingly tolerant toward resolutions designed to create or to strengthen international programs and activities for assisting countries, when requested, in dealing with demographic problems. Although there was evidence of growing concern about population in the international community, those clauses of the resolutions directed at member governments, in deference to national sovereignty, merely suggested that they examine their own population situations and take whatever action they considered appropriate. In no sense did the resolutions embody an international consensus on a strategy to reduce population growth. . . .

As the UN General Assembly and its subsidiary bodies developed a position of support for population activities, each of the major functional agencies—including WHO, UNESCO, FAO, ILO, and the World Bank—acquired mandates that roughly paralleled those emanating from the UN. Although they mildly endorsed the idea of targets, none of these international statements went as far as to propose specific targets for limiting population growth, nor did they establish a population strategy for recommendation to international organizations or national governments. Most of those responsible for drafting the World Population Plan of Action were prepared to take additional positive steps along these lines.

What has been referred to here as "the population ancestry" had an important development component as well. Invariably, United Nations resolutions and discussions on population linked demographic concerns with a vast range of other economic and social problems. The mandates of the various UN agencies dealt with, among other things, population and health, education, employment, rural development, and the status of women, and they emphasized the desirability of integrating population and development policies and programs. A development component was also reflected in the Draft Plan. Although population had always been considered in the UN within the context of development, the population ancestry evolved independently from the other ancestry of Bucharest.

The New International Economic Order Ancestry. Those who laid the groundwork for Bucharest, mainly population specialists in the UN and member governments, had been in many cases almost totally absorbed in population questions in the years preceding the Conference. As a result, they were often poorly attuned to other issues that the developing nations perceived as more salient to their interest than curbing population growth. . . .

During the 1960s, aware of the widening gap between rich and poor nations, Third World countries had become more and more frustrated with the slowness of development, a condition that they came to attribute in large measure to their disadvantaged position in world trade and to the economic policies of the rich countries toward them. Increasingly, they perceived the value of unifying with one another in their attempts to wrest concessions from the industrialized countries. Although this movement can be traced back to the 1955 Bandung Conference, it gained its first real impetus from the UN Conference on Trade and Development (UNCTAD I) held in 1964. At that conference a bloc of African, Asian, and Latin American nations (later to become known as the "Group of 77") united in supporting a series of "general propositions" that attempted to redefine the principles governing international economic relations. The Group of 77 had enough votes to establish UNCTAD as a permanent agency of the United Nations, but, lacking the means to implement its goals, UNCTAD remained much more a symbol than a reality.

In the decade from 1964 to 1974, the developing nations continually voiced their dissatisfaction with the lack of progress in improving terms of trade, reducing trade barriers, strengthening commodity agreements, and obtaining other concessions from the rich countries in order to promote economic development. The Third World position was set forth and elaborated in a series of conferences and meetings. . . .

The Sixth Special Session was prompted by the success in late 1973 of oil-producing nations in imposing a drastic increase in oil prices on the world market. This action by the Organization of Petroleum-Exporting Countries (OPEC) represented a psychological breakthrough for the developing nations in their relations with the industrialized world. For the first time, the industrialized nations were shown to be highly vulnerable to interruptions in the supply of vital resources controlled by Third World countries. . . .

Over the reservations and objections of a handful of developed nations, notably the United States, consensus was reached at the Sixth Special Session on a "Declaration on the Establishment of a New International Economic Order" and an associated "Programme of Action." The Declaration and Programme of Action touched on a wide spectrum of Third World concerns, including raw materials and primary commodities; food; trade; the international monetary system; industrialization; the transfer of technology; multinational corporations; strengthening the UN system; and special emergency assistance to developing nations unable to cope with price increases on imports necessary for development. These declarations are regarded as significant. . . .

Political Alignments and Perspectives on Population at Bucharest

Until the opening of the Bucharest Conference, there were grounds to believe that a consensus had been successfully achieved among governments on the question of the relationship between population and development and that the Draft World Population Plan of Action expressed this consensus. . . . This qualified consensus broke down in the opening days of the Conference. A group of Third World countries led by Algeria and Argentina attacked both the language and the basic premises of the Draft Plan and, in effect, insisted that it be rewritten to incorporate the principles of the New International Economic Order. Their actions changed the focus of the Conference from the question of population and development policies to the far more politically sensitive question of the merits of a restructured world economy. They raised issues that could not be accommodated within the preexisting consensus, and, moreover, raised them in terms that could not be easily negotiated and compromised within the context of the Conference.

The Conference became polarized, as those nations most involved in the formulation of the Draft Plan sought to defend it and prevent it from becoming an instrument of proponents of the New International Economic Order. Other nations whose views had previously been favorable toward the Draft Plan felt compelled at Bucharest to align themselves with the Third World and Socialist countries who challenged it. The cleavage between the positions represented by these two groups of nations, the former designated here as the "incrementalist" position and the latter designated as the "redistribution" position, dominated the early stages of the Conference. Toward the end of the Conference, however, a "conciliation" position emerged. This position was not simply a result of the disposition of countries to terminate the Conference on a note of good will, but rather, it too was based on political considerations, although they were significantly different from those behind the incrementalist and redistribution positions. Despite the many perspectives on population among countries at the Conference, demographic considerations were definitely subordinated to political interests at Bucharest.

The Incrementalist Position. The incrementalist position was principally identified with a group of Western powers, including the United States, the United Kingdom, Canada, and Germany, who felt that rapid population growth was a serious impediment to development. From their perspective, a principal objective of the Bucharest Conference was to build on the statements and resolutions of earlier international forums to increase the commitment of governments and international agencies to carry out population and family planning programs. Although they recognized that demographic behavior is also influenced by socioeconomic development, their policy recommendations were generally to strengthen population efforts by integrating population policy with development planning and by introducing population components into specific projects and programs in various development sectors. The incrementalists wanted the World Population Conference to confine discussion, debate, and resolutions within this policy framework. Correspondingly, they wanted to avoid discussion, debate, and resolutions dealing with broad economic, social, and political issues to which they were unprepared as well as disinclined to respond.

The United States was the most prominent and active representative of the incrementalist position. . . .

The US stance at Bucharest is linked to its strategy for dealing with an array of issues that have arisen in the international arena, including development, trade, the environment, food, energy, raw materials, and population. The Third World emphasizes the need to treat these issues as interrelated, whereas United States does not deny their interrelatedness but feels that there should be specific international forums to deal with each of these questions. . . . The United States may be prepared to make concessions in the areas of trade, aid, investment, and monetary reform, but it is determined to negotiate them in GATT, the International Monetary Fund, the Economic and Social

Council, and other specialized international forums where it is able to exercise greater influence and bring to bear the necessary expertise. The United States is opposed to negotiating these issues—or even discussing them openly—in a two-week conference on population.

Although the United States is willing to confront Third World demands in "appropriate forums," the United States—along with most other Western industrialized nations—is simply not prepared to accede to the radical transformation of the international economic system as proposed by the developing nations. The demand for a New International Economic Order is seen as ideologically objectionable as well as a threat to American wealth and power. From the American perspective, it is an attempt to improve economic conditions in the Third World by redistributing the existing wealth of the industrialized nations rather than by creating new wealth through development.

The Redistribution Position. The primary goal of the adherents of the redistribution position at Bucharest was to establish the principle that population problems are not a cause but a consequence of underdevelopment—and that the most effective solution for underdevelopment is a New International Economic Order. They took the view that if the West claims to be committed to curbing population growth in order to facilitate economic development, then for the same end it should be equally if not more committed to restructuring the international economic system and to paying "fair" prices for the products of the developing nations. If the West claims to be concerned about people of the developing nations having too many children, then it should be more concerned about its own "excessive" consumption of raw materials that cannot be replenished. If the West claims to be concerned about malnutrition and starvation in the Third World, then it is not enough to urge that fewer children be born; it is equally essential that the rich countries "more equitably" distribute their abundant food supplies.

Many delegations did not discover until after their arrival at Bucharest that a relatively small but critical group of Third World countries, with strong support and encouragement from Socialist nations, was intent upon making population a vehicle for advancing the goals of the New International Economic Order. While these goals had a natural attraction for Third World countries, there were other, more complex reasons leading them to line up behind the redistribution position. First, the Third World in recent years has increasingly tried to demonstrate its solidarity in confronting the industrial world. Second, among the most vigorous exponents of the redistribution position were oil producing nations, notably Algeria. Other developing countries felt a practical need to remain on good terms with the OPEC nations because many were seeking concessionary arrangements with OPEC for the purchase of oil and were also hopeful of economic assistance. Even India, for example, whose domestic and international record on population is close to the incrementalist position, found itself at Bucharest espousing the redistribution position without emphasizing the importance it has attached to population and family planning programs. Third, the redistribution position was compatible with the view that economic and social development is a necessary prerequisite to a reduction in population growth rates. Although this view is essentially sociological orthodoxy in its description of historical Western experience, it has been transformed into an ideological statement rather than a scholarly interpretation of the factors underlying the demographic transition. The contention that fertility decline cannot take place without prior economic development was further buttressed by the apparent lack of success of many countries with family planning programs. Fourth, the de-emphasis of population and family planning programs in the redistribution position had a special appeal for a group of nations, mainly from Africa, Latin America, and Eastern Europe, who were either pronatalist or largely disinterested in policies to limit population growth. . . .

The Conciliation Position. An analysis of Conference alignments solely in terms of the conflict between the redistribution and incrementalist positions obscures the complex variety of interests and motives of nations at Bucharest. Even the most ardent advocates of these positions had other interests that were best advanced by bringing the Conference to a conclusion with a semblance of consensus rather than by continuing to engage in confrontation politics. . . .

The advocates of the redistribution position, who were in the majority at Bucharest, theoretically could have voted for a Plan of their own choosing without making any concessions to the incrementalist position. However, to conclude the Conference without a Plan or to produce a Plan that did not have the approval of Western nations would have had adverse implications for the developing nations extending beyond Bucharest. They felt that endorsement of a Plan that was also acceptable to Western industrialized nations, especially the United States, would better serve their long run interest in strengthening the United Nations. The United Nations is presently an important vehicle for the Third World countries; because of their voting power in the United Nations, there is no other setting in which they can potentially exercise as much influence with the industrialized countries. The extent to which this voting power is an effective source of influence, however, depends on the importance that the developed countries assign to the United Nations as a setting in which meaningful negotiations can take place. If the policy initiatives of the developed countries in the United Nations are continually defeated, and if all United Nations policy instruments become merely expressions of the objectives of the developing nations, there is some danger that rich and powerful nations will simply "write off" the United Nations and find other means to advance and protect their global interests.

The conciliation position was also supported by a number of nations who both subscribed to the New International Economic Order and were aware of the inimical effects of rapid population growth on development. While these nations voted for the redistribution position in many of the changes in the Draft Plan, they did so with the knowledge that the revised Plan would leave nations free to pursue their own population policies. Those countries that were most prominent in upholding the conciliation position at Bucharest—Sweden, Mexico, and Egypt among others—showed a willingness to argue openly that there was no necessary incompatibility between a commitment to the New International Economic Order and active governmental intervention to limit population growth. Because of their affinity with both the redistribution and incrementalist positions, they were able to capitalize on the residual sentiment of most nations in favor of consensus and to exercise an influential voice in the negotiations resulting in the final Plan of Action.

C. World Population Plan of Action (1974)

The World Population Conference, having due regard for human aspirations for a better quality of life and for rapid socio-economic development, taking into consideration the interrelationship between population situations and socio-economic development, decides on the following World Population Plan of Action as a policy instrument within the broader context of the internationally adopted strategies for national and international progress.

A. Background to the Plan

1. The promotion of development and improvement of quality of life require coordination of action in all major socio-economic fields including that of population, which is the inexhaustible source of creativity and a determining factor of progress. At the international level a number of strategies and programmes whose explicit aim is to affect variables in fields other than population have already been formulated. . . . The Declaration on the Establishment of a New International Economic Order, and the Programme of Action to achieve it . . . provide the most recent overall framework for international co-operation. The explicit aim of the World Population Plan of Action is to help co-ordinate population trends and the trends of economic and social development. The basis for an effective solution

of population problems is, above all, socio-economic transformation. A population policy may have a certain success if it constitutes an integral part of socio-economic development; its contribution to the solution of world development problems is hence only partial, as is the case with the other sectoral strategies. Consequently, the Plan of Action must be considered as an important component of the system of international strategies and as an instrument of the international community for the promotion of economic development, quality of life, human rights and fundamental freedoms.

2. The formulation of international strategies is a response to universal recognition of the existence of important problems in the world and the need for concerted national and international action to achieve their solution. Where trends of population growth, distribution and structure are out of balance with social, economic and environmental factors, they can, at certain stages of development, create additional difficulties for the achievement of sustained development. Policies whose aim is to affect population trends must not be considered substitutes for socio-economic development policies but as being integrated with those policies in order to facilitate the solution of certain problems facing both developing and developed countries and to promote a more balanced and rational development. . . .

3. [Omitted]

4. The consideration of population problems cannot be reduced to the analysis of population trends only. It must also be borne in mind that the present situation of the developing countries originates in the unequal processes of socio-economic development which have divided peoples since the beginning of the modern era. This inequity still exists and is intensified by the lack of equity in international economic relations with consequent disparity in levels of living.

5. Although acceleration in the rate of growth of the world's population is mainly the result of very large declines in the mortality of developing countries, those declines have been unevenly distributed. . . .

6. While the right of couples to have the number of children they desire is accepted in a number of international instruments, many couples in the world are unable to exercise that right effectively. In many parts of the world, poor economic conditions, social norms, inadequate knowledge of effective methods of family regulation and the unavailability of contraceptive services result in a situation in which couples have more children than they desire or feel they can properly care for. In certain countries, on the other hand, because of economic or biological factors, problems of involuntary sterility and of subfecundity exist, with the result that many couples have fewer children than they desire. Of course, the degree of urgency attached

to dealing with each of these two situations depends upon the prevailing conditions within the country in question.

7. Individual reproductive behaviour and the needs and aspirations of society should be reconciled. In many developing countries, and particularly in the large countries of Asia, the desire of couples to achieve large families is believed to result in excessive national population growth rates and Governments are explicitly attempting to reduce those rates by implementing specific policy measures. On the other hand, some countries are attempting to increase desired family size, if only slightly.

8. Throughout the world, urban populations are growing in size at a considerably faster rate than rural populations. . . .

9. In most of the developing countries, although the rate of urban population growth is higher than the growth rate in rural areas, the latter is still significant . . . [and] . . . in many countries, the revitalization of the countryside is a priority goal.

10. For some countries international migration may be, in certain circumstances, an instrument of population policy. . . .

11. [Omitted]

12. Declining birth-rates also result in a gradual aging of the population. . . . There is an urgent need, in those countries where such programmes are lacking, for the development of social security and health programmes for the elderly.

13. Because of the relatively high proportions of children and youth in the populations of developing countries, declines in fertility levels in those countries will not be fully reflected in declines in population growth rates until some decades later. . . . Efforts made by developing countries to speed up economic growth must be viewed by the entire international community as a global endeavour to improve the quality of life for all people of the world, supported by a just utilization of the world's wealth, resources and technology in the spirit of the new international economic order. . . .

B. Principles and Objectives of the Plan

14. This Plan of Action is based on a number of principles which underlie its objectives and are observed in its formulation. The formulation and implementation of population policies is the sovereign right of each nation. This right is to be exercised in accordance with national objectives and needs and without external interference, taking into account universal solidarity in order to improve the quality of life of the peoples of the world. . . . The Plan of Action is based on the following principles:

(*a*) The principal aim of social, economic and cultural development, of which population goals and policies are integral parts, is to improve levels of living and the quality of life of the people. . . .

(*b*) True development cannot take place in the absence of national independence and liberation. Alien and colonial domination, foreign occupation, wars of aggression, racial discrimination, *apartheid,* and neo-colonialism in all its forms, continue to be among the greatest obstacles to the full emancipation and progress of the developing countries and all the people involved. . . .

(*c*) Population and development are interrelated: population variables influence development variables and are also influenced by them; thus the formulation of a World Population Plan of Action reflects the international community's awareness of the importance of population trends for socio-economic development, and the socio-economic nature of the recommendations contained in this Plan of Action reflects its awareness of the crucial role that development plays in affecting population trends;

(*d*) Population policies are constituent elements of socio-economic development policies, never substitutes for them: while serving socio-economic objectives, they should be consistent with internationally and nationally recognized human rights of individual freedom, justice and the survival of national, regional and minority groups;

(*e*) Independently of the realization of economic and social objectives, respect for human life is basic to all human societies;

(*f*) All couples and individuals have the basic right to decide freely and responsibly the number and spacing of their children and to have the information, education and means to do so; the responsibility of couples and individuals in the exercise of this right takes into account the needs of their living and future children, and their responsibilities towards the community;

(*g*) The family is the basic unit of society and should be protected by appropriate legislation and policy;

(*h*) Women have the right to complete integration in the development process particularly by means of an equal access to education and equal participation in social, economic, cultural and political life. . . .

(*i*) Recommendations in this Plan of Action regarding policies to deal with population problems must recognize the diversity of conditions within and among different countries;

(*j*) In the democratic formulation of national population goals and policies, consideration must be given, together with other economic and social factors, to the supplies and characteristics of natural resources and to the quality of the environment and particularly to all aspects of food supply including productivity of rural areas. . . .

(*k*) The growing interdependence among nations makes international action increasingly important to the solution of development and population problems. International strategies will achieve their objective only if they ensure that the underprivileged of the world achieve, urgently, through structural, social and economic reforms, a significant improvement in their living conditions. . . .

15. Guided by these principles, the primary aim of this Plan of Action is to expand and deepen the capacities of countries to deal effectively with their national and subnational population problems and to promote an appropriate international response to their needs by increasing international activity in research, the exchange of information, and the provision of assistance on request. In pursuit of this primary aim, the following general objectives are set for this Plan of Action:

(*a*) To advance understanding of population at global, regional, national and subnational levels, recognizing the diversity of the problems involved;

(*b*) To advance national and international understanding of the interrelationship of demographic and socio-economic factors in development . . .

(*c*) To promote socio-economic measures and programmes whose aim is to affect, *inter alia,* population growth, morbidity and mortality, reproduction and family formation, population distribution and internal migration, international migration, and, consequently, demographic structures;

(*d*) To advance national and international understanding of the complex relations among the problems of population, resources, environment and development . . .

(*e*) To promote the status of women and the expansion of their roles, their full participation in the formulation and implementation of socio-economic policy including population policies, and the creation of awareness among all women of their current and potential roles in national life;

(*f*) To recommend guidelines for population policies consistent with national values and goals and with internationally recognized principles;

(*g*) To promote the development and implementation of population policies where necessary . . .

(*h*) To encourage the development and good management of appropriate education, training, statistical research, information and family health services as well as statistical services in support of the above principles and objectives.

C. Recommendations for Action

1. *Population goals and policies*

a. *Population growth*

16. [Omitted]

17. Countries which consider that their present or expected rates

of population growth hamper their goals of promoting human welfare are invited, if they have not yet done so, to consider adopting population policies, within the framework of socio-economic development, which are consistent with basic human rights and national goals and values.

18. Countries which aim at achieving moderate or low population growth should try to achieve it through a low level of birth and death rates. Countries wishing to increase their rate of population growth should, when mortality is high, concentrate efforts on the reduction of mortality, and where appropriate, encourage an increase in fertility and encourage immigration.

19. Recognizing that *per capita* use of world resources is much higher in the developed than in the developing countries, the developed countries are urged to adopt appropriate policies in population, consumption and investment, bearing in mind the need for fundamental improvement in international equity.

b. *Morbidity and mortality*

20. The reduction of morbidity and mortality to the maximum feasible extent is a major goal of every human society. It should be achieved in conjunction with massive social and economic development. . . .

21. The short-term effect of mortality reduction on population growth rates is symptomatic of the early development process and must be viewed as beneficial. Sustained reductions in fertility have generally been preceded by reductions in mortality. Although this relationship is complex, mortality reduction may be a prerequisite to a decline in fertility.

22. It is a goal of this Plan of Action to reduce mortality levels, particularly infant and maternal mortality levels, to the maximum extent possible in all regions of the world and to reduce national and sub-national differentials therein. . . .

23. Countries with the highest mortality levels should aim by 1985 to have an expectation of life at birth of at least 50 years and an infant mortality rate of less than 120 per thousand live births. . . .

24. [Omitted]

25. It is recommended that health and nutrition programmes designed to reduce morbidity and mortality be integrated within a comprehensive development strategy and supplemented by a wide range of mutually supporting social policy measures. . . .

26. [Omitted]

c. *Reproduction, family formation and the status of women*

27. This Plan of Action recognizes the variety of national goals

with regard to fertility and does not recommend any world family-size norm.

28. This Plan of Action recognizes the necessity of ensuring that all couples are able to achieve their desired number and spacing of children and the necessity of preparing the social and economic conditions to achieve that desire. . . .

29. It is recommended that all countries:

(*a*) Respect and ensure, regardless of their overall demographic goals, the right of persons to determine, in a free, informed and responsible manner, the number and spacing of their children;

(*b*) Encourage appropriate education concerning responsible parenthood and make available to persons who so desire advice and the means of achieving it;

(*c*) Ensure that family planning, medical and related social services aim not only at the prevention of unwanted pregnancies but also at the elimination of involuntary sterility and subfecundity . . .

(*d*) Seek to ensure the continued possibility of variations in family size when a low fertility level has been established or is a policy objective;

(*e*) Make use, wherever needed and appropriate, of adequately trained professional and auxiliary health personnel, rural extension, home economics and social workers, and non-governmental channels, to help provide family planning services and to advise users of contraceptives;

(*f*) Increase their health manpower and health facilities to an effective level of effectiveness, redistribute functions among the different levels of professionals and auxiliaries in order to overcome the shortage of qualified personnel and establish an effective system of supervision in their health and family planning services;

(*g*) Ensure that information about, and education in, family planning and other matters which affect fertility are based on valid and proven scientific knowledge, and include a full account of any risk that may be involved in the use or non-use of contraceptives.

30. Governments which have family planning programmes are invited to consider integrating and co-ordinating those services with health and other services designed to raise the quality of family life. . . .

31. It is recommended that countries wishing to affect fertility levels give priority to implementing development programmes and educational and health strategies which, while contributing to economic growth and higher standards of living, have a decisive impact upon demographic trends, including fertility. . . .

32. While recognizing the diversity of social, cultural, political and economic conditions among countries and regions, it is nevertheless agreed that the following development goals generally have an effect

on the socio-economic context of reproductive decisions that tends to moderate fertility levels:

(*a*) The reduction of infant and child mortality . . .

(*b*) The full integration of women into the development process . . .

(*c*) The promotion of social justice . . . by means of a wide participation of the population in development and a more equitable distribution of income, land, social services and amenities;

(*d*) The promotion of wide educational opportunities for the young of both sexes . . .

(*e*) The elimination of child labour and child abuse and the establishment of social security and old age benefits;

(*f*) The establishment of an appropriate lower limit for age at marriage.

33. It is recommended that Governments consider making provision, in both their formal and nonformal educational programmes, for informing their people of the consequences of existing or alternative fertility behavior. . . .

34. Family size may also be affected by incentive and disincentive schemes. However, if such schemes are adopted or modified, it is essential that they should not violate human rights.

35. Some social welfare programmes, such as family allowances and maternity benefits, may have a positive effect on fertility and may hence be strengthened when such an effect is desired. However, such programmes should not, in principle, be curtailed if the opposite effect on fertility is desired.

36. The projections . . . of future declines in rates of population growth and . . . increased expectation of life are consistent with declines in the birth rate of the developing countries as a whole from the present level of 38 per thousand to 30 per thousand by 1985; in these projections, birth rates in the developed countries remain in the region of 15 per thousand. To achieve by 1985 these levels of fertility would require substantial national efforts, by those countries concerned, in the field of socio-economic development and population policies, supported, upon request, by adequate international assistance. . . .

37. In the light of the principles of this Plan of Action, countries which consider their birth rates detrimental to their national purposes are invited to consider setting quantitative goals and implementing policies that may lead to the attainment of such goals by 1985. Nothing herein should interfere with the sovereignty of any Government to adopt or not to adopt such quantitative goals.

38. Countries which desire to reduce their birth rates are invited to give particular consideration to the reduction of fertility at the extremes of female reproductive ages because of the salutary effects this may have on infant and maternal welfare.

39. The family is recognized as the basic unit of society. Governments should assist families as far as possible to enable them to fulfill their role in society. . . .

40. It is also recommended that: (a) Governments should equalize the legal and social status of children born in and out of wedlock as well as children adopted; (b) The legal responsibilities of each parent towards the care and support of all their children should be established.

41. Governments should ensure full participation of women in the educational, social, economic, and political life of their countries on an equal basis with men. . . .

42. Equal status of men and women in the family and in society improves the over-all quality of life. This principle of equality should be fully realized in family planning. . . .

43. [Omitted]

d. *Population distribution and internal migration*

44. [Omitted]

45. Policies aimed at influencing population flows into urban areas should be co-ordinated with policies relating to the absorptive capacity of urban centres. . . .

46. In formulating and implementing internal migration policies, Governments are urged to consider the following guidelines, without prejudice to their own socio-economic policies:

(*a*) Measures should be avoided which infringe the right of freedom of movement and residence . . .

(*b*) . . . Planned and more equitable regional development . . .

(*c*) In planning development, and particularly in planning the location of industry and business and the distribution of social services and amenities, Governments should take into account not only short-term economic returns or alternative patterns but also the social and environmental costs and benefits involved as well as equity and social justice in the distribution of the benefits of development among all groups and regions;

(*d*) . . . Efforts should be made to establish and strengthen networks of small and medium-size cities . . .

(*e*) Intensive programmes of economic and social improvement should be carried out in the rural areas through balanced agricultural development . . .

(*f*) Programmes should be promoted to make accessible to scattered populations the basic social services and the support necessary for increased productivity. . . .

47. Internal migration policies should include the provision of information to the rural population concerning economic and social conditions in the urban areas. . . .

48. In rural areas and areas accessible to rural populations, new

employment opportunities, including industries and public works programmes, should be created, systems of land tenure should be improved and social services and amenities provided. . . .

49-50. [Omitted]

e. *International migration*

51. It is recommended that Governments and international organizations generally facilitate voluntary international movement. However, such movements should not be based on racial considerations which are to the detriment of indigenous populations. . . .

52–53. [Omitted]

54. Countries that are concerned with the outflow of migrant workers and wish to encourage and assist those remaining workers or returning workers should make particular efforts to create favourable employment opportunities at the national level. . . .

55. Countries receiving migrant workers should provide proper treatment and adequate social welfare services for them and their families, and should ensure their physical safety and security. . . .

56. [Omitted]

57. Since the outflow of qualified personnel from developing to developed countries seriously hampers the development of the former, there is an urgent need to formulate national and international policies to avoid the "brain drain" and to obviate its adverse effects. . . .

58. Developing countries suffering from heavy emigration of skilled workers and professionals should undertake extensive educational programmes, manpower planning, and investment in scientific and technical programmes . . . and other programmes and measures. . . .

59–62. [Omitted]

f. *Population structure*

63. All Governments are urged, when formulating their development policies and programmes, to take fully into account the implications of changing numbers and proportions of youth, working-age groups and the aged, particularly where such changes are rapid. . . .

64. Specifically, developing countries are urged to consider the implications which the combination of the characteristically young age structure and moderate to high fertility has on their development. . . .

65. Developing countries are invited to consider the possible economic, social and demographic effects of population shifts from agriculture to non-agricultural industries. . . .

66–67. [Omitted]

2. ***Socio-economic policies***

68. This Plan of Action recognizes that economic and social devel-

opment is a central factor in the solution of population problems. National efforts of developing countries to accelerate economic growth should be assisted by the entire international community. . . .

69. In planning measures to harmonize population trends and socio-economic change, human beings must be regarded not only as consumers but also as producers. The investment by nations in the health and education of their citizens contributes substantially to productivity. Consequently, plans for economic and social development and for international assistance for this purpose should emphasize the health and education sectors. . . .

70. It is imperative that all countries, and within them all social sectors, should adapt themselves to more rational utilization of natural resources, without excess, so that some are not deprived of what others waste. . . . It is recommended that Governments give high priority to improving methods of food production, the investigation and development of new sources of food and more effective utilization of existing sources. . . .

3. ***Promotion of knowledge and policies***

71. [Omitted]

a. *Data collection and analysis*

72. . . . Countries that have not yet done so are urged to tabulate and analyze their census and other data and make them available to national policy-making bodies. . . .

73. [Omitted]

74. All countries that have not yet done so are encouraged to establish a continuing capability for taking multi-subject household sample surveys and to establish a long-term plan for regular collection of statistics on various demographic and interrelated socio-economic variables. . . .

75. . . . Countries are encouraged to establish or improve their vital registration system. . . .

76. Developing countries should be provided with technical co-operation, equipment and financial support to develop or improve the population and related statistical programmes mentioned above . . .

77. Governments that have not yet done so are urged to establish appropriate services for the collection, analysis and dissemination of demographic and related statistical information.

b. *Research*

78. . . . Although research designed to fill gaps in knowledge is very urgent and important, high priority should be given to research oriented to the specific problems of countries and regions, including methodological studies. Such research is best carried out in the coun-

tries and regions themselves and by competent persons especially acquainted with national and regional conditions. . . .

79–80. [Omitted]

c. *Management, training, education and information*

81. There is a particular need for the development of management in all fields related to population, with national and international attention and appropriate support given to programmes dealing with its promotion. . . .

82. A dual approach to training is recommended: an international programme for training in population matters concomitant with national and regional training programmes adapted and made particularly relevant to conditions in the countries and regions of the trainees. . . .

83–85. [Omitted]

86. . . . All countries are urged to further develop their formal and informal educational programmes; efforts should be made to eradicate illiteracy, to promote education among the youth and abolish factors discriminating against women.

87. Educational institutions in all countries should be encouraged to expand their curricula to include a study of population dynamics and policies, including, where appropriate, family life, responsible parenthood and the relation of population dynamics to socio-economic development and to international relations. . . .

88–89. [Omitted]

90. Voluntary organizations should be encouraged, within the framework of national laws, policies and regulations, to play an important role in disseminating population information and ensuring wider participation in population programmes, and to share experiences regarding the implementation of population measures and programmes.

91. International organizations, both governmental and non-governmental, should strengthen their efforts to distribute information on population and related matters. . . .

92–93. [Omitted]

d. *Development and evaluation of population policies*

94. Where population policies or programmes have been adopted, systematic and periodic evaluations of their effectiveness should be made. . . .

95. Population measures and programmes should be integrated into comprehensive social and economic plans and programmes and this integration should be reflected in the goals, instrumentalities and organizations for planning within the countries. In general, it is suggested that a unit dealing with population aspects be created and

placed at a high level of the national administrative structure and that such a unit be staffed with qualified persons from the relevant disciplines.

D. Recommendations for Implementation

1. ***Role of national Governments***

96. [Omitted]

97. This Plan of Action recognizes the responsibility of each Government to decide on its own policies. . . . However, national policies should be formulated and implemented without violating, and with due promotion of, universally accepted standards of human rights.

98. An important role of Governments with regard to this Plan of Action is to determine and assess the population problems and needs of their countries in the light of their political, social, cultural, religious and economic conditions; such an undertaking should be carried out systematically and periodically. . . .

99. [Omitted]

2. ***Role of international co-operation***

100. International co-operation, based on the peaceful coexistence of States having different social systems, should play a supportive role in achieving the goals of the Plan of Action. This supportive role could take the form of direct assistance, technical or financial, in response to national and regional requests. . . . Assistance should be provided on the basis of respect for sovereignty of the recipient country and its national policy. . . .

101–102. [Omitted]

103. There is a special need for training. . . . The United Nations system, Governments and, as appropriate, non-governmental organizations are urged to give recognition to that need and priority to the measures necessary to meet it, including information, education and services for family planning.

104. Developed countries, and other countries able to assist, are urged to increase their assistance to developing countries. . . . In this respect, it is recognized, in view of the magnitude of the problems and the consequent national requirements for funds, that considerable expansion of international assistance in the population field is required. . . .

3. ***Monitoring, review and appraisal***

107. It is recommended that monitoring of population trends and policies discussed in this Plan of Action should be undertaken continuously as a specialized activity of the United Nations and reviewed

biennially by the appropriate bodies of the United Nations system, beginning in 1977. . . .

108. A comprehensive and thorough review and appraisal of progress made towards achieving the goals and recommendations of this Plan of Action should be undertaken every five years by the United Nations system. . . .

109. It is urged that both the monitoring and the review . . . of this Plan of Action be closely co-ordinated with those of the International Development Strategy for the Second United Nations Development Decade and any new international development strategy that might be formulated.

D. Commentary and Issues

1. Population Growth: Vice or Virtue?

Historically, a large and growing population has been considered by nations to be a necessary condition for economic development, for political significance on the international scene, and for military power. "To govern is to populate," wrote Argentine statesman Juan Bautista Alberdi in the mid-nineteenth century, and certainly the subsequent political demography of most nations show due respect to that bit of political acumen. The economic history of the United States is replete with references to the large influx of immigrants which made industrialization and expansion possible in the nineteenth and early twentieth centuries. To take a current modern example, Brazilian political leaders and economists argue forcefully that Brazil has the space to not only absorb many more millions of people, but that it needs additional population to produce and consume goods in Brazil's growing economy and to give Brazil the worldwide importance only a very populous nation can have.[27]

The traditional theory is challenged by those who hold that rapid population growth impedes economic growth, particularly in the developing world. The pioneering work in analyzing the relationship between population and development was Coale and Hoover's classic study of India, which demonstrated that rapid population growth had a deleterious effect on economic development.[28] More

[27] For a clear exposition of this position, *see* P. Singer, *Population and Economic Development in Latin America,* 3 INTL. J. HLTH. SERV. 731 (1973).

[28] A. COALE & E. HOOVER, POPULATION GROWTH AND ECONOMIC DEVELOPMENT IN LOW-INCOME COUNTRIES: A CASE STUDY OF INDIA'S PROSPECTS (Princeton, 1958).

recently, Coale tested the model against data from Mexico and found it a reliable predictor.[29]

2. Family Planning and Development

At Bucharest, "Family planning programs can't work" became quite a popular slogan. Bumper stickers, posters, and other displays carried the message, "Development is the best contraceptive" and "Take care of the people and the people will take care of themselves."[30]

Can family planning programs work? In a larger context, what factors are responsible for fertility decline? These questions, critical to population policy analysis, were central to the discussions at the World Population Conference and have lost none of their relevance today.[31] They are examined below.

a. The Demographic Transition and Its Relevance. Those who argue that fertility decline naturally follows development—or, put differently, that development is a necessary and sufficient condition for fertility decline—point to the evidence of the "demographic transition." In its broad outlines demographic transition theory presents a plausible explanation of the change accompanying industrialization in nineteenth century Europe from an area of high mortality and high fertility to one of low mortality and low fertility. The theory holds that fertility decline "follows only after, and as the result of, a decline in mortality (particularly infant mortality) and an improvement in social and economic conditions or 'modern-

[29]A. Coale, *Population Growth and Economic Development: The Case of Mexico,* 56 FOREIGN AFFAIRS 415 (1978). Since the original Coale-Hoover study, considerable effort has been invested in model building; the models are reviewed in W. Arthur & G. McNicoll, *Large-Scale Simulation Models in Population and Development: What Use to Planners?* 1 POP. & DEV. REV. 251 (1975). *See also* W. Robinson, *Population Growth and Economic Welfare,* REP. ON POP./FAM. PLAN. No. 6 (1971).

[30]The thinking behind these slogans is acerbically analyzed in J. Stycos, *Demographic Chic and the United Nations,* 6 FAM. PLAN. PERSPECTIVES 160 (1974).

[31]The fundamental issues, as they emerged at Bucharest, were set forth in B. Berelson, *The Great Debate on Population: An Instructive Entertainment* (Pop. Council, 1975). The range of positions regarding population and development is also clearly presented in M. Teitlebaum, *Population and Development: Is a Consensus Possible?,* 53 FOREIGN AFFAIRS 742 (1974).

ization'."[32] Ironically, the World Population Conference elevated the theory of the demographic transition to political dogma at the same time it was undergoing increasing academic skepticism. Researchers investigating the demographic transition in Europe have found that although the theory holds in its general outline, in its specifics it varies from country to country and even within regions in a single country. In some places, for example, fertility decline preceded industrialization, while in others it followed only after considerable delay. After a comprehensive review of European demographic transition studies, Knodel and van de Walle concluded:

> In general, an examination of the social, economic, and mortality conditions at the time of the onset of the fertility decline in various European countries reveals no consistency in the level of development. . . . It seems safe to conclude that there was no clear threshold of social and economic development required for the fertility transition to begin. . . . Although a high level of social and economic development (as measured by the usual indexes) may often accompany a fall of fertility, it is clearly not a precondition.[33]

Even if the demographic transition were valid in its classical formulation as an explanation of demographic phenomenon in nineteenth century western Europe, whether it can be applied to the developing countries in today's world is questionable. Teitlebaum points to a number of conditions that militate against "natural" fertility declines in developing countries, including the rapidity of mortality decline in developing countries, contrasted with the more gradual reduction in Europe, the far higher fertility and rate of population growth in the developing countries of the twentieth cen-

[32]E. van de Walle & J. Knodel, *Europe's Fertility Transition: New Evidence and Lessons for Today's Developing World,* POP. BULL., vol. 34, no. 6, p. 5 (Pop. Ref. Bur., 1980). Demographic transition theory is set forth in A. Coale, *The Demographic Transition Reconsidered,* 1 PROCEEDINGS OF IUSSP INTL. POP. CONF., LIEGE, BELGIUM 53 (1973) and G. Stolnitz, *The Demographic Transition: From High to Low Birth Rates and Death Rates,* in POPULATION: THE VITAL REVOLUTION (R. Freedman, ed., Anchor, 1964). For variations on the theory, *see* J. Caldwell, *Toward a Restatement of Demographic Transition Theory,* 2 POP. & DEV. REV. 321 (1976): ——, *A Theory of Fertility: From High Plateau to Destabilization,* 4 POP. & DEV. REV. 553 (1978); R. Freedman, *Theories of Fertility Decline: A Reappraisal,* in WORLD POPULATION AND DEVELOPMENT: CHALLENGES AND PROSPECTS (P. Hauser, ed., Syracuse, 1979).

[33]J. Knodel & E. van de Walle, *Lessons from the Past: Policy Implications of Historical Fertility Studies,* 5 POP. & DEV. REV. 217, 224–225 (1979).

tury than in nineteenth century Europe, and the lack of emigration outlets for "excess" populations in developing countries, compared with the massive emigrations from Europe in the nineteenth century. On the other hand, he observes some factors that might speed fertility decline in developing countries, *e.g.,* the potential for rapid socio-economic development, improved methods of fertility control, and increased interest and capability in planning on the part of government.[34]

b. Desired Family Size. How many children people actually want is a thorny question with obvious implications for the family planning versus development controversy. Blake has argued that, even in the United States, women want more than a two or three child family and, therefore, more than just family planning is needed.[35] On the other hand, domestic fertility studies and evaluations of the federally funded family planning program have indicated that the desire for smaller families is widespread and that the decline in American fertility is due largely to the reduction in the number of unwanted children made possible through better and more easily available contraception.[36]

Internationally, findings from the World Fertility Survey have indicated that about half of all married women of reproductive age wanted no more children and more than one quarter of married women with at least one birth or currently pregnant did not want their last child or current pregnancy.[37] These findings lend some support to those who have argued that women want fewer children

[34]M. Teitlebaum, *The Relevance of the Demographic Transition for Developing Countries,* 188 SCIENCE 420 (1975). Freedman, *supra* n. 32 at 78–79, concluded:

> It is now known that, under current conditions, high levels of Western-type modernization are not a necessary condition of fertility decline . . . the cut and dried transition theory on which most demographers were nurtured does not seem to be enough.

[35]J. Blake, *Population Policy for Americans: Is the Government Being Misled?,* 164 SCIENCE 522 (1969); ____ & P. Das Gupta, *Reproductive Motivation Versus Contraceptive Technology,* 1 POP. & DEV. REV. 229 (1975).

[36]*See* C. Westoff, *The Decline of Unplanned Births in the United States,* 191 SCIENCE 38 (1976); ____, *The Yield of the Imperfect: The 1970 National Fertility Study,* 12 DEMOGRAPHY 573 (1975); ____ & N. RYDER, THE CONTRACEPTIVE REVOLUTION (Princeton, 1977); P. Cutright & F. Jaffe, *Family Planning Program Effects on the Fertility of Low-Income Women,* 8 FAM. PLAN. PERSPECTIVES 100 (1976).

[37]M. Kendall, *The World Fertility Survey: Current Status and Findings,* POPULATION REPORTS, series M, no. 3 (Johns Hopkins 1979).

and that the key to fertility decline is widespread availability of contraceptives.[38] This is not, however, inconsistent with the Davis-Blake thesis that women want more children than necessary for the socially desirable goal of zero population growth since initial results from the World Fertility Survey in ten countries indicated that women wanted between 3.7 and 4.8 children.[39] Some commentators have noted that the large number of illegal abortions presents a *prima facie* case that a considerable unserved population wants fewer children and would utilize family planning services were they available.[40]

c. Current Evidence from Developing Countries. Recent studies indicate that fertility in many developing countries has been falling. In some cases, the decline has been significant, even precipitous.[41] What conclusions can be drawn from the evidence? To what can the fertility declines be attributed? For analytical purposes, thought on the subject can be divided into three schools: (1) that family planning is responsible for fertility decline; (2) that family planning programs are not relevant and that fertility declines are due to socioeconomic development, and (3) that a combination of family planning and socio-economic development are responsible. Although the positions are separated herein for analytical purposes, in reality, there may be some overlap among them.

[38]*See* R. Ravenholt & J. Chao, *Availability of Family Planning Services—The Key to Rapid Fertility Reduction,* 6 FAM. PLAN. PERSPECTIVES 217 (1974). *See also* the conclusion of G. Rodriguez, *Family Planning Availability and Contraceptive Practice,* 4 INTL. FAM. PLAN. PERSPECTIVES & DIGEST 100, 114–115 (1978):

> Place of residence, education, and perceived availability and accessibility all have an important joint effect on contraceptive prevalence and unmet need. . . . In other words (other things being equal), increasing availability and accessibility alone in a country like Nepal, where services are few and distant, might bring about a substantial increase in use of contraception.

[39]J. Brackett, R. Ravenholt & J. Chao, *The Role of Family Planning in Recent Rapid Fertility Declines in Developing Countries,* 9 STUD. IN FAM. PLAN. 314 (1978). [Hereafter referred to as J. Brackett *et al.*]

[40]*See, e.g.,* B. VIEL, THE DEMOGRAPHIC EXPLOSION: THE LATIN AMERICAN EXPERIENCE 104–122 (Irvington, 1976).

[41]U.S. DEPT. OF COMMERCE, BUR. OF CENSUS, WORLD POPULATION 1977: RECENT DEMOGRAPHIC ESTIMATES FOR THE COUNTRIES AND REGIONS OF THE WORLD (1978); W. Mauldin, *Patterns of Fertility Decline in Developing Countries, 1950–1975,* 9 STUD. IN FAM. PLAN. 75 (1978); L. Tabah, *World Population Trends: A Stocktaking,* 6 POP. & DEV. REV. 355(1980).

(1) Family Planning as the Cause of Fertility Decline. Using three modes of statistical techniques, Tsui and Bogue analyzed fertility and socio-economic development in 113 developing countries, of which 95 (84 percent) had demonstrated fertility decline between 1968 and 1975. Their analysis led the authors to conclude:

> The results suggest that organized family planning efforts have been a major contributing factor in the fertility decline now evident in much of the developing world. . . . This leads to the prediction that the future course of world fertility may be determined in large part by the size, quality, and spread of the family planning campaign. . . .
>
> Along with such countries as Colombia, Egypt and Tunisia, Indonesia has experienced a notable fertility decline without a significant improvement in the standard of living. A strong family planning program to reduce fertility is believed to be associated with the birth rate decline.[42]

Similar conclusions were reached by Brackett, Ravenholt, and Chao:

> . . . The evidence to date from the World Fertility Survey indicates that level of socioeconomic development is not a dominant factor in determining the desire for fertility control . . . In the eight countries with vigorous family planning programs, more than 30 percent of the currently married women were using contraception. In one of these, the reported use rate was above 50 percent and in two others above 40 percent. These eight countries experienced declines in their fertility between the mid-1960s and mid-1970s of 25–35 percent. The two countries with weak programs reported very low contraceptive use rates—5 percent or less—and little or no change in fertility. . . . Most importantly the findings of the first ten national representative sample surveys performed under WFS auspices, and analyzed in this paper, show that a large proportion of married women of reproductive age in these poor countries do not want any more children and that there is a huge unmet demand for fertility control services. Until this existing demand is much more fully met, it is critical that adequate resources—both within these countries and from donor agencies—be allocated to support service programs.[43*]

[42] A. Ong Tsui & D. Bogue, *Declining World Fertility: Trends, Causes, Implications,* POP. BULL. vol. 33, no. 4 at 15–16 (Pop. Ref. Bur., 1978).

[43] J. Brackett *et al. supra* n. 39 at 322.

*Reprinted with the permission of The Population Council from J. Brackett, R. T. Ravenholt, and J. Chao, *The Role of Family Planning in Recent Rapid Fertility Declines in Developing Countries,* STUDIES IN FAMILY PLANNING 9, no. 12 (December 1978): p. 322.

The example of Indonesia is often cited by those who argue that family planning programs can work. In both Java and Bali acceptance of contraception has been remarkably high and fertility is said to have plummeted as a result.[44] All this in a country which is overwhelmingly rural, poor, not well educated, and not highly literate. Reviewing the Indonesian situation, Freedman commented:

> If it turns out that the data are reasonably valid, Indonesia could be the case of a large country in which a highly organized family-planning program, communicating to the village level, made a crucial difference in expanding the concept and practice of family limitation in improbable circumstances.[45]

(2) Development as the Cause of Fertility Decline. In a strong attack on the Tsui and Bogue paper *supra* n. 42., Demeny wrote:

> . . . The notion entertained by Bogue and Tsui that without organized family planning programs the natural course of events would see fertility declining at a snail's pace, replicating early historical precedents in modernization, is utterly fanciful. . . .
>
> Indeed, that program effort scores in the vast majority of cases on record are strongly dependent on the socioeconomic-institutional configuration of the countries in question is quite obvious, even though, once again, one would not expect that dependency to be fully registered by relating program effort scores to any set of aggregate statistical indicators of "development." As demand for birth control has emerged in the more successfully developing countries on a significant scale, it has been catered to by organized family planning programs. But in case after case—from Malaysia to Mauritius, from Taiwan to Trinidad—it can be shown that successful programs followed, rather than led, rapid expansion of practices aimed at limiting fertility—practices that were either home-produced, including postponement of marriage, or supported by services supplied through the private sector. Many of the successful programs were, in short, more a symptom of fertility change than its cause. . . . In contrast, where the conditions

[44] T. Hull, V. Hull & M. Singarimbun, *Indonesia's Family Planning Story: Success and Challenge,* POP. BULL., vol. 32, no. 6 (Pop. Ref. Bur., 1977); World Fertility Survey, *The Indonesia Fertility Survey, 1976: A Summary of Findings* (Intl. Stat. Inst., 1978).

[45] R. Freedman, *supra* n. 32 at 76.

are not right, where motivation is not present, programs do not work.[46*]

Demeny concluded by suggesting, under the heading of "Implications for Policy," that additional in-depth research on individual countries—concentrating on historical, socioeconomic, cultural, and institutional characteristics and factors—is necessary before policymakers will be able realistically to consider the alternatives available to them.

The philosophy expressed in the Demeny piece parallels much of the thinking that dominated the World Population Conference, namely, that since family planning programs have failed to reduce population growth, it is more fruitful to concentrate on the social and economic determinants of fertility.[47] Policy analysts have concentrated on a number of factors which correlate highly with—and thus might be inferred to have caused—fertility decline. The more salient ones include more equitable income distribution,[48] improvement of the status of women,[49] improved health, particularly maternal

*Reprinted with the permission of The Population Council from Paul Demeny, "On the end of the population explosion," *Population and Development Review* 5, no. 1 (March 1979): p. 151.

[46]P. Demeny, *On the End of the Population Explosion,* 5 POP. & DEV. REV. 141, 151 (1979). *See also,* ____, *Observations on Population Policy and Population Programs in Bangladesh,* 1 POP & DEV. REV. 307 (1975) and N. DEMERATH, BIRTH CONTROL AND FOREIGN POLICY (Harper & Row, 1976) for arguments de-emphasizing the importance of family planning.

[47]The literature on determinants of fertility is reviewed in N. Birdsall, *Analytical Approaches to the Relationship of Population Growth and Development,* 3 POP. & DEV. REV. 63 (1977); POPULATION AND DEVELOPMENT: THE SEARCH FOR SELECTIVE INTERVENTIONS (R. Ridker, ed., Johns Hopkins, 1976); R. Cassen, *Population and Development: A Survey,* 4 WORLD DEVELOPMENT 785 (1976); G. Simmons, *Family Planning Programs or Development: How Persuasive Is the New Wisdom,* 5 INTL. FAM. PLAN. PERSPECTIVES 101 (1979).

[48]*See particularly,* W. RICH, SMALLER FAMILIES THROUGH SOCIAL AND ECONOMIC PROGRESS (Overseas Dev. Council, 1973); J. KOCHER, RURAL DEVELOPMENT, INCOME DISTRIBUTION AND FERTILITY DECLINE (Population Council, 1973); R. Repetto, *Income Distribution and Fertility Change: A Comment,* 3 POP. & DEV. REV. 486 (1977).

[49]*See* R. Dixon, *Women's Rights and Fertility,* REP. ON POP. FAM. PLAN. No. 17 (Pop. Council, 1975); A Germain, *Status and Roles of Women as Factors in Fertility Behavior: A Policy Analysis,* 6 STUDIES IN FAM. PLAN. 192 (1975).

and child health,[50] better education,[51] and increased urbanization.[52]

3. Family Planning Plus Development as the Cause of Fertility Decline. An intermediate position has also emerged. Most closely associated with Berelson and Mauldin, the position maintains that both population and socioeconomic development are relevant to fertility decline and that the two have a synergistic effect.

Examining data from 94 developing countries, Mauldin and Berelson tried to distinguish the effects on fertility of family planning program effort from seven socioeconomic indicators (percent of literate adults, primary and secondary school enrollment as a percentage of the 5–19 age group, life expectancy, infant mortality rate, percentage of adult males in the nonagricultural labor force, GNP per capita, and percentage of population living in cities of more than 100,000). A grid, grouping countries by program effort and social setting, is presented in Table 8–1.[53]

Based on their analysis, the authors reached the following conclusions:

> The data and analyses show that the level of "modernization" as reflected by seven socioeconomic factors has a substantial relationship to fertility decline but also that family planning programs have a significant, independent effect over and above the effect of socioeconomic factors. The key finding probably is that the two—social setting and program effort—go together most effectively.[54]

[50]*See* T. Schultz, *Interrelationships between Mortality and Fertility,* in POPULATION AND DEVELOPMENT: THE SEARCH FOR SELECTIVE INTERVENTIONS 239 (R. Ridker, ed, Johns Hopkins, 1976); THE EFFECTS OF INFANT AND CHILD MORTALITY ON FERTILITY (S. Preston, ed., Academic, 1978): S. Scrimshaw, *Infant Mortality and Behavior in the Regulation of Family Size,* 4 POP. & DEV. REV. 383 (1978).

[51]*See* H. Graff, *Literacy, Education, and Fertility—Past and Present: A Critical Review,* 5 POP & DEV. REV. 105 (1979).

[52]*See* D. Goldberg, *Residential Location and Fertility* in POPULATION AND DEVELOPMENT: THE SEARCH FOR SELECTIVE INTERVENTIONS 387 (R. Ridker, ed., Johns Hopkins, 1976).

[53]W. Mauldin & B. Berelson, *Conditions of Fertility Decline in Developing Countries,* 9 STUDIES IN FAM. PLAN. 89, table 12 (1978). *See also* R. Freedman & B. Berelson, *The Record of Family Planning Programs,* 7 STUDIES IN FAM. PLAN. (1976), and K. SRIKANTAN, THE FAMILY PLANNING PROGRAM IN THE SOCIOECONOMIC CONTEXT (Pop. Council, 1977).

[54]*Id.* at 89.

Table 8–1 1965–75 Crude Birth Rate Declines (in Percents), by Social Setting and Program Effort: 94 Developing Countries*

Social setting	Program effort								
	Strong (20+)		*Moderate (10–19)*		*Weak (0–9)*		*None*		
	Country	*Decline*	*Country*	*Decline*	*Country*	*Decline*	*Country*	*Decline*	*Total*
High	Singapore	40	Cuba	40	Venezuela	11	Korea, North	5	
	Hong Kong	35	Chile	29	Brazil	10	Kuwait	5	
	Korea, South	32	Trinidad and		Mexico	9	Peru	2	
	Barbados	31	Tobago	29	Paraguay	6	Lebanon	2	
	Taiwan	30	Colombia	25			Jordan	1	
	Mauritius	29	Panama	22			Libya	−1	
	Costa Rica	29							
	Fiji	22							
	Jamaica	21							
	Mean	30	Mean	29	Mean	9	Mean	3	19
	Median	30	Median	29	Median	9.5	Median	2	22
Upper middle	China	24	Malaysia	26	Egypt	17	Mongolia	9	
			Tunisia	24	Turkey	16	Syria	4	
			Thailand	23	Honduras	7	Zambia	−2	
			Dominican		Nicaragua	7	Congo	−2	
			Republic	21	Zaire	6			
			Philippines	19	Algeria	4			
			Sri Lanka	18	Guatemala	4			
			El Salvador	13	Morocco	2			
			Iran	2	Ghana	2			
					Ecuador	0			
					Iraq	0			
	Mean	24	Mean	18	Mean	6	Mean	2	10
	Median	24	Median	20	Median	4	Median	1	7
Lower middle	Vietnam, North	23	India	16	Papua		Angola	4	
			Indonesia	13	New Guinea	5	Cameroon	3	
					Pakistan	1	Burma	3	
					Bolivia	1	Yemen,		
					Nigeria	1	P.D.R. of	3	
					Kenya	0	Mozambique	2	

					Liberia	0	Khmer/		
					Haiti	0	Kampuchea	2	
					Uganda	–4	Ivory Coast	1	
							Senegal	0	
							Saudi Arabia	0	
							Vietnam, South	0	
							Madagascar	0	
							Lesotho	–4	
	Mean	23	Mean	14	Mean	1	Mean	1	3
	Median	23	Median	14.5	Median	0.5	Median	1.5	1
Low					Tanzania	5	Laos	5	
					Dahomey	3	Central African		
					Bangladesh	2	Republic	5	
					Sudan	0	Malawi	5	
					Nepal	–1	Bhutan	3	
					Mali	–1	Ethiopia	2	
					Afghanistan	–2	Guinea	2	
							Chad	2	
							Togo	2	
							Upper Volta	1	
							Yemen	1	
							Niger	1	
							Burundi	1	
							Sierra Leone	0	
							Mauritania	0	
							Rwanda	0	
							Somalia	0	
					Mean	1	Mean	2	2
					Median	0	Median	1.5	1
Mean		29		21		4		2	0
Median		29		22		2		2	3

*Reprinted with the permission of The Population Council from W. Parker Mauldin and Bernard Berelson, "Conditions of fertility decline in developing countries, 1965–75," *Studies in Family Planning* Vol. 9, no. 5 (May 1978): p. 110 (Table 12).

This view is supported by a recent World Bank Working Paper which concluded that "both a positive socio-economic environment and a well-developed family planning program have been instrumental in the success of countries reducing their fertility."[55]

Yet, even this view, which appeals to common sense, is not without its weaknesses. To what extent, for example, can the effect of program be separated from that of socioeconomic forces? The International Review Group of Social Science Research on Population and Development has commented:

> Mauldin and Berelson . . . have made use of sophisticated statistical methodology, but not even the most powerful techniques can effectively distinguish the direction of causality.[56]

Another problem is the extent to which regression analysis must depend on easily available indicators for the largest number of countries in order to minimize statistical error. Dixon has observed that variables such as status of women and income distribution were omitted from the Mauldin-Berelson model because data were not available for all countries.[57] Finally, if both socioeconomic development and family planning do contribute to fertility, what does that tell a policymaker about allocating resources? In other words, should scarce resources be put into family planning programs or other developmental activities?[58]

3. Development Theory and the World Population Plan of Action

In the context of Bucharest, what does "development" mean? An analysis of the Plan of Action by Berelson shows that "development" covered not only growth in gross national product (GNP) and per capita income, but also a variety of economic and social factors, such as promotion of health and education, achievement of interna-

[55]R. Cuca, *Family Planning Programs: An Evaluation of Experience* xii (World Bank Staff Working Paper No. 345, 1979); *see also* N. Birdsall, *Population and Poverty in The Developing World* (World Bank Staff Working Paper No. 404, 1980).

[56]IRG, *supra* n. 9 at 100.

[57]R. Dixon, *On Drawing Policy Conclusions from Multiple Regressions: Some Queries and Dilemmas,* 9 STUDIES IN FAM. PLAN 286 (1978); *see also* W. Mauldin & B. Berelson, *Reply,* 9 STUDIES IN FAM. PLAN 288 (1978).

[58]B. Berelson and R. Haveman, *supra* n. 25, wrestled with the problem of resource allocation. *See also* B. Berelson, *Prospects and Programs for Fertility Reduction: What? Where?,* 4 POP. & DEV. REV. 579 (1978).

tional equity in consumption and investment, more rational utilization of natural resources, equal status for women, strengthening family life, establishment of social security systems, and the achievement of a balanced age structure.[59] In other words, the architects of the Plan of Action were referring to a political and social development and egalitarianism that goes far beyond the traditional concept of economic development. What are the consequences of this theory of development? Is it practicable to expect development in this broader sense to be achieved within the foreseeable future? If it is not feasible, what are the consequences for the Plan of Action adopted at Bucharest by which fertility decline is expected to follow development?

Traditional theories of development have stressed the need for economic growth in order to keep the economy humming, maintain high employment, and avoid recession.[60] This focus has tended to lead, in development priorities, to an emphasis on industrial production and to channelling money to the most productive sectors, on the assumption that benefits would ultimately "trickle down" to the great mass of society's needier people. These traditional theories of development have been under challenge for some time.[61]

One area of attack focuses on more equitable distribution of resources instead of, or as a prerequisite to, an emphasis on purely economic growth. It stresses the social and political nature of development, questions such traditional indicators of development as GNP or per capita income, and suggests a need for major institutional and structural changes; development is viewed as a "multidimensional process involving major changes in social structures, popular attitudes and both national and international institutions as a basis for the acceleration of economic growth, the reduction of inequality and the ultimate eradication of absolute poverty."[62] In this context, economists and planners have proposed alternative strategies of development, ranging from meeting "basic needs" to

[59]B. Berelson, *The World Population Plan of Action: Where Now?* 1 POP. & DEV. REV. 115 (1975).

[60]*See, e.g.,* C. KINDLEBERGER, ECONOMIC DEVELOPMENT (McGraw Hill, 1965) or W. ROSTOW, THE PROCESS OF ECONOMIC GROWTH (Norton, 1952).

[61]For an excellent, concise review of traditional development theory and the challenges to it, *see* M. Todaro, *Current Issues in Economic Development* (Center for Policy Studies Working Paper No. 24, Pop. Council, 1978).

[62]*Id.* at 5.

creation of a New International Economic Order to giving higher priority to agriculture.[63]

Another challenge to the traditional neo-classical model is from the left. Marxist economists, in general, have argued that societal revolution is necessary to end the dependence of developing countries on the neo-colonialist developed world. They emphasize the need for major structural changes to bring about a more just and egalitarian society.[64]

A third challenge is to "growth" itself, an attack made possible by the development of computer models of the world economy and spearheaded by two books sponsored by the Club of Rome: *The Limits To Growth*[65] *and Mankind At The Turning Point.*[66] Using a world simulation model programmed into a computer, the first book indicated that unless growth were halted, a catastrophe would occur by the middle of the next century. The model was severely criticized for having omitted regional distinctions and for underestimating the potential for growth of agriculture and other resources. The second book, using a more sophisticated model, distinguished between "organic" and "cancerous" growth, but produced only slightly less forbidding prospects. Writing along the same lines, economist Robert Heilbroner found that

> . . . the existing pace of industrial growth . . . holds out the risk of entering the danger zone of climatic change in as little as three or four

[63]Alternative development strategies are reviewed in M. Todaro, *supra* n. 61, and J. Weaver, K. Jameson & R. Blue, *Growth and Equity: Can They Be Happy Together?,* INTL. DEV. REV. vol. 20, no. 1, p. 20 (1978). A more comprehensive review is found in M. UL HAQ, THE POVERTY CURTAIN: CHOICES FOR THE THIRD WORLD (Columbia, 1976). J. SINGH, A NEW INTERNATIONAL ECONOMIC ORDER (Praeger, 1977) provides a readable analysis of the background to, and platform of, the New International Economic Order. P. Streeten presents a clear exposition of the basic needs approach in *The Distinctive Features of a Basic Needs Approach to Development,* INTL. DEV. REV. vol 19, no. 3, p. 8 (1977). *See also* B. WARD, PROGRESS FOR A SMALL PLANET (Norton, 1979); G. MYRDAL, AGAINST THE STREAM: CRITICAL ESSAYS ON ECONOMICS (Vintage 1975); INDEPENDENT COMMISSION ON INTERNATIONAL DEVELOPMENT ISSUES, NORTH-SOUTH: A PROGRAMME FOR SURVIVAL (MIT, 1980).

[64]*See, e.g.,* A. FRANK, CAPITALISM AND UNDERDEVELOPMENT IN LATIN AMERICA: HISTORICAL STUDIES OF CHILE AND BRAZIL (Monthly Review, 1969).

[65]D. MEADOWS, D. MEADOWS, J. RANDERS & W. BEHRENS III, THE LIMITS TO GROWTH (Universe, 1972).

[66]M. MESAROVIC & E. PESTEL, MANKIND AT THE TURNING POINT (Dutton, 1974).

> generations. If that trajectory is in fact pursued, industrial growth will then have to come to an immediate halt, for another generation or two along that path would literally consume human, perhaps all, life.[67]

The Leontief Report, using still another model, analyzed the possibility of attaining a meaningful reduction of income disparity between the rich and the poor nations by the year 2000 if the targets of the United Nations Development Decade were met. Because Leontief is widely considered an unbiased, objective analyst, his conclusions appear all the more discouraging:

> Target rates of growth of gross product in the developing regions, set by the International Development Strategy for the Second United Nations Development Decade, are not sufficient to start closing the income gap between the developing and the developed countries . . .
>
> The principal limits to sustained economic growth and accelerated development are political, social and institutional in character rather than physical. . . .
>
> To ensure accelerated development two general conditions are necessary: first, far reaching internal changes of a social, political and institutional character in the developing countries, and second, significant changes in the world economic order. Accelerated development leading to a substantial reduction of the income gap between the developing and developed countries can only be achieved through a combination of both these conditions.[68]

Is it likely that the two conditions mentioned in Leontief's last paragraph will be met? If not, what does this imply for development? For population growth?

[67]R. HEILBRONER, AN INQUIRY INTO THE HUMAN PROSPECT, 128 (Norton, 1974). For an analysis of the implications of zero population and economic growth, *see* THE NO GROWTH SOCIETY (M. Olson & H. Landsberg, eds., Norton, 1973) and L. Day, *What Will a ZPG Society Be Like,* POP. BULL., vol. 33, no. 3 (Pop. Ref. Bur., 1978). *Compare* Helibroner's pessimism with the viewpoint of HERMAN KAHN, THE NEXT 200 YEARS: A SCENARIO FOR AMERICA AND THE WORLD 4 (William Morrow, 1976), who, using a computer model developed at the Hudson Institute, concluded that:

> The application of a modicum of intelligence and good management in dealing with current problems can enable economic growth to continue for a considerable period of time, to the benefit, rather than the detriment, of mankind.

[68]W. Leontief, A. Carter & P. Petri, *The Future of the World Economy: Preface, Introduction and Summary* 29, 32 (U.N. Dept. of Econ. & Soc. Affairs, 1976). *See also* W. Leontief, *Population Growth and Economic Development: Illustrative Projections,* 5 POP. & DEV. REV. 1 (1979).

4. The World Population Conference in Retrospect and Implementation of the Plan of Action

In retrospect, how important was the World Population Conference? How, if at all, did the World Population Plan of Action influence the formulation of population or development policies?

Reactions, even several years after the event, are mixed. Compare the views of Leon Tabah, Director of the United Nations Population Division:

> It is remarkable how the situation has changed since Bucharest, for it would now be clearly incorrect to state that the governments of the Third World still are reticent on the topic of the regulation of births. What the countries of the Third World now lack is less a willingness to act than the technical, financial and administrative means to convert principles into concrete programmes.[69]

with those of Arthur McCormack:

> The real significance . . . was of course that the controversy at Bucharest on developmentalism versus immediate specific population programmes proved largely academic when it came to practice. Specific population programmes were opted for now. These were seen in the context of development, but there was no suggestion of postponement of needed population activities until development was achieved.[70]

Measham concluded the World Population Conference was both important and salutory because it *politicized* the population issue, *i.e.,* removed it from the narrow technical sphere of population specialists and made it part of ideology and international politics,[71] and Urquidi argued Bucharest was important because it created awareness of the importance of socioeconomic development and population planning and heightened interest in population policy.[72]

A logical way to assess the importance of the World Population Conference is to review its impact on (a) government policies

[69]L. Tabah, *A Deeper Understanding Since Bucharest,* PEOPLE, Vol. 6, no. 2, p. 5, 6 (1979).

[70]A. McCormack, *Population and Development at Bucharest and After,* INTL. DEV. REV., vol. 17, no. 3, p. 14 (1975).

[71]A. Measham, *Population Policy 1977: A Reexamination of the Issues,* 6 PREV. MED. 92 (1977).

[72]V. Urquidi, *On Implementing the World Population Plan of Action,* 2 POP. & DEV. REV. 91 (1976).

and attitudes, (b) later United Nations-sponsored conferences and actions, and (c) the policies and funding of the international donors.

a. Government Policies and Attitudes. Miro, after having evaluated the changes in population policy since Bucharest, concluded:

> . . . The number of countries whose governments have adopted [population] policies, with whatever content, remains essentially the same (around 40). . . . The Bucharest impact can be primarily detected in the efforts of several governments to streamline their programs . . . and to overhaul admininstrative machinery.[73]

Miro's conclusion is based partly upon the results of the United Nations' *Third Inquiry among Governments on Population Development.* A Fourth *Inquiry* was conducted in 1978 of population-related policies in 158 countries. The study indicated that of 116 developing countries, 51 judged their population growth rates to be too high, 53 found their growth rates to be satisfactory, and 12 deemed their population growth rates to be too low. This contrasts markedly with the perceptions of the developed world where out of 42 countries, 10 favored a higher rate of population growth, 31 found their population growth rates satisfactory, and only one country wanted to lower its population growth rate.[74]

Governmental attitudes toward population family planning and development have tended to differ by geographical region. This was nowhere better illustrated than by the five post-Bucharest regional "consultations," which were sponsored by the United Nations. The results of these meetings were summarized by Miro:

> 1. The Asia-Pacific region reiterated its support for the reduction of population growth, having set quantitative targets for declining rates of growth, mortality, and fertility. The statement of the regional report that "development is a central factor in the solution of population problems" may represent a new consensus as an outcome of Bucharest.
>
> 2. The Latin American countries, while recognizing that critical situations could arise from the demand for education, health, housing,

[73]C. Miro, *The World Population Plan of Action: A Political Instrument Whose Potential Has Not Been Realized,* 3 POP. & DEV. REV. 421, 435 (1977).

[74]United Nations, World Population Trends and Policies, 1979, Monitoring Report, Vol. II p. 29 (Dept. Econ. & Soc. Affairs, Pop. Studies No. 62 ST ESA SER.A 62 Add. 1, 1980).

and other services generated by population pressures in the region, persisted in refraining from making specific recommendations regarding the rate of population growth. No quantitative targets were proposed. Undoubtedly the most important recommendation adopted by the Latin American countries was to set up "high-level councils, commissions or other equivalent units, empowered to coordinate action in the field of population," in the countries of the region.

3. The African Consultation reflected more clearly than any other the intraregional diversity of situations and positions. The report represents a consensus between "countries with vast natural resources" where "a high rate of population growth could provide added benefits for development" and those "able to hold larger population" but in which "certain circumstances (economic, social, cultural or otherwise) may not make it possible." Many of the recommendations contained in the Plan were reiterated in the African context. The most prominent departure was in urging that African governments "pass legislation permitting qualified medical practitioners to perform abortion on request and on grounds of the health, *welfare* and survival of either mother and child or both of them." This recommendation is even more striking if one recalls that the subject of abortion was completely silenced at the World Population Conference.

4. The West Asia region took the most radical position in regard to population growth when it declared that "rapid population growth in the area does not constitute an obstacle in the way of socio-economic development," adding that "there are further indications that the development process may overcome the implications of the continued rise in reproduction rates and the natural increase of population." Their statement more than any other stressed the need for adequate statistical data on demographic variables.

5. The European countries agreed that the adoption of the Plan had "resulted in the speeding up of the enactment of legislation and the undertaking of organizational and research programmes that might otherwise have been allocated a lower priority." In the majority of countries it caused "Governments to realize that where previous approaches were not coordinated to resolve population problems, these approaches might be transformed into a considered comprehensive population policy, within the context of social and economic development strategies and plans." The representatives at the European Consultation also paid special attention to the Plan's recommendation to reduce "national and subnational differentials" in mortality (para. 22), calling on the World Health Organization to "initiate and coordinate studies of differen-

tial morbidity and mortality both in developed and developing countries."[75]*

b. The Seventh Special Session and United Nations' Conferences. Six United Nations' conferences and the Seventh Special Session of the General Assembly were held within four years of the World Population Conference. As far as the Seventh Special Session was concerned, one commentator noted that "the World Population Conference might never have occurred."[76] The World Food Conference (Rome, 1975) and the International Women's Year Conference (Mexico, 1975) reaffirmed the right to determine the number and spacing of children. The latter also emphasized the importance of improving the status of women. The other conferences (Human Settlements, Vancouver, 1976; Desertification, Nairobi, 1977; Employment, Geneva, 1976; and Technical Cooperation Among Nations, Buenos Aires, 1978) mention only in passing, if at all, the World Population Conference, or the principles enunciated in the World Population Plan of Action.

c. International Population Assistance. Perhaps the most significant impact of the World Population Conference was expanding the programmatic horizons of the major international donors, particularly those that fund population-related programs.[77] After Buchar-

[75]C. Miro, *supra* n. 73 at 427-428.

*Reprinted with the permission of The Population Council from Carmen A. Miro, *The World Population Plan of Action: A Political Instrument Whose Potential Has Not Been Realized,* POPULATION AND DEVELOPMENT REVIEW 3, no. 4 (December 1977): pp. 427–428.

[76]B. Baron, *Population and the Seventh Special Session: A Report,* 1 POP. & DEV. REV. 297 (1975).

[77]The donor institutions with budgets of more than $40 million in 1979 were:

The United States Agency for International Development (AID), which funds family planning programs, biomedical and demographic research and other population-related programs and agencies. Its 1979 contribution was approximately $177 million, allocated to international agencies and to national governments.

The United Nations Fund for Population Activities (UNFPA), the major funding agency of population-related activities within the United Nations. It funds a variety of population programs, generally through host national governments. Its 1979 budget was approximately $96 million.

The International Planned Parenthood Federation (IPPF), which provides funding and technical assistance to private family planning associations throughout the world. Its 1979 budget was estimated at approximately $46 million.

est, there appeared to be greater willingness to consider funding "development" activities thought to have an indirect effect on fertility and to consider population within a developmental framework, rather than as an isolated, outside factor. For example, the Population Council, after appointing a president with a "development" rather than a "population" background, began giving greater emphasis to non-family-planning projects, *e.g.,* those which would enhance the status of women. Similarly, the International Planned Parenthood Federation reconsidered its role as an agency devoted almost exclusively to family planning and set aside money for other activities that might indirectly affect fertility. The Agency for International Development indicated a greater willingness than previously to consider financing integrated health programs, and the United Nations Fund for Population Activities demonstrated increased receptivity to maternal-child health programs. The changes in donor attitudes, should not obscure, however, the fact that the greatest proportion of program money in the population field goes to fund family planning programs. For example, the UNFPA, the largest nongovernmental donor, allocated 59 percent of its 1977–1980 budget for family planning.[78]

Other international donors with budgets of more than $15 million in 1979 were: the Swedish government ($42 million), The Norwegian Government ($40 million), the World Health Organization ($38 million), the World Bank ($31 million), the Federal Republic of Germany ($17 million), and the Japanese government ($16 million). The total amount of international aid to population activities in 1979 was $394 million, excluding double counting.

The source of the budget figures is S. Isaacs, *Review of the Current Status of Family Planning,* Annex to the *Background Document* for the Conference on Family Planning in the 80's (1981) *See also* H. Gille, *Recent Trends in International Population Assistance,* Appendix D to R. SALAS, INTERNATIONAL POPULATION ASSISTANCE: THE FIRST DECADE (Pergamon, 1979). UNFPA, POPULATION PROGRAMMES AND PROJECTS: VOL. 1, GUIDE TO SOURCES OF INTERNATIONAL POPULATION ASSISTANCE (1979); IPPF, REPORT TO DONORS, 1979.

[78]C. Miro, *supra* n. 73 at 432.

CHAPTER 9

NATIONAL POPULATION LAWS AND POLICIES

I. INTRODUCTION

In general, it is the developing countries that have issued explicit population policies or laws. According to a Population Council report, 35 developing countries have promulgated official policies to reduce population growth rates.[1] This chapter examines explicit population policies with the following questions in mind: if a country wants to reduce population growth rates, what policy options are available to it? what are the advantages and disadvantages of an explicit policy? in what form should it be issued? what political considerations promote or impede issuance of an explicit policy? what program implications flow from promulgation of explicit policies?

Excerpts from the national population policy or law of three countries—Mexico, India, and Ghana—are presented below. Since treatment of population issues is highly idiosyncratic, these excerpts are not provided as models, but, rather, as examples of what coun-

[1]D. NORTMAN & E. HOFSTATTER, POPULATION AND FAMILY PLANNING PROGRAMS 17 (10th Ed., Pop. Council, 1980).

tries can and have done. The Mexican policy exemplifies a direct attack on the problem of rapid population growth within a developmental context; the Indian policy, which, with the change of government in 1977, is no longer in effect, demonstrates the radical measures that can be taken to deal with a population problem considered critical; and the Ghanaian policy is an example of a careful description of a country's demographic situation which offers a combination of family planning and incentives to reduce fertility. Although this chapter focuses on the specifics of policy, it should be read in the context of the global framework presented in Chapter 8 and the discussion of incentives and fertility regulation presented in the preceding chapters.

II. NATIONAL LAWS AND POLICIES—THREE CASE STUDIES

A. Population Law of Mexico, 1974[2]

Article 1

The provisions of this Law are of public order and for general observance in the Republic. Its purpose is to regulate the phenomena relating to the population in regard to its size, structure, dynamics and distribution within national territory, in order that it might partake justly and fairly in economic and social benefits.

Article 2

Through the Secretariat of the Interior, the Federal Executive shall dictate, promote and coordinate, as the case may be, adequate measures for the resolution of national demographic problems.

Article 3

For the purposes of this Law, the Secretariat of the Interior shall dictate and carry out, or when appropriate, promote before competent or corresponding dependencies, measures necessary:

I. To adapt the economic and social development programs to necessities which may arise due to the size, structure, dynamics and distribution of the population;

II. To carry out family planning programs through the educational and public health services available to the public, and to supervise said programs and those carried out by private organizations in order that these might be carried out with absolute respect for fundamental

[2]Source of this translation is the INTL. ADV. COMM. ON POP. & LAW., ANNUAL REVIEW OF POPULATION LAW, 1979 at 10 Law and Population Monograph No. 30 (Fletcher School of Law & Diplomacy, 1975).

human rights and the preservation of family dignity, so that population growth might be regulated rationally and stabilized, as well as to achieve a better exploitation of the human and natural resources to the nation;

III. To lower the death rate;

IV. To influence the dynamics of the population through systems of education, public health, professional and technical training, and the protection of infants, as well as to obtain participation of the mass of the people in the solution of problems affecting it;

V. To promote the complete integration of the woman into the economic, educational, social and cultural process;

VI. To promote the complete integration of fringe groups into the national development;

VII. To subject the immigration of foreigners to methods which it may deem pertinent, and to procure their best assimilation into national conditions as well as their appropriate distribution within the territory;

VIII. To restrict the emigration of nationals when required by national interests;

IX. To try to plan urban centers of population in such a way as to assure the efficient performance of required public services;

X. To stimulate establishment of strong national population centers in sparsely populated border areas;

XI. To promote mobilization of the population within the different areas of the Republic in order to adapt geographic distribution to the possibilities of regional development, based upon special settlement programs for said population;

XII. To promote the creation of towns in order to group together geographically isolated nuclei;

XIII. To coordinate the activities of dependencies of the federal, state and municipal public sectors as well as those pertaining to private organizations which help the population in those areas where a disaster is expected or has already happened; and

XIV. Any other objectives which may be determined by this Law or other legal provisions.

Article 4

Dependencies of the Federal Executive are responsible for putting the above Article into effect, while the application and execution of the necessary procedures for carrying out each one of the objectives of the national demographic policy correspond to the other entities of the Public Sector, in accordance with those attributes conferred upon them by law. However, the definition of the rules, joint initiatives and coordination of the programs of said dependencies in demographic matters is the exclusive concern of the Secretariat of the Interior.

Article 5

The National Population Council is created to be in charge of the demographic planning of the nation, in order to include the population in programs of economic and social development which may be formulated within government sectors, and to join their objectives to the needs arising from demographic phenomena.

Article 6

The National Population Council shall be composed of a representative of the Secretariat of the Interior who shall be the head of the division and shall act as president of the same, and by a representative from each one of the Secretariats of Public Education, Health and Public Assistance, of the Treasury and Public Credit, Foreign Relations, Labor and Social Security, and of the Presidency, as well as one from the Department of Agrarian Affairs and of Colonization, who shall be the heads of the same or the Subsecretaries and General Secretaries who they may designate. For each proprietor-representative, a substitute shall be designated who should have the same administrative level as the former, or that immediately below.

When dealing with subjects which are the concern of other dependencies or organizations of the public sector, the President of the Council may request the heads to attend the corresponding session or sessions or to name a representative to act in their behalf.

The Council may be assisted by technical consultants and may organize the advisory interdisciplinary units which it deems appropriate so as to include specialists in problems relating to development and demography.

B. Population Policy of India, 1976[3]

1. With 2.4 per cent of the world's land area, India has about 15 per cent of the world's people. It is estimated that our population as on 1st January, 1976 has crossed the 600 million mark, and is now rising at the rate of well over one million per month. Since independence 250 millions have been added, equivalent to the entire population of the Soviet Union with six times the land area of India. The increase every year is now equal to the entire population of Australia which is 2 1/2 times the size of our country. If the present rate of increase continues unchecked our population at the turn of the century may well reach the staggering figure of one billion. Indisputably we are facing a population explosion of crisis dimensions which has largely diluted the fruits of the remarkable economic progress that we have made over the last two decades. If the future of the nation is to be secured,

[3]Statement of Dr. Karan Singh, Minister of Health and Family Planning, April 16, 1976.

and the goal of removing poverty to be attained, the population problem will have to be treated as a top national priority and commitment.

2. Our real enemy is poverty, and it is as a frontal assault on the citadels of poverty that the Fifth Five-Year Plan has included the Minimum Needs Programme. One of its five items is integrated package of health, family planning and nutrition. Far reaching steps have been initiated to reorient the thrust of medical education so as to strengthen the community medicine and rural health aspects, and to restructure the health care delivery system on a three-tier basis going down to the most far-flung rural areas where the majority of our people reside and where child mortality and morbidity are the highest. Similarly, ignorance, illiteracy and superstition have got to be fought and eliminated. In the ultimate analysis it is only when the underlying causes of poverty and disease are eliminated that the nation will be able to move forward to its desired ideals.

3. Nonetheless it is clear that simply to wait for education and economic development to bring about a drop in fertility is not a practical solution. The very increase in population makes economic development slow and more difficult of achievement. The time factor is so pressing, and the population growth so formidable, that we have to get out of the vicious circle through a direct assault upon this problem as a national commitment. . . .

4. . . . After a thorough and careful consideration of all the factors involved as well as the expression of a wide spectrum of public opinion, Government have decided on a series of fundamental measures detailed below which, it is hoped, will enable us to achieve the planned target of reducing the birth rate from an estimated 35 per thousand in the beginning of the Fifth Plan to 25 per thousand at the end of the Sixth. Allowing for the steady decline in the death rate that will continue due to the improvement in our medical and public health services and the living standards of our people, this is expected to bring down the growth rate of population in our country to 1.4 per cent by 1984.

5. Raising the age of marriage will not only have a demonstrable demographic impact, but will also lead to more responsible parenthood and help to safeguard the health of the mother and the child. . . . The present law has not been effectively or uniformly enforced. It has, therefore, been decided that the minimum age of marriage should be raised to 18 for girls and 21 for boys, and suitable legislation to this effect will be passed. . . . The question of making registration of marriages compulsory is under active consideration.

6. It has been represented by some States that while on the one hand we are urging them to limit their population, those States which do well in this field face reduction of representation in Parliament while those with weak performance in family planning tend to get increasing

representation. It is obviously necessary to remedy this situation. It has, therefore, been decided that the representation in the Lok Sabha and the State Legislatures will be frozen on the basis of the 1971 census until the year 2001. This means in effect that the census counts of 1981 and 1991 will not be considered for purposes of adjustment of Lok Sabha Legislature seats. . . .

7. In a federal system the sharing of Central resources with the States is a matter of considerable importance. In all cases where population is a factor, as in the allocation of Central assistance to State Plans, devolution of taxes and duties and grants-in-aid, the population figures of 1971 will continue to be followed till the year 2001. In the matter of Central assistance to State Plans, eight per cent will be specifically earmarked against performance in family planning. . . .

8. While there is a direct correlation between illiteracy and fertility, this is particularly marked in the case of girls' education. Wherever female literacy improves, it has been seen that fertility drops almost automatically. It is, therefore, necessary that special measures be taken to raise the levels of female education, particularly above the middle level for girls as well as non-formal education plans for young women especially in certain backward States where the family planning performance so far has been unimpressive. The same is true with regard to child nutrition programmes, as high infant mortality and morbidity have a direct impact on fertility. The Ministry of Education is urging upon the State Governments the necessity to give these matters higher priority than has been accorded so far and fully earmarking adequate outlays both for girls education up to the middle level and child nutrition.

9. My Ministry is also in close touch with the Education Ministry with regard to the introduction of population values in the educational system, and the NCERT has already made a beginning in bringing out some textbooks on these lines. . . .

10. The adoption of a small family norm is too important a matter to be considered the responsibility of only one Ministry. It is essential that all Ministries and Departments of the Government of India as well as the States should take up as an integral part of their normal programme and budgets the motivation of citizens to adopt responsible reproductive behaviour both in their own as well as the national interest. A directive to this effect is being issued by the Prime Minister to all Ministries of the Government of India. . . .

11. Experience over the last 20 years has shown that monetary compensation does have a significant impact upon the acceptance of family planning, particularly among the poorer sections of society. In view of the desirability of limiting the family size to two or three it has been decided that monetary compensation for sterilization (both

male and female) will be raised to Rs. 150/— if performed with two living children or less, Rs.100/— if performed with three living children and Rs.70/— if performed with four or more children. . . .

12. In addition to individual compensation, Government is of the view that group incentives should now be introduced in a bold and imaginative manner so as to make family planning a mass movement with greater community involvement. It has, therefore, been decided that suitable group incentives will be introduced for the medical profession, for Zila and Panchayat Samitis, for teachers at various levels, for cooperative societies and for labour in the organized sector through their respective representative national organizations. . . .

13. Despite governmental efforts at Union, State and Municipal level, family planning cannot succeed unless voluntary organizations are drawn into its promotion in an increasing measure, particularly youth and women's organizations. There is already a scheme for aiding voluntary organizations, and it has been decided that this will be expanded. Also, full rebate will be allowed in the income tax assessment for amounts given as donations for family planning purposes to Government, local bodies or any registered voluntary organization approved for this purpose by the Union Ministry of Health.

14. Research in reproductive biology and contraception is under way. . . .

15. The question of compulsory sterilization has been the subject of lively public debate over the last few months. It is clear that public opinion is now ready to accept much more stringent measures for family planning than before. However, the administrative and medical infrastructure in many parts of the country is still not adequate to cope with the vast implications of nation-wide compulsory sterilization. We do not, therefore, intend to bring in Central legislation for this purpose, at least for the time being. Some States feel that the facilities available with them are adequate to meet the requirements of compulsory sterilization. We are of the view that where a State legislature, in the exercise of its own powers, decides that the time is ripe and it is necessary to pass legislation for compulsory sterilization, it may do so. Our advice to the States in such cases will be to bring in the limitation after three children, and to make it uniformly applicable to all Indian citizens resident in that State without distinction of caste, creed or community.

16. Some States have also introduced a series of measures directed towards their employees and other citizens in the matter of preferential allotment of houses, loans, etc. for those who have accepted family planning. In this sphere also we have decided to leave it to each individual State to introduce such measures as they consider necessary and desirable. Employees of the Union Government will be

expected to adopt the small family norm and necessary changes will be made in their service/conduct rules to ensure this.

17. In order to spread the message of family planning throughout the nation, a new multi-media motivational strategy is being evolved which will utilize all the available media channels including the radio, television (especially programmes aimed directly at rural audiences), the press, films, visual displays and also include traditional folk media such as the jatra, puppet shows, folk songs and folk dances. . . .

C. Population Policy of Ghana, 1969[4]

1.1 The population of Ghana is the nation's most valuable resource. It is both the instrument and the objective of national development. The protection and enhancement of its welfare is the Government's first responsibility. When that welfare is threatened, the Government must act.

1.2 The welfare of the nation is now endangered by a subtle, almost imperceptible demographic change. During the past three or four decades the death rate has been slowly falling, permitting more children to survive into adulthood and adding years to the life expectancy of our people. But while the death rate has been falling, there has been no noticeable change in the birth rate. Patterns of high fertility that were appropriate, perhaps even necessary, in an era of high mortality are continuing in a time when they have become inappropriate and unnecessary. Unless birth rates can be brought down to parallel falling death rates, Ghana's population will climb at a rate dangerous to continuing prosperity and the children of the next few generations will be born into a world where their very numbers may condemn them to life-long poverty. . . .

The Consequences Of Rapid Population Growth

3.3 Development at best is a slow and difficult process. Rapid population increase can adversely affect nearly every aspect of that process and can neutralize hard won gains. If development progress is to be made and economic gains achieved and consolidated, attention will have to be given to the problem of curbing population growth. . . .

3.5 It is obvious that rapid population growth in Ghana cannot continue indefinitely. But it is equally obvious that there are only three ways in which a decline in the growth rate can occur: by exporting people; by increasing death rates; or decreasing fertility. Forced or

[4]Excerpts from a policy paper of the government of Ghana entitled, *Population Planning for National Progress and Prosperity,* reprinted in STUDIES IN FAM. PLAN. no. 44 (1969).

voluntary emigration is not a practical solution. . . . Deliberate efforts to raise death rates or to delay health measures that would contribute to reduced mortality are morally unacceptable. . . . This leaves only the alternative of reducing births and this is the course that, sooner or later, will have to be taken.

3.6 Once started, a programme to reduce the number of births gathers momentum only slowly, so it is important to begin as early as possible. Benefits in terms of improved maternal and child health and decreasing child mortality show up first, but even these are somewhat delayed because no births can be prevented in the first nine months of a programme. The effects of fewer births on direct educational costs would normally not appear for five or six years, although there might be opportunity for earlier savings in educational planning and construction costs. The effect on the labour force would be felt only after 15 or 16 years; the children who will be moving into the labour force during that time are already born. Because of these inevitable delays in pay-off, a family planning programme must be seen in a long perspective. . . .

3.33 High fertility and its consequence, rapid population increase, are thus closely linked to many of the economic, social welfare, health and other problems of development. . . .

3.34 Population is an important variable of concern to development planning. It is as amenable to planned change and control as other variables that planners work with. Resources and effort devoted to population planning and programming—including fertility limitation—will pay off more handsomely in economic return than resources devoted to more conventional aspects of development. . . .

4.4 In the past there were valid reasons for high fertility. Infant and child mortality rates were very high and only a fraction of the children born were able to survive to adulthood. Cultural preferences for sons favoured the production of large numbers of children. Children surviving to adulthood offered the only possibility of support for parents grown old. Under conditions of rural life and subsistence agriculture children cost little and at an early age could be expected to begin to make small economic contributions. . . . Traditional expectations defined the value of women largely in terms of their ability to bear children and the weight of community and family pressures was on the side of high fertility.

4.5 Some of these reasons still persist but the conditions which established and sustained them are rapidly changing. . . .

4.8 Contraception is the preferred means for programmes of fertility limitation around the world. . . .

4.9 It is possible that, notwithstanding the effects of massive contraceptive programmes that have been introduced in a number of countries, abortion is still the most widely practised form of fertility limitation around the world. . . . Opposition to it is principally moral rather than technical. . . .

4.12 Unlike some other types of development projects, a fertility limitation programme can be relatively inexpensive and the benefits begin to appear rather quickly. . . .

4.14 Results [of a national KAP study] indicate that there are enough potential acceptors to justify starting a family planning programme and it is probable that a well planned information campaign could attract others about as rapidly as services could be expanded.

A Population Policy For Ghana

5.2 With these considerations in mind and with the conviction that present rates of population growth are detrimental to individual and family welfare and constitute major hindrances to the attainment of development objectives, the government believes that voluntary planning of the size of families and reductions in the rates of population growth are in the vital interest of the nation and proposes that a national policy be adopted to advance these interests.

5.3 The following paragraphs define and discuss the principal elements in such a policy:

5.4 I. A national population policy and programme are to be developed as organic parts of social and economic planning and development activity. . . .

5.5 Basic aims defined in Ghana's development programme are to build the foundations for self-generating growth, reduce the high rate of unemployment, check the rate of migration to the cities, and stimulate economic, social, and cultural progress in order to provide higher standards of living compatible with human dignity and based on equal and full opportunities for all. A population policy and programme are viewed as integral parts of efforts toward social and economic development, improvement of health and nutrition, elevation of quality and extension of the scope of education, wider employment opportunities, and better development and use of human resources in the interests of a more abundant life. . . .

5.8 II. The vigorous pursuit of further means to reduce the still high rates of morbidity and mortality will be an important aspect of population policy and programmes. . . .

5.10 III. Specific and quantitative population goals will be established on the basis of reliable demographic data and the determination of demographic trends. . . .

5.13 IV. Recognizing the crucial importance of a wide understanding of the deleterious effects of unlimited population growth and of the means by which couples can safely and effectively control their fertility, the Government will encourage and itself undertake programmes to provide information, advice, and assistance for couples wishing to space or limit their reproduction. These programmes will be educational and persuasive, and not coercive. . . .

5.16 V. Ways will be sought to encourage and promote wider productive and gainful employment for women; to increase the proportion of girls entering and completing school; to develop a wider range of non-domestic roles for women; and to examine the structure of Government perquisites and benefits and if necessary change them in such ways as to minimize their pro-natalist influences and maximise their anti-natalist effects. . . .

5.20 To discourage the unrestricted growth of families, the Government has decided to modify employment policies as follows:

1. Paid maternity leave will be granted only when the applicant has served for not less than one year.

2. The number of paid maternity leaves will be limited to three during the entire working life of those affected and no payment will be made in respect to any number of leaves beyond this limit.

3. Children allowances paid to Government officers will be limited to three only, and this will apply to all officers irrespective of whether they reside in or outside of Ghana.

4. The Government's responsibility for payment of traveling expenses of officer's children will be limited to three.

5.21 VI. The Government will adopt policies and establish programmes to guide and regulate the flow of internal migration, influence spatial distribution in the interest of development progress, and reduce the scale and rate of immigration in the interests of national welfare. . . .

5.23 It is recognized that there is need for an integrated programme for the solution of problems relating to the spatial distribution of the population. National and regional planning committees have been set up to help plan urban and suburban settlement and resettlement and to assist in the initiation of programmes to regulate rural to urban migration. . . .

5.26 The Government believes that development of ten towns with a population of 50,000 each, for example, will benefit the nation more than development confined largely to one city of 500,000.

5.27 The Government intends to intensify its efforts to supply rural areas with facilities such as safe pipe-borne water and improved means of refuse disposal. It is expected that the provision of these and other amenities will help to make rural life more attractive and thus slow down the rate of rural-urban migration.

5.28 The Government will take steps to evaluate and, as necessary, to control immigration and to assure that the permitted immigration is in the best interests of the country. A principal cause for concern has been the size of immigrants' remittances to their countries of origin. The effects of this outflow of capital will be studied and remedial action taken as necessary. . . .

III. COMMENTARY AND ISSUES

A. The Form of National Population Laws and Policies

The Mexican government issued its national policy in the form of a Population Law. What significance should be given to the promulgation of the policy in the form of a law rather than, say, a statement by the Health Minister? To what extent does enactment as a law serve to legitimize a policy? Will a policy endure longer if written as a law? Is the government more likely to take programmatic or budgetary action? In the same context, what importance should be given to the Mexican government's amending the Constitution in 1975. The constitutional provision states:

> The man and the woman are equal before the law, which shall protect the organization and development of the family.
>
> Every person has the right to decide in a free, responsible and informed manner with regard to the number and spacing of his or her children.[5]

Similar provisions are written into the constitutions of Yugoslavia, Ecuador, China, and Portugal.[6]

Given the generally agreed-upon socio-economic context of population policy, does it follow that a written population policy should be made part of a country's development plan? If a population policy is included in a national development plan, does the policy lapse when the plan ends?

In a parallel vein, how can demographic variables best be included in a national development plan? A recent study disclosed that distressingly little in the way of demographic considerations was included in the development plans of 60 developing countries. Although 80 percent of the countries estimated their population growth rates, only 68 percent estimated future population size and less than

[5]Article 4 of the Mexican Constitution. Source of this translation is the INT. ADV. COMM. ON POP. AND LAW., *supra* n. 2 at 9.

[6]IPPF, *Family Planning Policies* (wallchart published with PEOPLE, vol. 6, no. 2 [1979]).

half utilized fertility and mortality data in projecting school-age and working-age populations.[7]

B. The Substance of National Population Laws and Policies

What should a national population policy or law contain? In other words, what strategies are available to policymakers?

Berelson and Haveman have listed 12 strategies for fertility reduction available to policymakers:

Strategies Involving the Supply of Fertility Control Means

Improve public sector access to current contraceptive methods, *i.e.,* "family planning programs";
. . . plus sterilization;
. . . plus abortion;
. . . plus new and improved methods with better acceptability, continuity, and/or effectiveness;
Improve private-sector distribution of current means of fertility control.

Strategies Seeking to Influence the Demand for Fertility Control

Advance socio-economic determinants of fertility singly or collectively; *e.g.,* general development, popular education, infant/child mortality, income, industrialization, women's status, urbanization;
Promote information, education, propaganda on fertility control;
Manipulate incentives and disincentives affecting fertility behavior, *e.g.,* maternity costs, child assistance, housing, social security, social services;
. . .through direct payment of money or gifts for desired fertility performance;
Manage community "pressure" for an antinatalist consensus;
Impose legal sanctions on age at marriage, internal migration;
. . . limits on family size.[8]

[7]B. STAMPER, POPULATION AND PLANNING IN DEVELOPING NATIONS: A REVIEW OF 60 DEVELOPMENT PLANS FOR THE 1970's, 9–24 (Pop. Council, 1977).

[8]B. Berelson & R. Haveman, *On the Efficient Allocation of Resources for Fertility Reduction,* 5 INTL. FAM. PLAN. PERSPECTIVES 133, 134 (1979).*See also* the range of policy options set forth in L. CORSA & D. OAKLEY, POPULATION PLANNING 162–176 (Michigan, 1979); POPULATION POLICIES AND ECONOMIC DEVELOPMENT: A WORLD BANK STAFF REPORT 57–83 (Johns Hopkins, 1974), and B. Berelson, *Beyond Family Planning,* 163 SCIENCE 533 (1969).

How have the Mexican, Indian, and Ghanaian policies dealt with these strategies? How have they dealt with other considerations, such as:

Demographic objectives;
Establishing a coordinating mechanism;
Rights of minority groups;
Immigration and spacial distribution;
Tax deductions for contributions;
Legislative representation?

To a large extent, the content of a population policy will depend on what is politically acceptable. And, as Berelson and Haveman observe, what is most acceptable is not necessarily what is most feasible or effective.[9]

Isaacs and Sheffield, after reviewing population policies in Latin America, listed seven strategies which could safely (from the viewpoint of acceptability) be included in a population policy. These are:

Formation of a National Population Council.

A program of family planning services.

A public informational and motivational campaign which promotes responsible parenthood and family planning as a health measure for mothers and children.

Inclusion of family life education in school curricula.

A review of laws which could have an impact on population trends.

Gathering and correlation of relevant statistical data.

A stipulation that demographic variables be integrated into overall socio-economic development planning.[10]

C. Individual Versus Community Interests: The Issue of Coercion

The Indian Population Policy, although not itself adopting compulsory measures, suggested that states were free to invoke compulsory sterilization and set forth a series of incentives and disincen-

[9] *Id.* at 141.

[10] S. Isaacs & A. Sheffield, *Population Policy and Program Action: The Latin American Experience,* 1 J. INTL. & COMP. PUB. POL. 83 (1977)

tives to induce lowered fertility.[11] In contrast, both the Mexican and Ghanaian policies stressed the voluntary nature of fertility control.

The justification for compulsion is, of course, that the interests of the society as a whole, which are best served by limiting the number of children, must take precedence over the self-interests of individual families. How to relate individual self-interest to the best interests of the community has puzzled experts for many years and has emerged as a central issue in the population debate.[12]

The extent to which individual liberty may be curtailed for the benefit of society as a whole has, of course, ethical implications far beyond the population field alone. But when the issue is confined to population, the two sides are reasonably clear cut: on the one hand the right of couples to have the number of children they desire; on the other, the duty of government to protect the welfare of its people by reducing population growth. Yet this opposition contains complications. How serious is the population problem? Is it serious enough to justify compulsion? Is it serious enough to justify developed nations cutting off assistance to developing countries seen as hopeless or which refuse to take action to curb population growth?[13] Short of such drastic measures as these, what can or should developed countries do to encourage developing countries to adopt strong antinatal policies?[14] Should the developed countries do anything? Must non-coercive measures first be exhausted before compulsion can be justified? Do coercive measures range across a spectrum of acceptability, *e.g.*, are there differences in acceptability among compulsory sterilization of people with more than three children, a requirement

[11]D. Gwatkin, *Political Will and Family Planning: The Implications of India's Emergency Experience,* 5 POP. & DEV. REV. 29 (1979), notes that some states ordered government civil servants to be sterilized while other states instructed government employees to have *others* sterilized or to face penalties. He cites the orders of the state of Uttar Pradesh that teachers be sterilized or lose a month's salary and the decision of the same state to withhold the pay of family planning and health department workers who failed to produce the requisite number of acceptors. Sterilization in India is discussed *supra* pp. 193–198; incentives in India are examined *supra* pp. 316–325.

[12]This issue is explored allegorically in G. Hardin, *The Tragedy of the Commons, 162 SCIENCE 1243 (1968). See also,* K. Davis, *Population Policy: Will Current Programs Succeed?* 158 SCIENCE 730 (1967).

[13]This kind of "triage" was suggested by W. PADDOCK & P. PADDOCK, FAMINE 1975, (Little Brown, 1967).

[14]For a discussion of this question, *see* P. Hauser, *Population Criteria in Foreign Aid Programs,* in THE POPULATION CRISIS AND MORAL RESPONSIBILITY (P. Wogaman, ed., Public Affairs, 1973).

that people be licensed to have babies,[15] and adding a sterilizant to the water supply?[16] Governmentally-sanctioned peer pressure has been used successfully in China to limit births—is this conceptually and ethically different from compulsory birth control measures?[17]

After examining the major issues, Berelson put forward seven attributes of an "ideal" program:

> An ideal policy would permit a maximum of individual freedom and diversity. It would not prescribe a precise number of children for each category of married couple, nor lay down a universal norm to which all couples should conform; correlatively, it would move toward compulsion only very reluctantly and as the absolutely last resort. . . .
>
> An ideal program designed to affect the number of children people want would help promote other goals that are worth supporting on their own merits, or at least not conflict with such goals.
>
> An ideal program would not burden the innocent in an attempt to penalize the guilty—*e.g.,* would not burden the Nth child by denying him a free education simply because he *was* the Nth child of irresponsible parents.
>
> An ideal program would not weigh heavily upon the already disadvantaged—*e.g.,* by withdrawing maternal or medical benefits or free education from large families, policies that would tend to further deprive the poor.
>
> An ideal program would be comprehensible to those directly affected and hence subject to their responses.
>
> An ideal program would respect present values in family and children, which many people may not be willing to bargain away for other values in a cost-benefit analysis.
>
> An ideal program would not rest upon the designation of population control as the final value justifying all others. . . .[18]

D. National Population Councils

A common feature included in many population policies is establishment of a national population coordinating council.[19] Where

[15] K. BOULDING, THE MEANING OF THE TWENTIETH CENTURY: THE GREAT TRANSITION (Harper & Row, 1964)

[16] P. EHRLICH, THE POPULATION BOMB 135 (Ballantine, 1968).

[17] For a discussion of peer pressure in China, *see* J. Aird, *Fertility Decline and Birth Control in China,* 4 POP. & DEV. REV. 225, 236–247. *See also* materials cited *supra* p. 248, n. 73 and p. 312 n. 7.

[18] B. Berelson, *supra* n. 8 at 538.

[19] Article 95 of the World Population Plan of Action recommended establishment of high-level national population councils. Many observers felt that this would be the single most important clause in the Plan of Action if it were followed by governments.

in government is the optimal location for such a council? The Mexican government housed it in the Ministry of Interior, the Dominican Republic in the Health Ministry, and the Colombian government in the Office of the President. What are the advantages and disadvantages of housing a council in the Health Ministry, which delivers services, versus, say, the Ministry of Interior, which tends to have more political power? Can a coordinating council be expected to deal with technical issues? In this regard, the experience of El Salvador might be instructive; in 1974 the Salvadorean government established an interministerial council to oversee its population policy and a "technical committee" to handle questions of service delivery, service statistics, and other technical matters.

E. THE POLITICS OF POPULATION POLICY

In a number of countries, including many in Latin America and Africa, population policy remains a delicate issue. The economic benefits of a policy may not be readily observable for at least 15 years; the main beneficiaries often have little political power, and opposition to policy is easily generated from both the left and the right.[20] Thus, many public officials—even those who favor reducing population growth rates—consider articulation of an explicit population policy unnecessarily risky. Given this political framework, what is the best time and manner to announce a population policy? How can it be introduced to minimize potential opposition? The masterful performance of the Mexican government in introducing its policy has been comparatively well-documented.[21] In assessing events lead-

[20]The advantages and disadvantages of articulating an explicit population policy are discussed in L. Saunders, *Action Needs: The Relevance of Political Research,* in POLITICAL SCIENCE IN POPULATION STUDIES 1 (R. Clinton, W. Flash & R. Godwin, eds., Lexington, 1972). For analyses of the process of population policy, *see* RESEARCH IN THE POLITICS OF POPULATION (R. Clinton & R. Godwin, eds., Lexington, 1972); COMPARATIVE POLICY ANALYSIS: THE STUDY OF POPULATION POLICY DETERMINANTS IN DEVELOPING COUNTRIES (R. Godwin, ed., Lexington, 1975); POPULATION AND POLITICS: NEW DIRECTIONS IN POLITICAL SCIENCE RESEARCH (R. Clinton, ed., Lexington, 1973); THE DYNAMICS OF POPULATION POLICY IN LATIN AMERICA (T. McCoy, ed., Ballinger, 1974) [hereafter cited as T. McCoy, ed.]; A. MEASHAM, FAMILY PLANNING IN NORTH CAROLINA: THE POLITICS OF A LUKEWARM ISSUE, No. Carolina Pop. Center Monograph No. 17 (1972).

[21]*See* J. Nagel, *Mexico's Population Policy Turnaround,* POP. BULL. vol. 33, no. 5 (Pop. Ref. Bur., 1978); F. Turner, *Responsible Parenthood: The Politics of Mexico's New Population Policies* (Amer. Enterprise Inst. for Pub. Pol. Res., 1974); T. McCoy, *A Paradigmatic Analysis of Mexican Population Policy,* in T. McCoy, ed., *supra* n. 20 at 377.

ing up to Mexico's announcement of a population policy, Nagel observed the following important political considerations:[22]

> *Medical Involvement*
>
> . . . Mexico's medical profession, although not the organized leaders of the family planning movement as in Colombia during the mid-1960s, for instance, did help point the way through research findings and expressed concern over still high rates of infant and maternal mortality and illegal abortion—estimated as high as one for every five live births in 1969. For instance, a strong appeal in 1965 by Dr. John Rock of birth control pill fame to the Mexican Association of Gynecology and Endocrinology, urging efforts to deal with Mexico's high birth rate and more research, was widely publicized. . . .
>
> *Demographic Research*
>
> . . . Demographic-related research organizations helped fuel public discussion and understanding of population issues during the 1960s. The Institute of Social Research at Mexico City's large National Autonomous University began population studies in collaboration with El Colegio [de Mexico] demographic center. More influential, however, was the Mexican Institute of Social Studies (IMES). . . . IMES is a private non-profit organization of Catholic laymen focused on research on the Mexican family and community life. Among its studies reproduced in popular form and widely sold through bookstores was *Quien Escucha al Papa?* (*Who Listens to the Pope?*), in which Enrique Brito reported that half of a sample of women queried in Mexico's three largest cities a year after the 1968 publication of the papal encyclical *Humanae Vitae* rejected the encyclical with its condemnation of artifical contraception, "totally or partially." . . . Similarly provocative was the 1966 "Investigation of the Family in Mexico," a national survey by IMES founder and longtime director Luis Leñero Otero which revealed that 40 percent of the married women interviewed reported having had abortions, both induced and spontaneous, and 85 percent regarded some form of birth control as necessary.
>
> *The Press*
>
> Throughout the 1960s, the press took an essentially passive role in shaping public consciousness of the population problem. There were calls in the press as early as 1957 for government attention to national demographic trends but editorial coverage up to the 1972 policy change included opinion both for and against government family planning efforts. . . . However, the widespread press coverage of Mexi-

[22] J. Nagel, *supra* n. 21 at 15–20.

co's and the world's population explosion, and of such incidents as the closing of Dr. Edris Rice-Wray's clinic, doubtless affected the knowledge, attitudes and practices of the reading public, thus making it at least receptive to a shift in government population policy. When the shift came, the press response was extensive and appropriately laudatory for the most part.

Church Opposition: Real or Apparent?

Because of its traditional pronatalist stance and particularly after the Pope's rejection of artificial contraception in the *Humanae Vitae* of 1968, the Catholic Church has been perceived as the major obstacle to government family planning efforts in Latin America. Evidence of the Church's influence on public policy and private behavior in this area in Mexico during the 1960s is, however, unclear.

Figures on actual practicing Catholics in Mexico suggest that the Church's influence on individual behavior in most areas is less than might be supposed. . . .

The Church's influence on the government's continuing pronatalism in the 1960s and subsequent turnaround is still more uncertain. Formally separated from the state and stripped of much of its political power by the 1917 Constitution, the Church in Mexico has since then generally been politically cautious. Before publication of the *Humanae Vitae,* the uncertainty of what the Pope would decide also made it difficult for the Church in Mexico, as elsewhere, to take a firm stand that might influence public policy. The local Church hierarchy quickly fell in line with the encyclical once it appeared, but its presumed opposition to a shift in official policy did not last. In December 1972, a collective pastoral of the 80 Mexican bishops announced their support of the new government family planning policy. Justifying thier "reinterpretation" of the *Humanae Vitae* on the grounds of "what is the very real and excruciating emergency for most Mexican families: the population explosion," the bishops praised the new program as "a humane measure, wholly consistent with the Church's belief in the primacy of conscience and its concern for the family unit."

The bishops' letter came just two weeks before the government was to begin actual operation of its new program although some months after the original proclamation of the new policy. Thus it provided good publicity for the program at a strategic point and was carefully designed to demonstrate agreement with the government. . . .

The Political Left

In Mexico, as in other Latin American countries, the political left had been presumed to hold the Marxist view that problems of overpopulation, if they exist, can be solved only by the reorganization of a capitalist society into a "collective mode of production," where the "productive forces of the people would increase more rapidly than their numbers." In November 1971, Octavio Paz, Mexico's great poet, chided the Left for its resistance to government-organized family planning:

> "The adoption of a demographic policy is urgent. In this, the Left has been no less guilty, with its silence, than have been the Government and the Church with their hypocritical complacency."

Whatever its influence on Echeverria's early pronatalism, however, the Mexican Left, like the Church, quickly indicated support for the government turnaround once it came. . . .

Policy Turnabout

Presumably, persistent warnings from key advisors finally convinced Echeverria, too, that uncontrolled population growth threatened the Mexican "economic miracle" which had been central to the institutional revolutionary regime's success since its birth in 1917. In 1971 for the first time since 1930–34, Mexico's growth in gross national product appeared to fall below the population growth rate. Though partly due to Echeverria's institution of a 10 percent luxury tax in a mild attack on Mexico's skewed income distribution, the economic slump came as a warning. So, too, did the student riots of 1968, and further street fighting in Mexico City and stepped-up guerrilla activities in the countryside in 1971. Confronted with this evidence of rising discontent with the "revolutionary establishment," Echeverria and his advisors may have decided, as Terry McCoy speculates, to "gamble on a new approach . . . in effect broadening the revolutionary consensus to encompass a previously rejected policy in the hopes it would contribute to the maintenance of the regime itself." It has also been speculated that Echeverria's wife played a role. In February 1972, before the formal policy shift, Sra. Echeverria had inaugurated the government's first, well-attended series of family planning education lectures sponsored by the National Institute for the Protection of Children. Within weeks of the policy change, this mother of eight children observed, "If in my day there had been talk of family planning, I would have taught courses in it."

Cementing the Shift

The new official policy was cemented in a revised General Law of Population, passed unanimously by Congress in November 1973 and implemented at the beginning of 1974. . . .*

*Reprinted with permission from the Population Reference Bureau.

On a more general level, Corsa and Oakley have elaborated five stages in the development of population policy:

> Private sector interest, characterized by the establishment and activities of private family planning association, usually affiliated with the International Planned Parenthood Federation.
> Unofficial government interest expressed within administration and/or legislature. This is presaged by an administrative census or statistical activities.
> Gestation period in the public sector, "shrouded in the mystery of unrevealed meeting reports, committee discussions, and personal persuasion."
> Adoption of some policy by executive and/or legislature.
> Oscillation of policy measures, notably in developed countries, characterized by addition to and subtraction from the policy measures and occasional changes in the speed of implementation.[23]

F. Population Policy and Program Action

Program implementation may, but does not necessarily, follow policy announcement. On the other hand, active programs can exist in the absence of explicit policy. The gap between policies and programs can be seen by a review of family planning in some Latin American countries. The Mexican government's announcement of a population policy was followed by strong action including formation of a National Population Council, establishment of a National Family Planning Coordinating Council, initiation of an active program of family planning services, commencement of a widespread education campaign, and introduction of population and sex education into school textbooks. It is clear that in Mexico issuance of the population policy and its continued support at the presidential level has made it easier to implement large-scale governmental programs to reduce fertility. Peru, on the other hand, which issued a population policy in 1976, still does not permit widespread family planning services, even in the private sector.[24] Costa Rica, Cuba, and Chile, three countries without explicit policies, have had active governmental family planning programs; in all three countries fertility rates have fallen dramatically.[25]

[23]L. CORSA & D. OAKLEY, *supra* n. 8 at 183–187.

[24]The Peruvian policy, *Guidelines for a Population Policy in Peru,* appears in translation in IPPF/WHR, NEWS SERVICE, vol. 4, no. 5, p. 23 (1976).

[25]For a comprehensive review of Latin American policies and programs, *see* S. Isaacs & A. Sheffield, *supra* n. 10 and CELADE, LA POLITICA DE POBLACION EN AMERICA LATINA, 1974–1978 (in Spanish, 1979).

The Ghana policy, although beautifully written, was not followed by significant action. It did provide the basis for a national family planning program, but the percentage of women using contraception has not increased appreciably since 1970.[26] The Indian experience in implementing its population policy has been described by Gwatkin in the following terms:[27]

> The April 1976 national population policy statement . . . proved to be of only limited direct operational importance despite its formal approval by the cabinet. The eloquent general development orientation of its opening passages was completely ignored in practice; and with one significant exception—the increased incentive payments, which were made available immediately to sterilization acceptors—few of the specific measures were effectively implemented before the government's January 1977 decision to hold elections led it to drop the obviously unpopular family planning drive.
>
> The national population policy's famous provision opening the door to compulsory sterilization broke down in its first test. The April national policy statement had said that states wishing to pass compulsory sterilization legislation would be allowed to do so. But when the Maharashtra State government sought central government concurrence in its August legislation, which conformed carefully with the April statement's guidelines, the central government's response was an extended silence that lasted until January's declaration of elections. The measure was then returned to Maharashtra unapproved. The details of the revenue-sharing arrangement outlined in the April national policy statement were still being worked out as of the January election declaration, with the result that it was not implemented during the aggressive drive. The legislation necessary to raise the age of marriage was still on its way through parliament, so that it, too, went untested. The widely publicized proposed regulation requiring central government employees to limit the number of their offspring was still under review by potentially affected civil servants.*

On a worldwide level, Watson has compared family planning policies with family planning program action in developing countries. Using a one percent acceptance rate in the national family planning program, *i.e.,* at least one percent of all women of fertile age make use of the program, as the criterion of "real programmatic

[26]R. Cuca, *Family Planning Programs: An Evaluation of Experience,* World Bank Staff Working Paper No. 345 at 63 (1979).

[27]D. Gwatkin, *supra* n. 11 at 39.

*Reprinted with the permission of The Population Council from Davidson R. Gwatkin, "Political Will and Family Planning: The Implications of India's Emergency Experience," *Population and Development Review* 5, no. 1 (March 1979): p. 39.

support," he produced the following comparison of policy and program action:[28]

Table 9–1 Family Planning Policies and Program Support

Region	Countries with policy support			Countries with "real programmatic support"		
	Number	Population (in millions)	Percent of regional population	Number	Population (in millions)	Percent of regional population
South Asia	5	797	99+	5	797	99+
East Asia	4	892	98	4	892	98
Southeast Asia/ Oceania	15	299	90	12	266	80
Latin America/ Caribbean	22	277	93	20	161	54
West Asia/North Africa	12	197	89	4	96	43
Sub-Saharan Africa						
Angiophone countries	17	206	95	8	36	16
Francophone countries	6	43	38	1	1	0.4
Developing world total	81	2,712	94	54	2,249	78

What other criteria might be devised to measure programmatic effort? Consider the following index proposed by Lapham and Mauldin:[29]

Fertility reduction included in official planning policy

Favorable public statements by political leaders

Contraception readily and easily available, publicly and commercially throughout the country

Customs and legal regulations allow importation of contraceptives not manufactured locally

Vigorous effort to provide family planning services to all MWRA (married women of reproductive age)

Adequate family planning administration structure

Training facilities available and utilized

[28] W. Watson, *A Historical Overview,* in FAMILY PLANNING IN THE DEVELOPING WORLD: A REVIEW OF PROGRAMS 6 (W. Watson, ed., Pop. Council, 1977).

[29] R. Lapham & W. Mauldin, *National Family Planning Programs: Review and Evaluation,* 3 STUDIES IN FAM. PLAN. 29, 31 (1972).

Full-time home-visiting field workers

Postpartum information, education, and service program

Abortion services openly and legally available to all

Voluntary sterilization services (male and female) openly and legally available to all

Use of mass media on a substantial basis

Government provides substantial part of family planning budget from its own resources

Record keeping systems for clients at clinic level and for program service statistics

Serious and continuous evaluation effort

G. Population Policies in the Developed Countries

Up to this point, the discussion has concentrated primarily on national laws and policies in developing countries. What of the developed nations? Are their population concerns sufficiently different to require a distinct perception of population policy?

Berelson, after reviewing the population policies of 24 developed countries (defined as "the industrialized, healthier, better educated, better off, more 'modernized' societies—as a rough measure, those countries with annual per capita incomes of US $1,000 and above"), concluded that:

> Few developed countries have explicit population policies. Rather, demographic trends are evaluated within broader social, economic, environmental, political, and humanitarian concerns. And although population is of concern to a number of countries—as evidenced by the creation of numerous population commissions—it does not rank high on the agenda of national problems.
>
> Many of the developed countries, particularly those with fertility near the replacement level, are concerned with "too little growth for national well being." The majority of developed countries are seeking to move in a more pronatalist way.
>
> Within many developed countries, there is concern with the existence and fertility levels of different communities within the same society.
>
> There is concern with internal distribution of population, more particularly the issues of great and sometimes rapid urbanization.
>
> Finally, there appears to be a growing concern with qualitative population issues now that the quantitative range seems to have narrowed

—with issues of population distribution, with the amenities and esthetics of space, with environmental cleanliness, with age structure, even with genetic considerations over the long run. So while the developing world struggles with numbers, the developed struggles with the translation of low rates into human values.[30]

With regard to the recrudescence of pronatalist policies, recall that most developed countries have expressed a desire to maintain their current rate of population growth or to increase it.[31] This is particularly true of the socialist countries of Eastern Europe, France, and West Germany, all of which are concerned with the effects of negative growth and aging populations and all of which have enacted measures to increase fertility.[32]

The United States does not have an explicit population policy, although a policy to reduce or eliminate unwanted births could be inferred from the actions of the American government.[33] Some groups, such as Zero Population Growth (ZPG), have advocated that the United States assert world leadership by declaring a policy goal of population stabilization. The Commission on Population Growth and the American Future, although not recommending adoption of an explicit population policy, did conclude that the slowing and eventual stopping of population growth would be in the best interests of the United States.[34] In 1978 more than 30 members of the U.S. House of Representatives sponsored a bill that recommended enactment of a population policy and creation of a national Office of Population Policy.[35] No action was taken on the bill, and it was reintroduced in 1979 and 1981.[36]

[30]B. Berelson, *Summary,* in POPULATION POLICY IN DEVELOPED COUNTRIES 771 (B. Berelson, ed., McGraw-Hill, 1974). *See also,* C. Westoff, *Marriage and Fertility in the Developed Countries,* 239 SCIENTIFIC AMERICAN 51 (1978).

[31]*See* U.N., WORLD POPULATION TRENDS AND POLICIES: 1979 MONITORING REPORT, Vol. II, (Dept. Econ. & Soc. Affairs, Pop. Studies No. 62, ST/ESA/SER.A/62/Add.1, 1980) discussed p. 395, *supra*.

[32]*See* discussion *supra* pp. 326–336. *See also Europe's Falling Birth Rates* in PEOPLE, vol. 7, no. 1, pp. 3–23 (1980).

[33]For discussion of population policy in the United States, *see* F. Jaffe, *Public Policy on Fertility Control,* 229 SCIENTIFIC AMERICAN 17 (1973); T. LITTLEWOOD, THE POLITICS OF POPULATION CONTROL (Notre Dame, 1977); P. BACHRACH & E. BERGMAN, POWER AND CHOICE: THE FORMULATION OF AMERICAN POPULATION POLICY (Lexington, 1973).

[34]COMM. ON POP. GROWTH & THE AMER. FUTURE, POPULATION AND THE AMERICAN FUTURE (Signet, 1972).

[35]H.R. 13223 (1978).

[36]H.R. 5062 (1979) and H.R. 907 (1981).

INDEX